Dorothy,

Your wisdom, understanding and assistance has been greatly appreciated.

Rodger
Oct 1/92.

Canadian Parks Service
Classification System for Historical Collections

National Historic Sites

Parks Service

Environment Canada

© Minister of Supply and Services Canada 1992

Available in Canada through
your local bookseller
or by mail from
Canada Communication Group — Publishing
Ottawa, Canada   K1A 0S9

Published under the authority of the Minister of the Environment, Ottawa, 1992.

Design: Louis D. Richard
Electronic page layout: Canada Communication Group — Publishing

Canadian Cataloguing in Publication Data
Canadian Parks Service
Canadian Parks Service classification system for historical collections

Issued also in French under title: Système de
classification des collections historiques du
Service canadien des parcs.
Includes bibliographical references.
ISBN 0-660-14666-5
DSS cat. no. R61-2/15-1E

1. Museum registration methods.
2. Classification — Museums.
3. Antiques — Canada — Classification.
4. Art objects — Canada — Classification.
I. Title

AM139.C32 1992   069'.52   C92-099734-1

Canada	Groupe
Communication	Communication
Group	Canada
Publishing	Édition

Cover illustration:
Cornelius Krieghoff (1815-1872), *Officer's Trophy Room*, 1846.
Oil, Royal Ontario Museum.

TABLE OF CONTENTS

III. Thesaurus

INTRODUCTION

In the past ten years the Collections Management Group of the Canadian Parks Service (CPS) has developed a number of tools that are used, in various ways, for documenting and managing collections. Several dozen documents written since 1980 have focussed on disseminating our analysis and research results in order to better manage our artifact collections on display or used for animation in our parks and historic sites. There are numerous types of these documents, such as:

- exhibition catalogues;
- descriptive catalogues;
- statements of collection projects;
- period animation guides;
- period furnishing plans;
- management policies and directives;
- management reports;
- inventories of historical artifacts;
- Artifact Information System (AIS);
- Classification system for historical collections (nomenclature).

The CPS classification system has revolutionized artifact management in recent years. This system's nomenclature makes it possible to categorize all of the artifacts in our historical collections on the basis of a thesaurus of over 6,000 keywords drawn from our cataloguing records. It uses as its basic reference the classification system developed by R.G. Chenhall, *Nomenclature for Museum Cataloging*. Being a second-generation tool, with all of the advantages that entails in comparison to other existing tools, the CPS classification system is more than a theoretical instrument. It is the foundation of our automated collections management system. Its performance currently compares extremely favourably with that of other systems currently in use in the Canadian museum community. In our 114 historic sites, 5 regional offices, and headquarters in Ottawa, the effectiveness of our computerized system more than met the expectations established at the beginning of the decade.

Unlike many other users of automated systems in museum facilities who have experienced difficulty adapting to new technology (some have even gone back to manual card files), our collections managers, curators, and other users employ this system not only as a quick reference tool, but also to research, select, analyse, and locate artifacts. Our computerized records (Artifact Information System) provide access to over 500,000 artifacts on display or in storage throughout the country, and this data bank may be consulted simultaneously from any point in the network. Users may also access other information associated with specific themes or the function of an artifact, thereby facilitating and considerably speeding research into our collections.

In response to the many requests for consultation and the positive comments we received from various museums and universities, we decided to produce a reference edition, *Canadian Parks Service Classification System for Historical Collections*.

In establishing our system, we drew up a list of terms (see THESAURUS), which of course raised the problem of standardizing the vocabulary. Moreover, having to translate terms into French or English forced us to study definitions in depth in order to grasp nuances and choose the most appropriate term. The terms were selected by group consensus.

This list of terms is not immutable. Comparing the present updated list with the initial list that launched the system three years ago indicates that adjustments have already been undertaken within CPS.

Partners from museums are currently working to automate management of their collections, using this thesaurus as a reference. Their comments will, we hope, enable us to design together a version that meets all users' needs. We now have at our disposal a key tool that would allow all museums with collections of ethnographic artifacts to manage these collections effectively and facilitate museum-to-museum communications.

The next step will be to add illustrations and definitions for each term in the Thesaurus. This *Visual Dictionary* will constitute a complete scientific tool for identifying artifacts and managing historical collections. Once completed, this project will provide museums across Canada and researchers in the material culture field with an original and exceptional scientific tool.

Richard Gauthier
Chief Curator
Historical and Archaeological Collections
Quebec Region
Québec City

Rodger McNicoll
Chief Curator
Interpretive Collections
Program Headquarters
Ottawa

BONNET, MILITARY	C080:03-00062	BONNET ÉCOSSAIS MILITAIRE
Headdress with high crown made of plumes and with a diced edged headband. Part of the uniform in military Scottish corps.	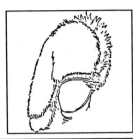	*Haute coiffure de plumes, à bandeau quadrillé.* *Partie de l'uniforme dans les corps militaires écossais.*

CAP	C080:03-00063	CASQUETTE
Headgear with soft crown, brimless, sometimes with a visor and flaps to protect the head, the ears and forehead, made of different material (felt, fur, cloth). Protects the head from the elements. **Synonym:** Windsor cap; frontiersman's cap. **Exclusion:** All other specific CAPs; CAP (H120:09-00115); GLENGARRY (C080:03-00072).		*Coiffure souple, sans rebord, faite de matériaux divers (feutre, fourrure, tissu), garnie d'une visière et parfois de rabats protégeant la nuque, les oreilles et le front.* *Protège la tête des intempéries.* *Exclusion:* *KÉPI, CASQUETTE (H120:09-00115); GLENGARRY (C080:03-00072).*

CLOG	C060:03-00031	GALOCHE
Footwear with thick wooden sole or iron skate and leather or fabric vamp fastened over a shoe or foot. Protects the shoe or the foot by raising it over the mud. **Synonym:** Patten. **Exclusion:** SABOT (C080:03-00038).		*Chaussure à semelle de bois épaisse ou de fer en forme de patin et à empeignes de gros cuir ou de tissu se portant sur un soulier ou directement sur le pied.* *Protège le soulier ou le pied en le haussant au-dessus de la boue.* *Synonyme:* *Socque.* *Exclusion:* *SABOT (C080:03-00038).*

Sample page of *Visual Dictionary*

ACKNOWLEDGEMENTS

This project started in 1989 and is the result of the combined efforts of Canadian Parks Service curators and registrars, linguists, translators from Secretary of State, and members of the scientific community. It is in this collegial spirit that the working group was established:

Rosemary Campbell
  National Collections Manager
Paul-Aimé Lacroix
  Registrar of Collections
Yves Bergeron
  Curator from 1987 to 1991
Glen Purdy
  Senior Cataloguer
Jean-Luc Vincent
  Special Project Assistant
Élaine Bouchard
  Project Assistant
Yvon Legendre
  Project Assistant

Extended Working Group from:
  Atlantic Region
  Prairie and Northern Region
  Ontario Region
  Western Region

Partners in the scientific community*:

Yves Bergeron
  Chief Curator
  Musée du Séminaire de Québec

Annie Brisset
  Director
  School of Translators and Interpreters
  University of Ottawa

Anne-Marie Desdouits
  Ethnolinguist
  Professor of Ethnology
  Laval University

Jean-Claude Dupont
  Professor of Ethnology
  Laval University

Raymond Pepermans
  Guest Professor
  Terminology and Museography Project
  University of Ottawa

Trainees from Laval University:
(Ethnology and museology programs)

  Élaine Bouchard
  Yvon Legendre
  Lucie Chabot-Roy
  Sylie Robitaille
  Valérie Desmeules
  Nadia Ringuet
  Jasmine Fréchette

Trainee from the University of Ottawa:
(History Department)

  Terrence Gartland

---

* We wish to thank Robert Innes. While working as a consultant, he designed on a volunteer basis the computerized data base for the preparation of the *Visual Dictionary*. We also which to thank the EDP specialists of the Atmospheric Environment Service in Downsview, Ontario.

I

THE CANADIAN PARKS SERVICE

CLASSIFICATION SYSTEM

FOR HISTORICAL COLLECTIONS

A SCIENTIFIC TOOL FOR COLLECTIONS MANAGEMENT

To date, the national collection of the Canadian Parks Service has an inventory of almost 500,000 artifacts. Apart from the size of the collection, the diversity of the artifacts should be emphasized. In order to adequately manage this large national collection containing artifacts from all sectors of traditional material life it was necessary to adopt a fairly extensive classification system and to ensure standardization of terms.

Few specialized and standardized tools for identifying artifacts existed until the end of the 1970s. Often curators and registrars were the only ones who truly knew their collections, and artifacts were recorded in files under whatever specific name the curator happened to choose.

In 1979 CPS started to use and promote Robert G. Chenhall's classification system. Then, in 1983, upon the registrars' recommendations, CPS officially adopted Chenhall's work as the prime reference for classifying historical artifacts in the national collection.

Given the extent of its network of sites and the diversity of its historical collections, CPS developed the Canadian Parks Service Classification System for Historical Collections, upon which the automated management of historical artifacts is based. Its nomenclature differs from Chenhall's in several respects. Although it contains the same categories, it specifically reflects the CPS national collection and contains only the names of artifacts in that collection. Accordingly, some components of this classification system are more elaborate than their equivalents in Chenhall, e.g., military artifacts, costumes, and packaging and containers.

THE CLASSIFICATION SYSTEM
AND THE COMPUTERIZATION OF COLLECTIONS

In 1980 a number of sites in the Canadian Parks Service began automating their collections of historical artifacts. Without any real coordination, these individual initiatives were undertaken to improve access to documentation and enhance the effectiveness of collections management. In 1985, for example, Quebec Region, with the assistance of the Université de Sherbrooke, developed a computer program to manage its collections; Prairie and Northern Region as well as Western region, meanwhile, began to develop a computerized collections inventory system for internal management purposes, and a short time later, CPS studied the feasibility of establishing one common system for the entire network.

The Canadian Parks Service developed the Artifact Information System (AIS), a computerized system specifically adapted to the needs of the Parks network. It proved highly effective. This flexible and open system provides rapid access to the entire national collection. It contains technical data, broken down into about 20 fields, that are essential to collections management:

- Major Category
- Classification
- Nomenclature Code
- Object Name
- Suffix
- Common Name and Description

- Registration Number
- Batch Number

- Acquisition Date
- Method of Acquisition
- Region of Acquisition
- Unit Cost
- Cost of Acquisition

- Status
- Period

- Special Condition
- Condition Code
- Conservation Flag

- Location
  Building
  Room
  Section
  Location Date

More-detailed information that cannot be expressed as readily in computer language, such as exhaustive descriptions, legal documents, and photographs, are kept in a card file.

During 1986 we started transferring data from card files to AIS. This automation has made it possible to prepare an exhaustive inventory of the entire CPS collection, both on display and in storage. AIS facilitates collections management and above all simplifies research.

The cornerstone of any classification system, the standardization of terms, is particularly important in automating collections management. One curator may identify a given cast-iron vessel as a "pan," a colleague records a similar artifact as a "pot," a third calls it a "cauldron," and a fourth a "baking dish"; in the end, none is incorrect. Individuals name and describe artifacts on the basis of their own empirical and scientific knowledge. When it comes time to conduct research using card files, it soon becomes clear that a single artifact appears under different names and in different categories. The same problems occur with computerized catalogues. As long as each card contains a photograph of the artifact and the collection does not grow much

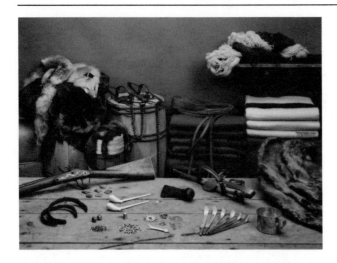

Thanks to AIS, very little time was required to locate and assemble the artifacts in the above photograph, prepared for an exhibition catalogue for *Montréal et le Québec au temps de la révolution française* [Montréal and Québec during the French revolutionary period].
000/INF/PR6/A-92

beyond a few thousand artifacts, researchers can generally find their way.

But for vast collections held in several locations, system users had to learn to speak the same language, and a list of preferred terms was needed to link artifacts and to conduct research. CPS has been engaged in preparing this list since 1983.

Robert G. Chenhall, in the first edition of *Nomenclature*, warned his readers:

> *No book, no list of terms, no written words, can ever do the actual job of identifying any object. The process of identification, per se, is one of the key functions implied by the job title 'Curator.'* *

Chenhall's classification system also conveyed a new idea: establishing for material culture collections preferred terms similar to those used for scientific collections. This would solve problems arising out of the automation of collection records and make possible information exchanges between museums.

CPS faced problems in standardizing terms and coping with English and French terms. The English-language terminology was based on the list Chenhall published in 1978. Quebec Region was charged with the responsibility of preparing a verified list of French terms while respecting the parameters of Chenhall's work.

To rationalize communications between the various regions of the network and to ensure that the same terms are used in French and in English, Rosemary Campbell of Program Headquarters in Ottawa was given responsibility for coordinating this work, and the successful operation of the system depends on this fundamental task. Hence one single person is responsible for noting new terms and disseminating conventions to AIS users.[†]

After the initial translation phase, we used alphanumeric coding as a bridge between artifacts inventoried in both languages. Artifacts recorded as "CASQUETTE" and "CAP," for example, are identified according to category, class, and object, which are expressed by the same alphanumeric code C080:03-00063 for both. Anyone wishing to identify all the caps in the collection, therefore, may use this code to locate all such headgear regardless of whether their records are in French or English.

Now that the computerization of CPS collections has been completed, a researcher can find out in only a few minutes how many, say, caps are in the network, what condition they are in, where they are stored or displayed, and whether they are available. After querying the data bank, the researcher is certain that he or she has the records for every caulking tool in the collection and is therefore able to make more informed choices than in the past.

---

* Robert G. Chenhall, *Nomenclature for Museum Cataloging. A System for Classifying Man-Made Objects*, American Association for State and Local History, Nashville, 1978, p. 7.

[†] Our work led the American Association for State and Local History to invite CPS to participate in its committee to revise Chenhall's nomenclature; the resulting publication benefited from CPS experience:
James R. Blackaby, Patricia Greeno, and The Nomenclature Committee, *The Revised Nomenclature for Museum Cataloguing. A Revised and Expanded Version of Robert G. Chenhall's System for Classifying Man-Made Objects*, AASLH Press, 1988.

MORPHOLOGY OF THE CLASSIFICATION SYSTEM

How is a system for classifying material culture arti-facts vital to managing an ethnographic collection? Any collection consists of series of objects, but only a classification system makes it possible to establish a primary level of organization and analysis. Such a sys-tem becomes increasingly necessary as a collection develops.

Classification systems simply provide indexing terms; they do not give names to all the artifacts involved. They make it possible to sort artifacts by category and class according to specific perspectives. Strict rules facilitate identifying and locating artifacts and, by extension, managing and controlling them. This approach opens the door to data automation. Classification systems become the key to accessing artifacts.

CPS nomenclature, like Chenhall's, contains a hierar-chical structure established according to each artifact's primary function. Each of the 500,000 artifacts in the national ethnographic collection has a place in this nomenclature, which has been specifically tailored to CPS needs.

A HIERARCHICAL SYSTEM

In science, classification systems establish hierarchies through direct observation of the physical characteris-tics of natural things. CPS followed this principle to develop its classification system for historical artifact collections. To create simple and useful divisions, man-agers of historical collections have established hierar-chical levels on the basis of an object's original func-tion.

ORIGINAL FUNCTION OF AN OBJECT

Artifacts of material culture all have one thing in com-mon: they were created for a specific purpose. This is the original function.

As Chenhall wrote,

> The lexicon in this book is based upon the assump-tion that every man-made object was originally created to fulfill some function or purpose and, further, that original function is the only common denominator that is present in all of the artifacts of man, however simple or complex. At the top or highest level in any hierarchy of classifying and naming man-made artifacts there can be no con-sistent organizing principle other than the known (or presumed) reason why each object was origi-nally created.*

An object's primary function must always be taken into account and should not be confused with other possible but subsequent functions. The issue arises because arti-facts tend to evolve over time and acquire different functions.†

---

* Robert G. Chenhall, *Nomenclature for Museum Cataloging. A System for Classifying Man-Made Objects*, American Association for State and Local History, Nashville, 1978, p. 8.

† *See* Marcel Moussette, "Sens et contresens: l'étude de la culture matérielle au Québec," in *Canadian Folklore canadien*, Vol. 4, 1-2, 1982, pp. 10-16.

When an artifact has several functions, it is classified in the appropriate main category that comes first in the hierarchical listing. For example, a blacksmith's apron will be classified in CLOTHING, OUTERWEAR and not METALWORKING TOOLS & EQUIPMENT. Similarly, a watercolour picture entitled "Canadian Infantrymen on the March," will be placed in DOCUMENTARY ARTIFACT and not ART.

In some cases, the system makes it possible to classify artifacts according to a function other than the original function:

• an artifact's original function is not known, but its use at the time it was acquired by CPS is known;

• the secondary function takes precedence over the original function. For example, a gun used for trade will be classified in EXCHANGE MEDIUM, not in FIREARM;

• an artifact no longer fulfills the function for which it was created because it has been modified/altered for adaptation to another function. For example, a used tin can (CONTAINER [G020]) that has been modified to serve as an ashtray (HOUSEHOLD ACCESSORY [B080]) will be classified according to its most recent function.

In some specific cases, the system permits one artifact to be included in up to three classes to facilitate research and cover all aspects of the artifact, e.g.,

• a try square bearing the inscription "Pascal Hardware" (WOODWORKING TOOLS & EQUIPMENT and ADVERTISING MEDIUM);

• a sword bearing an inscription commemorating victory in a battle in which the sword was used (ARMAMENT T&E, EDGED and DOCUMENTARY ARTIFACT).

THE ORGANIZATIONAL STRUCTURE

The structure of the nomenclature is organized into three levels:

• categories,
• classes and subclasses, and
• names of objects.

There are ten categories of artifacts:

01: Structures
02: Furnishings
03: Personal Artifacts
04: Tools & Equipment for Materials
05: Tools & Equipment for Science and Technology
06: Tools & Equipment for Communication
07: Distribution and Transportation Artifacts
08: Communication Artifacts
09: Recreational Artifacts
10: Unclassifiable Artifacts

These ten categories could be divided into four groups:

SHELTER

01: Structures
02: Furnishings
03: Personal Artifacts

TOOLS AND EQUIPMENT

04: Tools & Equipment for Materials
05: Tools & Equipment for Science and Technology
06: Tools & Equipment for Communication
07: Distribution and Transportation Artifacts

COMMUNICATION

08: Communication Artifacts
09: Recreational Artifacts

UNKNOWN

10: Unclassifiable Artifacts

Within categories, artifacts are sorted into classes and subclasses, both of which are listed according to alphanumeric codes.

ARTIFACTS THAT ARE DIFFICULT TO IDENTIFY

It is sometimes difficult to identify artifacts correctly. A certain number of possibilities nonetheless exist for recording information in the data base.

For example, an unidentified kind of shovel used in a foundry could be classified as:

SHOVEL and METALWORKING T&E.

An unidentified shovel that cannot be associated with a specific activity could be designated as:

SHOVEL and MUTIPLE USE ARTIFACTS.

In an extreme case, where the artifact is not identified and cannot be associated with an activity, the record would read:

PROBLEMATICAL and FUNCTION UNKNOWN.

ARTIFACTS THAT ARE DIFFICULT TO CLASSIFY

Some artifacts are difficult to classify because they serve more than one purpose. Scout knives, for example, have multiple uses. Other objects are designed to have two uses, such as rulers or ballpoint pens bearing company or retailer names, or clothing emblazoned with a corporate sponsor's name.

Museums often contain artifacts that have been altered to adapt to new functions. Barrels converted into flower boxes are one example of this.

Artifacts that have been transformed intentionally should be classified according to their most recent function. Thus, the converted barrels should be classified in SITE FEATURE.

LIST OF TERMS

In any classification system, it is essential to distinguish between the *names of objects* and the *terms used to describe objects*. Object names include all common names used to designate objects of material culture. Object terms, however, refer back to the preferred words or expressions used in the classification system. Thus, object names such as "cauldron," "pot," "pan," or "casserole dish" all refer in the classification system to a single preferred artifact term: cooking receptacle. Of course, the common names are part of an object's history; they indicate that it is part of material culture. For this reason, common names must be given under a specific heading in the cataloguing record.

Object terms are generally selected by consensus; thus, they may sometimes correspond to a common name. This method does generate a certain ambiguity.

SELECTING AND ADDING TERMS

Object terms used in the CPS Classification system have been approved by a consensus of registrars and curators. The English spelling conforms to *Webster's Third International Dictionary*, while the French spelling is that given in the Robert dictionary.

New object terms must be selected according to the rules of the classification system. They must specify a useful generic distinction, and they must be binominal if at all possible (i.e., a substantive and a single qualifier).

Secondary data such as the style, manufacturer, or era of an artifact cannot be used to create new object terms.

RULES OF WRITING

Wherever possible, categories are identified by terms in the plural, while classification terms and artifact names are usually in the singular.

Categories, classification terms, and object names are always written in capital letters. Lower-case letters are used only in written documentation (registration and worksheet records) and are reserved for the artifact's common name (i.e., names in common use, scientific names, and regionalisms).

RULES OF SYNTAX

The general rule for name entry in the lexicon is to invert it. The noun or substantive of the object term is placed first, followed by a comma, followed by a word or phrase qualifier.

There are a few exceptions to this rule:

• words that make no sense if inverted such as NIDDY NODDY, CHEST OF DRAWERS;

• parts, accessories, and fragments of objects such as LAMP BURNER;

• assemblages such as MORTAR & PESTLE.

THE HIERARCHICAL CATEGORIES, CLASSES, AND SUBCLASSES

Category 01
STRUCTURES

A020 BUILDING

A040 BUILDING COMPONENT

A060 SITE FEATURE

A080 OTHER STRUCTURE

Category 02
FURNISHINGS

B020 BEDDING

B040 FLOOR COVERING

B060 FURNITURE

B080 HOUSEHOLD ACCESSORY

B100 LIGHTING DEVICE

B120 PLUMBING FIXTURE

B140 TEMPERATURE CONTROL DEVICE

B160 WINDOW OR DOOR COVERING

Category 03
PERSONAL ARTIFACTS

C020 ADORNMENT

CLOTHING
C060 CLOTHING, FOOTWEAR
C080 CLOTHING, HEADWEAR
C100 CLOTHING, OUTERWEAR
C120 CLOTHING, UNDERWEAR
C140 CLOTHING ACCESSORY

C160 PERSONAL GEAR

C180 TOILET ARTICLE

Category 04
TOOLS & EQUIPMENT FOR MATERIALS

D020 AGRICULTURAL T&E

D040 ANIMAL HUSBANDRY T&E

D060 FISHING & TRAPPING T&E

FOOD T&E
D100 FOOD PROCESSING T&E
D120 FOOD SERVICE T&E

D140 FORESTRY T&E

D160 GLASS, PLASTICS, CLAYWORKING T&E

D180 LEATHER, HORN, SHELLWORKING T&E

D200 MASONRY & STONEWORKING T&E

D220 METALWORKING T&E

D240 MINING & MINERAL HARVESTING T&E

D260 PAINTING T&E

D280 PAPERMAKING T&E

D300 TEXTILEWORKING T&E

D320 WOODWORKING T&E

OTHER T&E FOR MATERIALS
D550 BASKET, BROOM, BRUSH MAKING T&E
D600 CIGAR MAKING T&E
D650 LAPIDARY T&E
D680 SOAPMAKING T&E
D700 WIGMAKING T&E

Category 05
TOOLS & EQUIPMENT FOR SCIENCE AND TECHNOLOGY

E020   ACOUSTICAL T&E

ARMAMENT T&E
E060   ARMAMENT, FIREARM
E080   ARMAMENT, EDGED
E100   ARMAMENT, BLUDGEON
E120   ARMAMENT, ARTILLERY
E140   ARMAMENT, AMMUNITION
E160   ARMAMENT, BODY ARMOR
E180   ARMAMENT ACCESSORY

E200   ASTRONOMICAL T&E

E220   BIOLOGICAL T&E

E240   CHEMICAL T&E

E260   CONSTRUCTION T&E

E280   ELECTRICAL & MAGNETIC T&E

E300   ENERGY PRODUCTION T&E

E320   GEOLOGICAL T&E

E340   MAINTENANCE T&E

E360   MECHANICAL T&E

E380   MEDICAL & PSYCHOLOGICAL T&E

E400   MERCHANDISING T&E

E420   METEOROLOGICAL T&E

E440   NUCLEAR PHYSICS T&E

E460   OPTICAL T&E

E480   REGULATIVE & PROTECTIVE T&E

E500   SURVEYING & NAVIGATIONAL T&E

E520   THERMAL T&E

E540   TIMEKEEPING T&E

E560   WEIGHTS & MEASURES T&E

E600   OTHER T&E FOR SCIENCE & TECHNOLOGY

Category 06
TOOLS & EQUIPMENT FOR COMMUNICATION

F020   DATA PROCESSING T&E

F040   DRAFTING T&E

F060   MUSICAL T&E

F080   PHOTOGRAPHIC T&E

F100   PRINTING T&E

F120   SOUND COMMUNICATION T&E

F140   TELECOMMUNICATION T&E

F160   VISUAL COMMUNICATION T&E

F180   WRITTEN COMMUNICATION T&E

F500   OTHER T&E FOR COMMUNICATION

Category 07
DISTRIBUTION & TRANSPORTATION ARTIFACTS

G020   CONTAINER

AEROSPACE TRANSPORTATION
G060   AEROSPACE TRANSPORTATION EQUIPMENT
G080   AEROSPACE TRANSPORTATION ACCESSORY

LAND TRANSPORTATION
G120   LAND TRANSPORTATION, ANIMAL POWERED
G140   LAND TRANSPORTATION, HUMAN POWERED
G160   LAND TRANSPORTATION, MOTORIZED
G180   LAND TRANSPORTATION ACCESSORY

RAIL TRANSPORTATION
G220   RAIL TRANSPORTATION EQUIPMENT
G240   RAIL TRANSPORTATION ACCESSORY

WATER TRANSPORTATION
G280   WATER TRANSPORTATION EQUIPMENT
G300   WATER TRANSPORTATION ACCESSORY

Category 08
COMMUNICATION ARTIFACTS

H020	ADVERTISING MEDIUM
H040	ART
H060	CEREMONIAL ARTIFACT
H080	DOCUMENTARY ARTIFACT
H100	EXCHANGE MEDIUM
H120	PERSONAL SYMBOL

Category 09
RECREATIONAL ARTIFACTS

I020	GAME
I040	PUBLIC ENTERTAINMENT DEVICE
I060	RECREATIONAL DEVICE
I080	SPORTS EQUIPMENT
I100	TOY

Category 10
UNCLASSIFIABLE ARTIFACTS

J020	ARTIFACT REMNANT
J040	FUNCTION UNKNOWN
J060	MULTIPLE USE ARTIFACTS

II

DEFINITIONS OF THE CATEGORIES,

CLASSES, AND SUBCLASSES

(Adapted from *Revised Nomenclature*)

Category 01
STRUCTURES

Artifacts originally created to define space for human activities or to be used as components of space-defining artifacts.

A020
BUILDING

An artifact originally created primarily to provide or define a space with a controllable climate, usually through enclosure, for human activities. This classification may include permanent structures, such as garages or office buildings, or portable structures, such as tents. This classification includes most human-made structures. Houses, barns, warehouses, train stations, and jails are all primarily intended to provide spaces that can be kept warm or cool and dry. Architectural samples integral to buildings, such as wall sections or roof sections, should be catalogued in this classification as parts of buildings. Separable, distinct, and interchangeable components, such as doorknobs or window sashes, should be classified as BUILDING COMPONENT (A040). This classification includes interpretive models of buildings.

A040
BUILDING COMPONENT

An artifact originally created as a separate, distinct, and generally interchangeable structural or decorative part of a building (though such artifacts as hinges, for example, can be used on non-building artifacts such as gates or tables). Though building components are distinct objects, they function as parts of larger structures rather than as independent units. This classification includes such things as mantels and window frames, but excludes parts of buildings or other structures that lack distinctiveness or interchangeability, such as roofs, chimneys, or joists. Also excluded from this classification are parts of buildings that are not integral parts of a structure, such as furnishings, lighting devices, and plumbing fixtures, all of which are listed in the FURNISHINGS category.

A060
SITE FEATURE

An artifact originally created as a distinct element that is associated with a site, a building, or other structure. Rather than functioning simply as a part of a larger structure, a site feature is an independent entity that complements other structures. This classification includes such things as birdbaths, flagpoles, gates, and fences.

A080
OTHER STRUCTURE

An artifact originally created primarily to modify the environment or landscape or to define a space for some reason besides climate control. This classification includes dams, mines, and bridges. Structures such as sports complexes that are primarily intended to provide controlled access and convenient seating should be placed in this classification. Some other structures may have climate-controlled spaces, such as the space under a dome in a stadium or the generating room of a hydro-electric dam, but these spaces serve a secondary role to the function of the structures.

Category 02
FURNISHINGS

Artifacts originally created to facilitate human activity and to meet physical needs of people generally by offering comfort, convenience, or protection. Clothing is excluded from this classification as it addresses only the needs of specific individuals. Furnishings are not artifacts used as active agents in other processes such as tools or equipment; they passively enable human activity.

B020
BEDDING

An artifact originally created to be used on a bed or in association with sleeping, such as blankets, pillows, and sleeping bags.

B040
FLOOR COVERING

An artifact originally created as portable or temporary covering for a building floor. This classification includes rugs and carpeting, but not permanently attached tile or linoleum, which are included in the BUILDING COMPONENT (A040) classification.

B060
FURNITURE

An artifact originally created to answer the physical requirements and comforts of people in their living and work spaces. This classification includes outdoor furniture, desks, tables, beds, and chairs, but excludes appliances or tools such as washing machines or ladders.

B080
HOUSEHOLD ACCESSORY

An artifact originally created to be placed in or around a building for the convenience of people to enchance, complement, or facilitate the maintenance of their environment. This classification includes small furnishings such as soap dishes and spittoons, special household containers such as vases and wastebaskets, and objects, such as antimacassars and table covers, that protect furniture. The classification does not include artifacts intended primarily to communicate, they are classified as ART (H040) in COMMUNICATION ARTIFACTS, nor does it include devices used in productive housekeeping activities such as cooking or maintenance.

B100
LIGHTING DEVICE

An artifact originally created to provide illumination. This classification includes lighting accessories such as candlesnuffers or wick trimmers, general-purpose portable lighting devices such as kerosene lanterns, and specialized fixtures such as streetlamps and theatre lighting devices and lighthouse lamp accessories.

B120
PLUMBING FIXTURE

An artifact originally created to be attached as an integral component to water and sewer lines, often within a building. Portable objects that serve comparable purposes are HOUSEHOLD ACCESSORIES (B080). Pipes and pipe fittings are BUILDING COMPONENTS (A040), not PLUMBING FIXTURES (B120).

B140
TEMPERATURE CONTROL DEVICE

An artifact originally created to enable people to control the temperature of their immediate environment according to their needs. This classification does not include devices to control temperature for purposes other than human comfort, as is the case with bake ovens and kilns, nor does it include relatively permanent structural parts of a building, such as fireplaces or flues.

e.g., stove, woodbin, ember carrier.

B160
WINDOW OR DOOR COVERING

An artifact originally created to cover or adorn a window, door, or doorway. This classification does not include relatively permanent structural parts of buildings that are BUILDING COMPONENTS (A040), such as doors or window sashes.

e.g., curtain, valance, curtain ring.

Category 03
Personal Artifacts

Artifacts originally created to serve an individual's personal needs as clothing, adornment, body protection, or grooming aids.

C020
ADORNMENT

An artifact originally created to be worn on the human body or on clothing for ornamentation rather than for protection or simply as body covering. Adornment lacks the communicative aspect of objects in the PERSONAL SYMBOL (H120) classification and is more decorative than those in the PERSONAL GEAR (C160) classification.

e.g., ring, necklace, pendant.

CLOTHING

An artifact originally created as a covering for the human body. This classification includes underwear, outerwear, headwear, footwear, and accessories such as belts or cuff links.

C060: CLOTHING FOOTWEAR

Clothing and other protective items that are worn on the feet for protection or cover. This classification includes boots, stockings, gaiters.

C080: CLOTHING, HEADWEAR

Clothing that protects or covers the head. This classification includes bonnets, tricorn hats, and turbans.

C100: CLOTHING, OUTERWEAR

Clothing that is worn on the body over undergarments or as an exterior layer of dress. This classification includes coats, overcoats, dresses.

C120: CLOTHING, UNDERWEAR

Clothing that is worn beneath outerwear to protect or cover the body. Underwear is the layer of clothing that is closest to the skin. This classification includes petticoats, corsets.

C140: CLOTHING ACCESSORY

An artifact, such as a belt or cuff link, created originally to be used in association with clothing. Accessories include artifacts that are worn, such as ascots, as well as those that are used for minor care of clothing, such as shoe-polish applicators.

C160
PERSONAL GEAR

An artifact originally created to be used by an individual as a personal carrying device such as a wallet or a knapsack, as a protective apparatus such as an umbrella or goggles, as a personal or physical aid such as a cane or eyeglasses, or as personal smoking equipment and supplies such as a pipe. This classification includes military accoutrements such as canteens and pouches used as personal accessories not directly associated with armament.

C180
TOILET ARTICLE

An artifact originally created to be used for personal care, hygiene, or grooming. This classification includes razors, toothbrushes, cosmetics.

Category 04

TOOLS & EQUIPMENT FOR MATERIALS

Tools, equipment, and supplies originally created to manage, oversee, capture, harvest, or collect resources and to transform or modify particular materials, both raw and processed. These artifacts are normally created in response to problems inherent in the materials themselves. Wood requires certain kinds of cutting devices, fish require certain lures, food requires certain serving utensils.

D020
AGRICULTURAL T&E

Tools, equipment, and supplies originally created for farming or gardening. This classification includes implements used in planting, tending, harvesting, and storing crops and in processing food for animals but not food for humans (*see* FOOD PROCESSING T&E [D100]). This classification does not include tools and equipment used in caring for animals (*see* ANIMAL HUSBANDRY T&E [D040]), working with forest products (*see* FORESTRY T&E [D140]), or in preparing fibres for textiles from agricultural products (*see* TEXTILEWORKING T&E [D300]). Tools and equipment used in tobacco harvesting are found in this classification.

D040
ANIMAL HUSBANDRY T&E

Tools, equipment, and supplies originally created for the care, breeding, and study of animals. This classification includes instruments used in the practice of veterinary medicine, in the psychological study of animals, and in the care of animals, such as the tools a farrier uses to shoe animals. This classification excludes equipment used in processing animal products for human use (*see* FOOD PROCESSING T&E [D100] or LEATHER, HORN, & SHELLWORKING T&E [D180]). Also excluded are the tools of trades related to animal husbandry; these tools are not used directly with animals, such as a farrier's metalworking tools.

e.g., hoof chisel, hobble, muzzle.

D060
FISHING & TRAPPING T&E

Tools, equipment, and supplies originally created for capturing aquatic and terrestrial animals by any means other than weaponry, such as nets, traps, and fishhooks.

FOOD T&E

D100: FOOD PROCESSING T&E

Tools, equipment, and supplies originally created for processing, storing, and preparing food or beverages for human consumption. This classification does not include tools for gathering, producing, or managing food materials.

e.g., churn, sugar cutter, cheese slicer.

D120: FOOD SERVICE T&E

Tools, equipment, and supplies originally created for the service, presentation, or consumption of food or beverages by humans, such as saucers, cups, and silent butlers.

D140
FORESTRY T&E

Tools, equipment, and supplies originally created for cutting, handling, or processing timber or for harvesting forest crops such as bark, sap, gum, resin, or rubber (bark shredder, felling ax). This classification does not include equipment for cartage, which is classified under TRANSPORTATION ARTIFACTS, or for manufacturing products from wood, which is classified under WOODWORKING T&E (D320) or PAPERMAKING T&E (D280).

D160
GLASS, PLASTICS, & CLAYWORKING T&E

Tools, equipment, and supplies originally created for fabricating objects from homogenous complex compounds, such as glass, clay, rubber, synthetic resins, plastics, or waxes. This classification also includes the tools, equipment, and supplies used for producing such homogenous complex compounds. These compounds differ from other materials because they generally require elaborate processing at some point during their use. As compounds, they differ from other processed materials, such as leather, because they are not discrete units; they differ from aggregate materials, such as masonry, because of their homogeneity and their need for elaborate processing. This classification includes candle molds, glazier points.

D180
LEATHER, HORN, & SHELLWORKING T&E

Tools, equipment, and supplies originally created for processing materials that are animal in origin. This classification includes tools and equipment for processing furs or hides, for preparing leather, for fabricating leather products, for working shell, horn, bone, and ivory, and tools for making things from quills or feathers. This classification also includes artifacts for processing materials that are the products of insects and bacteria.

e.g., beaming knife, awl, harness maker's bench.

D200
MASONRY & STONEWORKING T&E

Tools, equipment, and supplies originally created for working with natural stone or with aggregate materials such as concrete, mortar, brick, or plaster. These aggregate materials can be of natural or manufactured origin. They differ from materials related to GLASS, PLASTICS, & CLAYWORKING T&E (D160) because they lack the homogeneity and the need for complex processing of those materials.

e.g., bushhammer, zax, trowel.

D220
METALWORKING T&E

Tools, equipment, and supplies originally created for casting, forging, machining, or fabricating metals or metal products. This classification does not include tools, equipment, and supplies used in mining or preliminary ore processing (see MINING & MINERAL HARVESTING T&E [D240]).

e.g., anvil, sheet metalworker's snips, vise.

D240
MINING & MINERAL HARVESTING T&E

Tools, equipment, and supplies originally created for extracting materials in solid, liquid, or gaseous state from the natural environment. This classification includes equipment used for underground and surface mines, quarries, and oil and water wells, for prospecting, and for supplemental processing operations such as breaking, milling, washing, cleaning, or grading. It also includes tools used for ice and salt harvesting.

e.g., ice saw, spoon, double-pointed pick.

D260
PAINTING T&E

Tools, equipment, and supplies originally created for working with materials that mask large surfaces by depositing a residual film, such as a paint film, or by using adhesives to attach a thin covering, such as wallpaper or gold leaf, to a surface. This classification includes tools, equipment, and supplies used in decorative, artistic, and protective applications. Excluded are tools and equipment that are used with thicker coatings, such as wood veneers or plastic laminates, and tools and equipment used for metal plating. Also excluded are tools and equipment, such as ink knives and silk screens, associated with printing processes.

e.g., putty knife, palette, wallpaper brush.

D280
PAPERMAKING T&E

Tools, equipment, and supplies originally created for manufacturing materials formed from the residue of suspensions or fabricating products made of such materials. Paper, whether made from wood pulp, textile fibres, or plastic fibres, is the principle product that falls in this classification. Particles mixed with liquids form suspensions. Though felt is made of materials that are matted like paper, tools and felting fall under TEXTILEWORKING T&E (D300) because felt is not formed from a suspension.

D300
TEXTILEWORKING T&E

Tools, equipment, and supplies originally created for preparing materials made from fibres and preparing woven fabrics. Also included in this category are tools, equipment, and supplies used for manufacturing objects from fibres or cloth. This classification includes tools, such as hatchels and cotton gins, specific to fibre preparation, but excludes tools, such as sheep shears and cotton balers, that are related to fibre sources.

e.g., sewing needle, embroidery scissors, reel, spool.

D320
WOODWORKING T&E

Tools, equipment, and supplies originally created for fabricating objects from wood. This classification includes artifacts used with and to create physically modified wood by-products such as plywood, chipboard, and masonite. This classification excludes tools and equipment for making objects out of chemically modified wood by-products such as paper, rayon, and rubber.

e.g., clamp, felloe saw, plane.

OTHER T&E FOR MATERIALS

D550: BASKET, BROOM, BRUSH MAKING T&E

Tools, equipment, and supplies for fabricating objects out of fibrous materials that are generally coarser than those used for textiles. This subclass includes tools used for basket making, broom making, brush making, and thatching.

D600: CIGAR MAKING T&E

Tools, equipment, and supplies for fabricating nonfood products for human consumption out of tobacco and related vegetable products. This subclass includes tools for handling harvested tobacco and manufacturing tobacco products. Smoking accessories and supplies are under PERSONAL GEAR (C160).

D650: LAPIDARY T&E

Tools, equipment, and supplies for fabricating objects out of crystalline materials, primarily precious and semi-precious stones. This subclass includes jewellers' gem-cutting tools, but excludes tools that are used in jewellry manufacture but that are for working non-crystalline materials such as metal, wood, or plastic.

D680: SOAPMAKING T&E

Tools, equipment, and supplies, such as a potash caldron or soap stick, used in manufacturing soap from hardwood ash residue.

D700: Wigmaking T&E

Tools, equipment, and supplies used in fabricating wigs and hair pieces from fibres. This subclass includes tools for preparing and arranging fibres and for sewing wigs, and special tools for finishing wigs. Excluded are tools that might be generally used for grooming, such as combs and brushes, unless they are specifically designed for wigmaking.

Category 05

TOOLS & EQUIPMENT FOR SCIENCE & TECHNOLOGY

Tools, equipment, and supplies used to observe natural phenomena or to apply knowledge gained from such observation. Tools in this category tend to be made to enlarge or record our understanding of the world or to help express such understanding. Classifications in this category are related by virtue of the fact that they contain artifacts created to employ a particular body of knowledge. ASTRONOMICAL T&E (E200) covers tools used to examine distant phenomena. TIMEKEEPING T&E (E540) covers things that people have developed to measure time. MAINTENANCE T&E (E340) covers tools developed in response to a body of knowledge about how to take care of things. These classifications are based on knowledge rather than on materials.

E020
ACOUSTICAL T&E

Tools, equipment, and supplies originally created for studying sound and its effect upon hearing. Artifacts in ACOUSTICAL T&E differ from those in SOUND COMMUNICATION EQUIPMENT (E020) in that the function of the former is to study sound, not to transmit or receive it. They differ from some related items in MEDICAL AND PSYCHOLOGICAL T&E (E380) in that the function of items in ACOUSTICAL T&E is to examine the nature and effects of sound, not to diagnose or treat medical situations.

e.g., tuning fork.

ARMAMENT T&E

Tools, equipment, and supplies originally created to be used for hunting, target shooting, warfare, or self-protection. This classification includes firearms, artillery, bladed weapons, and striking weapons. It does not include objects designed for transporting troops or supplies. For convenience it is divided into several subclasses based on weapon forms.

E060: ARMAMENT T&E, FIREARM

This subclass includes all projectile-firing weapons than can be easily deployed by one person. It excludes ammunition, firearm accessories, and crew-served heavy armament.

e.g., rifle, pistol, blunderbuss.

E080: ARMAMENT T&E, EDGED

This subclass includes all armament intended to cut or pierce by cutting. It includes edged weapons such as bayonets that are accessories to firearms and tools such as crossbows that launch edged weapons.

E100: ARMAMENT T&E, BLUDGEON

This subclass includes all armament designed to batter or crush by weight or momentum. It also includes arms such as sling-shots that propel missiles that are neither explosive nor penetrating.

e.g., blackjack, club.

E120: ARMAMENT T&E, ARTILLERY

This subclass includes all heavy weapons that employ combustion or explosion to fire a projectile. Artillery may be portable and it may be employed by only one person, but typically it is fired by a crew from a more or less stationary position.

e.g., cannon, carronade.

E140: ARMAMENT T&E, AMMUNITION

This subclass includes all ammunition for armament whether intended for particular weapons, such as BBs or cartridges, or intended to be deployed alone, such as missiles or bombs.

E160: ARMAMENT T&E, BODY ARMOR

This subclass includes clothing worn as defensive armament. It includes the formal parts of a "suit of armour" and protective devices used in combat.

E180: ARMAMENT T&E, ACCESSORY

This subclass includes all accessories used for hunting, target shooting, warfare, or self-protection. This subclass includes arms and artillery accessories and personal accoutrements, such as cartridge belts, cartridge boxes, and sword belts, associated with armament.

E200
ASTRONOMICAL T&E

Tools, equipment, and supplies originally created to observe, measure, and document objects and events outside the earth's atmosphere. Artifacts within ASTRONOMICAL T&E differ from those within OPTICAL T&E (E460) in that the former are not intended to address particular problems associated with vision. And they differ from those under SURVEYING AND NAVIGATIONAL T&E (E500) in that they are concerned with observation rather than with practical uses for such observation.

e.g., astrolabe, achromatic telescope, orrery.

E220
BIOLOGICAL T&E

Tools, equipment, and supplies originally created to observe, measure, and document physiological or anatomical aspects of organisms for purposes other than diagnosis or treatment. Tools for diagnosing and treating people are classified under MEDICAL AND PSYCHOLOGICAL T&E (E380); those for animals are under ANIMAL HUSBANDRY T&E (D040).

e.g., petri dish.

E240
CHEMICAL T&E

Tools, equipment, and supplies originally created for studying or manufacturing substances based upon their molecular composition, structure, and properties. The study of atomic and subatomic particles is classified under NUCLEAR PHYSICS T&E (E440); study of the interaction of physical objects, under MECHANICAL T&E (E360).

e.g., flash, beaker, still.

E260
CONSTRUCTION T&E

Tools, equipment, and supplies originally created for moving earth and building structures. This classification includes paving machines and equipment that modifies by demolition, such as wrecking balls and jackhammers. It also includes tools, such as pile drivers, used for constructing highways and structural facilities. It does not include specialized tools, such as hammers or cement mixers, listed in other classifications and used in the construction industries.

E280
ELECTRICAL & MAGNETIC T&E

Tools, equipment, and supplies originally created to observe, measure, and document electrical and magnetic phenomena. This classification also includes tools, equipment, and components, such as electrician's pliers or oscilloscopes, used in the manufacture, installation, and repair of electrical and electronic devices. It does not include electrical or electronic devices created to serve other specific purposes, such as sound communication or data processing, nor does it include electrical motors or generators (*see* ENERGY PRODUCTION T&E [E300]).

e.g., ammeter, resistor, fuseboard.

E300
ENERGY PRODUCTION T&E

Tools, equipment, and supplies originally created to generate, convert, or distribute energy or power.

e.g., motor, generator.

E320
GEOLOGICAL T&E

Tools, equipment, and supplies originally created to observe, measure, and document geological phenomena. This classification includes geologists' picks and seismic measuring devices, but excludes tools used for harvesting or mining rock or mineral materials.

E340
MAINTENANCE T&E

Tools, equipment, and supplies originally created for cleaning or laundering activities, whether carried on in homes or public buildings, whether performed privately or professionally. This classification includes specialized tools used for restoring and conserving objects.

e.g., clothes wringer, iron, sock stretcher.

E360
MECHANICAL T&E

Tools, equipment, and supplies originally created for the study, measurement, or utilization of the static and dynamic properties of solids, liquids, and gases. This classification includes general-purpose mechanical devices, such as wedges and hoists, and specialized devices, such as tensiometers and pressure gauges, used to measure mechanical properties.

E380
MEDICAL & PSYCHOLOGICAL T&E

Tools, equipment, and supplies originally created for examining, testing, diagnosing, and treating humans. This classification includes dental tools, objects used for testing sight and hearing, and objects used for psychological testing or treatment. It does not include objects used to study physical phenomena (*see* OPTICAL T&E [E460], ACOUSTICAL T&E [E020], BIOLOGICAL T&E [E220], and CHEMICAL T&E [E240]), or tools for veterinary medicine (*see* ANIMAL HUSBANDRY T&E [D040]).

e.g., splint, forceps, dose spoon.

E400
MERCHANDISING T&E

Tools, equipment, and supplies originally created to facilitate or enable the exchange of goods or services. This classification includes artifacts used to present goods, such as counters, as well as specific product packages. General product packages that are primarily intended for transporting goods rather than for marketing them fall within CONTAINERS (G020) in the DISTRIBUTION & TRANSPORTATION ARTIFACTS category.

E420
METEOROLOGICAL T&E

Tools, equipment, and supplies originally created to observe, measure, and document atmospheric phenomena.

e.g., weather vane, barometer.

E440
NUCLEAR PHYSICS T&E

Tools, equipment, and supplies originally created to study atomic structure and elementary particles as well as the physical properties of the universe.

E460
OPTICAL T&E

Tools, equipment, and supplies originally created to observe, measure, and record light. This classification includes commonly used equipment, such as binoculars and microscopes. It excludes specialized artifacts created for other scientific observation, such as visual-acuity charts and telescopes that are used particularly for astronomy (E200).

E480
REGULATIVE & PROTECTIVE T&E

Tools, equipment, and supplies originally created for controlling the behaviour of people, providing security or protection for property, and carrying out non-ceremonial activities of governmental organizations (including fire protection, police protection, and voting).

e.g., handcuffs, whip, shackle.

E500
SURVEYING & NAVIGATIONAL T&E

Tools, equipment, and supplies originally created to determine the position of an observer relative to known reference points or to indicate the form and extent of a region, such as land surface. This classification includes instruments for taking linear and angular measurements. It excludes devices for making calculations (*see* DATA PROCESSING T&E [F020]) or for recording data graphically (*see* DRAFTING T&E [F040]). This classification differs from ASTRONOMICAL T&E (E200) in that the objects in this classification are used for applied purposes, not for scientific study.

e.g., astrolabe, sextant, theodolite.

E520
THERMAL T&E

Tools, equipment, and supplies originally created to observe, measure, and document heat and its effects. Specialized artifacts created to serve specific purposes, such as a meteorological thermometer, are excluded from this classification.

E540
TIMEKEEPING T&E

Tools, equipment, and supplies originally created for recording and measuring time. This classification does not include timekeeping artifacts created for specialized purposes, such as chronometers.

e.g., clock, sundial.

E560
WEIGHTS & MEASURES T&E

Tools, equipment, and supplies originally created to observe, record, and measure mass (weight) or physical dimensions such as length, area, and volume. This classification includes general-purpose measuring devices such as precision balances or folding rules. It excludes artifacts created to measure time and to measure particular scientific data. Also excluded are specialized measuring devices and gauges such as sextants or carpenters' squares.

E600
OTHER T&E FOR SCIENCE & TECHNOLOGY

Category 06

TOOLS & EQUIPMENT FOR COMMUNICATION

Tools, equipment, and supplies used to enable communication. This category includes those classifications for literal and abstract communication, PRINTING T&E (F100) and MUSICAL T&E (F060). This category does not include things produced as communication, such as works of art and documents. These are the artifacts created by the tools of this category, and they are listed in Category 08, COMMUNICATION ARTIFACTS.

F020
DATA PROCESSING T&E

Tools, equipment, and supplies originally created for processing data by manual, mechanical, or electronic means. This classification includes numerical and word-processing devices such as abacuses and digital computers, process-control devices such as analog computers; and learning devices such as teaching machines.

F040
DRAFTING T&E

Tools, equipment, and supplies, such as T-squares or drafting tables, originally created to be used for precision drawing. This classification includes instruments used to record surveying and navigational observations. It does not include general-purpose writing or lettering tools.

F060
MUSICAL T&E

Tools, equipment, and supplies originally created to produce musical sounds. This classification includes devices actively employed in musical performance. It excludes equipment that simply transmits sound, as well as acoustical tools and equipment for studying sound.

e.g., piano, drum, violin.

F080
PHOTOGRAPHIC T&E

Tools, equipment, and supplies, such as cameras, film-processing tanks, or enlargers, originally created to capture permanent visual images by optical and chemical means.

F100
PRINTING T&E

Tools, equipment, and supplies originally created to reproduce written, photographic, or artistic material. This classification includes specialized tools such as handpresses, engraver's blocks, and photocopiers that are used for bookbinding, engraving, etching, lithography, and silk-screening.

F120
SOUND COMMUNICATION T&E

Tools, equipment, and supplies originally created to amplify or store music, spoken words, or other sounds that are meaningful for human communication.

e.g., foghorn, megaphone, speaking tube.

F140
TELECOMMUNICATION T&E

Tools, equipment, and supplies originally created to facilitate communicating at a distance, usually by means of electronic equipment. This classification includes the telephone, telegraph, radio, and television.

F160
VISUAL COMMUNICATION T&E

Tools, equipment, and supplies originally created to be used as visual signs or signalling devices or as means of viewing photographic or other visual images.

e.g., railroad lantern, signal flag, motion-picture projector.

F180
WRITTEN COMMUNICATION T&E

Tools, equipment, and supplies originally created to facilitate communication between people by means of written documents. This classification includes tools and supplies used for writing, such as pens, ink, and paper. Excluded are artifacts produced by writing, such as letters, and artifacts that are written upon but that were created for another purpose, such as postcards. These particular exclusions are both DOCUMENTARY ARTIFACTS (H080).

F500
OTHER T&E FOR COMMUNICATION

Category 07

DISTRIBUTION & TRANSPORTATION ARTIFACTS

Artifacts originally created to transport or distribute animate and inanimate things. This category also includes artifacts originally created to facilitate such transportation or as an adjunct to such transportation. This category includes propelled vehicles such as automobiles and wheelbarrows as well as containers that facilitate distribution. Because transportation equipment is complex and parts are often collected independently, subclasses for accessories are offered for some classifications. Scaled and design models are featured in this category.

G020
CONTAINER

Artifacts originally created for packing, shipping, or holding goods and commodities. Containers created for particular products and used for marketing and merchandising products are listed in MERCHANDISING T&E (E400).

AEROSPACE TRANSPORTATION

G060: AEROSPACE TRANSPORTATION EQUIPMENT

An artifact originally created to transport people or goods above the surface of the earth.

e.g., airplane, kite.

G080: AEROSPACE TRANSPORTATION ACCESSORY

An artifact originally created as an accessory to be used in conjunction with the transportation of people or goods above the surface of the earth.

e.g., engine, fixed-pitched propeller, propeller hub.

LAND TRANSPORTATION

G120: LAND TRANSPORTATION, ANIMAL POWERED

An artifact, powered by animal energy, originally created to transport people or goods on land without restriction to a fixed route determined by a track or other guidance device.

e.g., dogcart, cart, stagecoach.

G140: LAND TRANSPORTATION, HUMAN POWERED

An artifact, powered by human energy alone, originally created to transport people or goods on land without restriction to a fixed route determined by a track or other guidance device.

e.g., stretcher, bicycle, snowshoe.

G160: LAND TRANSPORTATION, MOTORIZED

An artifact, powered by some kind of self-acting mechanism such as a motor, originally created to transport people or goods on land without restriction to a fixed route determined by a track or other guidance device.

e.g., automobile.

G180: Land Transportation Accessory

An artifact originally created as an accessory used in the transportation of people or goods on land without restriction to a fixed route determined by a track or other guidance device.

e.g., hame, wheel chock, riding crop.

RAIL TRANSPORTATION

G220: Rail Transportation Equipment

An artifact originally created to transport people or goods on or along a fixed route determined by a track or some similar device.

e.g., train truck, locomotive.

G240: Rail Transportation Accessory

An artifact originally created as an accessory to the transportation of people or goods on or along a fixed route determined by a track or some similar device.

e.g., switch iron, steam locomotive throttle.

WATER TRANSPORTATION

G280: Water Transportation Equipment

An artifact originally created to transport people or goods on or under water.

e.g., canoe, scow, lobster boat.

G300: Water Transportation Accessory

An artifact originally created as an accessory for the transportation of people or goods on or under water.

e.g., life ring, rope capstan, paddle.

Category 08
COMMUNICATION ARTIFACTS

Artifacts originally created as expressions of human thought. COMMUNICATION ARTIFACTS comment on, interpret, or enhance people's environments. COMMUNICATION ARTIFACTS can function symbolically or literally. This category excludes the tools and equipment used to create communication artifacts.

H020
ADVERTISING MEDIUM

An artifact originally created to call public attention to a product, service, or event and to elicit a specific response in regard to products, services, or events. Generally the intended response is to urge people to acquire, use, or participate in the product, service, or event that is being advertised.

e.g., poster, banner, catalogue.

H040
ART

An artifact originally created for expressing and communicating ideas, values, or attitudes through images, symbols, and abstractions. It often reflects aesthetic pleasure or demonstrates creative skills and dexterity. Art can be uniquely created or it can be produced in a medium that allows many duplicates to be made.

e.g., picture, statue, gravure, painting.

H060
CEREMONIAL ARTIFACT

Artifacts originally created for carrying on governmental, fraternal, religious, or other organized and sanctioned societal activities. These artifacts are intended to evoke, symbolize, or express certain aspects of the traditions or heritage of a community or group of people. Usually they are associated with rituals or ceremonies. This classification includes: (1) any religious artifact, such as communication cups and altar pieces (note, though, that personal devotional objects such as religious medals and talismans are classified under PERSONAL SYMBOL [H120]); (2) any object used in a ceremony concerned with major personal events or crises, such as birth, puberty, sickness, or death, or concerned with community events or crises, such as harvest festivals or the need for rain; and (3) any object, such as a Girl Scout troop pennant, used in the ceremonial activities of a fraternity, lodge, club, governmental, or military organization.

H080
DOCUMENTARY ARTIFACT

An artifact originally created to communicate information to people. Unlike ADVERTISING MEDIUM

(H020), DOCUMENTARY ARTIFACTS are not generally intended to elicit specific responses in regards to products, services, or events. Instead, they present points of view, images, or sets of ideas, often with the aim of enlightening or swaying people's attitudes. This classification includes documents and also artifacts displaying commemorative information on materials other than paper, such as commemorative coins and souvenir plates.

H100
EXCHANGE MEDIUM

An artifact originally created to be used as a medium of exchange, such as coins, currency, or shell money, or as a means of obtaining specific services, such as postage stamps or transportation tokens.

H120
PERSONAL SYMBOL

An artifact originally created to communicate a particular personal belief, achievement, status, or membership. This classification includes articles of adornment or clothing worn primarily for their symbolism, such as fraternal rings, academic gowns, or crowns. PERSONAL SYMBOLS differ from CEREMONIAL ARTIFACTS (H060) in that they express individual ideas, not the ideas of a group.

Category 09
RECREATIONAL ARTIFACTS

Artifacts originally created to be used as toys or to carry on the activities of sports, games, gambling, or public entertainment.

I020
GAME

An artifact originally created for a competitive activity based upon chance, problem solving, or calculation rather than physical effort and conducted according to stated rules. This category also includes all forms of gambling devices.

e.g., dominoes, marble, card deck.

I040
PUBLIC ENTERTAINMENT DEVICE

An artifact originally created for the production of non-competitive spectator entertainment.

I060
RECREATIONAL DEVICE

An artifact originally created for a participatory, usually non-competitive, recreational activity other than an athletic game or exercise. This classification includes entertainment equipment such as a carousel, a pinball machine, a swing, or a slide, whether such equipment is publicly or privately owned and whether or not charges are associated with its use.

I080
SPORTS EQUIPMENT

An artifact originally created for a physical activity that is often competitive. This classification includes equipment used in all forms of athletic games and exercises, including individual and team sports.

e.g., dumbbell, tennis net, ice skate.

I100
TOY

An artifact originally created as a plaything. Toys often represent functional objects, such as toy hammers and toy ships, or living things, such as baby dolls and stuffed animals. Toys also include objects developed primarily for play, such as balls, tops, and kites.

Category 10

UNCLASSIFIABLE ARTIFACTS

Artifacts originally created to serve purposes that cannot be identified at the time the objects are catalogued.

J020
ARTIFACT REMNANT

A segment or incomplete part of an artifact originally created to fulfill a purpose that cannot be determined or inferred from the fragment.

J040
FUNCTION UNKNOWN

An artifact originally created to serve an unknown purpose.

J060
MULTIPLE USE ARTIFACT

An artifact originally created to serve a variety of purposes that extend beyond the range of one classification. Tools that have multiple attachments that enable them to serve a range of functions fall into this classification, as do hybrid tools that are made of several disparate parts that are used together to perform a particular function, such as fence mending.

III

THESAURUS

INTRODUCTION

Terms in the thesaurus are presented in two ways: in alphabetical order and in hierarchical order by category and class.

At the time of cataloguing, a primary consultation may be carried out by simply consulting the alphabetical list. If the term is not found there, the hierarchical list may then be used to locate the appropriate term by way of a series of filters.

HIERARCHICAL

LIST OF TERMS

Class A020: BUILDING

Total: 27

Object, suffix

BALUSTRADE
BEAM, TRUSS
BLOCKHOUSE, MODEL
BUILDING, MODEL OFFICE
CEILING
COVER, TEPEE
FIREPLACE
FIREPLACE FACADE
FLOOR
FORT, MODEL
HABITATION, MODEL
HANDRAIL
HOUSE
HOUSE, MINIATURE

Object, suffix

MAUSOLEUM, MODEL
MUSEUM, MODEL
PLANT, MODEL INDUSTRIAL
ROOF
SHED
TEMPLE, MODEL
TENT
TENT PEG
TIMBER
TIMBER, INSTRUCTIONAL MODEL
WALL
WIGWAM
WIGWAM, MODEL

Class A040: BUILDING COMPONENT

Total: 69

Object, suffix

ASSEMBLY, LATCH
BALUSTER
BAR
BASEBOARD
BOARD
BRACKET
BRACKET, MILITARY
BRICK
CABINET, MEDICINE
COLUMN
CORNERSTONE
CORNICE
COVER, FLUE
CROSS
DOOR
DOOR, BAKEOVEN
DOOR, FIREPLACE
DOORBELL
DOORFRAME
DOORKNOB
DOORPLATE
DOORSPRING
DUMBWAITER
ESCUTCHEON
FINIAL
FLUE
FRAME, WINDOW
GRILL, VENTILATOR
GRILL, WINDOW
GUDGEON
HANGER, PIPE
HASP
HINGE
HOLDER, FLAG
HOOK, CEILING

Object, suffix

KNOCKER
LATCH
LIFT, WINDOW
LINOLEUM
LOCK
LOCK, DOOR
LOCK, MILITARY DOOR
LOCK, WINDOW
MANTEL
MOLDING
NEWEL CAP
PAINT FRAGMENT
PANELING
PILLAR
PINTLE
PIPE
POT, CHIMNEY
PULPIT
RAIL, BAR
ROD, LIGHTNING
ROD, STAIR
SHELF
SHINGLE
STAPLE
TILE
TRACK, DOOR
VENTILATOR
WALLPAPER
WALLPAPER FRAGMENT
WEIGHT, DOOR
WINDOW
WINDOW, SALES MODEL
WINDOWPANE
WINDOWPANE, LEADED

Class A060: SITE FEATURE

Total: 8

Object, suffix

BARBWIRE
BIRDHOUSE
CISTERN
FENCE

Object, suffix

FLAGPOLE
FOUNTAIN, WATER
POST, HITCHING
POST RING, HITCHING

Class A080: OTHER STRUCTURE

Total: 6

Object, suffix

BILLBOARD
BOX, SENTRY
HYDRANT

Object, suffix

POLE, UTILITY
SLUICE
TOWER

Class B020: BEDDING

Total: 34

Object, suffix

BAG, POLICE SLEEPING
BAG, SLEEPING
BEDSPREAD
BEDSPRINGS
BELT, MILITARY BEDDING
BLANKET
BLANKET, MILITARY
BLANKET, MINIATURE
BLANKET, POLICE
BLANKET/SHEET
BOLSTER
BOLSTER, MILITARY
CANOPY
COMFORTER
COVER, BOLSTER
COVER, MATTRESS
COVER, MILITARY BOLSTER

Object, suffix

COVER, MILITARY MATTRESS
COVER, PILLOW
COVER, POLICE SLEEPING BAG
COVER, SLEEPING BAG
CURTAIN, BED
HAMMOCK
MAT, SLEEPING
MATTRESS
MATTRESS, MILITARY
PILLOW
PILLOWCASE
QUILT
RUFFLE, DUST
SHAM, PILLOW
SHEET
SHEET, MILITARY
SHEET, MINIATURE

Class B040: FLOOR COVERING

Total: 11

Object, suffix

CARPET
COVER, STAIR
DOORMAT
FLOORCLOTH
MAT
MAT, BATH

Object, suffix

RUG
RUG, MILITARY MAGAZINE
RUG, THROW
RUNNER
UNDERLAY

Class B060: FURNITURE

Total: 173

Object, suffix

BED
BED, CHILD'S
BED, FOLDING
BED, FOUR-POSTER
BED, MILITARY
BED, MINIATURE CHILD'S
BED, MINIATURE FOUR-POSTER
BED, POLICE
BED, SOFA
BED HEADBOARD
BED LEG
BED POST
BED POST FINIAL
BED RAIL
BENCH
BENCH, BUCKET
BENCH, GARDEN
BENCH LEG
BENCH, MILITARY
BENCH, MINIATURE
BOOKCASE
BOOKCASE, MILITARY
CABINET
CABINET, CHINA
CABINET, CORNER
CABINET, DISPLAY

Object, suffix

CABINET, FILING
CABINET, HANGING
CABINET, KEY
CABINET, PHONOGRAPH
CABINET, PHONOGRAPH/RADIO
CABINET, POLICE HANGING
CABINET, RADIO
CANDLESTAND
CANTERBURY
CASE, DRESSING
CELLARETTE
CHAIR
CHAIR, BARBER'S
CHAIR, CHILD'S
CHAIR, CHILD'S ROCKING
CHAIR, DESK
CHAIR, DINING
CHAIR, EASY
CHAIR, FOLDING
CHAIR, GARDEN
CHAIR, HALL
CHAIR, INVALID
CHAIR, MILITARY
CHAIR, MILITARY FOLDING
CHAIR, MINIATURE
CHAIR, OCCASIONAL

Class B060: FURNITURE — *(Continued)*

Object, suffix

CHAIR, PILOT'S	RACK, BOOT
CHAIR, PLATFORM ROCKING	RACK, GUN
CHAIR, POLICE DESK	RACK, HARNESS
CHAIR, POTTY	RACK, HAT
CHAIR, RECLINING	RACK, MAGAZINE
CHAIR, ROCKING	RACK, MILITARY GUN
CHAIR, SPEAKER'S	RACK, PLANT
CHAIR BACK	RACK, STORAGE
CHAIR SEAT	RACK, TOWEL
CHAIR/TABLE	RACK BAND, MILITARY GUN
CHEST	SAFE
CHEST, BLANKET	SCREEN
CHEST, MILITARY	SCREEN, POLE
CHEST, MINIATURE	SEAT, LOVE
CHEST HANDLE	SECRETARY
CHEST OF DRAWERS	SECRETARY-BOOKCASE
CHEST OF DRAWERS, CHILD'S	SETTEE
CHEST ON FRAME	SETTLE
CHIFFOROBE	SIDEBOARD
COAT-TREE	SIDEBOARD, MINIATURE
COATRACK	SOFA
COATRACK, MILITARY	STALL
COMMODE	STAND, SHAVING
CONFESSIONAL	STAND, TELEVISION
COVER, FOOTSTOOL	STEPS, BED
CRADLE	STOOL
CRADLE/ROCKER	STOOL, MILITARY
CRIB	STOOL, MILKING
CRIB, MINIATURE	SUITE, BEDROOM
CUPBOARD	TABLE
CUPBOARD, HANGING	TABLE, CARD
CUPBOARD, MILITARY HANGING	TABLE, CENTER
CUPBOARD, MINIATURE	TABLE, CENTER PEDESTAL
CUPBOARD, PRESS	TABLE, COFFEE
DESK	TABLE, CONSOLE
DESK, DROP-FRONT	TABLE, CORNER
DESK, MILITARY	TABLE, DINING
DESK, MILITARY CAMPAIGN	TABLE, DRESSING
DESK, ROLLTOP	TABLE, FOLDING
DESK, SCHOOL	TABLE, GAME
DESK, SLANT-TOP	TABLE, GARDEN
EASEL	TABLE, KITCHEN
ETAGERE	TABLE, LIBRARY
FENDER	TABLE, MILITARY
FOOTSTOOL	TABLE, MINIATURE
HALLSTAND	TABLE, MORTICIAN'S
HIGHCHAIR	TABLE, NIGHT
KNEELER	TABLE, PIER
LOUNGE	TABLE, SERVING
MIRROR	TABLE, SEWING
MIRROR, CHEVAL	TABLE, TEA
MIRROR, DRESSER	TABLE, TIER
MIRROR, WALL	TABLE, TILT-TOP
OTTOMAN	TABLE, TRIPOD
PEDESTAL	TABLE, VESTING
PEW	TABLE, WRITING
PEW HEADBOARD	TABLE LEAF
PODIUM	WARDROBE
POST, MILITARY CURTAIN	WASHSTAND
PRIE-DIEU	WASHSTAND, MILITARY
PULL, DOOR/DRAWER	

Class B080: HOUSEHOLD ACCESSORY

Object, suffix

Object, suffix

ANTIMACASSAR	HOLDER, TOILET PAPER
AQUARIUM	HOLDER, TREE
ASHTRAY	HOLDER, UMBRELLA
BAG, TABLE LEAF	HOLDER, WATCH
BANK, COIN	HOOK, BIRDCAGE
BATHTUB	HOOK, COAT
BEDKEY	HUMIDOR
BELLPULL	JAR, BELL
BIRDCAGE	JAR, POTPOURRI
BOOKEND	JAR, SLOP
BOOTJACK	JARDINIERE
BOTTLE, HOT-WATER	KEY
BOWL, FLOWER	LADDER
BOX, BIBLE	LADDER, MILITARY
BOX, CIGARETTE	LAMBREQUIN
BOX, DEED	LANTERN, PAPER
BOX, JEWELRY	LAVABO
BOX, MISSAL	MAT, TABLE
BOX, TRINKET	MOUSETRAP
BOX, WALL	NAIL, PICTURE FRAME
BRACKET, PICTURE FRAME	NAILHEAD, PICTURE FRAME
BURNER, INCENSE	PADLOCK
CACHEPOT	PADLOCK, MILITARY
CAN, WATERING	POCKET, WALL
CAP, BOTTLE	RACK, KEY
CASE, DISPLAY	RACK, NEWSPAPER
CASE, DOILY	RACK, PIPE
CASTER	RACK, SPOON
CHAIN, PICTURE FRAME	RACK, TIE
CHEST, SILVER	RATTRAP
COASTER, FURNITURE	RECEIVER, CARD
COATHANGER	RUNNER, BENCH
COATHANGER, MILITARY	RUNNER, TABLE
COVER, CHAIR SEAT	SAFE, MATCH
COVER, CUSHION	SAUCER, FLOWERPOT
CURTAIN, SPLASH	SCARF, BUREAU
CUSHION	SCARF, PIANO
CUTTER, CIGAR	SCRAPER, BOOT
DISPENSER, TOWEL	SET, ANTIMACASSAR
DOILY	SET, BUREAU SCARF
DOORSTOP	SLIPCOVER
FAN, FLY	SPITTOON
FILTER, WATER	STAND, BOOK
FLOWERPOT	STAND, SMOKER'S
FLOWERPOT, MINIATURE	STEPLADDER
FLYPAPER	STOPPER, BOTTLE
FLYTRAP	STRONGBOX
FRAME, PICTURE	STRONGBOX, POLICE
FROG	SWATTER, FLY
GLASS, PICTURE FRAME	THROW
HANGER, PICTURE FRAME	THROW, TABLE
HOLDER, MATCH	URN
HOLDER, PLATE	VASE
HOLDER, RING	WARMER, BED
HOLDER, SPILL	WARMER, FOOT
HOLDER, TISSUE	WASTEBASKET

Class B100: LIGHTING DEVICE

Total: 85

Object, suffix

BOBECHE
BOX, CANDLE
BULB, LIGHT
CANDELABRUM
CANDLE
CANDLESNUFFER
CANDLESNUFFER & TRAY
CANDLESTICK
CANDLESTICK, MILITARY
CANDLESTICK, MINER'S
CANDLESTICK, MINIATURE
CASE, ELECTRIC LAMP
CHANDELIER
CHANDELIER, CANDLE
CHANDELIER, ELECTRIC
CHANDELIER, GAS
CHANDELIER, KEROSINE
COVER, LAMP ROSETTE
COVER, LIGHTHOUSE LENS
CRESSET
EXTINGUISHER, CANDLE
FLASHLIGHT
GIRANDOLE
GRISETTE
HOLDER, LAMP
HOLDER, LANTERN
HOLDER, MILITARY LAMP
HOLDER, RUSHLIGHT
HOLDER, SHADE
HOLDER, SPLINT
HOLDER, TAPER
LAMP
LAMP, BURNING-FLUID
LAMP, CAMPHENE
LAMP, CANDLE
LAMP CHIMNEY
LAMP COUNTERWEIGHT
LAMP, ELECTRIC
LAMP, ELECTRIC MINER'S
LAMP FONT
LAMP, GAS
LAMP, GASOLINE
LAMP, KEROSINE

Object, suffix

LAMP, MILITARY OIL
LAMP, MINER'S CARBIDE
LAMP, MINER'S OIL
LAMP, MINIATURE SEMILIQUID
LAMP, OIL
LAMP, SEMILIQUID
LAMP BASE
LAMP BURNER
LAMP BURNER, LIGHTHOUSE
LAMP BURNER DEFLECTOR
LAMP GLOBE
LAMP GLOBE GALLERY
LAMP MANTLE
LAMP PENDANT
LAMP REFLECTOR
LAMP SHADE
LAMP SHADE, MILITARY
LANTERN
LANTERN, CANDLE
LANTERN, CARBIDE
LANTERN, ELECTRIC
LANTERN, FISHERMAN'S
LANTERN, GAS
LANTERN GLOBE
LANTERN, KEROSINE
LANTERN, MILITARY
LANTERN, MINIATURE CANDLE
LANTERN, OIL
LANTERN, SHIP'S
LANTERN FONT, MILITARY
LIGHT SOCKET
LIGHTER, GAS LAMP
RUSHLIGHT
SCONCE
SCONCE, MIRRORED
SEARCHLIGHT
SPOTLIGHT
STREETLAMP
TRAY, CANDLESNUFFER
TRIMMER, WICK
WICK
WRENCH, LAMP

Class B120: PLUMBING FIXTURE

Total: 11

Object, suffix

BATHTUB
FAUCET
HEATER, WATER
PUMP, WATER
SHOWER
SHOWER HEAD

Object, suffix

SINK
STAND, WATER HEATER
TOILET
TOILET FLUSH CHAIN
TOILET SEAT

Class B140: TEMPERATURE CONTROL DEVICE

Total: 69

Object, suffix

Object, suffix

ANDIRON

ANDIRON, MINIATURE

BELLOWS

BIN, COAL

BOARD, MILITARY STOVE

BOARD, STOVE

BOX, ASH

BOX, MILITARY ASH

BRACKET, FIRESET

BRIQUETTE

BROOM, FIREPLACE

CARRIER, EMBER

CARRIER, LOG

DRILL, FIREMAKING

FIREBACK

FIREBOARD

FIRESET

FIRESET, MILITARY

FLINT

FORK, FIREPLACE

GRATE, FIREPLACE

HEATER

HEATER, ALCOHOL

HEATER, BURNING-FLUID

HEATER, COAL

HEATER, LAMP

HEATER, WOOD

LOG, ARTIFICIAL

MATCH

POKER

POKER, MINIATURE

PUNK

RACK, STOVEPIPE

RADIATOR

RAKE, FIREPLACE

RAKE, STOVE

REDUCER, STOVE LID

SCOOP, FIREPLACE

SCRAPER, FIREPLACE

SCREEN, FIRE

SCUTTLE, COAL

SHAKER, GRATE

SHOVEL, FIREPLACE

SHOVEL, MINIATURE FIREPLACE

SHOVEL, STOVE

STAND, BELLOWS

STAND, FIRESET

STEEL

STOVE

STOVE, MILITARY

STOVE, MINIATURE

STOVE, WOOD

STOVE DOOR

STOVE DOOR, MILITARY

STOVE GRATE

STOVE LEG

STOVE LID

STOVE URN

STOVEPIPE

STOVEPIPE COLLAR

STOVEPIPE DAMPER

TINDERBOX

TINDERPISTOL

TONGS, FIREPLACE

TONGS, MILITARY FIREPLACE

TUB, MILITARY COAL

WICK

WOODBIN

WOODBIN, MILITARY

Class B160: WINDOW OR DOOR COVERING

Total: 20

Object, suffix

Object, suffix

BLIND, VENETIAN

BRACKET, ROD

BRACKET, SHADE

CLEAT, AWNING

CURTAIN

CURTAIN, DOOR

DRAPERY

HINGE, AWNING

HOOK, CURTAIN

LOOP, CURTAIN

PULL, SHADE

PULLEY, CURTAIN

RING, CURTAIN

ROD, CURTAIN

ROD FINIAL, CURTAIN

ROLLER, SHADE

SHADE, SPRING-PULL

SWAG

VALANCE

WEIGHT, CURTAIN

Class C020: ADORNMENT

Total: 21

Object, suffix

ANKLET
ARMLET
BEAD
BRACELET
BRELOQUE
BROOCH
CHATELAINE
CORSAGE
EARRING
FOB
HAIRPIECE

Object, suffix

HOLDER, LAPEL PIN
LABRET
LOCKET
NECKLACE
ORNAMENT, HAIR
PENDANT
PIN, LAPEL
RING
STAND, WIG
WIG

Class C060: CLOTHING, FOOTWEAR

Total: 31

Object, suffix

BOOT
BOOT, HIP
BOOT, MILITARY
BOOT, POLICE
BOOT, RIDING
BOOT, WELLINGTON
BOOTEE
BOTTE SAUVAGE
CLOG
CREEPER
CREEPER, MILITARY
GAITER
GAITER, MILITARY
MOCCASIN
MUKLUK
PUTTEE, MILITARY

Object, suffix

RUBBER
SABOT
SABOT, FOUNDER'S
SHOE
SHOE, CHILD'S
SHOE, MILITARY
SHOE HEEL
SHOE IRON
SHOE SOLE
SHOELACE
SLIPPER
SLIPPER, MILITARY MAGAZINE
SOCK
SPAT
STOCKING

Class C080: CLOTHING, HEADWEAR

Total: 59

Object, suffix

AMICE
BALMORAL
BERET
BIRETTA
BOATER
BONNET
BONNET, INDOOR
BONNET, INFANT'S
BONNET, MILITARY
CAP
CAP, BATHING
CAP, BOUDOIR
CAP, FORAGE
CAP, MILITARY
CAP, POLICE
CAP, SMOKING
DERBY
FEDORA
GLENGARRY
GLENGARRY, MILITARY
HAIRNET
HAT

Object, suffix

HAT, HARD
HAT, MILITARY BICORN
HAT, MILITARY TRICORN
HAT, PANAMA
HAT, POLICE
HAT, RAIN
HAT, TOP
HAT, TRICORN
HAT BODY
HATBAND
HATBAND, MILITARY
HATBAND, POLICE
HAVELOCK, MILITARY
HEADBAND
HELMET, AVIATOR'S
HELMET, FIREMAN'S
HELMET, MILITARY
HELMET, MILITARY PITH
HELMET, MINER'S
HELMET, POLICE PITH
HOMBERG
HOOD

Class C080: CLOTHING, HEADWEAR — *(Continued)*

Total: 59

Object, suffix

KERCHIEF
LAPPET
NIGHTCAP
PILLBOX
PILLBOX, MILITARY
PILLBOX, POLICE
SCARF
SHAKO, MILITARY

Object, suffix

SHAKO CHIN STRAP, MILITARY
SUNBONNET
SWEATBAND
TOQUE
TUQUE
TURBAN
VEIL

Class C100: CLOTHING, OUTERWEAR

Total: 110

Object, suffix

ALB
APRON
APRON, BLACKSMITH'S
APRON, MILITARY DRUMMER'S
BLOUSE
BLOUSE, CHILD'S
BLOUSE, MILITARY
BODICE
BOLERO
BREECHES
BREECHES, CHILD'S
BREECHES, MILITARY
BREECHES, MILITARY RIDING
BREECHES, POLICE RIDING
BUNTING
CAPE
CAPE, MILITARY
CAPOTE
CASSOCK
CHAPS
CHASUBLE
CLOAK
COAT
COAT, AUTOMOBILE
COAT, CUTAWAY
COAT, FROCK
COAT, LABORATORY
COAT, MILITARY
COAT, MILITARY FROCK
COATEE, MILITARY
COSTUME, SEASONAL
COVERALLS
DALMATIC
DOUBLET, MILITARY
DRESS
DRESS, CHILD'S
DRESS, INSTRUCTIONAL MODEL
GOWN, BAPTISMAL
GOWN, DRESSING
GOWN, WEDDING
GREATCOAT, MILITARY
HABIT, RELIGIOUS
HABIT, RIDING
HOUSECOAT
JACKET
JACKET, BED
JACKET, CHILD'S

Object, suffix

JACKET, MILITARY
JACKET, MILITARY FATIGUE
JACKET, MILITARY MESS
JACKET, MOURNING
JACKET, PEA
JACKET, POLICE PEA
JACKET, PRISONER
JACKET, SMOKING
JACKET, SUIT
JACKET, WAITER
JERKIN
JUSTAUCORPS, MILITARY
KILT
KIMONO
KNICKERS
LEGGING
LOINCLOTH
MANIPLE
NIGHTGOWN
OVERCOAT
OVERCOAT, MILITARY
OVERCOAT, POLICE
PAJAMAS
PANTS
PANTS, INSTRUCTIONAL MODEL
PANTS, MILITARY
PANTS, POLICE
PARKA
PINAFORE
PLAID, MILITARY FLY
RAINCOAT
ROMPER
SACK
SET, BAPTISMAL
SET, COAT & BONNET
SET, SWEATER
SHAWL
SHIRT
SHIRT, INSTRUCTIONAL MODEL
SHIRT, MILITARY
SHIRT, POLICE
SHORTS
SKIRT
SKIRT, CHILD'S
SMOCK
STOLE
SUIT

Class C100: CLOTHING, OUTERWEAR — (Continued)
Total: 110

Object, suffix

SUIT, BATHING
SUIT, CHILD'S
SUIT, JUMP
SUIT, MILITARY MAGAZINE
SURPLICE
SWEATER
TIGHTS
TUNIC

Object, suffix

TUNIC, MILITARY
TUNIC, POLICE
UNIFORM
UNIFORM, MILITARY
VEIL, HUMERAL
WAISTCOAT
WAISTCOAT, MILITARY
WAISTCOAT, POLICE

Class C120: CLOTHING, UNDERWEAR
Total: 25

Object, suffix

BELT, GARTER
BINDER
BRASSIERE
BUSTLE
CAMISOLE
COMBINATION
COMBINATION, CHILD'S
CORSET
CORSET, CHILD'S
COVER, CORSET
DIAPER
DRAWERS
DRAWERS, CHILD'S

Object, suffix

GIRDLE
IMPROVER, BUST
LACE, CORSET
PANTALETTES
PETTICOAT
PETTICOAT, CHILD'S
PETTICOAT, HOOP
SLIP
SLIP, CHILD'S
SLIP YOKE
SUIT, UNION
UNDERSHIRT

Class C140: CLOTHING ACCESSORY
Total: 77

Object, suffix

APPLICATOR, SHOE-POLISH
ARMBAND
ARMBAND, MILITARY
ASCOT
BELT
BELT, MILITARY
BELT, MILITARY SAM BROWNE
BELT, MILITARY SHOULDER
BELT, POLICE
BELT, POLICE SAM BROWNE
BIB
BOA
BOX, BOOTBLACKING
BRUSH, CLOTHES
BRUSH, HAT
BRUSH, SHOE
BUCKLE
BUFFER, BUTTON
BUFFER, SHOE
BUTTON
BUTTONHOOK
CLASP
CLIP, TIE
COLLAR
COLLAR, POLICE
COLLAR, ROMAN
CRAVAT
CRAVAT, MILITARY

Object, suffix

CUFF
DICKEY
FICHU
GARTER
GLOVE
GLOVE, FISHERMAN'S
GLOVE, POLICE
HATPIN
HOLDER, HATPIN
HOOK, BOOT
JABOT
KIT, MILITARY BUTTON POLISHING
KIT, SHOESHINE
LINK, CUFF
MITT
MITTEN
MITTEN, POLICE
MUFF
MUFFLER
NECKERCHIEF
NECKTIE
NECKTIE, POLICE
PRESS, PANTS
SACHET
SASH
SASH, MILITARY
SCARF, MILITARY NECK
SET, BUCKLE

Class C140: CLOTHING ACCESSORY — *(Continued)*

Total: 77

Object, suffix

SET, CLOTHES BRUSH	STOCK, MILITARY
SET, COLLAR & CUFF	STRETCHER, GLOVE
SET, COLLAR & MUFF	STUD
SET, COLLAR & SLEEVE	SUSPENDERS
SET, TIE CLIP	SUSPENDERS, MILITARY
SHOEHORN	SUSPENDERS, POLICE
SLEEVE	TIE, BOW
STAY, COLLAR	TREE, SHOE
STICK, MILITARY BUTTON	WEIGHT, MILITARY PANTS
STICKPIN	WRISTLET
STOCK	

Class C160: PERSONAL GEAR

Total: 137

Object, suffix

AID, HEARING	CASE, KEY
BACKPACK	CASE, MEDICINE
BACKPACK, MILITARY	CASE, MEDICINE BOTTLE
BAG, DITTY	CASE, MILITARY SABRETACHE
BAG, DUFFLE	CASE, MIRROR
BAG, GARMENT	CASE, NIGHTGOWN
BAG, MILITARY DUFFLE	CASE, PHOTOGRAPH
BAG, PIPE	CASE, PIPE
BAG, POLICE DUFFLE	CASE, SLIPPER
BAG, SCHOOL	CASE, STOCKING
BAG, SHOE	CASE, STUD
BANDBOOK	CASE, THERMOMETER
BASKET, TRINKET	CASE, TIE
BELT, MILITARY BACKPACK	CASE, VACCUM BOTTLE
BELT, MILITARY BLANKET	CHAIN, KEY
BELT, MILITARY CANTEEN	CHAIN, WATCH
BELT, MILITARY DRUM	CHEST
BELT, MILITARY MESS TIN	CHEST, MINIATURE
BELT, MILITARY MONEY	CHEST, SEA
BELT, MILITARY POUCH	CLEANER PIPE
BELT, MILITARY SABRETACHE	CLIP, MONEY
BELT, MONEY	CONDOM
BELT, POLICE POUCH	COVER, MILITARY CANTEEN
BOTTLE, MEDICINE	COVER, MILITARY POUCH
BOTTLE, OPIUM	COVER, MILITARY SABRETACHE
BOTTLE, SMELLING	COVER, PARASOL
BOTTLE, SNUFF	COVER, POLICE POUCH
BOX, TOBACCO	COVER, SHOE
BRIEFCASE	CRUTCH
CANE	CUTTER, CIGAR
CANTEEN	ETUI
CANTEEN, MILITARY	EYEGLASSES
CARRIER, LUGGAGE/SHAWL	FAN
CASE, CARD	FLASK, POCKET
CASE, CIGAR	FRAME, PACK
CASE, CIGAR HOLDER	GOGGLES
CASE, CIGARETTE	GOGGLES, SNOW
CASE, CLOTHES BRUSH	GOGGLES FILTER
CASE, COLLAR	GRATER, TOBACCO
CASE, EAR TRUMPET	HANDKERCHIEF
CASE, EYEGLASSES	HATBOX
CASE, GLOVE	HATBOX, MILITARY
CASE, HANDKERCHIEF	HATBOX, POLICE
CASE, JEWELRY	HAVERSACK

Class C160: PERSONAL GEAR — *(Continued)*

Total: 137

Object, suffix

HAVERSACK, MILITARY
HAVERSACK, POLICE
HOLDER, CIGAR
HOLDER, CIGARETTE
HOLDER, COIN
HOLDER, NOSEGAY
HOLDER, SHOE
KIT, SHOESHINE
KNAPSACK
KNIFE, PIPE
KNIFE, POCKET
LIGHTER
LOCK, TRUNK
MACHINE, CIGARETTE
MONOCLE
PARASOL
PARASOL HANDLE
PARFLECHE
PILLBOX
PIPE
POCKET
POUCH, FIRE
POUCH, MILITARY
POUCH, POLICE
POUCH, TOBACCO

Object, suffix

PROSTHESIS
PURSE
PURSE FRAME
RING, KEY
RING, MILITARY KEY
SABRETACHE
SABRETACHE, MILITARY
SABRETACHE, POLICE
SAFE, MATCH
SATCHEL
SET, MILITARY ACCOUTREMENT
SNUFFBOX
SPORRAN, MILITARY
STICK, MILITARY SWAGGER
SUITCASE
TAMPER, PIPE
TOBACCO
TRUMPET, EAR
TRUNK
TRUNK, MILITARY
UMBRELLA
WALKER
WALLET
WARMER, HAND

Class C180: TOILET ARTICLE

Total: 81

Object, suffix

BASIN
BASIN, MILITARY
BEDPAN
BIDET
BLADE, RAZOR
BOTTLE, TOILET
BOWL, BARBER'S
BOX, PUFF
BOX, RAZOR
BRUSH HANDLE, SHAVING
BRUSH, NAIL
BRUSH, SHAVING
BUFFER
CASE, COMPACT
CASE, SHAVING BRUSH
CASE, SOAP
CASE, TOILET BOTTLE
CASE, TOOTHBRUSH
CLIPPERS, HAIR
COMB
COMPACT
COVER, CHAMBER POT
CURLER
DISH LID, SOAP
DISH, SOAP
DUSTER, BARBER'S
EYECUP
FILE, NAIL
HAIRBAG, MILITARY
HAIRBRUSH

Object, suffix

HAIRPIN
HEATER, CURLING IRON
HOLDER, TOOTHBRUSH
IRON, CURLING
IRON, STRAIGHTENING
JAR, COSMETIC
KNIFE, CUTICLE
MIRROR, HAND
MUG, SHAVING
OINTMENT CONTAINER
PENCIL, EYEBROW
PIN, BOBBY
PITCHER
PLANTER
POMANDER
POT, CHAMBER
POT LID, CHAMBER
POT, MINIATURE CHAMBER
PUFF, POWDER
RACK, TOOTHBRUSH
RAZOR
RECEIVER, HAIR
SCISSORS, BARBER'S
SCISSORS, MANICURE
SET, DRESSER
SET, HAIRBRUSH
SET, MANICURE
SET, RAZOR
SET, SHAVING
SET, TOILET

Class C180:   TOILET ARTICLE — *(Continued)*

Total: 81

Object, suffix

SHAKER, POWDER	TOWEL, FACE
SHAPER, NAIL	TOWEL, FINGERTIP
SHARPENER, RAZOR BLADE	TOWEL, HAND
SPOON, EAR	TOWEL, POLICE
STROP	TOWEL, ROLLER
TOOTHBRUSH	TRAY, DRESSER
TOOTHBRUSH, MILITARY	TWEEZERS
TOOTHPICK	URINAL
TOWEL	URINAL, MILITARY
TOWEL, BATH	WASHCLOTH
TOWEL, BEACH	

Class D020: AGRICULTURAL T&E   Total: 98
Object, suffix

BASKET, GATHERING
BASKET, WINNOWING
BILLHOOK
CAN, WATERING
CHISEL, PRUNING
CHOPPER, FEED
CORNHUSKER, HAND
CULTIVATOR, GARDEN
CULTIVATOR, HAND
CULTIVATOR, WALKING
CULTIVATOR HANDLE
CUTTER, ENSILAGE
DIBBLE
DIGGER, POTATO
DUSTER, DRY-POWDER
EDGER, TURF
FLAIL
FORK
FORK, ALFALFA
FORK, HAY-LIFTING
FORK, MANURE
FORK, SPADING
FORK, VEGETABLE SCOOP
GRINDER, FEED
GUARD, MOWER SICKLE BAR
HARROW, DISK
HARROW, SPIKE-TOOTH
HAYFORK
HOE
HOE, GARDEN
HOE, GRUB
HOE, TURNIP
HOE BLADE
HOOK, BRUSH
HOOK, CORN
HOOK, GRASS
HOOK, HAY-BALE
HOOK, MANURE
HOOK, POTATO
KNIFE, HAY
KNIFE, PRUNING
KNIFE, TOBACCO
MACHETE
MACHINE, THRESHING
MATTOCK
MATTOCK HANDLE
MILL, FANNING
MOWER
MOWER, LAWN

Object, suffix

MOWER BLADE
MOWER HANDLE
NEEDLE, BAGGER'S
NOZZLE, GARDEN HOSE
PICKER, FRUIT
PINCERS, GARDEN
PLOW
PLOW, BOG-CUTTER
PLOW, MOLDBOARD
PLOW, SALES MODEL
PLOW BEAM
PLOW COULTER
PLOW HANDLE
PLOW GAUGE WHEEL
PLOWSHARE
PULLER, STUMP
RAKE
RAKE, GARDEN
RAKE, HAND HAY
REAPER, MODEL
RIDDLE, GRAIN
ROLLER, GARDEN
SAW, PRUNING
SCOOP, FEED
SCYTHE
SCYTHE, CRADLE
SCYTHE BLADE
SCYTHE SNATH
SEEDER, HAND CENTRIFUGAL
SEEDER, HAND SEEDBOX
SEEDER, SEEDBOX
SHEARS, HEDGE
SHEARS, PRUNING
SHELLER, CORN
SHOVEL, GRAIN
SHOVEL, SCOOP
SICKLE
SPADE, DITCHING
SPADE, DRAIN-TILE
SPADE, GARDEN
SPADE, PEAT
SPRAYER, HAND
SPRINKLER, IRRIGATION
SPUD, WEEDING
STICK, TOBACCO
STONEBOAT
TRACTOR, FARM
TROWEL, GARDEN
WEEDER, ROD

Class D040: ANIMAL HUSBANDRY T&E   Total: 66
Object, suffix

BASKET, PET
BEEHIVE
BLANKET
BLOCK, CLINCHING
BOOT, ANKLE
BOWL, PET

Object, suffix

BOX, FARRIER'S NAIL
BOX, SHOEING
BROODER, POULTRY
BRUSH, ANIMAL
BUFFER, HOOF
CHISEL, HOOF

Class D040: ANIMAL HUSBANDRY T&E — (Continued)

Total: 66

Object, suffix

CLIPPER, ANIMAL	LANCET
CLIPPER PLATE, ANIMAL	LEADER, LIVESTOCK
COLLAR, PET	LEASH
COMB, ANIMAL	MUZZLE
COOP, POULTRY-SHIPPING	NAIL, HORSESHOE
COWBELL	NEST, EGG
CURRYCOMB	NET, ANIMAL
DOCKER	OXSHOE
FEEDBAG	PARER, HOOF
FEEDER, LIVESTOCK	PICK, HOOF
FEEDER, POULTRY	PIN, PICKET
FLOAT, DENTAL	PINCERS, FARRIER'S
FRAME, OX-SHOEING	POKE
GAG, HORSE'S MOUTH	RASP, HOOF
HAMMER, FARRIER'S DRIVING	SET, SURGICAL INSTRUMENT
HAMMER, FARRIER'S FITTING	SHEARS, FETLOCK
HOBBLE	SHEARS, SHEEP
HORSESHOE	SMOKER, BEE
HORSESHOE PAD	STAND, SHOEING
HORSESHOE TOE-CALK	SYRINGE
INCUBATOR, FISH	SYRINGE, DOSE
IRON, BRANDING	TIE, CATTLE
IRON, HOOF-SEARING	TONGS, CLINCHING
IRON, HORSE'S MOUTH	TOWEL
KIT, SYRINGE	TRIMMER, HOOF
KNIFE, HOOF	TWISTER, NOSE
LAMP, SINGEING	WATERER, LIVESTOCK

Class D060: FISHING & TRAPPING T&E

Total: 45

Object, suffix

BAG, WHALER'S	KNIFE, SNOW
BASKET, OYSTER	LINE, FISH
BOX, BAIT	LURE
BOX, LOBSTER PEG	NET
BOX, TACKLE	NET, DIP
BUCKET, BAIT	NET, DRIFT
BUOY, LOSBTER POT	NET, POUND
CAPSTAN	PEG, LOBSTER
CASE, FISHING ROD	PLOW
CHEST, FISHING	POT, LOBSTER
CLAMP, TRAP SETTING	REEL, FISHING
CLUB, FISH	ROD FERRULE, FISHING
CREEL	ROD, FISHING
DREDGE, SHRIMP	ROD SWIVEL, FISHING
FISHHOOK	SINKER
FLOAT	STRAINER, ICE
GAFF, FISH	TRAP
GAFF, MINIATURE SEALING	TRAP, FISH
GAUGE, LOBSTER	TRAP CHAIN
HOE, CLAMMING	WEIGHT, MINIATURE NET
JIG	WEIGHT, NET
KIT, FISHING	WINDER, FISHING
KNIFE, MINCING	

Class D100: FOOD PROCESSING T&E

Object, suffix

AUGER, SUGAR
AX, SLAUGHTERING
BAKEBOARD
BASKET, COOKING
BASKET, DOUGH-RISING
BASKET, STORAGE
BENCH, SLAUGHTERING
BISCUIT
BLENDER, PASTRY
BLOCK, CHOPPING
BOARD, CUTTING
BOILER, DOUBLE
BOULOIR
BOWL
BOWL, BUTTER-WORKING
BOWL, CHOPPING
BOWL, MINIATURE BUTTER-WORKING
BOWL, MIXING
BOX, BREAD
BOX, CAKE
BOX, CHEESE
BOX, DOUGH-RISING
BOX, FOOD-STORAGE
BOX, MINIATURE SALT
BOX, SALT
BOX, SPICE
BOX LID, CHEESE
BRACKET, TEAKETTLE
BRAZIER
BROILER
BRUSH, KITCHEN
BRUSH, PASTRY
CABINET, FOOD-STORAGE
CADDY
CALDRON
CALDRON, MINIATURE
CALDRON HANDLE
CAN, CREAM
CAN, MILK
CANISTER
CANISTER, BAKING POWDER
CANISTER, BARLEY
CANISTER, COCOA
CANISTER, COFFEE
CANISTER, FLOUR
CANISTER, MILK POWDER
CANISTER, NUT
CANISTER, RICE
CANISTER, SUGAR
CANISTER, TEA
CAP, PRESERVING JAR
CAPPER, BOTTLE
CARRIER, BOTTLE
CASK, FISH DRESSER'S
CASK, RUM
CASK, WINE
CASSEROLE
CHISEL, ICE
CHOPPER, FOOD
CHURN
CHURN, BUTTER

Object, suffix

CHURN, MINIATURE
CHURN LID, BUTTER
CLEAVER
COLANDER
COLANDER, MILITARY
CORER, FRUIT
CORKER, BOTTLE
CORKSCREW
COVER, FOOD
COVER, ROLLING PIN
CRANE
CROCK
CROCK, MINIATURE
CROCK LID
CUP, MEASURING
CUTTER, CABBAGE
CUTTER, COOKIE
CUTTER, DOUGHNUT
CUTTER, PASTRY
CUTTER, SUGAR
DASHER
DECORATOR, CAKE
DIPPER
DISH, BAKING
DISH, CHAFING
DREDGER
DRYER, CORN
DRYER, HERB
EGGBEATER
FIRKIN
FORK, FISH
FORK, MILITARY TOASTING
FORK, TOASTING
FREEZER, ICE-CREAM
FUNNEL
FUNNEL, WINE
GAMBREL
GRATER
GRATER, SPICE
GRIDDLE
GRINDER, BONE
GRINDER, MEAT
HAMMER, SUGAR
HAND, SCOTCH
HEATER, MILK
HOOK, MEAT
ICEBOX
INFUSER, MILITARY TEA
INFUSER, TEA
IRON, WAFER
IRON, WAFFLE
JACK, BOTTLE
JAR, COOKIE
JAR, FOOD-STORAGE
JAR, PRESERVING
JUG
KETTLE
KNIFE
KNIFE, BONING
KNIFE, BREAD
KNIFE, BUTCHER

Class D100: FOOD PROCESSING T&E — *(Continued)*

Total: 294

Object, suffix

KNIFE, CHEESE
KNIFE, CHEF'S
KNIFE, CHOPPING
KNIFE, OYSTER
KNIFE, PARING
KNIFE, SKINNING
KNIFE, SPLITTING
KNIFE, THROATING
KNIFEBOARD
LADLE
LICORICE
LIFTER, PIE
LIFTER, STOVE
LINER, PRESERVING JAR
LOGGERHEAD
MAKER, COFFEE
MASHER
MASHER, POTATO
MAUL, MEAT
MILL, BUHR
MILL, COFFEE
MILL, FLOUR
MILL, NUT
MILL, SPICE
MIXER, DOUGH
MOLD
MOLD, BUTTER
MOLD, CHEESE
MOLD, CONFECTION
MOLD, COOKIE
MOLD, GELATIN
MOLD, JELLY
MOLD, PUDDING
MORTAR
MORTAR AND PESTLE
OPENER, BOTTLE
OPENER, CAN
OVEN, REFLECTOR
PADDLE
PAIL, LARD
PAIL, MILKING
PAN, BREAD
PAN, CAKE
PAN, DOUGH
PAN, FRYING
PAN, MILK
PAN, MINIATURE FRYING
PAN, MUFFIN
PAN, PIE
PAN, PUDDING
PAN, ROASTING
PAN, TUBE
PARER, FRUIT
PEEL
PEELER, VEGETABLE
PESTLE
PEW
PICK, ICE
PIN, ROLLING
PITTER, FRUIT
PLATE, HOT

Object, suffix

POACHER
POACHER, FISH
POPPER, CORN
POT, CROCK
POT, MINIATURE CROCK
POTHOLDER
PRESS, BUTTER
PRESS, CHEESE
PRESS, FRUIT
PRESS, LARD
PUMP, LIQUID
RACK, COOLING
RACK, KNIFE
RACK, MEAT
RACK, PIE
RACK, SCHNITZ
RACK, SPICE
RACK, SPIT
RACK, UTENSIL
RACK, WINE
RAMEKIN
REAMER, JUICE
REFRIGERATOR
REST, SPOON
RICER
ROASTER, APPLE
ROASTER, CHESTNUT
ROASTER, COFFEE
ROTISSERIE
SALAMANDER
SAUCEPAN
SAUCEPAN LID
SAUCEPOT
SAW, MEAT
SCALE, EGG
SCALER, FISH
SCOOP
SCOOP, ICE-CREAM
SCOOP, MELON
SCOOP, SALT
SCRAPER, DOUGH
SCRAPER, HOG
SEEDER, RAISIN
SEPARATOR, CREAM
SEPARATOR, EGG
SET, CANISTER
SET, MILITARY MESS
SET, MILITARY SKEWER
SET, SKEWER
SET, UTENSIL
SHEET, COOKIE
SIEVE
SIFTER
SINK, DRY
SKEWER
SKEWER, MILITARY
SKIMMER
SKIMMER, CREAM
SLAB, CANDY MAKING
SLICER, CHEESE
SLICER, EGG

Class D100: FOOD PROCESSING T&E — *(Continued)*

Total: 294

Object, suffix

SLICER, VEGETABLE
SPADE, BUTTER-WORKING
SPATULA
SPATULA, MILITARY
SPIDER
SPOON
SPOON, BASTING
SPOON, CADDY
SPOON, MEASURING
SPOON, MILITARY
SQUEEZER, FRUIT
STAND, CASK
STEAMER
STIRRER
STOVE
STOVE, PORTABLE
STRAINER
STRAINER, GRAVY
STRAINER, MILITARY
STRAINER, MILK
STRAINER, WHEY
STUFFER, SAUSAGE
SWAB, BAKER'S OVEN
TABLE, SPLITTING
TABLE, STEAM

Object, suffix

TAMPER
TANK, WATER
TEAKETTLE
TEAKETTLE LID
THERMOMETER
THERMOMETER, MILK
TILTER, TEAKETTLE
TIMER, KITCHEN
TOASTER
TONGS, ICE
TONGS, KITCHEN
TRAMMEL
TRAMMEL, MINIATURE
TROUGH, DOUGH
TROUGH, MINIATURE DOUGH
TUB, MILITARY SALTING
TUB, SALTING
TUBE, THIEF
VAT, BUTTER
VAT, FISH
WARMER, BRANDY
WARMER, PLATE
WHEEL, JAGGING
WHISK
WORKER, BUTTER

Class D120: FOOD SERVICE T&E

Total: 235

Object, suffix

BASKET, BREAD
BASKET, CAKE
BASKET, FRUIT
BASKET, PICNIC
BASKET, WINE
BOTTLE, NURSING
BOTTLE, SELTZER
BOTTLE, VACUUM
BOTTLE, WATER
BOWL
BOWL, CEREAL
BOWL, CREAM
BOWL, FINGER
BOWL, FRUIT
BOWL, MILITARY
BOWL, PUNCH
BOWL, SALAD
BOWL, SOUP
BOWL, SUGAR
BOWL LID
BOWL LID, SUGAR
BOX, KNIFE
CARAFE
CASE, FLATWARE
CASE, NAPKIN
CASTER
CHARGER
CHOPSTICK
CLOTH, KNIFE BOX
COASTER

Object, suffix

COFFEEPOT
COFFEEPOT LID
COMPOTE
COOLER, WATER
COOLER, WINE
COVER, MILITARY MESS TIN
COZY
CROSS, DISH
CRUET
CRUET STOPPER
CUP
CUP, COFFEE
CUP, DEMITASSE
CUP, INVALID'S
CUP, MILITARY
CUP, MUSTACHE
CUP & SAUCER
CUP & SAUCER, DEMITASSE
CUP & SAUCER, MINIATURE
CUP, WATER
DECANTER
DECANTER STOPPER
DISH
DISH, BONBON
DISH, BONE
DISH, BUTTER
DISH, CANDY
DISH, CHEESE
DISH, FISH
DISH, HONEY

Class D120: FOOD SERVICE T&E — *(Continued)*

Total: 235

Object, suffix

Object, suffix

DISH, HOT-WATER	NAPKIN
DISH, RELISH	NAPKIN, BREAD BASKET
DISH, VEGETABLE	NAPPY
DISH, WASTE	NIPPLE, NURSING BOTTLE
DISH LID, BUTTER	NUTCRACKER
DISH LID, VEGETABLE	NUTPICK
DOME, FOOD	PAD, TABLE
EGGCUP	PAIL, DINNER
EPERGNE	PAIL, MILITARY SOUP
FLAGON	PAIL, MINIATURE WATER
FORK	PAIL, WATER
FORK, CARVING	PITCHER
FORK, COLD-MEAT	PITCHER, CREAM
FORK, DESSERT	PITCHER, MILK
FORK, DINNER	PITCHER, MINIATURE
FORK, FISH	PITCHER, SYRUP
FORK, FISH-SERVING	PITCHER, WATER
FORK, FRUIT	PITCHER, WINE
FORK, LUNCHEON	PLATE
FORK, MINIATURE	PLATE, BUTTER
FORK, OYSTER	PLATE, CHILD'S
FORK, PICKLE	PLATE, CUP
FORK, SALAD	PLATE, DESSERT
GLASS	PLATE, DINNER
GLASS, CHAMPAGNE	PLATE, LUNCHEON
GLASS, COCKTAIL	PLATE, MILITARY
GLASS, CORDIAL	PLATE, MILITARY DESSERT
GLASS, MALT-BEVERAGE	PLATE, MILITARY SERVING
GLASS, DESSERT	PLATE, MINIATURE
GLASS, SHOT	PLATE, SALAD
GLASS, SWEETMEAT	PLATE, SAUCEBOAT
GLASS, WINE	PLATE, SERVING
GOBLET	PLATE, SOUP
GOBLET, MINIATURE	PLATTER
HOLDER, CORNCOB	PLATTER, MILITARY
HOLDER, PLACECARD	PORRINGER
HOLDER, TOOTHPICK	POT, CHOCOLATE
HORN, DRINKING	POT, MUSTARD
JAR	RACK, TOAST
JAR, GINGER	REST, KNIFE
JAR, PICKLE	RING, DISH
JAR LID	RING, NAPKIN
KNIFE	SALTCELLAR
KNIFE, BUTTER	SALTSHAKER
KNIFE, CAKE	SALVER
KNIFE, CARVING	SAUCEBOAT
KNIFE, DESSERT	SAUCER
KNIFE, DINNER	SCOOP, CHEESE
KNIFE, FISH	SERVER, CHEESE
KNIFE, FRUIT	SERVER, PIE
KNIFE, LUNCHEON	SERVER, SALAD
KNIFE HANDLE	SERVICE, COFFEE
KNIFE, MINIATURE TABLE	SERVICE, TEA
LABEL, DECANTER	SET, BEVERAGE
LADLE	SET, CARVING
LINER, PLATTER	SET, CONDIMENT
MAT, PLACE	SET, CRUET
MILL, PEPPER	SET, DAIRY
MUG	SET, DECANTER
MUG, CHILD'S	SET, DESSERT
MUG, MILITARY	SET, EGG

Class D120: FOOD SERVICE T&E — *(Continued)*

Total: 235

Object, suffix

Object, suffix	Object, suffix
SET, FLATWARE	STAND, SERVING TRAY
SET, FORK & KNIFE	STAND, VEGETABLE DISH
SET, MILITARY FORK & KNIFE	STEIN
SET, SALT & PEPPER	TABLECLOTH
SET, TABLEWARE	TABLESPOON
SHAKER, PEPPER	TANKARD
SHAKER, SUGAR	TANTALUS
SHEARS, GRAPE	TAZZA
SLICE, FISH	TEACUP
SNIFTER	TEAPOT
SPOON	TEAPOT LID
SPOON, COFFEE	TEASPOON
SPOON, DESSERT	TIN, MILITARY MESS
SPOON, GRAPEFRUIT	TONGS
SPOON, MARROW	TONGS, SUGAR
SPOON, MILITARY	TRAY, BED
SPOON, MINIATURE	TRAY, BREAD
SPOON, MUSTARD	TRAY, FLATWARE
SPOON, SALT	TRAY, SERVING
SPOON, SERVING	TRIVET
SPOON, SHERBET	TUMBLER
SPOON, SOUP	TUREEN
SPOON, SUGAR	TUREEN LID
SPOONER	URN, COFFEE
STAND, CAKE	URN, TEA
STAND, CARAFE	VASE, CELERY
STAND, CRUET	

Class D140: FORESTRY T&E

Total: 34

Object, suffix

Object, suffix	Object, suffix
AUGER, RAFT	HOOK, CANT
AX, BARKING	PEAVY
AX, FELLING	PICKAROON
AX, MARKING	PIKE, FORK
AX BLADE, FELLING	PIKE, POLE
AX HANDLE	POLE HANDLE, PIKE
AX HANDLE, MILITARY	RING, SNUB
BUCKET, SAP	RULE, LOG
BUCKSAW	SAW, TWO-HANDED CROSSCUT
CALIPERS, TIMBER	SAW HANDLE, TWO-HANDED CROSSCUT
CANTHOOK HANDLE	SCRAPER, TREE
CASE, BUCKSAW	SCRIBE, TIMBER
DOG, LOG	SHREDDER, BARK
DOG, RING	SPOUT, SAP
DOG, SPAN	SPUD, BARKING
HAMMER, MARKING	TONGS
HAMMER HEAD, MARKING	TROUGH, SAP

Class D160: GLASS, PLASTICS, CLAYWORKING T&E

Total: 15

Object, suffix

Object, suffix	Object, suffix
CUTTER, GLASS	MOLD, GUNPOWDER TIN
FUNNEL, WAX	MOLD, MINIATURE CANDLE
MOLD, BOTTLE	MOLD, SOAP
MOLD, CANDLE	PATTERN, DICTAPHONE CYLINDER
MOLD, DICTAPHONE CYLINDER	POINT, GLAZIER'S

Class D160: GLASS, PLASTICS, CLAYWORKING T&E — *(Continued)*

Total: 15

Object, suffix	Object, suffix
POT	STICK, CANDLE DIPPING
REEL, CANDLE-DIPPING	TOOL, LOOP
ROULETTE	

Class D180: LEATHER, HORN, SHELLWORKING T&E

Total: 125

Object, suffix	Object, suffix
AWL	HOOK, LAST
AWL, CLICKER'S	HORSE, STITCHING
AWL, COLLAR	IRON, EDGE
AWL, GARNISH	KNIFE
AWL, HARNESS	KNIFE, BEAMING
AWL, PANEL	KNIFE, BEVEL-POINT SKIVING
AWL, PEGGING	KNIFE, CURRIER'S
AWL, SADDLER'S	KNIFE, FLESHING
AWL, SADDLER'S STITCHING	KNIFE, HEAD
AWL, SCRATCH	KNIFE, HEEL
AWL, SEAT	KNIFE, PEG
AWL, SEWING	KNIFE, ROUND-HEAD
BENCH, COBBLER'S	KNIFE, SKIVING
BENCH, HARNESS MAKER'S	KNIFE, SQUARE-POINT
BEVELER, EDGE	LAST
BREAKER, SEAT	LAST, COBBLER'S
BRISTLE, SEWING	LEATHER
BURNISHER, STRIP	MACHINE, DIE-CUTTING
CASE, PUNCH	MACHINE, SPLITTING
CHANNELER	MOLD, LEATHER
CHEST, TOOL SADDLER'S	NAIL, SHOE
CHISEL, THONGING	NEEDLE
CLAMP	NEEDLE, GLOVER'S
CLAMP, STRETCHING	NEEDLE, HARNESS
CREASER	PALMIRON
CREASER, BEVEL	PEG, SHOE
CREASER, EDGE	PINCERS, LASTING
CREASER, SCREW	PITCH
CREASER, SINGLE	PLIERS, PAD-SCREW
CUTTER, EDGE	PLIERS, SETTING
CUTTER, REVOLVING-WHEEL	POINT, AWL
CUTTER, WASHER	PRESS, FUR
CUTTER, WELT	PRICK, SINGLE STITCH
CUTTER BLADE	PRICKER, SINGLE-STITCH
FID	PRICKER, WHEEL
FINGERSTALL	PUNCH, ASYMMETRIC OBLONG
FORK, STRAINING	PUNCH, BUTTON-HOLE
GAUGE, DRAW	PUNCH, HAND
GLAZER	PUNCH, HEEL LIFT
GOUGE	PUNCH, LINE
GOUGE, V	PUNCH, OBLONG-HOLE
GRAVER	PUNCH, PIERCING
GROOVER, STITCHING	PUNCH, RECTANGULAR DRIVE
GROOVER, MARTINGALE	PUNCH, ROUND-HOLE
GROOVER BLADE	PUNCH, SCALLOPING
HAFT, AWL	PUNCH, SQUARE DRIVE
HAFT, PEGGING AWL	PUNCH, STRAP-END U
HAFT, SEWING AWL	PUNCH, STRAP-END V
HAMMER, COBBLER'S	RASP
HAMMER, SADDLER'S	RASP, PEG
HANGER, PELT	ROLL, FILLET
HOLDER, STRAP	ROLL, PATTERN

Class D180: LEATHER, HORN, SHELLWORKING T&E — *(Continued)*

Total: 125

Object, suffix

SCRAPER
SEATIRON
SET, SADDLER'S STITCHING AWL
SET, STUFFING ROD
SETTER, GROMMET
SETTER, RIVET
SHAVE, SKIRT
SLICKER
SLICKER, EDGE
SPOKESHAVE
STAMP, CLOSING

Object, suffix

STAMP, MILITARY BRANDING
STAND, LAST
STIRRUP
STRETCHER, PELT
THREAD, BOOTMAKER'S
TREE, BOOT
TRIMMER, EDGE
TURNER, SEAM
VISE, COLLAR
WHEEL, CROW

Class D200: MASONRY & STONEWORKING T&E

Total: 58

Object, suffix

AX, BRICK
AX, TOOTH
BIT, SCUTCH
BOX, MASON'S TOOL
BRUSH, MASON'S
BUSHHAMMER
CHISEL
CHISEL, CUTTING
CHISEL, PITCHING
CHISEL, POINT
CHISEL, STRAIGHT
CHISEL, TOOTH
DOG, RING
DRILL, ROUND
FEATHER
FLOAT
HAMMER
HAMMER, FACE
HAMMER, PATENT
HAMMER, SLATER'S
HAMMER, SPALLING
HAWK
HOD
HOE, MILITARY MORTAR
HOE, MORTAR
JOINTER
LEVEL, MASON'S
LEVEL, MILLSTONE
LINE, CHALK

Object, suffix

MALLET, MASON'S
PALM, MASON'S
PICK
PICK, FLINTING
PICK, MASON'S
PICK, MILL
PICK, SLATE
PIN, LINE
PLUG
POKER, KILN
RASP
REEL, CHALK
RIPPER, SLATER'S
SAW, MASON'S
SCUTCH
SET, FEATHER & PLUG
SET, MILL PICK
SLEDGE, MASON'S BIT
SPATULA, PLASTERER'S
SQUARE, MASON'S
SQUARE, MASON'S TRY
TOOL, PLASTERER'S MODELING
TROUGH, MIXING
TROWEL
TROWEL, POINTING
TROWEL, SMOOTHING
TUBE, GROUTING
WEDGE
ZAX

Class D220: METALWORKING T&E

Total: 269

Object, suffix

ANVIL
ANVIL, NAILMAKER'S
BAR, COPPER
BAR, GRAPHITE
BASKET, ORE
BEAD-TOOL, BOILER TUBE
BELLOWS, BLACKSMITH'S
BENDER, PIPE
BIN, MILITARY CHARCOAL

Object, suffix

BIT, FLAT
BIT, LATHE
BIT, TWIST
BLOCK, SWAGE
BOLT
BRACE
BRAKE
BRUSH, FILE
BRUSH, METAL

Class D220: METALWORKING T&E — *(Continued)*   **Total: 269**

Object, suffix

Object, suffix	Object, suffix
BURNISHER	HAMMER, RIVETING
CARRIER, WHETSTONE	HAMMER, SET
CHISEL, COLD	HAMMER, SETTING
CHISEL, HOT	HAMMER, SHIPWRIGHT'S COPPERING
CHISEL, MILITARY COLD	HAMMER, STRAIGHT-PEEN
CHUCK, LATHE	HARDY
CLOTH, EMERY	HARDY, HALF-ROUND
COREBOX, ANVIL	HARDY, STRAIGHT
COREBOX, CALDRON	HOLDER, DIE
COREBOX, CANNON CARRIAGE	HOOK, PLATE BENDING
COREBOX, CANNON CARRIAGE TRUCK LEVER	HORN, SPRUE MOLDER'S
COREBOX, GUN	INGOT
COREBOX, LATCH ASSEMBLY	IRON, PIG
COREBOX, MILITARY CARRONADE	IRON, SMOOTHING
COREBOX, MORTAR	IRON, SOLDERING
COREBOX, RACK	JIG, ASSEMBLING
COREBOX, SHELL	JIG, CUTTING
COREBOX, STOVE LID	JIG, DRILLING
COREBOX, SWIVEL GUN	JOINTER, SAW
CREASER, HOT	LADLE, HOT-METAL
CRUCIBLE	LATHE, HAND
CRUCIBLE LID	LIFTER
CUPEL	MACHINE, BURRING
CUTTER, BOILER SHEET	MACHINE, DIE-CUTTING
CUTTER, BOILER TUBE	MACHINE, FORMING
CUTTER, BOLT	MACHINE, GROOVING
CUTTER, FLUE	MACHINE, PIPE THREADING
CUTTER, PIPE	MACHINE, RIVETING
CUTTER, RIVET	MACHINE, SETTING-DOWN
CUTTER, WIRE	MACHINE, SHEARING
DIE	MACHINE, TIRE-BENDING
DIE, FISHHOOK	MACHINE, TURNING
DIE, MILITARY BUTTON	MANDREL
DIE, MILITARY MESS-PLATE	MOLD
DIE, MILITARY SHAKO PLATE	MOLD, BELL CLAPPER
DIE, STAMP	MOLD, BOILER
DIE, TOE-CALK WELDING	MOLD, GOLD BULLION
DRESSER, GRINDING WHEEL	MOLD, LURE
FILE, FLAT	MOLD, MILITARY CAP BADGE
FILE, MILL	MOLD, MILITARY SHOULDER BELT PLATE
FILE, ROUND	MOLD, MULTIPLE CONNECTOR
FILE, SAW	MOLD, NET WEIGHT
FILE, TRIANGULAR	MOLD, POLICE CREST
FILE HANDLE	MOLD, PROPELLER
FLASK, MOLDING	MOLD, SPOON
FLATTER	MOLD, STEERING WHEEL
FORGE, BLACKSMITH'S	NIPPERS, NAIL
FORK, BENDING	OVEN, AMALGAM DRYING
FULLER, BOTTOM	PATTERN, ANVIL
FULLER, TOP	PATTERN, ASHPAN
GAUGE, BOILER TUBE DIAMETER	PATTERN, BOILER
GAUGE, FLUE DIAMETER	PATTERN, CANNON CARRIAGE
GRINDER	PATTERN, CANNON CARRIAGE TRUCK LEVER
GRINDSTONE	PATTERN, CANNONBALL
GROOVER, HAND	PATTERN, CARD HOLDER
HACKSAW	PATTERN, CLOTHES HOOK
HACKSAW BLADE	PATTERN, GEAR
HAMMER	PATTERN, GRAPESHOT
HAMMER, BALL-PEEN	PATTERN, GUN
HAMMER, CROSS-PEEN	PATTERN, GUN WHEEL
HAMMER, RAISING	PATTERN, HEATER

Class D220: METALWORKING T&E — (Continued)

Object, suffix

PATTERN, HORSESHOE
PATTERN, KETTLE
PATTERN, KNIFE
PATTERN, LATCH ASSEMBLY
PATTERN, MILITARY BASIN
PATTERN, MILITARY CARRONADE
PATTERN, MILITARY SHELL VISE
PATTERN, MORTAR
PATTERN, MULTIPLE CONNECTOR
PATTERN, PIE PAN
PATTERN, RACK
PATTERN, SADIRON
PATTERN, SHELL
PATTERN, SHOT GARLAND
PATTERN, SPONTOON
PATTERN, STEERING WHEEL
PATTERN, STOVE
PATTERN, STOVE DOOR
PATTERN, STOVE LID REDUCER
PATTERN, STOVEPIPE COLLAR
PATTERN, STOVE PLATE CENTER
PATTERN, SWIVEL GUN
PATTERN, TEAKETTLE LID
PATTERN, TRAP
PIN, DRIFT
PIN, LIFTING
PLATE, BENCH
POKER
POST, MILITARY BEAKIRON
PRESS, DRILL
PUNCH
PUNCH, CENTRE
PUNCH, DRIFT
PUNCH, HOLLOW
RABBLE
RACK, BIT
RACK, MOLD
RACK, STOCK-METAL
RACK, TONGS
RAKE, BLACKSMITH'S
RAMMER
REAMER
REAMER, BOILER TUBE
RIVET
ROD, STIRRING
SAW, BAND
SAW, BLITZ
SCRAPER
SET, BUTTON DIE
SET, DIE
SET, MILITARY BUTTON DIE
SET, MILITARY DIE
SET, TAP & DIE
SETTER, RIVET
SHEARS, BENCH
SHOVEL, BLACKSMITH'S
SKID
SKIMMER
SLEDGE
SLEDGE, CROSS-PEEN
SLEDGE, DOUBLE-FACE

Object, suffix

SLEDGE, MILITARY STRAIGHT-PEEN
SLEDGE HANDLE
SNIPS, SHEET METALWORKER'S
SPOON, BLACKSMITH'S
SPRINKLER, BLACKSMITH'S
SPRUE
STAKE, BEAK
STAKE, BEAKHORN
STAKE, CANDLEMOLD
STAKE, COOPER'S
STAKE, CREASING
STAKE, DOUBLE-HORN
STAKE, HATCHET
STAKE, ROUND-HEAD
STAKE, SEAMING
STAKE, SQUARE
STAMP
STAND, BLACKSMITH'S
STAND, CRUCIBLE
STEEL
STOCK, DIE
STONE, SCYTHE-SHARPENING
SWAGE
SWAGE, BOTTOM
SWAGE, HALF-ROUND TOP
SWAGE, TOP
TAP
TEMPLATE
TONGS
TONGS, BOLT
TONGS, CLIP
TONGS, CRUCIBLE
TONGS, FLAT
TONGS, HAMMER
TONGS, HOLLOW-BIT
TONGS, HOOP
TONGS, PICKUP
TONGS, PINCER
TONGS, SHOE
TONGS, SIDE
TONGS, TIRE
TOOL, BOLT HEADING
TOOL, NAIL HEADING
TORCH, GASOLINE
TORCH, KEROSINE
TORCH, PROPANE
TRAVELER
TRIP-HAMMER
TUB, SLACK
TUYERE
UPSETTER, TIRE/AXLE
VISE
VISE, BENCH
VISE, HAND
VISE, LEG
VISE, PIPE
WHETSTONE
WRENCH, ALLEN
WRENCH, BOX
WRENCH, CARRIAGE NUT
WRENCH, CRESCENT

Total: 269

Class D220: METALWORKING T&E — *(Continued)*

Total: 269

Object, suffix

Object, suffix

WRENCH, MONKEY
WRENCH, OPEN-END
WRENCH, PIPE
WRENCH, SLIP

WRENCH, SOCKET
WRENCH, TAP
WRENCH, TORQUE

Class D240: MINING & MINERAL HARVESTING T&E

Total: 54

Object, suffix

Object, suffix

BAG, ORE
BAR, MINER'S
BENDER, POINT
BENDER, RAIL
BOILER
BOX, SLUICE
BUCKET, DRAGLINE
BUCKETLINE
CAR, MINE
CAR WHEEL, MINE
CLASSIFIER
DREDGE
DRILL, PERCUSSIVE AIR
DRILL, PLACER
DRILL, ROTARY
DRIVER, POINT
FAN, VENTILATION
FORK, SLUICE
HAMMER, HAND
HOIST, MINE
CASK
KIBBLE
LADLE, PITCH
LOCOMOTIVE, MINE
MAT, GOLD
MINER, CONTINUOUS
MONITOR, HYDRAULIC

NOZZLE, HYDRAULIC
PAN, MINER'S
PICK
PICK, DOUBLE-POINTED
PICK, MILITARY
PICK HANDLE
PICK HEAD
PICKAROON
PIN, DREDGE BUCKET
POINT, COLD WATER THAWING
POINT, STEAM THAWING
POLE, GIN
POUCH, BLASTING CAP
POUCH, GOLD
PRICKER
PULLER, COLD WATER POINT
PUMP
PUMP, SINGLE-ACTION
RIFFLES
SAW, ICE
SAW HANDLE, ICE
SCOOP, SAMPLING AMALGAMATING
SCREEN, TROMMEL
SELENIUM
SEPARATOR
SLUSHER
SPOON

Class D260: PAINTING T&E

Total: 21

Object, suffix

Object, suffix

BOX, ARTIST'S
BRUSH, GRAINING
BRUSH, LETTERING
BRUSH, PAINT
BRUSH, WALLPAPER
COMB, GRAINING
CRAYON
KNIFE
KNIFE, GRAINING
KNIFE, PALETTE
KNIFE, PUTTY

KNIFE, WALLPAPER
MILL, ROLLER
PAINT
PALETTE
PESTLE
ROLLER
ROLLER, GRAINING
SCRAPER, WALL
SET, GRAINING COMB
SPATULA

Class D280: PAPERMAKING T&E

Total: 0

Class D300: TEXTILEWORKING T&E

Total: 118

Object, suffix

Object, suffix

ATTACHMENT, SEWING MACHINE	MACHINE, SEWING
BAG, BUTTON	MALLET, SERVING
BAG, NEEDLEWORK	MARKER, HEM
BASKET, NEEDLEWORK	MARLINSPIKE
BENCH, WEAVER'S	MILL, STRAW ROLLING
BLOCK, HAT	MILL, WARPING
BLOCK, WOOD	MOLD, PURSE
BOARD, SCUTCHING	NEEDLE, DARNING
BOBBIN	NEEDLE, KNITTING
BODKIN	NEEDLE, NETMAKING
BOLT, CLOTH	NEEDLE, RUGMAKING
BOLT, MILITARY CLOTH	NEEDLE, SAILMAKER'S
BOX, NEEDLEWORK	NEEDLE, SEWING
BREAKER, FLAX	NEEDLE, SNOWSHOEMAKING
CARD, HAND	NEEDLE, UPHOLSTERER'S
CASE, CROCHET HOOK	NIDDY NODDY
CASE, KNITTING NEEDLE	PADDLE
CASE, MILITARY NEEDLEWORK	PALM, SAILMAKER'S
CASE, NEEDLE	PATTERN
CASE, NEEDLEWORK	PIECE, QUILT
CASE, PIN	PIN, HATTER'S
CASE, SCISSORS	PIN, SAFETY
CASE, THREAD	PIN, STRAIGHT
CHALK, TAILOR'S	PINCUSHION
CLAMP, QUILTING-FRAME	PLIERS, BUTTON
CLAMP, SEWING	PUNCH, GROMMET
COMB, HAND	REED
COVER, PINCUSHION	REEL
CURVE/SQUARE, PATTERN DRAFTING	REEL, CLOCK
CUSHION, EMERY	RIPPLE
DISTAFF	SCISSORS
DRYER, YARN	SCISSORS, BUTTONHOLE
EGG, DARNING	SCISSORS, EMBROIDERY
FID	SHEARS
FORM, DRESS	SHEARS, DRESSMAKER'S
FRAME, QUILTING	SHUTTLE
FRAME, TENTER	SHUTTLE, NETTING
FRAME, WARPING	SPINDLE
GAUGE, NET	SPOOL
GLOBE, LACEMAKER'S	SPOOLER
HATCHEL	STILETTO
HOLDER, SPOOL	STRETCHER, HAT
HOOK, CROCHET	SUPPLIES, MILITARY SEWING
HOOK, RUG	SUPPLIES, SEWING
HOOK, SAILMAKER'S	SWIFT
HOOP, EMBROIDERY	SYSTEM, PATTERN DRAFTING
IRON, HATTER'S	TEMPLATE, MITTEN
KNIFE, HATTER'S	TEMPLE
KNIFE, SCUTCHING	THIMBLE
LOOM	TWISTER
LOOM, BEAD	WEIGHT, LOOM
LOOM, CARPET	WHEEL, FLAX SPINNING
LOOM, HAND	WHEEL, SPINNING
LOOM, RIGID HEDDLE	WHEEL, TRACING
LOOM, TABLET	WHEEL, WOOL SPINNING
LOOM, TAPE	WHORL, SPINDLE
MACHINE, CRIMPING	WINDER, BOBBIN
MACHINE, KNITTING	WINDER, LACE
MACHINE, PLEATING	WINDER, THREAD

Class D320: WOODWORKING T&E

Object, suffix

Object, suffix

ADZ	CLAMP, C
ADZ, CARPENTER'S	CLAMP, FURNITURE
ADZ, COOPER'S	CLAMP, JOINER'S
ADZ, COOPER'S NOTCHING	CLAMP, SAW
ADZ, HOLLOWING	CLUB, FROE
ADZ, SHIPWRIGHT'S	COMPASS, BEAM
ADZ BLADE	COMPASS, COOPER'S WING
ADZ HANDLE	CRAYON, LUMBER
AUGER	CRESSET
AUGER, SHELL	CROWBAR
AUGER, SNAIL	CROZE
AUGER, SPIRAL	CUTTER, COOPER'S
AUGER, TAPER	CUTTER, PEG
AUGER HANDLE	DOG, HOOPING
AWL	DOG, SPOKE
AWL, MARKING	DOWNSHAVE, COOPER'S
AWL, SQUARE	DRAWKNIFE
AX	DRAWKNIFE, BOXING
AX, COOPER'S	DRAWKNIFE, COOPER'S
AX, MORTISING	DRAWKNIFE, COOPER'S CHAMFERING
AX, SHIPWRIGHT'S	DRAWKNIFE, COOPER'S HEADING
AX, SIDE	DRAWKNIFE, COOPER'S HOLLOWING
AX HANDLE, SIDE	DRILL
BEETLE	DRILL, BOW
BENCH, CARPENTER'S	DRIVER, HOOP
BENCH, WHEELWRIGHT'S	EXTRACTOR, BUNG
BIT	FILE
BIT, CENTER	FRAME, WHEELWRIGHT'S WHEEL
BIT, COUNTERSINK	FROE
BIT, GIMLET	GAUGE, CLAPBOARD
BIT, MORTISE	GAUGE, CUTTING
BIT, SHELL	GAUGE, MARKING
BIT, SPOKE-TRIMMER	GIMLET
BIT, SPOON	GLUEPOT
BIT, TAPER	GOUGE
BIT, TWIST	GOUGE, CARVING
BLOCK, BEVEL	GOUGE, FIRMER
BLOCK, SANDING	GOUGE, PARING
BLOCK, WHEELWRIGHT'S CHOPPING	GOUGE, TURNING
BOILER, BOATBUILDER'S	HAMMER
BOLT	HAMMER, CLAW
BOX, CARPENTER'S TOOL	HAMMER, COOPER'S
BOX, MITRE	HAMMER, JOINER'S
BOX, SCREW	HAMMER, SETTING
BRACE	HAMMER, TACK
BRADAWL	HATCHET
BROADAX	HATCHET, LATHING
BROADAX BLADE	HATCHET, SHINGLING
BUNGSTART	HATCHET, SIDE
CASE, BIT	HOLDER, CAULKING IRON
CHALK, CARPENTER'S	HOLDFAST
CHISEL	HOOK, BENCH
CHISEL, CARVING	HOOK, CAULKING SHIPWRIGHT'S
CHISEL, CORNER	HOOK, COOPER'S BLOCK
CHISEL, FIRMER	HOOP, TRUSS
CHISEL, MORTISE	HORSE, SHAVING
CHISEL, PARTING	IRON, FLAGGING
CHISEL, RIPPING	IRON, SHIPWRIGHT'S CAULKING
CHISEL, TURNING	IRON, VENEERING
CHISEL HANDLE	IRON, WHEELWRIGHT'S BURNING
CLAMP	JIG

Class D320: WOODWORKING T&E — *(Continued)*

Object, suffix

JIG, BASKETMAKER'S
JIGSAW
JOINTER-PLANER
KNIFE, BLOCK
KNIFE, CARVING
LATHE
LATHE SPUR CENTER
LEVEL
LEVEL, PLUMB
LINE, CHALK
MACHINE, BORING
MACHINE, MORTISING
MACHINE, SAW SHARPENING
MALLET
MALLET, CARPENTER'S
MALLET, CARVER'S
MALLET, SHIPWRIGHT'S CAULKING
MAUL, CLEAVING
MAUL, POST
MOP, PITCH
NAIL
PADDLE, PITCH
PATTERN
PEG
PENCIL, CARPENTER'S
PLANE
PLANE, ASTRAGAL
PLANE, BLOCK
PLANE, BOX-SCRAPER
PLANE, CHAMFERING
PLANE, COMPASS
PLANE, DADO
PLANE, EDGE
PLANE, FILLISTER
PLANE, FLOOR
PLANE, FORKSTAFF
PLANE, GROOVING
PLANE, GUTTERING
PLANE, HOLLOW
PLANE, JACK
PLANE, LONG-JOINTER
PLANE, MAST-AND-SPAR
PLANE, MITER
PLANE, MOLDING
PLANE, NOSING
PLANE, PANEL
PLANE, PLOW
PLANE, RABBET
PLANE, ROUND
PLANE, ROUNDER
PLANE, ROUTER
PLANE, SASH
PLANE, SHORT-JOINTER
PLANE, SMOOTHING
PLANE, SPILL
PLANE, SUN
PLANE, TONGUE-AND-GROOVE
PLANE, TONGUEING
PLANE, TOOTHING
PLANE, TRYING
PLANE BLADE

Object, suffix

PLANE FENCE, CHAMFERING
PLANE HANDLE
PLANE WEDGE
POT, GREASE
POT, PITCH
POUCH, NAIL
PRESS, CORK
PULLER, NAIL
PULLER, TACK
PUNCH
PUNCH, CARVER'S
PUNCH, COOPER'S
PUNCH, MARKING
PUNCH, NAIL
RACK, DRAWKNIFE
RACK, GIMLET
RASP
REAMER
REAMER, WHEELWRIGHT'S
REEL, CHALK
RIPSAW
ROUTER
RULE, BENCH
SAW
SAW, BAND
SAW, BENCH
SAW, BOW
SAW, COMPASS
SAW, COPING
SAW, CROSSCUT
SAW, DOVETAIL
SAW, DOWEL
SAW, FELLOE
SAW, FLOORING
SAW, FRAMED-PIT
SAW, KEYHOLE
SAW, OPEN-PIT
SAW, TENON
SAW BLADE, BENCH
SAW BLADE, CROSSCUT
SAW HANDLE
SAW HANDLE, CROSSCUT
SAW-SET
SAWHORSE
SCORPER, CLOSED
SCORPER, OPEN
SCRAPER
SCRAPER, SHIPWRIGHT'S
SCREW
SCRIBER
SET, AWL PAD
SLICK
SPIKE
SPOKESHAVE
SQUARE
SQUARE, BEVEL
SQUARE, CARPENTER'S
SQUARE, MITER
SQUARE, SET
SQUARE, TRY
STOP, BENCH

Class D320: WOODWORKING T&E — *(Continued)*   Total: 260

Object, suffix	Object, suffix
STRETCHER, CANOE CANVAS	VISE
TAP, SCREW	VISE, SAW SHARPENING
TEMPLATE, ANIMAL YOKE	WASHER
TEMPLATE, BOAT HULL	WEDGE, CLEAVING
TEMPLATE, COFFIN	WEDGE, HANDLE
TEMPLATE, SNOWSHOE	WHEEL, CAULKING
TOOL, HOOP BENDING	WICKER
TWIBIL	WINDLASS, HOOPING

Class D550: BASKET, BROOM, BRUSH MAKING T&E   Total: 1

Object, suffix	Object, suffix
FORK, THATCHING	

Class D600: CIGAR MAKING T&E   Total: 0

Class D650: LAPIDARY T&E   Total: 0

Class D680: SOAPMAKING T&E   Total: 3

Object, suffix	Object, suffix
CALDRON, POTASH	STRAINER, LYE
STICK, SOAP	

Class D700: WIGMAKING T&E   Total: 0

CATEGORY 05 : TOOLS & EQUIPMENT FOR SCIENCE AND TECHNOLOGY

Class E020: ACOUSTICAL T&E
Object, suffix   **Object, suffix**   Total: 1

FORK, TUNING

Class E060: ARMAMENT, FIREARM
Object, suffix   **Object, suffix**   Total: 67

BLUNDERBUSS	PISTOL, MILITARY PERCUSSION
CARBINE	PISTOL, PERCUSSION
CARBINE, MILITARY BREECHLOAD	PISTOL, POCKET
CARBINE, MILITARY CENTER-FIRE	PISTOL, POCKET CENTER-FIRE
CARBINE, MILITARY FLINTLOCK	REVOLVER
CARBINE, MILITARY PERCUSSION	REVOLVER, CENTER-FIRE
CARBINE, MILITARY RIM-FIRE	REVOLVER, MILITARY
CARBINE BREECH MECHANISM	REVOLVER, MILITARY CENTER-FIRE
DERRINGER	REVOLVER, MILITARY PERCUSSION
FLINTLOCK MECHANISM	REVOLVER, PERCUSSION
GUN, MACHINE	REVOLVER, POLICE CENTER-FIRE
HARQUEBUS	RIFLE
LAUNCHER, GRENADE	RIFLE, BREECHLOAD
MUSKET	RIFLE, CENTER-FIRE
MUSKET, FLINTLOCK	RIFLE, LONG
MUSKET, MILITARY FLINTLOCK	RIFLE, MILITARY BREECHLOAD
MUSKET, MILITARY MATCHLOCK	RIFLE, MILITARY CENTER-FIRE
MUSKET, MILITARY PERCUSSION	RIFLE, MILITARY FLINTLOCK
MUSKET, PERCUSSION	RIFLE, MILITARY PERCUSSION
MUSKET BARREL	RIFLE, MILITARY RIM-FIRE
MUSKET BUTT PLATE	RIFLE, MINIATURE
MUSKET STOCK	RIFLE, PERCUSSION
MUSKET TRIGGER	RIFLE, POLICE CENTER-FIRE
MUSKET TRIGGER GUARD	RIFLE, RIM-FIRE
MUSKETOON, MILITARY	RIFLE BARREL
PEPPERBOX	RIFLE BREECH MECHANISM
PERCUSSION LOCK MECHANISM	SET, DUELLING PISTOL
PISTOL	SHOTGUN BREAKCATCH LEVER
PISTOL, AUTOMATIC	SHOTGUN, CENTER-FIRE
PISTOL, DUELLING	SHOTGUN, DOUBLE-BARREL
PISTOL, FLINTLOCK	SHOTGUN, DOUBLE-BARREL CENTER-FIRE
PISTOL, HORSEMAN'S	SHOTGUN, DOUBLE-BARREL PERCUSSION
PISTOL, MILITARY AUTOMATIC	SHOTGUN, PERCUSSION
PISTOL, MILITARY FLINTLOCK	

Class E080: ARMAMENT, EDGED
Object, suffix   **Object, suffix**   Total: 80

ARROW	BAYONET, MILITARY SOCKET SPIKE
ARROWHEAD	BAYONET, MILITARY SOCKET SWORD
AX, BOARDING	BAYONET, MILITARY SOCKET TRIANGULAR
AX, MILITARY BOARDING	BAYONET, SOCKET
BACKSWORD, MILITARY	BAYONET MOUNT SPRING
BAYONET	BILL
BAYONET, HILTED SWORD	BOLO
BAYONET, MILITARY HILTED KNIFE	BOW
BAYONET, MILITARY HILTED SWORD	BROADSWORD
BAYONET, MILITARY HILTED TRIANGULAR	BROADSWORD, MILITARY
BAYONET, MILITARY PLUG KNIFE	BROADSWORD TASSEL
BAYONET, MILITARY PLUG SWORD	CASE, ARROW
BAYONET, MILITARY SOCKET CRUCIFORM	CASE, MILITARY SWORD
BAYONET, MILITARY SOCKET KNIFE	CROSSBOW

Class E080: ARMAMENT, EDGED — *(Continued)*

Total: 80

Object, suffix

CUTLASS	PIKE, MILITARY
CUTLASS, MILITARY	PIKE, MILITARY BOARDING
DAGGER	POINT, PROJECTILE
DAGGER, MILITARY	RAPIER
DAGGER HANDLE	RAPIER, MILITARY
DIRK, MILITARY	RAPIER, MILITARY CANE
FOIL	SABER
GLADIUS, MILITARY	SABER, MILITARY
HALBERD	SMALLSWORD, MILITARY
HALBERD, MILITARY	SPEAR
HANGER, MILITARY	SPEAR, EEL
HARPOON	SPEAR, FISH
HARPOON, MINIATURE	SPEAR, MUSKRAT
HARPOON HEAD	SPONTOON
KNIFE	SPONTOON, MILITARY
KNIFE, BOWIE	SWORD
LANCE	SWORD, HUNTING
LANCE, MILITARY	SWORD, MILITARY
LANCE, MINIATURE WHALE	SWORD, MINIATURE
LANCE, POLICE	SWORD, POLICE
LANCE, WHALE	SWORD BLADE, MILITARY
LANCE BARB, MINIATURE	SWORD BOW
LINER, BROADSWORD HILT	SWORD GUARD, MILITARY
PARTISAN	SWORD HILT
PIKE	SWORD POMMEL
PIKE, BOARDING	TOMAHAWK

Class E100: ARMAMENT, BLUDGEON

Total: 3

Object, suffix

BLACKJACK	KNUCKLES, BRASS
CLUB	

Class E120: ARMAMENT, ARTILLERY

Total: 22

Object, suffix

CANNON	GUN, MILITARY
CARRIAGE AXLE PIN, CANNON	GUN, MILITARY ANTIAIRCRAFT
CARRIAGE AXLE WASHER, CANNON	GUN, MILITARY FIELD
CARRIAGE, MILITARY CANNON	GUN, MILITARY GARRISON
CARRIAGE WHEEL, MILITARY CANNON	GUN, MILITARY SEA-COAST
CARRONADE	GUN, SWIVEL
CARRONADE, MINIATURE	LAUNCHER, MISSILE
CATAPULT, MINIATURE	MORTAR
FALCONET	MORTAR, MODEL
GUN, ANTITANK	PLATFORM PINTLE, TRAVERSING
GUN, GATLING	STAND, MILITARY FALCONET

Class E140: ARMAMENT, AMMUNITION

Total: 37

Object, suffix

BALL, MUSKET	CAP, MILITARY FUSE
BULLET	CARTRIDGE
CANNONBALL	CARTRIDGE, BAG
CANNONBALL, MILITARY	CARTRIDGE CASE

Class E140: ARMAMENT, AMMUNITION — *(Continued)*

Total: 37

Object, suffix

CARTRIDGE, CASELESS
CARTRIDGE, CENTER-FIRE
CARTRIDGE, MINIATURE BAG
FUSE, MILITARY DETONATING
GRAPESHOT
GRAPESHOT, MILITARY
GRAPESHOT, MINIATURE
GRENADE
GRENADE, ANTIPERSONNEL
KIT, INSTRUCTIONAL MODEL AMMUNITION
MISSILE, DESIGN MODEL
PETARD
PRIMER
SABOT, CANNONBALL
SHELL, ARTILLERY

Object, suffix

SHELL CASE, ARTILLERY
SHELL, SHOTGUN
SHELL, SHRAPNEL
SHOT, BAR
SHOT, CASE
SHOT, CHAIN
SHOT, LEAD
SHOT, MILITARY CASE
SHOT, MILITARY CHAIN
SHOT, MINIATURE CASE
TORPEDO, DESIGN MODEL
TORPEDO, MODEL
TUBE, MILITARY FRICTION
WAD, GUN

Class E160: ARMAMENT, BODY ARMOR

Total: 7

Object, suffix

BACKPLATE
BREASTPLATE
HELMET
HELMET, MILITARY

Object, suffix

MAIL
NET, MILITARY HELMET CAMOUFLAGE
VAMBRACE

Class E180: ARMAMENT ACCESSORY

Total: 175

Object, suffix

BAG, HUNTING
BELT, CARTRIDGE
BELT, MILITARY BAYONET
BELT, MILITARY CARTRIDGE
BELT, MILITARY CARTRIDGE-BOX
BELT, MILITARY POWDER HORN
BELT, MILITARY SWORD
BELT, POLICE CARTRIDGE
BELT, POLICE HOLSTER
BOX, AMMUNITION
BOX, CARTRIDGE
BOX, MILITARY AMMUNITION
BOX, MILITARY CARTRIDGE
BOX, MILITARY FUSE
BOX, POLICE CARTRIDGE
BRUSH, MILITARY CANNON
BRUSH, MILITARY GUNNER'S
BUCKET, MILITARY
BUCKET, MILITARY LANCE
BUCKET, MILITARY SADDLE
BUCKET, MINIATURE MILITARY
BUCKET, POLICE SADDLE
CALIPERS, MILITARY GUNNER'S
CALL, GAME
CALTROP
CAP, PERCUSSION
CAP, SNAP
CARRIAGE, ARTILLERY SLING
CASE, ARTILLERY CARTRIDGE
CASE, GUN

Object, suffix

CASE, GUNPOWDER
CASE, MILITARY GUN
CASE, MILITARY GUNNER'S QUADRANT
CASK, GUNPOWDER
CASK, MILITARY GUNPOWDER
CLINOMETER, MILITARY GUNNER'S
CLIP, CARTRIDGE
CLIP, MILITARY CARTRIDGE
CONTAINER, GREASE
COVER, MILITARY CARTRIDGE-BOX
COVER, POLICE CARTRIDGE-BOX
CUTTER, WAD
DECOY
DECOY, MINIATURE
FINDER, RANGE
FLASK, POWDER
FLASK, PRIMING
FLASK, SHOT
FLINT
FLOAT, MINIATURE
FROG, MILITARY BAYONET
FROG, MILITARY SWORD
FROG STUD, MILITARY
GARLAND, MILITARY SHOT
GIN, ARTILLERY
HAMMER, MAGAZINE COOPER'S
HANDSPIKE, MILITARY
HOLSTER
HOLSTER, MILITARY
HOLSTER, POLICE

Class E180: ARMAMENT ACCESSORY — *(Continued)*

Total: 175

Object, suffix

HORN, MILITARY POWDER
HORN, POWDER
JAG, MILITARY
KEY, MILITARY TRUNNION
KIT, GUN-CLEANING
LADLE, HOT-SHOT
LADLE, MILITARY ARTILLERY
LANYARD, MILITARY
LANYARD, POLICE REVOLVER
LEVER, CANNON CARRIAGE TRUCK
LEVER, MINIATURE CANNON CARRIAGE TRUCK
LIMBER, MILITARY
LINCHPIN, MILITARY
LINSTOCK, MILITARY
MAGAZINE
MALLET, MAGAZINE
MEASURE, POWDER
MOLD, BALL
MOLD, BULLET
MOLD, MILITARY BALL
NET, TORPEDO
OILCAN
PAIL, MAGAZINE WATER
PIPE, RAMROD
POST, MILITARY AIMING
POUCH, BALL
POUCH, MILITARY BALL
POUCH, MILITARY CAP
POUCH, MILITARY MAGAZINE
POUCH, MILITARY SHOT
POUCH, SHOT
PRESS, CARTRIDGE-CASE
PRESS, PRIMING
PRICKER, MILITARY
PRICKER, MINIATURE MILITARY
PROTECTOR, MILITARY NIPPLE
PULLER, BULLET
PULLER, GUN WHEEL
QUADRANT, MILITARY GUNNER'S
QUIVER
QUOIN, MILITARY
QUOIN, MINIATURE MILITARY
RACK, ARMS
RACK, MILITARY SHOT
RAKE, HOT-SHOT
RAMMER, MILITARY
RAMROD
RAMROD, MILITARY
REST, MUSKET
ROD, CLEANING
ROD, MILITARY CLEANING
SCABBARD, BAYONET
SCABBARD, DAGGER
SCABBARD, MILITARY BACKSWORD
SCABBARD, MILITARY BAYONET
SCABBARD, MILITARY BROADSWORD
SCABBARD, MILITARY CANE RAPIER
SCABBARD, MILITARY CUTLASS

Object, suffix

SCABBARD, MILITARY DIRK
SCABBARD, MILITARY GLADIUS
SCABBARD, MILITARY HANGER
SCABBARD, MILITARY HILTED KNIFE BAYONET
SCABBARD, MILITARY HILTED SWORD BAYONET
SCABBARD, MILITARY HILTED TRIANGULAR BAYONET
SCABBARD, MILITARY PLUG KNIFE BAYONET
SCABBARD, MILITARY PLUG SWORD BAYONET
SCABBARD, MILITARY RAPIER
SCABBARD, MILITARY SABER
SCABBARD, MILITARY SMALLSWORD
SCABBARD, MILITARY SOCKET CRUCIFORM BAYONET
SCABBARD, MILITARY SOCKET KNIFE BAYONET
SCABBARD, MILITARY SOCKET SPIKE BAYONET
SCABBARD, MILITARY SOCKET SWORD BAYONET
SCABBARD, MILITARY SOCKET TRIANGULAR BAYONET
SCABBARD, MILITARY SWORD
SCABBARD, MINIATURE SWORD
SCABBARD, POLICE SWORD
SCABBARD, SWORD
SCRAPER, MILITARY BARREL
SET, LOADING TOOL
SHEATH
SHEATH, TOMAHAWK
SHIELD
SIEVE, MILITARY POWDER
SIGHT
SIGHT, MILITARY
SIGHT, MILITARY ARTILLERY
SIGHT, MILITARY TELESCOPE
SLING
SLING, MILITARY MUSKET
SLING, MILITARY RIFLE
SLING SWIVEL, MILITARY MUSKET
SLING THONG, MILITARY MUSKET
SPONGE
SPONGE, MILITARY
STARTER, BULLET
STICK, MILITARY PORTFIRE
STOPPER, MILITARY MUZZLE
STRUT, MILITARY TARGET
SWORD KNOT, MILITARY
SWORD KNOT, POLICE
TACKLE, MILITARY CANNON
TAMPION, MILITARY
TAMPION, MINIATURE MILITARY
THUMBSTALL, MILITARY GUNNER'S
TONGS, HOT-SHOT
TOOL, CARTRIDGE LOADING
TOOL, LOADING
TOOL, MILITARY HOT-SHOT
TOW, CLEANING
VISE, MILITARY SHELL
WAD-HOOK, MILITARY
WORM
WORM, MINIATURE
WRENCH, MILITARY NIPPLE

CATEGORY 05: TOOLS & EQUIPMENT FOR SCIENCE AND TECHNOLOGY

Class E200: ASTRONOMICAL T&E

Total: 5

Object, suffix

ASTROLABE
ORRERY
TELESCOPE, ACHROMATIC

Object, suffix

TELESCOPE, GALILEAN
TELESCOPE, REFLECTING

Class E220: BIOLOGICAL T&E

Total: 1

Object, suffix

DISH, PETRI

Class E240: CHEMICAL T&E

Total: 30

Object, suffix

BEAKER
BURNER, BUNSEN
CLAMP, HOSECOCK
CONDENSER
COVER, BEAKER
CRUCIBLE
DISH, EVAPORATING
EYEDROPPER
FLASK
FUNNEL
FUNNEL, FILTER
GRADUATE
MORTAR
MORTAR & PESTLE
PAD, HOT

Object, suffix

PAPER, FILTER
PESTLE
RACK, TEST TUBE
RETORT
STILL
STILL, SOLAR
STOPPER
SUPPORT, RING
TONGS, BEAKER
TONGS, FLASK
TRIANGLE
TRIPOD
TUBE, TEST
TUBING
TWEEZERS

Class E260: CONSTRUCTION T&E

Total: 9

Object, suffix

PITCH
PLIERS, FENCING
PUMP, WATER
SCRAPER
SHOVEL, ENTRENCHING

Object, suffix

SHOVEL, POWER
STRETCHER, FENCE-WIRE
TAMPER
TOOL, MILITARY ENTRENCHING

Class E280: ELECTRICAL & MAGNETIC T&E

Total: 19

Object, suffix

AMMETER
BATTERY, DRY-CELL
BATTERY, WET-CELL
BOX, CONTROL
CABLE, ELECTRICAL
CAPACITOR, ELECTROLYTIC
CLAMP, SPLICING
COUNTER
COVER, OUTLET BOX
FUSEBOARD

Object, suffix

INSULATOR
MAGNET
PLIERS, NEEDLENOSE
REGULATOR, VOLTAGE
RELAY
RESISTOR
RHEOSTAT
TRANSISTOR
TUBE, X-RAY

Class E300: ENERGY PRODUCTION T&E

Total: 35

Object, suffix

BEARING
BELT
BOILER, STEAM
BOX, OUTLET
CLAMP, STEAM HOSE
COMPRESSOR, DUPLEX AIR
CORD, ELECTRICAL
COUNTERSHAFT
COVER, STEAM BOILER INSPECTION
DYNAMOTOR
ENGINE, DESIGN MODEL
ENGINE, GASOLINE
ENGINE, STEAM
GENERATOR
GOVERNOR
GRIP, SERVICE CABLE
INJECTOR, LUBRICATING OIL
INSULATOR

Object, suffix

MAGNETO
MANOMETER, STEAM BOILER
MOTOR, ELECTRIC
PILLOWBLOCK
PLUG
PLUG, SPARK
PUMP, STEAM BOILER
RECTIFIER
SHEET, STEAM BOILER
STEAMLINE
SWITCH
TRANSFORMER
TREADLE
TUBE-EXPANDER
VALVE, STEAM
VALVE, STEAM BOILER
WATERWHEEL AXLE

Class E320: GEOLOGICAL T&E

Total: 0

Class E340: MAINTENANCE T&E

Total: 85

Object, suffix

ASHPAN
BAG, LAUNDRY
BAG, LAUNDRY BLUEING
BASKET, LAUNDRY
BEATER, LAUNDRY
BEATER, RUG
BENCH, LAUNDRY
BOARD, IRONING
BROOM
BROOM, MINIATURE
BROOM, WHISK
BRUSH
BRUSH, FLUE
BRUSH, MILITARY SCRUB
BRUSH, POLISH
BRUSH, SCRUB
BUTLER, SILENT
CAN, KEROSINE
CAN, TRASH
CLEANER, LAMP CHIMNEY
CLEANER, VACUUM
CLEANSER
CLOTH, CLEANING
CLOTHESLINE
CLOTHESPIN
COVER, IRONING BOARD
DISHPAN
DIVIDER, CLOTHESLINE
DOLLY, WASH
DRYER

Object, suffix

DUSTER
DUSTPAN
FORK, LAUNDRY
GRATER, SOAP
HAMPER
HOLDER, CLOTHESPIN
HOLDER, DUSTER
HOLDER, WHISK BROOM
INCINERATOR
IRON
IRON, FLUTING
IRON HANDLE
KNOCKER, SNOW
MACHINE, WASHING
MANGLE
MOP
PADDLE, LAUNDRY
PAIL
PAIL, MILITARY
PAIL & WRINGER
PAPER, SHELF
PLUNGER
PLUNGER, WASH
POLISHER, FLOOR
PRESS, LINEN
RACK, DRYING
REEL, CLOTHESLINE
SADIRON
SAVER, SOAP
SCOOP, ICE

Class E340: MAINTENANCE T&E — *(Continued)*

Total: 85

Object, suffix

SCOOP, SNOW
SCRAPER, BOILER SCALE
SCRAPER, SNOW
SCRUBBER
SIFTER, ASH
SOAP
SPONGE
SPRINKLER
SQUEEGEE
STOPPER, SINK
STRAINER, LAUNDRY BLUEING
STRAINER, SINK
STRETCHER, CARPET

Object, suffix

STRETCHER, CURTAIN
STRETCHER, GLOVE
STRETCHER, SOCK
SWEEPER, CARPET
TONGS, LAUNDRY
TOWEL, DISH
TRIVET
WASHBOARD
WASHBOILER
WASHTUB
WRINGER, CLOTHES
WRINGER, MOP

Class E360: MECHANICAL T&E

Total: 27

Object, suffix

APPARATUS, PERMEABILITY
BLOWER
CELL, TETRAHEDRAL
CONNECTOR, MULTIPLE
FLYWHEEL
GAUGE, AIR-PRESSURE
GAUGE, STEAM-PRESSURE
GEAR
GYROSCOPE
HOIST
HYDROMETER
JACK, LIFTING
JACK, PULLING
LAUNCHER, PROPELLER

Object, suffix

LEVER
NUT
NUT, TETRAHEDRAL
PULLEY
PUMP, HYDROSTATIC TEST
REGULATOR, GAS
SLING
SPRING, SPIRAL
TANK, TEST
TURNBUCKLE
WASHER, TURNBUCKLE
WINDER, MOTOR
WINDLASS

Class E380: MEDICAL AND PSYCHOLOGICAL T&E

Total: 67

Object, suffix

APPARATUS, PNEUMOTHORAX
APPLICATOR, LINIMENT
ATOMIZER
AUTOCLAVE
BANDAGE
BOWL, BLEEDING
BRUSH, TREPANNING
CASE, PNEUMOTHORAX APPARATUS
CASE, SPECIMEN
CASE, SURGICAL INSTRUMENT
CHART, VISUAL-ACUITY
CHISEL, TREPANNING
CURETTE
DEPRESSOR, TONGUE
DIRECTOR
DISH
DOUCHE, NASAL
ELEVATOR, MALAR
ELEVATOR, TREPANNING
EXTRACTOR, LITHOTOMY
FORCEPS
FORCEPS, ASSALINI

Object, suffix

FORCEPS, BONE-CUTTING
FORCEPS, DENTAL
GALLIPOT
KIT, FIRST-AID
KIT, INSTRUCTIONAL MODEL ACUPUNCTURE
LANCET, BLOOD
MACHINE, PILL
MASK, ANAESTHESIA
MIRROR, HEAD
MIRROR, ORAL EXAMINING
MODEL, ANATOMICAL
MORTAR & PESTLE
NEEDLE, SUTERING
PAD, HEATING
PERFORATOR, TREPANNING
PIN, TREPHINE
PLASTER, COUGH
PROBE
PUMP, BREAST
PUMP, EMBALMING
RESPIRATOR
SAW, SURGICAL

Class E380: MEDICAL AND PSYCHOLOGICAL T&E — *(Continued)*

Object, suffix

Object, suffix	Object, suffix
SCALPEL	SPOON, DOSE
SCISSORS, SURGICAL	STRIPPER, RIB
SCOOP, TREPANNING BONE	SYRINGE
SCRAPER, PERIOSTEUM	TAPE, ADHESIVE
SET, EMBALMING INSTRUMENT	THERMOMETER
SET, SCALPEL	THREAD, SUTERING
SET, SURGICAL INSTRUMENT	TOURNIQUET
SHEARS, RIB	TOURNIQUET, MILITARY
SHIELD, X-RAY	TRAY, KIDNEY
SPECULUM	TREPHINE
SPECULUM, AURAL	VAPORIZER
SPLINT	

Class E400: MERCHANDISING T&E

Object, suffix

Object, suffix	Object, suffix
BAG, BEAN	BOTTLE, BOOT POLISH
BAG, CEMENT	BOTTLE, BORACIC ACID
BAG, CEREAL	BOTTLE, BRANDY
BAG, COAL	BOTTLE, CANDLE
BAG, COFFEE	BOTTLE, CARBOLIC ACID
BAG, DYE	BOTTLE, CASTOR OIL
BAG, FEED	BOTTLE, CHEMICAL
BAG, FLOUR	BOTTLE, CLEANING FLUID
BAG, GLOVE	BOTTLE, CLOVE
BAG, GLUE	BOTTLE, COD LIVER OIL
BAG, GRAIN	BOTTLE, COFFEE SYRUP
BAG, GUNPOWDER	BOTTLE, COGNAC
BAG, JEWELRY	BOTTLE, CONDIMENT SAUCE
BAG, LEAD SHOT	BOTTLE, CONFECTION
BAG, NAIL	BOTTLE, CORN OIL
BAG, POTATO	BOTTLE, COSMETIC
BAG, RICE	BOTTLE, COTTON SEED OIL
BAG, SALT	BOTTLE, COUGH DROP
BAG, SAND	BOTTLE, CREAM
BAG, SEED	BOTTLE, CURRY
BAG, STOCKING	BOTTLE, DECONGESTANT
BAG, SUGAR	BOTTLE, DISH SOAP
BAG, TANKAGE	BOTTLE, DYE
BAG, TOBACCO	BOTTLE, EMBALMING FLUID
BAG, TRADE	BOTTLE, EYEWASH
BALE, BLANKET	BOTTLE, FLAVORING
BALE, CARPET	BOTTLE, FOOD COLORING
BALE, CLOTH BOLT	BOTTLE, FORMALDEHYDE
BALE, PANTS	BOTTLE, FRUIT JUICE
BALE, PELT	BOTTLE, GIN
BALE, ROPE	BOTTLE, GINGER
BARRIER, DISPLAY	BOTTLE, GINGER ALE
BIN, STORAGE	BOTTLE, GINGER BEER
BOTTLE, ALCOHOLIC BEVERAGE	BOTTLE, GLUE
BOTTLE, AMMONIA	BOTTLE, GLYCERIN
BOTTLE, ANALGESIC	BOTTLE, GRAPE JUICE
BOTTLE, ANTACID	BOTTLE, GUN BLUEING
BOTTLE, ANTISEPTIC	BOTTLE, HAIR TONIC
BOTTLE, APOTHECARY	BOTTLE, HORSERADISH
BOTTLE, ASTRINGENT	BOTTLE, HYDROGEN PEROXIDE
BOTTLE, BEER	BOTTLE, INK
BOTTLE, BEVERAGE	BOTTLE, INSECT REPELANT
BOTTLE, BITTERS	BOTTLE, INSECTICIDE

Class E400: MERCHANDISING T&E — *(Continued)*

Total: 1197

Object, suffix

Object, suffix

BOTTLE, IODINE	BOX, AIR FRESHENER
BOTTLE, KETCHUP	BOX, AMMONIA
BOTTLE, LAUNDRY BLEACH	BOX, ANALGESIC
BOTTLE, LAUNDRY BLUEING	BOX, ANTACID
BOTTLE, LAXATIVE	BOX, ANTISEPTIC
BOTTLE, LEATHER DRESSING	BOX, ARMBAND
BOTTLE, LEMON JUICE	BOX, ASTRINGENT
BOTTLE, LEMONADE	BOX, ATOMIZER
BOTTLE, LIME JUICE	BOX, AXLE WASHER
BOTTLE, LINIMENT	BOX, BAKING SODA
BOTTLE, LIQUEUR	BOX, BANDAGE
BOTTLE, LUBRICATING OIL	BOX, BEAD
BOTTLE, MALT EXTRACT	BOX, BELT
BOTTLE, MANDRAKE	BOX, BISCUIT
BOTTLE, MEAT EXTRACT	BOX, BONING KNIFE
BOTTLE, MEDICINAL	BOX, BOOT POLISH
BOTTLE, MEDICINAL SYRUP	BOX, BORACIC ACID
BOTTLE, MILK	BOX, BREATH FRESHENER
BOTTLE, MINERAL OIL	BOX, BUTTER
BOTTLE, MINERAL WATER	BOX, BUTTON
BOTTLE, MOUTHWASH	BOX, BUTTON CARD
BOTTLE, MUSTARD	BOX, CAKE DECORATOR
BOTTLE, NAIL POLISH	BOX, CAKE MOLD
BOTTLE, NON-ALCOHOLIC BEVERAGE	BOX, CANDLE
BOTTLE, OINTMENT	BOX, CARD DECK
BOTTLE, OLIVE	BOX, CARTRIDGE
BOTTLE, OLIVE OIL	BOX, CARTRIDGE LOADING TOOL
BOTTLE, OPIUM	BOX, CARVING SET
BOTTLE, PAINT	BOX, CELERY SEED
BOTTLE, PECTIN	BOX, CEREAL
BOTTLE, PHOTOGRAPHIC DEVELOPER	BOX, CHALK
BOTTLE, PICKLE	BOX, CHEESECLOTH
BOTTLE, PIGMENT	BOX, CHEMICAL
BOTTLE, PILL	BOX, CHEWING GUM
BOTTLE, POISON	BOX, CIGAR
BOTTLE, SALT	BOX, CIGARETTE
BOTTLE, SAVORY	BOX, CIGARETTE PAPER
BOTTLE, SCOTCH	BOX, CINNAMON
BOTTLE, SHAMPOO	BOX, CITRIC ACID
BOTTLE, SHELLAC	BOX, CLASP
BOTTLE, SKIN LOTION	BOX, CLEANSER
BOTTLE, SMELLING SALTS	BOX, CLOTHING
BOTTLE, SNUFF	BOX, CLOTHING FASTENER
BOTTLE, SODA WATER	BOX, CLOVE
BOTTLE, SPICE	BOX, COCOA
BOTTLE, STIMULANT	BOX, COD LIVER OIL
BOTTLE, STOVE POLISH	BOX, COFFEE
BOTTLE, THYME	BOX, COFFIN PLATE
BOTTLE, TOILET	BOX, COIN ENVELOPE
BOTTLE, TOOTHPASTE	BOX, COLLAR
BOTTLE, TRANQUILIZER	BOX, COLLAR & CUFF
BOTTLE, TURPENTINE	BOX, COMB
BOTTLE, VARNISH	BOX, CONFECTION
BOTTLE, VERMIFUGE	BOX, CORN STARCH
BOTTLE, VINEGAR	BOX, CORSET
BOTTLE, WHISKEY	BOX, COSMETIC
BOTTLE, WINE	BOX, COUGH DROP
BOTTLE, WOOD POLISH	BOX, CRAYON
BOTTLE, YEAST	BOX, CREAM OF TARTAR
BOWL, SHAVING SOAP	BOX, CREAM SKIMMER
BOX, ABSORBENT COTTON	BOX, CUFF

Class E400: MERCHANDISING T&E — *(Continued)*
Object, suffix   Object, suffix

BOX, CURLER	BOX, LEMONADE
BOX, CURTAIN RING	BOX, LIGHT SOCKET
BOX, CUSTARD	BOX, LIGHTER FLINT
BOX, DANCE FLOOR WAX	BOX, LINEN MARKING SET
BOX, DECONGESTANT	BOX, LINIMENT
BOX, DINNER MIX	BOX, LUBRICATING GREASE
BOX, DRILL	BOX, LUBRICATING OIL
BOX, DRILL BIT	BOX, LUGGAGE/SHAWL CARRIER
BOX, DYE	BOX, MATCH
BOX, EMBALMING FLUID	BOX, MEAT EXTRACT
BOX, ERASER	BOX, MEAT TENDERIZER
BOX, EYE CAP	BOX, MEDICINAL
BOX, EYECUP	BOX, MEDICINAL SYRUP
BOX, EYEGLASSES	BOX, METAL POLISH
BOX, EYEWASH	BOX, MILITARY FRICTION TUBE
BOX, FILE	BOX, MILITARY SIGHT
BOX, FILM	BOX, MILK
BOX, FISHHOOK	BOX, MILK POWDER
BOX, FLASHLIGHT	BOX, MITT
BOX, FLATWARE	BOX, MONEY
BOX, FLAVORING	BOX, MOP
BOX, FLOUR	BOX, MUSTARD
BOX, FLYPAPER	BOX, NAIL
BOX, FOOD COLORING	BOX, NAIL POLISH
BOX, FUNNEL	BOX, NAPKIN
BOX, GAITER	BOX, NASAL DOUCHE
BOX, GARTER	BOX, NECKTIE
BOX, GELATIN	BOX, NEWSPAPER CLIP
BOX, GINGER	BOX, NOISEMAKER
BOX, GLOVE	BOX, NURSING BOTTLE
BOX, GLUE	BOX, NURSING BOTTLE NIPPLE
BOX, GOGGLES FILTER	BOX, NUTMEG
BOX, GRAVY MIX	BOX, OINTMENT
BOX, GREETING CARD	BOX, PAINT
BOX, GUN GREASE	BOX, PAPER CLIP
BOX, GUN WAD	BOX, PASTA
BOX, GUNPOWDER	BOX, PEANUT
BOX, HAIR CLIPPERS	BOX, PEN
BOX, HAIR TONIC	BOX, PENCIL
BOX, HAIRPIN	BOX, PENCIL SHARPENER
BOX, HANDKERCHIEF	BOX, PEPPER
BOX, HARMONICA	BOX, PERCUSSION CAP
BOX, HAT	BOX, PHONOGRAPH NEEDLE
BOX, HOOK	BOX, PHOTOGRAPHIC DEVELOPER
BOX, HOPS	BOX, PHOTOGRAPHIC FILM
BOX, ICE CREAM MIX	BOX, PHOTOGRAPHIC FIXER
BOX, INK	BOX, PICTURE FRAME HANGER
BOX, INSECTICIDE	BOX, PIGMENT
BOX, INSTANT POTATO	BOX, PILL
BOX, JELLY	BOX, PIPE FILTER
BOX, JEWELRY	BOX, POCKET KNIFE
BOX, LABEL	BOX, POPCORN
BOX, LAMP CHIMNEY	BOX, PORTABLE STOVE
BOX, LAMP GLOBE	BOX, POULTRY GRIT
BOX, LAMP MANTLE	BOX, PRESERVING JAR LINER
BOX, LANTERN	BOX, PRESERVING JAR SEAL
BOX, LARD	BOX, PRINTER'S LEADS
BOX, LAUNDRY BLUEING	BOX, PRINTER'S TYPE
BOX, LAUNDRY SOAP	BOX, RAISIN
BOX, LAXATIVE	BOX, RAZOR
BOX, LEATHER DRESSING	BOX, RAZOR BLADE

Class E400: MERCHANDISING T&E — *(Continued)*

Object, suffix

Object, suffix

Total: 1197

BOX, RAZOR BLADE SHARPENER	BOX, VAPORIZER
BOX, RESPIRATOR FILTER	BOX, VARNISH
BOX, ROSIN	BOX, VEHICLE LIGHT SWITCH
BOX, RUBBER BOOT	BOX, VERMIFUGE
BOX, SADIRON	BOX, VIOLIN STRING
BOX, SALT	BOX, WATCH
BOX, SAW JOINTER	BOX, WELDING FLUX
BOX, SAW-SET	BOX, WHETSTONE
BOX, SCRUBBER	BOX, WHITEWASH
BOX, SEALING WAX	BOX, WICK
BOX, SEED	BOX, WINDOW LIFT
BOX, SELENIUM	BOX, WINE GLASS
BOX, SERUM	BOX, YEAST
BOX, SEWING SUPPLIES	CAN, ANCHOVY
BOX, SHAMPOO	CAN, APPLE
BOX, SHAVING SOAP	CAN, APPLESAUCE
BOX, SHIRT	CAN, APRICOT
BOX, SHOE	CAN, ARTICHOKE
BOX, SHROUD	CAN, ASBESTOS
BOX, SHUTTLECOCK	CAN, ASPARAGUS
BOX, SKATE	CAN, BEAN
BOX, SKATE BLADE	CAN, BEEF
BOX, SKIN LOTION	CAN, BEET
BOX, SNUFF	CAN, BELT DRESSING
BOX, SODA BISCUIT	CAN, CABBAGE
BOX, SOLDER FLUX	CAN, CARROT
BOX, SPARK PLUG	CAN, CAULIFLOWER
BOX, SPICE	CAN, CAUSTIC SODA
BOX, STAPLER	CAN, CHERRY
BOX, STARCH	CAN, CHICKEN
BOX, STATIONERY	CAN, CHILI CON CARNE
BOX, STOCKING	CAN, COFFEE
BOX, STORAGE	CAN, CONDENSED MILK
BOX, STOVE MICA	CAN, CORN
BOX, STOVE POLISH	CAN, CREAM
BOX, STOVEPIPE COLLAR	CAN, EVAPORATED MILK
BOX, STRAIGHT PIN	CAN, FRUIT
BOX, STROP	CAN, GOULASH
BOX, SUGAR	CAN, GRAPE
BOX, SUPPOSITORY	CAN, HAM
BOX, SUSPENDER	CAN, JAM
BOX, SYRINGE	CAN, LOBSTER
BOX, TALCUM POWDER	CAN, LUBRICATING GREASE
BOX, TAPER	CAN, LUNCHEON MEAT
BOX, TEA	CAN, MEAT BALL
BOX, TEAT DILATOR	CAN, MILK POWDER
BOX, TEST TUBE	CAN, MIXED VEGETABLES
BOX, THIMBLE	CAN, NUT
BOX, THREAD	CAN, ONION FLAKE
BOX, TISSUE	CAN, PAINT
BOX, TOBACCO	CAN, PEA
BOX, TOILET BOTTLE	CAN, PEACH
BOX, TOILET SOAP	CAN, PEAR
BOX, TOILETRY SET	CAN, PINEAPPLE
BOX, TONIC	CAN, PLUM
BOX, TOOTHBRUSH	CAN, PORK
BOX, TOOTHPASTE	CAN, POTATO
BOX, TOOTHPICK	CAN, RASPBERRY
BOX, TYPEWRITER RIBBON	CAN, SALMON
BOX, UNDERWEAR	CAN, SARDINE
BOX, VALVE	CAN, SAUERKRAUT

Class E400: MERCHANDISING T&E — *(Continued)*

Total: 1197

Object, suffix

Object, suffix

CAN, SOUP	CASK, BUTTER
CAN, SPAGHETTI SAUCE	CASK, COFFEE
CAN, SPINACH	CASK, COGNAC
CAN, STRAWBERRY	CASK, FIG
CAN, TOMATO	CASK, FLOOR CLEANER
CAN, TOMATO JUICE	CASK, FLOUR
CAN, TURNIP	CASK, GUNPOWDER
CAN, VARNISH	CASK, KEROSENE
CARBOY, LUBRICATING OIL	CASK, LEAD SHOT
CARD, BUCKLE	CASK, LIME
CARD, BUTTON	CASK, MADEIRA
CARD, CLOTHING FASTENER	CASK, MEAT
CARD, FISHHOOK	CASK, MILITARY GUNPOWDER
CARD, HAIRPIN	CASK, MOLASSES
CARD, HANDKERCHIEF	CASK, NAIL
CARD, HATPIN	CASK, OYSTER SHELL
CARD, PEN	CASK, PAINT
CARD, RIBBON	CASK, PICKLE
CARD, SEWING SUPPLIES	CASK, PIGMENT
CARD, STRAIGHT PIN	CASK, PINE TAR
CARRIER, MONEY	CASK, PLASTER
CARTON, ANALGESIC	CASK, POISON
CARTON, BUTTER	CASK, PORK
CARTON, CANNED FOOD	CASK, POTASH
CARTON, CHALK	CASK, RICE
CARTON, CIGARETTE	CASK, RUM
CARTON, CIGARETTE PAPER	CASK, SALMON
CARTON, COFFEE	CASK, SULFUR
CARTON, COLLAR STAY	CASK, TABLEWARE
CARTON, CONDENSED MILK	CASK, VINEGAR
CARTON, CONFECTION	CASK, WATER
CARTON, EGG	CASK, WHISKEY
CARTON, EVAPORATED MILK	CASK, WINE
CARTON, HOOPS	CASK HEAD, PORK
CARTON, KETCHUP	CASK HEAD, WINE
CARTON, LIGHTER FLINT	CLIP, NEWSPAPER
CARTON, LIME JUICE	COUNTER
CARTON, MILK POWDER	COVER, BOTTLE STOPPER
CARTON PANEL, EVAPORATED MILK	CRATE, ANALGESIC
CARTON, PASTA	CRATE, APPLE
CARTON, PEPPER	CRATE, ART OBJECT
CARTON, RENNET	CRATE, AX BLADE
CARTON, SKIN LOTION	CRATE, BAKING POWDER
CARTON, SPONGE	CRATE, BANANA
CARTON, STOVE POLISH	CRATE, BEAN
CARTON, TOILET SOAP	CRATE, BISCUIT
CARTON, TOOTHPASTE	CRATE, BITTERS
CARTON, VACUUM BOTTLE	CRATE, BOOT
CASE, COLLAR	CRATE, BOOT POLISH
CASE, COLLAR & CUFF	CRATE, BOTTLE STOPPER
CASE, CUFF	CRATE, BUTTER
CASE, DISPLAY	CRATE, CANDLE
CASE, DOILY	CRATE, CARTRIDGE
CASE, JEWELRY	CRATE, CEREAL
CASE, MILITARY CARTRIDGE	CRATE, CHALK
CASE, NEEDLE	CRATE, CHEESE
CASE, SHOELACE SALES-SAMPLE	CRATE, CHOCOLATE
CASE, STOVE POLISH	CRATE, CLEANSER
CASK, APPLE	CRATE, CLOTH BOLT
CASK, BEER	CRATE, COCOA
CASK, BISCUIT	CRATE, COD

Class E400: MERCHANDISING T&E — *(Continued)*

Total: 1197

Object, suffix

CRATE, COFFEE
CRATE, COGNAC
CRATE, OONDENSED MILK
CRATE, CONDIMENT SAUCE
CRATE, CONFECTION
CRATE, CORN
CRATE, CRAYON
CRATE, DATE
CRATE, DRIED APPLE
CRATE, DRIED FRUIT
CRATE, EGG
CRATE, EMBALMING FLUID
CRATE, EVAPORATED CREAM
CRATE, EVAPORATED MILK
CRATE, FAN
CRATE, FISH
CRATE, FLAVORING
CRATE, FOOD SYRUP
CRATE, FOOTWEAR
CRATE, FRUIT
CRATE, GASOLINE
CRATE, GIN
CRATE, GLUE
CRATE, GRAPEFRUIT
CRATE, HAIR TONIC
CRATE, HARDWARE
CRATE, HATCHET
CRATE, INK
CRATE, JIG
CRATE, KEROSENE
CRATE, KETCHUP
CRATE, LARD
CRATE, LAUNDRY BLUEING
CRATE, LAUNDRY SOAP
CRATE, LEMON
CRATE, LEMON PEEL
CRATE, LIME JUICE
CRATE, LIQUEUR
CRATE, LOBSTER
CRATE, LUBRICATING GREASE
CRATE, LUBRICATING OIL
CRATE, MATCH
CRATE, MEAT
CRATE, MEDICINAL
CRATE, MILK
CRATE, MILKPOWDER
CRATE, MUSTARD
CRATE, NAIL
CRATE, NON-ALCOHOLIC BEVERAGE
CRATE, NUT
CRATE, ORANGE
CRATE, OYSTER
CRATE, PEA
CRATE, PEAR
CRATE, PENCIL
CRATE, PHONOGRAPH RECORD
CRATE, PORT
CRATE, PRUNE
CRATE, RADIO
CRATE, RAISIN
CRATE, RIFLE

Object, suffix

CRATE, RUM
CRATE, SALMON
CRATE, SALT
CRATE, SARDINE
CRATE, SAW
CRATE, SAW BLADE
CRATE, SEED
CRATE, SHELLAC
CRATE, SKIN LOTION
CRATE, SODA BISCUIT
CRATE, SOFT DRINK
CRATE, SPICE
CRATE, STARCH
CRATE, STEAM GAUGE
CRATE, STOVE POLISH
CRATE, STOVEPIPE
CRATE, SUGAR
CRATE, TEA
CRATE, TOBACCO
CRATE, TOILET
CRATE, TOILET SOAP
CRATE, TOMATO
CRATE, TONIC
CRATE, VARNISH
CRATE, VEGETABLE
CRATE, VERMIFUGE
CRATE, VINEGAR
CRATE, WELDING FLUX
CRATE, WELDING ROD
CRATE, WHISKEY
CRATE, WINDOWPANE
CRATE, WINE
CRATE, YEAST
CRATE PANEL, GASOLINE
CRATE PANEL, OYSTER
CUTTER, STRING
CUTTER, TOBACCO
DEMIJOHN, WINE
DISPENSER, WRAPPING PAPER
DRUM, DIESEL OIL
DRUM, GASOLINE
DRUM, KEROSINE
HOLDER, BAG
HOLDER, SIGN
HOLDER, STRING
JAR, ANTACID
JAR, ANTISEPTIC
JAR, APOTHECARY
JAR, BAKING POWDER
JAR, BANDAGE
JAR, BLACKCURRANT JAM
JAR, CAPER
JAR, CELERY SALT
JAR, CHEESE
JAR, CHEMICAL
JAR, CINNAMON
JAR, COFFEE
JAR, COLA SEED
JAR, COLD CREAM
JAR, CONFECTION
JAR, CONFECTIONER'S

Class E400: MERCHANDISING T&E — *(Continued)*   **Total: 1197**

Object, suffix   **Object, suffix**

Object, suffix	Object, suffix
JAR, COSMETIC	LABEL, ASTRINGENT
JAR, CURRY	LABEL, AXLE CLIP
JAR, DECONGESTANT	LABEL, BACON
JAR, DEODORANT	LABEL, BAKING POWDER
JAR, FISH PASTE	LABEL, BAKING SODA
JAR, FLAVORING	LABEL, BANDAGE
JAR, GELATINE	LABEL, BEAN
JAR, GOOSEBERRY JAM	LABEL, BEEF
JAR, HAIR TONIC	LABEL, BEER
JAR, HONEY	LABEL, BEET
JAR, JAM	LABEL, BISCUIT
JAR, KETCHUP	LABEL, BITTERS
JAR, MARJORAM	LABEL, BITUMINIZED PAPER
JAR, MARMALADE	LABEL, BLACKBERRY
JAR, MEAT PASTE	LABEL, BLACKBERRY JAM
JAR, MEDICINAL	LABEL, BLACKCURRANT
JAR, METAL POLISH	LABEL, BLUEBERRY
JAR, MUSTARD	LABEL, BOLOGNA
JAR, MUSTARD PLASTER MIX	LABEL, BOLT
JAR, OINTMENT	LABEL, BOOT POLISH
JAR, OLIVE	LABEL, BRANDY
JAR, OLIVE OIL	LABEL, BUTTER
JAR, PEANUT	LABEL, BUTTON
JAR, PEANUT BUTTER	LABEL, CALK
JAR, PETROLEUM JELLY	LABEL, CANDLE
JAR, PICKLE	LABEL, CARROT
JAR, PICKLE SPICE	LABEL, CARTRIDGE
JAR, PIGMENT	LABEL, CARTRIDGE LOADING TOOL
JAR, POISON	LABEL, CASTER
JAR, POULTRY SPICE	LABEL, CASTOR OIL
JAR, SALAD DRESSING	LABEL, CEILING HOOK
JAR, SALT	LABEL, CEREAL
JAR, SHAMPOO	LABEL, CHEESE
JAR, SHAVING SOAP	LABEL, CHEMICAL
JAR, SKIN LOTION	LABEL, CHERRY
JAR, SNUFF	LABEL, CHEWING GUM
JAR, SPICE	LABEL, CHICKEN
JAR, STRAWBERRY JAM	LABEL, CHILI CON CARNE
JAR, SYRUP	LABEL, CHOP SUEY
JAR, TALCUM POWDER	LABEL, CIGAR
JAR, THYME	LABEL, CIGARETTE
JAR, TOILET	LABEL, CINNAMON
JAR, TOOTHPASTE	LABEL, CITRUS FRUIT
JAR LID, ANTISEPTIC	LABEL, CLAM
JAR LID, COLD CREAM	LABEL, CLOTH BOLT
JAR LID, COSMETIC	LABEL, CLOTHING
JAR LID, TOOTHPASTE	LABEL, COCOA
JUG, ALCOHOLIC BEVERAGE	LABEL, COD LIVER OIL
JUG, MUSTARD	LABEL, COFFEE
JUG, VARNISH	LABEL, COGNAC
JUG, VINEGAR	LABEL, COLD CREAM
JUG, WHISKEY	LABEL, CONDENSED MILK
LABEL, ANAESTHETIC	LABEL, CONDIMENT SAUCE
LABEL, ANALGESIC	LABEL, CONFECTION
LABEL, ANTACID	LABEL, CORN
LABEL, ANTISEPTIC	LABEL, COSMETIC
LABEL, APPLE	LABEL, COUGH DROP
LABEL, APRICOT	LABEL, CRAB
LABEL, APRICOT JAM	LABEL, CUSTARD
LABEL, ARTICHOKE	LABEL, DISINFECTANT
LABEL, ASPARAGUS	LABEL, DOOR/DRAWER PULL

Class E400: MERCHANDISING T&E — *(Continued)*

Total: 1197

Object, suffix

LABEL, DRILL BIT
LABEL, EGG
LABEL, EMBALMING FLUID
LABEL, EVAPORATED MILK
LABEL, EXPLOSIVE
LABEL, FLAVORING
LABEL, FOOD
LABEL, FRUIT
LABEL, GAME
LABEL, GIN
LABEL, GINGER
LABEL, GINGER BEER
LABEL, GLUE
LABEL, GOOSEBERRY
LABEL, GRAPE
LABEL, GRAPEFRUIT
LABEL, GUNPOWDER
LABEL, HAIR TONIC
LABEL, HAM
LABEL, HORSESHOE NAIL
LABEL, INK
LABEL, JELLY
LABEL, KETCHUP
LABEL, LAMP BURNER
LABEL, LARD
LABEL, LAUNDRY BLUEING
LABEL, LAUNDRY SOAP
LABEL, LAXATIVE
LABEL, LEMON
LABEL, LETTUCE
LABEL, LIME JUICE
LABEL, LINIMENT
LABEL, LOBSTER
LABEL, LOGANBERRY JAM
LABEL, LUBRICATING OIL
LABEL, MARMALADE
LABEL, MATCH
LABEL, MEAT PASTE
LABEL, MEDICINAL
LABEL, METAL POLISH
LABEL, MILITARY FRICTION TUBE
LABEL, MUSTARD
LABEL, NAIL
LABEL, NUT
LABEL, NUTMEG
LABEL, OINTMENT
LABEL, OLIVE
LABEL, OLIVE OIL
LABEL, ORANGE
LABEL, PAINT
LABEL, PANCAKE MIX
LABEL, PASTA
LABEL, PEA
LABEL, PEACH
LABEL, PEAR
LABEL, PEN
LABEL, PENCIL
LABEL, PEPPER
LABEL, PICKLE
LABEL, PILL
LABEL, PINEAPPLE

Object, suffix

LABEL, PLUM
LABEL, PLUM JAM
LABEL, POPCORN
LABEL, PRUNE
LABEL, PUMPKIN
LABEL, QUINCE
LABEL, RASPBERRY
LABEL, ROOF SHEATHING
LABEL, RUM
LABEL, SALAD DRESSING
LABEL, SALMON
LABEL, SANDWICH SPREAD
LABEL, SARDINE
LABEL, SAUERKRAUT
LABEL, SEALING WAX
LABEL, SEDATIVE
LABEL, SEWING NEEDLE
LABEL, SHAFT SEAL
LABEL, SHOE
LABEL, SHOE BRUSH
LABEL, SHORTENING
LABEL, SKIN LOTION
LABEL, SODA BISCUIT
LABEL, SOLVENT
LABEL, SOUP
LABEL, SPAGHETTI SAUCE
LABEL, SPICE
LABEL, SPINACH
LABEL, STARCH
LABEL, STATIONERY
LABEL, STOVE POLISH
LABEL, STRAIGHT PIN
LABEL, STRAWBERRY
LABEL, STRAWBERRY JAM
LABEL, SUGAR
LABEL, SYRUP
LABEL, TEA
LABEL, TEAKETTLE
LABEL, THREAD
LABEL, TOBACCO
LABEL, TOILET BOTTLE
LABEL, TOILET PAPER
LABEL, TOILET SOAP
LABEL, TOMATO
LABEL, TOMATO JUICE
LABEL, TOMATO SAUCE
LABEL, TONIC
LABEL, TOOL HANDLE
LABEL, TOOTHPASTE
LABEL, VARNISH
LABEL, VEGETABLE
LABEL, VINEGAR
LABEL, WHISKEY
LABEL, WINE
LABEL, WOOD POLISH
LABEL, WOODSCREW
LABEL, YARN
LABEL, YEAST
MACHINE, VENDING
MANIKIN
NIPPERS, TICKET

Class E400: MERCHANDISING T&E — *(Continued)*

Object, suffix   Total: 1197

Object, suffix

PACKAGE, ADDRESS LABEL	PACKAGE, PILL
PACKAGE, ALLSPICE	PACKAGE, PIPE CLEANER
PACKAGE, ANALGESIC	PACKAGE, POUNCE
PACKAGE, ANTACID	PACKAGE, PRESERVING JAR SEAL
PACKAGE, ASTRINGENT	PACKAGE, PROMISSORY NOTE
PACKAGE, BAKING SODA	PACKAGE, RAZOR BLADE
PACKAGE, BANDAGE	PACKAGE, RENNET
PACKAGE, BOOT POLISH	PACKAGE, ROSIN
PACKAGE, BREAD	PACKAGE, SAFFRON
PACKAGE, BUTTER	PACKAGE, SEED
PACKAGE, CARD DECK	PACKAGE, SEWING NEEDLE
PACKAGE, CARTRIDGE	PACKAGE, SEWING SUPPLIES
PACKAGE, CHEMICAL FILTER	PACKAGE, SHAMPOO
PACKAGE, CHESTNUT LEAF	PACKAGE, SHOELACE
PACKAGE, CHEWING GUM	PACKAGE, SLEEVE GARTER
PACKAGE, CIGARETTE	PACKAGE, SPICE
PACKAGE, CIGARETTE PAPER	PACKAGE, STARCH
PACKAGE, CLASP	PACKAGE, STATIONERY
PACKAGE, CLEANSER	PACKAGE, STOVE MICA
PACKAGE, CLOTH BOLT	PACKAGE, STOVE POLISH
PACKAGE, COD LIVER OIL	PACKAGE, STRAIGHT PIN
PACKAGE, COFFEE	PACKAGE, STRING
PACKAGE, COLLAR	PACKAGE, TEA
PACKAGE, CONDIMENT SAUCE	PACKAGE, THREAD
PACKAGE, COSMETIC	PACKAGE, THYME
PACKAGE, COUGH DROP	PACKAGE, TISSUE
PACKAGE, DECAL	PACKAGE, TOBACCO
PACKAGE, DYE	PACKAGE, TOILET PAPER
PACKAGE, EGG SUBSTITUTE	PACKAGE, TOILET SOAP
PACKAGE, FISH LINE	PACKAGE, TOILETRY SET
PACKAGE, FISHHOOK	PACKAGE, TONIC
PACKAGE, FRUIT	PACKAGE, VERMIFUGE
PACKAGE, GAUGE PIN	PACKAGE, VIOLIN STRING
PACKAGE, GLAZIER'S POINT	PACKAGE, WAX PAPER
PACKAGE, GUN WAD	PAPER, WRAPPING
PACKAGE, HAIRPIN	RAKE, NAIL
PACKAGE, HATPIN	REGISTER, CASH
PACKAGE, JELLY	SALES-SAMPLE, BUCKLE
PACKAGE, LACE	SALES-SAMPLE, BUTTON
PACKAGE, LAMP WICK	SALES-SAMPLE, CARPET
PACKAGE, LAUNDRY BLUEING	SALES-SAMPLE, CARTRIDGE
PACKAGE, LAUNDRY SOAP	SALES-SAMPLE, CLOTH
PACKAGE, LEMONADE	SALES-SAMPLE, CROCHET HOOK
PACKAGE, LIGHT BULB	SALES-SAMPLE, FISHHOOK
PACKAGE, LINIMENT	SALES-SAMPLE, LACE
PACKAGE, MACE	SALES-SAMPLE, LINOLEUM
PACKAGE, MARJORAM	SALES-SAMPLE, PAINT
PACKAGE, MASTERWORT ROOT	SALES-SAMPLE, PEN
PACKAGE, MATCH	SALES-SAMPLE, SEWING SUPPLIES
PACKAGE, MEDICINAL	SALES-SAMPLE, WALLPAPER
PACKAGE, MEDICINAL SYRUP	SEAL, CARGO
PACKAGE, METAL POLISH	STAND, DISPLAY
PACKAGE, MUSTARD	TIN, ADHESIVE TAPE
PACKAGE, MUSTARD PLASTER MIX	TIN, ALLSPICE
PACKAGE, NAIL	TIN, ANALGESIC
PACKAGE, PAINT	TIN, ANTACID
PACKAGE, PEN	TIN, ANTISEPTIC
PACKAGE, PENCIL	TIN, APPLE & STRAWBERRY JAM
PACKAGE, PEPPER	TIN, ASBESTOS
PACKAGE, PHONOGRAPH NEEDLE	TIN, BAKING POWDER
PACKAGE, PHOTOGRAPHIC FILM	TIN, BAKING SODA

Class E400: MERCHANDISING T&E — *(Continued)*

Total: 1197

Object, suffix

TIN, BANDAGE
TIN, BEVERAGE MIX
TIN, BISCUIT
TIN, BOOT POLISH
TIN, BUTTER
TIN, CAMPHOR
TIN, CANDLE
TIN, CARBIDE
TIN, CAULKING COMPOUND
TIN, CAYENNE
TIN, CELERY SALT
TIN, CHALK
TIN, CHEMICAL
TIN, CIGARETTE
TIN, CIGARETTE PAPER
TIN, CINNAMON
TIN, CLEANSER
TIN, CLOVE
TIN, COCOA
TIN, COCONUT
TIN, COFFEE
TIN, COLLAR STAY
TIN, CONFECTION
TIN, COSMETIC
TIN, COUGH DROP
TIN, CREAM OF TARTAR
TIN, CURTAIN ROD
TIN, DEODORANT
TIN, FILM
TIN, FILM PLATE
TIN, FOOD RATION
TIN, GASOLINE
TIN, GINGER
TIN, GLUE
TIN, GRAVY MIX
TIN, GUM ARABIC
TIN, GUNPOWDER
TIN, HACKSAW BLADE
TIN, HAIR TONIC
TIN, HONEY
TIN, INK
TIN, INKPAD
TIN, INSECTICIDE
TIN, JAM
TIN, KEROSENE
TIN, LANTERN
TIN, LARD
TIN, LAUNDRY SOAP
TIN, LAXATIVE
TIN, LEATHER DRESSING
TIN, LUBRICATING GREASE
TIN, LUBRICATING OIL
TIN, LYE
TIN, MACE
TIN, MARJORAM
TIN, MATCH
TIN, MEAT EXTRACT
TIN, MEDICINAL
TIN, METAL POLISH
TIN, MILITARY DETONATING FUSE
TIN, MILITATY FRICTION TUBE

Object, suffix

TIN, MILK POWDER
TIN, MOLASSES
TIN, MUSTARD
TIN, NON-ALCOHOLIC BEVERAGE
TIN, NUTMEG
TIN, OINTMENT
TIN, PAINT
TIN, PAPER CLIP
TIN, PEANUT
TIN, PEANUT BUTTER
TIN, PEMMICAN
TIN, PEPPER
TIN, PERCUSSION CAP
TIN, PETROLEUM JELLY
TIN, PHONOGRAPH NEEDLE
TIN, PIE FILLING
TIN, PILL
TIN, PINE TAR
TIN, PIPE
TIN, PLUM JAM
TIN, POULTRY GRIT
TIN, PUTTY
TIN, RASPBERRY JAM
TIN, RIVET
TIN, SAGE
TIN, SALTPETER
TIN, SEWING NEEDLE
TIN, SHAVING SOAP
TIN, SHELLAC
TIN, SHORTENING
TIN, SKIN LOTION
TIN, SNUFF
TIN, SODA BISCUIT
TIN, SOLDER
TIN, SOLDER FLUX
TIN, SPICE
TIN, STARCH
TIN, STOVE POLISH
TIN, STRAIGHT PIN
TIN, STRAWBERRY JAM
TIN, SUGAR
TIN, SUPPOSITORY
TIN, SYRUP
TIN, TALCUM POWDER
TIN, TEA
TIN, TIRE PATCH
TIN, TOBACCO
TIN, TOILET SOAP
TIN, TOOTHPASTE
TIN, TURPENTINE
TIN, TYPEWRITER RIBBON
TIN, VARNISH
TIN, VEGETABLE OIL
TIN, VIOLIN FITTING
TIN, WATCH
TIN, WOOD POLISH
TONGS, SHELF
TRAY, MONEY
TRAY, STORAGE
TUB, CONFECTION
TUB, LARD

Class E400: MERCHANDISING T&E — *(Continued)*

Total: 1197

Object, suffix

TUB, PICKLE
TUB, RASPBERRY JAM
TUBE, COSMETIC
TUBE, DENTURE ADHESIVE
TUBE, DEODORANT
TUBE, FLAVORING
TUBE, GLUE

Object, suffix

TUBE, GUN GREASE
TUBE, MEDICINAL
TUBE, PAINT
TUBE, SHAVING SOAP
TUBE, TOOTHPASTE
WAX, SEALING

Class E420: METEOROLOGICAL T&E

Total: 6

Object, suffix

ANEMOMETER
BAROMETER
BAROMETER, ANEROID

Object, suffix

BAROMETER, MERCURY
THERMOMETER
WEATHERVANE

Class E440: NUCLEAR PHYSICS T&E

Total: 0

Class E460: OPTICAL T&E

Total: 10

Object, suffix

BINOCULARS
CASE, BINOCULARS
CASE, MILITARY BINOCULARS
GLASS, MAGNIFYING
GLASSES, FIELD

Object, suffix

LENS, MICROSCOPE
MICROSCOPE
PERISCOPE
SET, MICROSCOPE
TELESCOPE

Class E480: REGULATIVE & PROTECTIVE T&E

Total: 20

Object, suffix

ARROW
ARROWHEAD
AX, BOARDING
AX, MILITARY BOARDING
BACKSWORD, MILITARY
BAYONET
BAYONET, HILTED SWORD
BAYONET, MILITARY HILTED KNIFE
BAYONET, MILITARY HILTED SWORD
BAYONET, MILITARY HILTED TRIANGULAR

Object, suffix

BAYONET, MILITARY PLUG KNIFE
BAYONET, MILITARY PLUG SWORD
BAYONET, MILITARY SOCKET CRUCIFORM
BAYONET, MILITARY SOCKET KNIFE
BAYONET, MILITARY SOCKET SPIKE
BAYONET, MILITARY SOCKET SWORD
BAYONET, MILITARY SOCKET TRIANGULAR
BAYONET, SOCKET
BAYONET MOUNT SPRING
BILL

Class E500: SURVEYING & NAVIGATIONAL T&E

Total: 24

Object, suffix

ASTROLABE, MARINER'S
BOARD, TRAVERSE
CASE, ASTROLABE
CASE, SEXTANT
CASE, TRANSIT

Object, suffix

CHAIN, SURVEYOR'S
CHEST, SURVEYOR'S
CIRCUMFERENTOR
COMPASS
COMPASS, SURVEYOR'S

Class E500: SURVEYING & NAVIGATIONAL T&E — *(Continued)*   Total: 24

Object, suffix

Object, suffix	Object, suffix
CROSS-STAFF	ROD, STADIA
FINDER, RANGE	SCALE, NAVIGATIONAL
HORIZON, ARTIFICIAL	SET, SURVEYING INSTRUMENT
LEVEL, SURVEYOR'S	SEXTANT
MARKER, CONCRETE	SUNSTONE
OCTANT	THEODOLITE
QUADRANT	TRIPOD, SURVEYOR'S

Class E520: THERMAL T&E   Total: 1

Object, suffix

THERMOGRAPH

Class E540: TIMEKEEPING T&E   Total: 19

Object, suffix

Object, suffix	Object, suffix
BAND, WRISTWATCH	CLOCKWORK
CLOCK	HOURGLASS
CLOCK, CASE	KEY, CLOCK
CLOCK, SHELF	KEY, POCKET WATCH
CLOCK, TALL CASE	KEY, TIME CLOCK
CLOCK, TIMERECORDING	METRONOME
CLOCK, TRAVEL	SUNDIAL
CLOCK, WALL	WATCH, POCKET
CLOCK PENDULUM	WRISTWATCH
CLOCK WEIGHT	

Class E560: WEIGHTS & MEASURES T&E   Total: 25

Object, suffix

Object, suffix	Object, suffix
CALIPERS, DOUBLE	PAN, BALANCE
CALIPERS, INSIDE	RULE, FOLDING
CALIPERS, OUTSIDE	RULER
CASE, WEIGHT	SCALE, BALANCE
GAUGE	SCALE, COMPUTING
GAUGE, PRESSURE	SCALE, MILITARY COMPUTING
GAUGE, SNOW	SCALE, PLATFORM
GAUGE, WATER	SCALE, SPRING
MEASURE, DRY	SCOOP, BALANCE
MEASURE, FATHOM	STEELYARD
MEASURE, LIQUID	WEIGHT, BALANCE
MEASURE, MILITARY LIQUID	YARDSTICK
MEASURE, TAPE	

Class E600: OTHER FOR SCIENCE & TECHNOLOGY   Total: 0

Class F020: DATA PROCESSING T&E

Total: 6

Object, suffix

ABACUS
CALCULATOR
CASE, SLIDE RULE

Object, suffix

MACHINE, ADDING
MACHINE, TEACHING
RULE, SLIDE

Class B040: DRAFTING T&E

Total: 15

Object, suffix

COMPASS
COMPASS, BEAM
COMPASS, BOW
COMPASS POINT
DIVIDERS
PANTOGRAPH
PEN, RULING
PROTRACTOR

Object, suffix

RULE, PARALLEL
SCALE, ARCHITECT'S
SET, DRAFTING INSTRUMENT
STRAIGHTEDGE
T-SQUARE
TABLE, DRAFTING
TRIANGLE

Class F060: MUSICAL T&E

Total: 58

Object, suffix

ACCORDION
ACCORDION, MINIATURE
BAGPIPE, MILITARY
BANJO
BASSOON
BEATER, DRUM
BELL
BENCH, ORGAN
BENCH, PIANO
BOW, VIOLIN
BOW, VIOLONCELLO
BUGLE
BUGLE, MILITARY
BUGLE MOUTHPIECE
BUGLE, POLICE
CASE, BASS VIOL
CASE, MILITARY FIFE
CASE, VIOLIN
CLARINET
CONCERTINA
DRUM
DRUM HEAD
DRUM, MILITARY
DRUMSTICK
DRUMSTICK, MILITARY
FIFE
FIFE, MILITARY
FLAGEOLET
FLAGEOLET, MILITARY

Object, suffix

FLUTE
GONG
GUITAR
HARMONICA
HARP, JEW'S
HARPSICHORD
HORN, ALTO
HORN, COACH
HORN, HUNTING
HORN, POST
HURDY-GURDY
LYRE
OBOE
ORGAN, PIPE
ORGAN, REED
ORGANETTE
PIANO
PIANO, GRAND
PIANO, SQUARE
PIPE, PITCH
STAND, MUSIC
STICK, STAMPING
STOOL, ORGAN
STOOL, PIANO
TRUMPET, NATURAL
TUBA
VIOLIN
VIOLIN STRING
VIOLONCELLO

Class F080: PHOTOGRAPHIC T&E

Total: 20

Object, suffix

BAG, CHANGING
CAMERA
CAMERA, BOX

Object, suffix

CAMERA, FOLDING
CAMERA, OBSCURA
CASE, CAMERA

Class F080: PHOTOGRAPHIC T&E — *(Continued)*

Total: 20

Object, suffix

CLOTH, FOCUSING
FILTER
HOLDER, ROLL-FILM
LENS
METER, LIGHT
PLATE, FILM
PLATEHOLDER

Object, suffix

ROLL-FILM
SAFELIGHT
SHUTTER, DARK-SLIDE
TANK, FILM-PROCESSING
TIMER, DARKROOM
TRAY, PRINT-PROCESSING
TRIPOD

Class F100: PRINTING T&E

Total: 47

Object, suffix

AWL
BOARD, MATRIX
BOX, CASTING
BRAYER
BRUSH
CABINET, TYPE CASE
CASE, FILLET
CASE, TYPE
CHASE
CLAMP, BOOKBINDING
CUTTER, SLUG
DECAL
ENDPAPER
FURNACE, SMELT
FURNITURE
GALLEY
HANDPRESS
KEY, QUOIN
LETTERPRESS
MACHINE, FOLDING
MATRIX
PERFORATOR
PIN, GAUGE
PLANER

Object, suffix

PLANER, LINOTYPE
PLATE, ENGRAVING
POT, GLUE
PRESS, BLOCKING
PRESS, CYLINDER
PRESS, PLATEN
QUOIN
RACK, DRYING
REGLET
RESHAPER, LINOTYPE MATRIX
RULE, COMPOSING
RULE, TYPESETTING
SET, STENCIL
STENCIL
STICK, COMPOSING
STICK, SIDE
STITCHER
TABLE, GALLEY
TABLE, IMPOSING
TRAY, MATRIX
TRAY, REGLET
TRIMMER, SAW
TYPE

Class F120: SOUND COMMUNICATION T&E

Total: 33

Object, suffix

ALBUM, PHONOGRAPH RECORD
BELL
BELL, CHURCH
BELL, COUNTER
BELL, SCHOOL
BELL, SERVICE
BOX, DICTAPHONE CYLINDER
CASE, INTERCOM
CHIME
CLAPPER
CYLINDER, DICTAPHONE
CYLINDER, MUSIC-BOX
CYLINDER, ORGANETTE
DICTAPHONE, EDISON
EARPHONE
FOGHORN
GONG

Object, suffix

HORN, PHONOGRAPH
INTERCOM
JUKEBOX
MALLET, CHIME
MEGAPHONE
MICROPHONE
NEEDLE, PHONOGRAPH
PHONOGRAPH
RATTLE, GAS
RECORD, PHONOGRAPH
SHAVER, EDISON DICTAPHONE
SPEAKER
SPEAKER, POLICE
TAPE, POLICE
TUBE, SPEAKING
WHISTLE

Class F140: TELECOMMUNICATION T&E
Total: 18

Object, suffix

Object, suffix

CABLE, SUBMARINE	RECEIVER, TELEGRAPH
CABLE, SUBMARINE INSTRUCTIONAL MODEL	SWITCHBOARD, TELEPHONE
CASE, TELEPHONE BATTERY	TELEPHONE
COHERER	TELEPHONE, MODEL
KEY, TELEGRAPH	TELEVISION
OSCILLATOR, FREQUENCY	TRANSCEIVER
PHOTOPHONE	TRANSMITTER
PHOTOPHONE, DESIGN MODEL	TRANSMITTER, RADIO
RADIO	TRANSMITTER, TELEGRAPH

Class F160: VISUAL COMMUNICATION T&E
Total: 17

Object, suffix

Object, suffix

BUOY, SIGNAL	PROJECTOR, LANTERN-SLIDE
FLAG, SIGNAL	PROJECTOR, MOTION-PICTURE
HELIOGRAPH	PROJECTOR, SLIDE
LANTERN, RAILROAD	SEMAPHORE
LANTERN, SIGNAL	SIGN, MILITARY TRAFFIC
LOCKER, FLAG	SIGN, TRAFFIC
PISTOL, MILITARY SIGNAL	SIGNAL, STORM
PISTOL, SIGNAL	STEREOSCOPE
POINTER	

Class F180: WRITTEN COMMUNICATION T&E
Total: 106

Object, suffix

Object, suffix

AGENDA	DESK, MILITARY PORTABLE
BINDER	DESK, PORTABLE
BINDER, RING	ERASER
BLOTTER	FILE, PORTABLE
BOOK, ACCOUNT	FOLDER, FILE
BOOKMARK	FORM, ACCOUNT STATEMENT
BOX, CHALK	FORM, BANK DEPOSIT
BOX, FILE	FORM, BANK WITHDRAWAL
BOX, MARKING STAMP	FORM, DEATH CERTIFICATE
BOX, POUNCE	FORM, DEATH REGISTRATION
BOX, SIGNET	FORM, EMPLOYMENT
BOX, STAMP	FORM, FUNERAL RECORD
BRUSH	FORM, GOLD RECOVERY
CARD, GREETING	FORM, MEDICAL
CARD, SYMPATHY	FORM, ORDER
CARD, TIME CLOCK	FORM, POLICE ISSUE
CASE, DOCUMENT	FORM, PROMISSORY NOTE
CASE, PEN	FORM, SHIPPING
CASE, PENCIL	FORM, TIME SHEET
CASE, PENCIL LEAD	HOLDER, CALENDAR
CASE, SEALING WAX	HOLDER, CARD
CASE, TYPEWRITER	HOLDER, DESK-BLOTTER
CASE, WRITING	HOLDER, PAPER CLIP
CHALK	HOLDER, PEN
CHALKBOARD	HOLDER, PENCIL
CHART, THERMOGRAPH	HOLDER, STAMP
CLAMP, MAILBAG	INKPAD
CLIP, PAPER	INKSTAND
CLIPBOARD	INKWELL
COVER, LEDGER	IRON, BRANDING
CUTTER, PAPER	IRON, MILITARY BRANDING

Class F180: WRITTEN COMMUNICATION T&E — *(Continued)*   **Total: 106**

Object, suffix   **Object, suffix**

Object, suffix	Object, suffix
JOURNAL	RACK, STAMP
KEY, WRITING CASE	RIBBON, TYPEWRITER
KIT, LAUNDRY MARKING	SET, DESK
KNIFE, PAPER	SET, POSTCARD
LEDGER	SET, STAMP
LINER, INKWELL	SHARPENER, PENCIL
LOCK, MAILBAG	SIGNET
MAILBAG	SPINDLE
MAILBOX	STAMP
MAKER, LABEL	STAMP, CANCELLATION
NOTEBOOK	STAMP, DATE
PAGE, LEDGER	STAMP, MARKING
PAPER, CARBON	STAMP, NOTARY
PAPERWEIGHT	STAPLE
PEN	STAPLER
PEN, FOUNTAIN	STATIONERY
PENCIL	STENCIL
PORTFOLIO	TAG, SHIPPING
POSTCARD	TRAY, DESK
PUNCH, PAPER	TYPEWRITER, MANUAL
RACK, LETTER	WAX, SEALING
RACK, PEN	WIPER, PEN

Class F500: OTHER T&E FOR COMMUNICATION   **Total: 0**

Class G020: CONTAINER
Total: 30

Object, suffix

Object, suffix	Object, suffix
BAG	CASK, SLACK
BALE	CASK, WET-TIGHT
BASKET	CASK BUNG
BOTTLE	CASK HEAD
BOTTLE, MINIATURE	CASK HOOP
BOWL	CASK STAVE
BOX	CRATE
BUCKET, WELL	DEMIJOHN
CAN	JAR
CARBOY	JAR LID
CARTON	JUG
CASE	TIN
CASK	TUB
CASK, DRY-TIGHT	TUB, MILITARY
CASK, MINIATURE	TUBE

Class G060: AEROSPACE TRANSPORTATION EQUIPMENT
Total: 14

Object, suffix

Object, suffix	Object, suffix
AIRPLANE	AIRPLANE UNDERCARRIAGE, DESIGN MODEL
AIRPLANE, DESIGN MODEL	AIRPLANE WING, DESIGN MODEL
AIRPLANE, MODEL	AIRPLANE WING RIB
AIRPLANE AILERON	AIRPLANE WING STRUT
AIRPLANE RADIATOR	AIRSHIP
AIRPLANE RUDDER	GLIDER, DESIGN MODEL
AIRPLANE UNDERCARRIAGE	KITE

Class G080: AEROSPACE TRANSPORTATION ACCESSORY
Total: 12

Object, suffix

Object, suffix	Object, suffix
AIRFRAME, DESIGN MODEL	PROPELLER, DESIGN MODEL FIXED-PITCH
ENGINE	PROPELLER, FIXED-PITCH
LAUNCHER, KITE	PROPELLER HUB
PROPELLER, ADJUSTABLE-PITCH	SKI
PROPELLER, DESIGN MODEL	WHEEL, STEERING
PROPELLER, DESIGN MODEL ADJUSTABLE-PITCH	WINDER, KITE LINE

Class G120: LAND TRANSPORTATION, ANIMAL POWERED
Total: 49

Object, suffix

Object, suffix	Object, suffix
AMBULANCE	PUMPER, STEAM
BUCKBOARD	RUNABOUT
CARRIAGE	RUNABOUT BRAKE
CARRIAGE STEP	RUNABOUT CANOPY
CART	RUNABOUT CONNECTING ROD
CART, DOG	RUNABOUT DASH BRACKET
CART, TIP	RUNABOUT SEAT
CART SHAFT	RUNABOUT SHAFT
CUTTER	RUNABOUT TOE RAIL
CUTTER RUNNER	SLEDGE
DOGSLED	SLEIGH
DOGSLED SEAT	SLEIGH, MINIATURE
DRAY	STAGECOACH
OXCART	STAGECOACH WHEEL
PUMPER, HAND	WAGON

Class G120: LAND TRANSPORTATION, ANIMAL POWERED — *(Continued)*

Total: 49

Object, suffix	Object, suffix
WAGON AXLE	WAGON SEAT SPRING
WAGON AXLE-BED	WAGON SHAFT
WAGON BODY-HANGER	WAGON SHAFT BRACE
WAGON BOLSTER PLATE	WAGON SHAFT COUPLING
WAGON BRAKESHOE	WAGON SPRING
WAGON CAP	WAGON TONGUE
WAGON, DELIVERY	WAGON TURNTABLE
WAGON HITCH	WAGON WHEEL
WAGON HOUND	WAGON WHEEL HUB
WAGON KING BOLT	

Class G140: LAND TRANSPORTATION, HUMAN POWERED

Total: 20

Object, suffix	Object, suffix
BARROW	SNOWSHOE
BICYCLE, ORDINARY	SNOWSHOE FRAME
CARRIAGE, BABY	SNOWSHOE LACING
CRADLE, BOARD	SNOWSHOE, SALES MODEL
CRADLE, SLAT	STRETCHER
DOLLY	STROLLER
HANDBARROW	VELOCIPEDE
SEDAN	WHEELBARROW
SLEDGE	WHEELBARROW WHEEL
SLEDGE RUNNER	YOKE

Class G160: LAND TRANSPORTATION MOTORIZED

Total: 2

Object, suffix	Object, suffix
AUTOMOBILE, MILITARY	AUTOMOBILE WHEEL

Class G180: LAND TRANSPORTATION ACCESSORY

Total: 87

Object, suffix	Object, suffix
BELL, BICYCLE	COUPLING, WHIFFLETREE
BELL, SLEIGH	CROP, MILITARY RIDING
BIT	CROP, POLICE RIDING
BLINDER	CROP, RIDING
BREECHING	CRUPPER
BRIDLE	CUSHION, CARRIAGE
BUCKLE, COMMON-ROLLER	DOUBLETREE
BUCKLE, CONWAY	DOUBLETREE, LOGGER'S
BUCKLE, HALTER	GIRTH
BUCKLE, LOOP	HALTER
BUCKLE, ROLLER-AND-LOOP	HAME
CAN, MILITARY FUEL	HARNESS
CHAIN, HAME	HARNESS, DOG
CHAIN, STAY	HARNESS, FARM
CHAIN, WHIFFLETREE	HOLDBACK
CHOCK, WHEEL	HOOK, CARRIAGE CLOTHES
CINCH	HOOK, HAME
CLEVIS	HOOK, WHIFFLETREE
COCKEYE, SCREW	HORN
COLLAR, DOG	JACK, WAGON
COLLAR, HORSE	KIT, AUTOMOBILE TOOL
CONNECTOR, TRACE	LAMP, CARRIAGE

Class G180: LAND TRANSPORTATION ACCESSORY — *(Continued)*

Total: 87

Object, suffix

Object, suffix

LARIAT	SLIDE, BREAST STRAP
LOOP, HARNESS	SNAP, HARNESS
MOUNT, BRIDLE	SNAP, ROLLER
ORNAMENT, AUTOMOBILE HOOD	SOCKET, WHIP
ORNAMENT, HARNESS	SPUR
PAD, HORSE COLLAR	SPUR, MILITARY
PAD, SADDLE	SPUR, POLICE
PARASOL, CARRIAGE	STEPS, CARRIAGE
PIN, YOKE	STIRRUP
PLATE, LICENSE	STRAP, BREAST
PUMP, TIRE	STRAP, CHOKE
QUIRT	STRAP, HAME
REINS	STRAP, SPUR
RING, GIRTH	TRACE
ROBE, LAP	TUG, HARNESS
SADDLE	TUG, SHAFT
SADDLE, HARNESS	TUMPLINE
SADDLE, MILITARY PACK	WEIGHT, HITCHING
SADDLE, MILITARY RIDING	WHIFFLETREE
SADDLE, PACK	WHIP
SADDLE, POLICE	YOKE, ANIMAL
SADDLEBAG	

Class G220: RAIL TRANSPORTATION EQUIPMENT

Total: 3

Object, suffix

Object, suffix

HANDCAR	TRUCK, TRAIN
LOCOMOTIVE, MINIATURE	

Class G240: RAIL TRANSPORTATION ACCESSORY

Total: 8

Object, suffix

Object, suffix

BELL, LOCOMOTIVE	PIN, COUPLING
CROSSTIE	SPIKE
GOVERNOR, STEAM LOCOMOTIVE	THROTTLE, STEAM LOCOMOTIVE
IRON, SWITCH	TRACK SECTION

Class G280: WATER TRANSPORTATION EQUIPMENT

Total: 43

Object, suffix

Object, suffix

BATEAU, EXHIBITION MODEL	CORVETTE, MODEL
BATEAU, MINIATURE	CRUISER, MODEL STEAM
BOAT, DESIGN MODEL	DORY
BOAT, DESIGN MODEL PADDLE	DORY, MODEL
BOAT HULL, DESIGN MODEL	FERRY, MODEL
BOAT, LOBSTER	FISHERMAN
BOAT WHEEL, DESIGN MODEL PADDLE	FISHERMAN, MINIATURE
CANOE	FISHERMAN, MODEL
CANOE, DUGOUT	FISHERMAN, MODEL SCHOONER
CANOE, ICE	GALLEY, MODEL VIKING
CANOE, MINIATURE	HYDROPLANE
CANOE, MODEL	HYDROPLANE, DESIGN MODEL
CANOE, MODEL DUGOUT	HYDROPLANE, MODEL
CANOE, MODEL ICE	KAYAK, MODEL
CATAMARAN, MODEL	LONGSHIP, MODEL VIKING

Class G280: WATER TRANSPORTATION EQUIPMENT — *(Continued)*

Total: 43

Object, suffix	Object, suffix
PONTOON	VESSEL, MODEL 3-MAST GENERAL CARGO
PONTOON, DESIGN MODEL	VESSEL, MODEL BARK CARGO
SAILBOAT, INSTRUCTIONAL MODEL	VESSEL, MODEL CARGO
SAILBOAT, MODEL	VESSEL, MODEL SCHOONER CARGO
SCOW	VESSEL, MODEL SQUARE-RIGGED CARGO
SKIFF	WHALEBOAT
VESSEL, MINIATURE CARGO	

Class G300: WATER TRANSPORTATION ACCESSORY

Total: 77

Object, suffix	Object, suffix
ANCHOR	LEAD, SOUNDING
ANCHOR, GRAPNEL	LIGHT, RUNNING
ANCHOR, SEA	LOG
BAILER	MAST
BASKET, ROPE	MAT, CANOE
BELL, SHIP'S	MAUL, SHACKLE PIN
BLOCK	MOTOR, OUTBOARD
BOARD, NAME	OAR
BOLLARD	OARLOCK
BOX, SHIP'S LOG	PADDLE, CANOE
BRACKET, SHIP'S BELL	PADDLE, MINIATURE
BUOY, MOORING	PIN, BELAYING
CAPSTAN	PIN, THOLE
CAPSTAN, MINIATURE	PINTLE, RUDDER
CHAIN	PLATE, CHAIN
CHAIR, BOATSWAIN'S	PROPELLER
CHEST, CHART	PUMP
CHOCK	PUMP, BILGE
CLEAT	PUMP WHEEL, BILGE
COVER, MOTOR	RACK, POLICE KEY
CRADLE, DESIGN MODEL BOAT	RAFT, LIFE
DEADEYE	RATLINE
DODGER	RING, LIFE
FENDER	ROPE
FIDDLE, MESS TABLE	ROPE, SHIP'S BELL
FIGUREHEAD	RUDDER
FLOAT, LIFE	SAIL
GANGPLANK	SEACOCK HANDLE
HAMMER, SHACKLE PIN	SHACKLE
HOLYSTONE	SHACKLE, SWIVEL
HOOK, BOAT	SHEAVE
HOOP, MAST	SKID
HOSE, FIRE	STRAP, DODGER
HYDROFOIL	TANK, GASOLINE
HYDROFOIL, DESIGN MODEL	TURNTABLE
INDICATOR, MODEL ENGINE-ROOM TELEGRAPH	WHEEL, STEERING
JACKET, LIFE	WHISTLE, STEAM
KILLICK	WINDLASS
KIT, CANOE REPAIR	

Class H020: ADVERTISING MEDIUM

Total: 22

Object, suffix

AD, MAGAZINE
BAG, TRADE
BANNER
BLOTTER
BOARD, BULLETIN
BOARD, MILITARY BULLETIN
BOOKLET
CARD, TRADE
CATALOG
COUPON
FAN

Object, suffix

HANDBILL
LABEL, TRADE
MEASURE, TAPE
NOTEBOOK
POSTER
POSTER, MILITARY
POSTER, POLITICAL
SIGN, PRICE
SIGN, TRADE
SQUARE, TRY
STICKER

Class H040: ART

Total: 43

Object, suffix

ASSEMBLAGE
BOUQUET, FLORAL
BOX, SHADOW
BRIC-A-BRAC
BUST
COLLAGE
DIORAMA
DRAWING
FIGURINE
FIGURINE, MILITARY
FISH, ARTIFICIAL
FLOWER, ARTIFICIAL
FOOD, MISCELLANEOUS ARTIFICIAL
FRAME, PICTURE
FRUIT, ARTIFICIAL
GROUP, FIGURINE
HANGING
MAQUETTE
MEAT, ARTIFICIAL
ORNAMENT, CHRISTMAS TREE
ORNAMENT, EASTER
PAINTING

Object, suffix

PICTURE
PICTURE, BARK
PICTURE, CUT-PAPER
PICTURE, FLORA
PICTURE, HAIR
PICTURE, LEAF
PICTURE, NEEDLEWORK
PICTURE, RIBBON
PICTURE, SHELL
PICTURE, SILK
PICTURE, WAX
PLAQUE
PRINT
PRINT, MINIATURE
PRINT, PHOTOGRAPHIC
SAMPLER
SAMPLER, INSTRUCTIONAL MODEL
STATUE
TAPESTRY
WHIMSEY
WREATH, FLORAL

Class H060: CEREMONIAL ARTIFACT

Total: 121

Object, suffix

ALTAR
ALTARPIECE
AMPULLA
ASPERGILLUM
ASPERSORIUM
BAG, CEREMONIAL
BALDACHIN
BANNER
BELL, ALTAR
BELT, CEREMONIAL
BLANKET, DANCE
BOARD, TOBACCO CUTTING
BOTTLE, HOLY WATER
BOX, LUNULA
BOX, RELIGIOUS STATUE
BUNDLE, MEDICINE

Object, suffix

BURSE
CALUMET
CANDELABRUM
CANDLE, BIRTHDAY CAKE
CANDLE, RELIGIOUS
CANDLESTICK
CARD, ALTAR
CARD, PRAYER
CASE, CALUMET
CASE, CHALICE
CASE, CIBORIUM
CASE, MONSTRANCE
CATAFALQUE
CENSER
CHALICE
CHARCOAL, CENSER

Class H060: CEREMONIAL ARTIFACT — *(Continued)*

Total: 121

Object, suffix

CIBORIUM
CLOTH, ALTAR
COFFIN
COFFIN HANDLE
COFFIN LOCK
CORDELIERE, FLAGPOLE
CORPORAL
CRECHE
CROSS
CRUCIFIX
CUP, BRIDE'S
DISH, CEREMONIAL
DRUM, CEREMONIAL
FAVOR, POTLATCH
FIGURINE, RELIGIOUS
FLABELLUM
FLAG
FLAG, MILITARY
FLAGPOLE
FLAGPOLE FINIAL
FONT, BAPTISMAL
FONT, HOLY WATER
FOUNTAIN, HOLY WATER
FRONTAL
HOLDER, BIRTHDAY CANDLE
HOLDER, LAMPION
HOST
HYMNAL
INCENSE
KIT, SICK CALL
LAMP, CEREMONIAL
LAMPION
LANTERN, CEREMONIAL
LOOP, MARRIAGE
MANUTERGIUM
MASK
MISSAL
MONSTRANCE
MONUMENT
MONUMENT, MODEL
NAVETTE
NICHE, RELIGIOUS STATUE
PALL
PALM
PATEN

Object, suffix

PENNANT
PENNON
PICTURE, RELIGIOUS
PILLOW, COFFIN
PLAQUE
PLAQUE, POLICE
PLAQUE, RELIGIOUS
PLATE, COFFIN
PLATE, OFFERING
PURIFICATOR
PYX
PYXIS
RACK, LAMPION
RATTLE
RELIC, RELIGIOUS
RELIQUARY
SACRARIUM
SADDLEBAG, CEREMONIAL
SET, ALTAR CARD
SET, CRUET
SET, FUNERAL DRAPERY
SHROUD
SPOON, CEREMONIAL
STAND, COFFIN
STAND, MISSAL
STATIONS OF THE CROSS
STATUE, RELIGIOUS
STOCKING, CHRISTMAS
STONE, ALTAR
TABERNACLE
TOMBSTONE
TONGS, CENSOR CHARCOAL
TOTEM
TOWEL, CEREMONIAL
TRAY, CEREMONIAL
TUBE, SUCKING
VASE
VEIL
VEIL, CHALICE
VEIL, CIBORIUM
VEIL, TABERNACLE
WAND, DANCE
WHISTLE, CEREMONIAL
WREATH

Class H080: DOCUMENTARY ARTIFACT

Total: 228

Object, suffix

ALBUM, AUTOGRAPH
ALBUM, MILITARY PHOTOGRAPH
ALBUM, PHOTOGRAPH
ALBUM, POSTCARD
ALBUM, STAMP
ALBUM, TINTYPE
ALMANAC
AMBROTYPE
ANNOUNCEMENT
ANNOUNCEMENT, FUNERAL

Object, suffix

BANNER, COMMEMORATIVE
BILL-OF-LADING
BILL-OF-SALE
BLUEPRINT
BLUEPRINT, MILITARY
BOND
BOOK
BOOK, ACCOUNT
BOOK, ADDRESS
BOOK, CHILD'S

Class H080: DOCUMENTARY ARTIFACT — *(Continued)*

Object, suffix

BOOK, MILITARY
BOOK, MILITARY ACCOUNT
BOOK, POLICE ACCOUNT
BOOKLET
BOOKLET, MILITARY
BOWL, COMMEMORATIVE
BOX, COMMEMORATIVE
BOX, MILITARY COMMEMORATIVE
BUST, COMMEMORATIVE
CADDY, COMMEMORATIVE
CALENDAR
CARD, BASEBALL
CARD, CALLING
CARD, COMMUNION
CARD, DANCE
CARD, GREETING
CARD, IDENTIFICATION
CARD, INDEX
CARD, MEMBERSHIP
CARD, MOURNING
CARD, TALLY
CARTE-DE-VISITE
CARTE-DE-VISITE, MILITARY
CASE, DAGUERREOTYPE
CASE, MAP
CERTIFICATE, ACHIEVEMENT
CERTIFICATE, APPOINTMENT
CERTIFICATE, BAPTISMAL
CERTIFICATE, BIRTH
CERTIFICATE, BURIAL
CERTIFICATE, DISCHARGE
CERTIFICATE, FIRST COMMUNION
CERTIFICATE, FREE MINER
CERTIFICATE, MARRIAGE
CERTIFICATE, MEMBERSHIP
CERTIFICATE, MILITARY
CERTIFICATE, MILITARY COMMISSION
CERTIFICATE, MILITARY DISCHARGE
CERTIFICATE, MILITARY ENLISTMENT
CERTIFICATE, PAROLE
CERTIFICATE, PENSION
CERTIFICATE, POLICE DISCHARGE
CERTIFICATE, SIGNATURE
CERTIFICATE, STOCK
CERTIFICATE, TESTIMONIAL
CHART
CHART, MILITARY NAVIGATIONAL
CHART, NAVIGATIONAL
CHART, POLICE NAVIGATIONAL
CHECK, BANK
CITATION, MILITARY
CLIPPING, MAGAZINE
CLIPPING, NEWSPAPER
COIN, COMMEMORATIVE
COLLECTION, COIN
COLLECTION, STAMP
CONTRACT
COVER, BOOK
COVER, PHOTOGRAPH
COVER, POLICE BOOK
CUP, COMMEMORATIVE

Object, suffix

DAGUERREOTYPE
DEED
DIAGRAM, MILITARY
DIARY
DIORAMA
DIPLOMA
DIRECTORY, TELEPHONE
DRAWING, MILITARY TECHNICAL
DRAWING, TECHNICAL
ENDPAPER, BOOK
ENVELOPE
ENVELOPE, COMMEMORATIVE
EXERCISE, SCHOOL
FIGURE
FIGURE, INSTRUCTIONAL MODEL
FIGURINE
FIGURINE, MILITARY
FILM
FORM, BANK DEPOSIT
FORM, WILL
GLOBE
HANDBILL
HANDKERCHIEF, COMMEMORATIVE
INSURANCE POLICY
INVENTORY
INVENTORY, MILITARY
INVITATION
JACKET, BOOK
JOURNAL
JOURNAL, POLICE
KEY, COMMEMORATIVE
LEDGER
LETTER
LETTER, POLICE
LETTER, TESTMONIAL
LETTERS PATENT
LICENSE
LICENSE, MARRIAGE
LICENSE, OCCUPATIONAL
LICENSE, RADIO
LIST, MILITARY
LIST, POLICE
LOG
LOG, POLICE SHIP'S
LOG, SHIP'S
MAGAZINE
MAGAZINE, POLICE
MANUSCRIPT
MANUSCRIPT, MILITARY
MAP
MAP, ROAD
MEDAL, COMMEMORATIVE
MEMORANDUM
MEMORANDUM, MILITARY
MEMORANDUM, POLICE
MENU
MICROFILM
MODEL, TOPOGRAPHIC
MUG, COMMEMORATIVE
MUSIC, SHEET
NAMEPLATE

Class H080: DOCUMENTARY ARTIFACT — *(Continued)*

Total: 228

Object, suffix

Object, suffix

NAMEPLATE, MILITARY	PRINT, PHOTOGRAPHIC
NEGATIVE, FILM	PRINT, POLICE PHOTOGRAPHIC
NEGATIVE, MILITARY FILM	PRINT, SOLAR
NEWSPAPER	PROGRAM
NOTE	RADIOGRAPH
NOTE, MILITARY	RECEIPT
NOTE, PROMISSORY	RECEIPT, MILITARY
NOTEBOOK	RECIPE
NOTEBOOK, MILITARY	RECORDS, MILITARY
NOTEBOOK, POLICE	RELEASE, NEWS
NUMBERPLATE	REPORT
ORDERS, MILITARY	RIBBON, COMMEMORATIVE
ORDERS, POLICE	ROLL, MILITARY MUSTER
PADDLE, COMMEMORATIVE	ROSTER, MILITARY DUTY
PAGE, ACCOUNT BOOK	SCORECARD
PAGE, BOOK	SCRAPBOOK
PAGE, LEDGER	SCROLL
PAGE, MAGAZINE	SEAL, DEED
PAGE, MILITARY BOOK	SIGN
PAPERS	SPEECH
PASSPORT	SPOON, COMMEMORATIVE
PATENT	STATEMENT, ACCOUNT
PAYROLL	STATEMENT, BANK
PENNANT	STATUTE
PENNANT, COMMEMORATIVE	STEREOGRAPH
PERMIT	TABLET
PETITION	TAG, IDENTIFICATION
PETITION, MILITARY	TAG, MERCHANDISE
PICTURE	TELEGRAM
PICTURE, MILITARY	TELEGRAM, POLICE
PICTURE, POLICE	TIMETABLE
PIN	TINTYPE
PIN, COMMEMORATIVE	TINTYPE, MILITARY
PLAQUE	TOWEL, COMMEMORATIVE
PLAQUE, COMMEMORATIVE	TRANSCRIPT
PLATE, COMMEMORATIVE	TRANSPARENCY
POEM	TRANSPARENCY, LANTERN-SLIDE
POSTCARD	TRAY, COMMEMORATIVE
POSTER, COMMEMORATIVE	TUMBLER, COMMEMORATIVE
POSTER, INSTRUCTIONAL	VASE, COMMEMORATIVE
POWER OF APPOINTMENT	VOUCHER, AUDITOR'S
POWER OF ATTORNEY	VOUCHER, BANK
PRINT, MILITARY PHOTOGRAPHIC	WILL

Class H100: EXCHANGE MEDIUM

Total: 42

Object, suffix

Object, suffix

COIN	TRADE ITEM, AX
COUPON	TRADE ITEM, BASKET
CURRENCY	TRADE ITEM, BEAD
STAMP	TRADE ITEM, BELL
STAMP, POSTAGE	TRADE ITEM, BLANKET
STAMP, TAX	TRADE ITEM, BROOCH
STAMP, TRADING	TRADE ITEM, BUTTON
TICKET	TRADE ITEM, CASTOREUM
TOKEN	TRADE ITEM, COAT
TOKEN, TRANSPORTATION	TRADE ITEM, CONE
TRADE ITEM, ARMBAND	TRADE ITEM, CURLER
TRADE ITEM, AWL	TRADE ITEM, EARRING

Class H100: EXCHANGE MEDIUM — (Continued)

Total: 42

Object, suffix

TRADE ITEM, FIGURINE
TRADE ITEM, FISHHOOK
TRADE ITEM, HATCHET
TRADE ITEM, HIDE
TRADE ITEM, KETTLE
TRADE ITEM, KNIFE
TRADE ITEM, KNIFE SHEATH
TRADE ITEM, MIRROR
TRADE ITEM, MUSKET

Object, suffix

TRADE ITEM, PELT
TRADE ITEM, PENDANT
TRADE ITEM, PIGMENT
TRADE ITEM, PISTOL
TRADE ITEM, RING
TRADE ITEM, SHELL
TRADE ITEM, TOBACCO
TRADE ITEM, TOKEN
TRADE ITEM, WIRE

Class H120: PERSONAL SYMBOL

Total: 92

Object, suffix

AMULET
APRON
ARMBAND, MOURNING
BADGE, CAP
BADGE, FIREMAN"S
BADGE, MILITARY
BADGE, MILITARY BONNET
BADGE, MILITARY CAP
BADGE, MILITARY SHOULDER BELT
BADGE, POLICE
BEADS, ROSARY
BELT
BELT, MILITARY PRESENTATION SWORD
BLANKET, SHOULDER
BONNET
BUCKLE, MILITARY
BUCKLE, POLICE
BUTTON
BUTTON, MILITARY
BUTTON, POLICE
CAPE
CASE, MEDAL
CASE, MILITARY EPAULET
CASE, MILITARY PRESENTATION SWORD
CASE, MILITARY SHAKO PLUME
CASE, POLICE HELMET PLUME
CASE, ROSARY BEADS
CLOAK
COCKADE, MILITARY
COLLECTION, BADGE
COLLECTION, MILITARY BADGE
COLLECTION, MILITARY BUTTON
CRAVAT, MAGISTRATE
CUP, LOVING
EPAULET
EPAULET, MILITARY
EPAULET, POLICE
GORGET, MILITARY
GOWN, ACADEMIC
HAT
HEADDRESS
KNOT, MILITARY PRESENTATION SWORD
LOOP, SHOULDER
MACE
MEDAL
MEDAL, ACHIEVEMENT

Object, suffix

MEDAL, FRATERNAL
MEDAL, MILITARY
MEDAL, MILITARY CAMPAIGN
MEDAL, MILITARY GOOD CONDUCT
MEDAL, MILITARY SERVICE
MEDAL, MILITARY SERVICE & GOOD CONDUCT
MEDAL, MILITARY VALOR
MEDAL, RELIGIOUS
MEDAL, SERVICE
NECKLACE, RELIGIOUS
PATCH
PATCH, MILITARY
PENDANT, MINIATURE RELIGIOUS
PENDANT, RELIGIOUS
PIN
PIN, FRATERNAL
PLAQUE
PLAQUE, MILITARY
PLAQUE, RELIGIOUS
PLATE, MILITARY BACKPACK
PLATE, MILITARY CARTRIDGE-BOX
PLATE, MILITARY HELMET
PLATE, MILITARY SHAKO
PLATE, MILITARY SHOULDER BELT
PLUME, MILITARY
PLUME, MILITARY BICORN HAT
PLUME, MILITARY BONNET
PLUME, MILITARY CAP
PLUME, MILITARY SHAKO
PLUME, POLICE HELMET
POUCH
RIBBON, MEMBERSHIP
RIBBON, MILITARY SERVICE
RIBBON, POLICE SERVICE
RING, SIGNET
SASH
SCABBARD, MILITARY PRESENTATION SWORD
SCALP
SKIRT
SPIKE, POLICE HELMET
SPIKE FERRULE, MILITARY HELMET
SWORD, MILITARY PRESENTATION
TALISMAN
TROPHY
WAISTCOAT
WHISTLE, MILITARY

Class I020: GAME

Total: 42

Object, suffix

BAG, MARBLE	QUOITS
BOARD, ALPHABET GAME	SET, BACKGAMMON
BOARD, CHECKER	SET, BOWLING
BOARD, CRIBBAGE	SET, CHECKER
BOARD, GAME	SET, CHESS
BOX, GAME	SET, CLOCK GOLF
CARD, GAME	SET, CRIBBAGE
CHIP, POKER	SET, CROKINOLE
CUP, DICE	SET, DICE CUP
DECK, CARD	SET, DUCK & EGGS
DICE	SET, FORT
DIE	SET, GAME
DOMINOES	SET, MARBLE
HALMA	SET, OUIJA
KAKEE	SET, PARCHESI
LOTTO	SET, SCRABBLE
MACHINE, SLOT	SET, SOLITAIRE
MARBLE	SET, TIDDLYWINK
NABAHON	STICK, GAMBLING
PIECE, CHESS	TABLE, BAGATELLE
PIECE, GAME	WALTES

Class I040: PUBLIC ENTERTAINMENT DEVICE

Total: 0

Class I060: RECREATIONAL DEVICE

Total: 2

Object, suffix

MUTASCOPE	SWING

Class I080: SPORTS EQUIPMENT

Total: 47

Object, suffix

BAG, GOLF CLUB	LUGE, CHILD'S
BAG, SKATE	MASK, FENCING
BALL, BILLIARD	NET, TENNIS
BALL, BOWLING	PIN, BOWLING
BALL, CARPET	POLE, SNOW SKI
BALL, CROQUET	POST, TENNIS
BALL, TENNIS	RACK, BILLIARD CUE
BAT, BASEBALL	RACKET, TENNIS
BAT, CRICKET	SET, BILLIARD
BINDING, SNOW SKI	SET, CROQUET
BOBSLED	SET, SHUFFLEBOARD
CHALK, BILLIARD CUE	SET, TABLE TENNIS
CLUB, GOLF	SHUTTLECOCK
CLUB, INDIAN	SKATE, ICE
COVER, TENNIS RACKET	SKATE, ROLLER
CRAMPON	SKATE BLADE, ICE
CUE, BILLIARD	SKI, SNOW
DUMBBELL	SLED
GLOVE, BOXING	SLED RUNNER
GUARD, ICE SKATE	STAPLE, LAWN TENNIS
LUGE	STICK, LACROSSE

Class I080:   SPORTS EQUIPMENT — *(Continued)*

Total: 47

Object, suffix

STONE, CURLING
SYSTEM, DIVER'S
TABLE, BILLIARD

Object, suffix

TAPE, LAWN TENNIS
TOBOGGAN

Class I100:   TOY

Total: 151

Object, suffix

ANIMAL
ANIMAL, MECHANICAL
ANIMAL, STUFFED
ARK, NOAH'S
BALL
BANK, STILL
BATEAU
BATHTUB
BED
BED, FOUR-POSTER
BEDSPREAD
BLANKET
BLOCK
BLOCK, PARQUETRY
BOLSTER
BONNET
BOOK, DRAWING
BOOT
BOWL, SUGAR
BOX, TRINKET
CAGE, ANIMAL
CANNON
CANOE
CAP
CARRIAGE
CARRIAGE, DOLL
CART
CHAIR
CHAIR, ROCKING
CHEST
CHEST, BLANKET
CHEST OF DRAWERS
COAT
COMFORTER
CRADLE
CRAYON
CUE, BILLIARD
CUP & BALL
CUTTER
DISH
DISH, BUTTER
DOGSLED
DOLL
DOLL HEAD
DOLL, PAPER
DOLLHOUSE
DRESS
DUSTPAN
ENGINE, STEAM
EXPLODER, CAP
FAN
FIGURE

Object, suffix

FLAGEOLET
FORGE
GAUNTLET
GUN
GUN, AIR
HAMMER
HANDPRESS
HARNESS
HATCHET, SHINGLING
HIGHCHAIR
HOBBYHORSE
HOE
HOLSTER
HOOP
HORN
HORSE, ROCKING
JACK, JUMPING
LANTERN
LANTERN, MAGIC
LOCOMOTIVE
LUGE
MACHINE, SEWING
MALLET
MATTRESS
MOCCASIN
MUG
NIGHTGOWN
NOISEMAKER
PANTS
PETTICOAT
PILLOW
PILLOWCASE
PIPE, BUBBLE
PISTOL, CAP
PITCHER
PLATE
POPGUN
PUPPET, HAND
PUZZLE
QUILT
RAKE
RATTLE
RING, LIFE
ROPE, JUMP
RUG
SADIRON
SAILBOAT
SAUCEPAN
SAW
SCALE, BALANCE
SCOOP
SERVICE, TEA

Class I100: TOY — *(Continued)*   **Total: 151**

Object, suffix

Object, suffix	Object, suffix
SET, BLOCK	TABLE, BILLIARD
SET, FIGURE	TOP
SET, NOAH'S ARK	TOY, DOLL
SET, PICTURE BLOCK	TOY, MECHANICAL
SET, STAMP	TOY, PULL
SET, TOILET	TOY, TRUNDLE
SET, WOODEN CONSTRUCTION	TRICYCLE
SHAM, PILLOW	TRIVET
SHEET	TRUCK
SHIRT	TRUMPET
SHOE	TRUNK
SKIRT	UMBRELLA
SLEIGH	VICTORIA
SLINGSHOT	VILLAGE
SLIP	WAGON
SOCK	WASHBOARD
SPOON	WASHSTAND
SPOONER	WATCH, PENDANT
STAGECOACH	WHEELBARROW
STOVE	WHIRLIGIG
SUIT, JUMP	WHISTLE
SWEEPER, CARPET	WINDMILL
SWORD	YO-YO
TABLE	

Class J020: ARTIFACTS REMNANT

Total: 17

Object, suffix

Object, suffix

BONE FRAGMENT	RUBBER FRAGMENT
CORDAGE FRAGMENT	SHERD
FUR FRAGMENT	SHERD, HEAD
GLASS FRAGMENT	STONE, WORKED
IVORY, WORKED	TEXTILE FRAGMENT
LEATHER FRAGMENT	WHALEBONE FRAGMENT
LITHIC FRAGMENT	WOOD, WORKED
METAL FRAGMENT	WOOD FRAGMENT
PAPER FRAGMENT	

Class J040: FUNCTION UNKNOWN

Total: 1

Object, suffix

Object, suffix

PROBLEMATICAL

Class J060: MULTIPLE USE ARTIFACTS

Total: 65

Object, suffix

Object, suffix

AUGER, POST-HOLE	KNIFE, LINOLEUM
BELLOWS	KNIFE, UTILITY
BOB, MILITARY PLUMB	OILCAN
BOB, PLUMB	PALLET, CARGO
BOLT, U	PAPER, WAX
BOX, TOOL	PICK
BREAKER, ICE	PLIERS
BRUSH	PLIERS, VISE-GRIP
BRUSH, GLUE	PRESS, BARREL
BRUSH, WIRE	PUMP, BARREL
CAULKING	RACK, TOOL
CHAIN	RESPIRATOR
CHAIN, BUCKET	RING, UTILITY
CHEST, TOOL	RIVET
CLEVIS	ROPE
COUPLING, PNEUMATIC HOSE	SCISSORS
CRIMPER, SEAL	SCREWDRIVER
DIGGER, POST-HOLE	SCREWDRIVER HANDLE
DISPENSER, TAPE	SHOVEL
FUNNEL	SHOVEL BLADE
GRIPPER, BARREL	SHOVEL HANDLE
GROMMET	SINEW
GUN, GREASE	SPIGOT
HAMMER	STRAP
HAMMER HANDLE	SWIVEL, FLAG
HAMMERSTONE	TANK, H.P.G.
HOOK	TANK, L.P.G.
HOOK, BUCKET	TAPE, ADHESIVE
HOOK, CARGO	TARPAULIN
HOOK, CUP	VALVE
HOOK, HARNESS	WIRE
HOOK, JAMB	WORKBENCH
KIT, TOOL	

ALPHABETICAL

LIST OF TERMS

Class. Code	Object, suffix	Objet, suffixe
F020	ABACUS	*BOULIER COMPTEUR*
F060	ACCORDION	*ACCORDEON*
F060	ACCORDION, MINIATURE	*ACCORDEON MINIATURE*
H020	AD, MAGAZINE	*ANNONCE PUBLICITAIRE DE REVUE*
D320	ADZ	*HERMINETTE*
D320	ADZ, CARPENTER'S	*HERMINETTE DE CHARPENTIER*
D320	ADZ, COOPER'S	*DOLOIRE DE TONNELIER*
D320	ADZ, COOPER'S NOTCHING	*COCHOIR DE TONNELIER*
D320	ADZ, HOLLOWING	*CURETTE DE TONNELIER*
D320	ADZ, SHIPWRIGHT'S	*HERMINETTE DE CHARPENTIER DE CHANTIER NAVAL*
D320	ADZ BLADE	*LAME D'HERMINETTE*
D320	ADZ HANDLE	*MANCHE D'HERMINETTE*
F180	AGENDA	*AGENDA*
C160	AID, HEARING	*APPAREIL AUDITIF*
G080	AIRFRAME, DESIGN MODEL	*CELLULE MODELE DE PROJET*
G060	AIRPLANE	*AEROPLANE*
G060	AIRPLANE AILERON	*AILERON D'AEROPLANE*
G060	AIRPLANE, DESIGN MODEL	*AEROPLANE MODELE DE PROJET*
G060	AIRPLANE, MODEL	*AEROPLANE MODELE REDUIT*
G060	AIRPLANE RADIATOR	*RADIATEUR D'AILE*
G060	AIRPLANE RUDDER	*GOUVERNE DE DIRECTION*
G060	AIRPLANE UNDERCARRIAGE	*TRAIN D'ATTERRISSAGE*
G060	AIRPLANE UNDERCARRIAGE, DESIGN MODEL	*TRAIN D'ATTERRISSAGE MODELE DE PROJET*
G060	AIRPLANE WING, DESIGN MODEL	*AILE D'AEROPLANE MODEL DE PROJET*
G060	AIRPLANE WING RIB	*NERVURE D'AILE D'AEROPLANE*
G060	AIRPLANE WING STRUT	*HAUBAN D'AEROPLANE*
G060	AIRSHIP	*AERONEF*
C100	ALB	*AUBE*
H080	ALBUM, AUTOGRAPH	*KEEPSAKE*
H080	ALBUM, MILITARY PHOTOGRAPH	*ALBUM DE PHOTOS MILITAIRE*
F120	ALBUM, PHONOGRAPH RECORD	*ALBUM DE DISQUES DE PHONOGRAPHE*
H080	ALBUM, PHOTOGRAPH	*ALBUM DE PHOTOS*
H080	ALBUM, POSTCARD	*ALBUM DE CARTES POSTALES*
H080	ALBUM, STAMP	*ALBUM DE TIMBRES*
H080	ALBUM, TINTYPE	*ALBUM DE FERROTYPIES*
H080	ALMANAC	*ALMANACH*
H060	ALTAR	*AUTEL*
H060	ALTARPIECE	*RETABLE*
H080	AMBROTYPE	*AMBROTYPE*
G120	AMBULANCE	*AMBULANCE*
C080	AMICE	*AMICT*
E280	AMMETER	*AMPEREMETRE*
H060	AMPULLA	*AMPOULE*
H120	AMULET	*AMULETTE*
G300	ANCHOR	*ANCRE*
G300	ANCHOR, GRAPNEL	*ANCRE A GRAPPIN*
G300	ANCHOR, SEA	*ANCRE FLOTTANTE*
B140	ANDIRON	*CHENET*
B140	ANDIRON, MINIATURE	*CHENET MINIATURE*
E420	ANEMOMETER	*ANENOMETRE*
I100	ANIMAL	*ANIMAL*
I100	ANIMAL, MECHANICAL	*ANIMAL MECANIQUE*
I100	ANIMAL, STUFFED	*ANIMAL REMBOURRE*
C020	ANKLET	*BRACELET DE CHEVILLE*
H080	ANNOUNCEMENT	*AVIS*
H080	ANNOUNCEMENT, FUNERAL	*AVIS DE DECES*
B080	ANTIMACASSAR	*TETIERE DE FAUTEUIL*
D220	ANVIL	*ENCLUME*
D220	ANVIL, NAILMAKER'S	*ENCLUME DE CLOUTIER*
E360	APPARATUS, PERMEABILITY	*APPAREIL POUR TEST DE PERMEABILITE*
E380	APPARATUS, PNEUMOTHORAX	*APPAREIL DE PNEUMOTHORAX*

Class. Code	Object, suffix	Objet, suffixe
E380	APPLICATOR, LINIMENT	APPLICATEUR POUR LINIMENT
C140	APPLICATOR, SHOE-POLISH	APPLICATEUR DE CIRAGE A CHAUSSURES
C100	APRON	TABLIER
H120	APRON	TABLIER
C100	APRON, BLACKSMITH'S	TABLIER DE FORGERON
C100	APRON, MILITARY DRUMMER'S	TABLIER DE TAMBOUR MILITAIRE
B080	AQUARIUM	AQUARIUM
I100	ARK, NOAH'S	ARCHE DE NOE
C140	ARMBAND	BRASSARD
C140	ARMBAND, MILITARY	BRASSARD MILITAIRE
H120	ARMBAND, MOURNING	BRASSARD DE DEUIL
C020	ARMLET	BRASSARD
E080	ARROW	FLECHE
E080	ARROWHEAD	POINTE DE FLECHE
C140	ASCOT	ASCOT
E340	ASHPAN	GARDE-CENDRES
B080	ASHTRAY	CENDRIER
H060	ASPERGILLUM	GOUPILLON
H060	ASPERSORIUM	BENITIER PORTATIF
H040	ASSEMBLAGE	INSTALLATION
A040	ASSEMBLY, LATCH	ASSEMBLAGE DE LOQUET
E200	ASTROLABE	ASTROLABE
E500	ASTROLABE, MARINER'S	ASTROLABE DE MARIN
E380	ATOMIZER	PULVERISATEUR
D300	ATTACHMENT, SEWING MACHINE	ACCESSOIRE DE MACHINE A COUDRE
D320	AUGER	TARIERE
J060	AUGER, POST-HOLE	BECHE TARIERE
D140	AUGER, RAFT	TARIERE A RADEAU DE BILLES
D320	AUGER, SHELL	TARIERE A CUILLERE
D320	AUGER, SNAIL	TARIERE A BOIS HELICOIDALE
D320	AUGER, SPIRAL	TARIERE SPIRALEE
D100	AUGER, SUGAR	VRILLE A SUCRE
D320	AUGER, TAPER	TARIERE CONIQUE
D320	AUGER HANDLE	MANCHE DE TARIERE
E380	AUTOCLAVE	STERILISATEUR
G160	AUTOMOBILE, MILITARY	AUTOMOBILE MILITAIRE
G160	AUTOMOBILE WHEEL	ROUE D'AUTOMOBILE
D180	AWL	ALENE
F100	AWL	POINCON
D320	AWL	POINTE
D180	AWL, CLICKER'S	ALENE A POINCONNER
D180	AWL, COLLAR	ALENE A COUDRE LES COLLETS
D180	AWL, GARNISH	PERCOIR A POSER LES GARNITURES
D180	AWL, HARNESS	ALENE DE HARNAIS
D320	AWL, MARKING	POINTE A TRACER
D180	AWL, PANEL	ALENE A DECOUPER LES PANNEAUX
D180	AWL, PEGGING	ALENE DE CHEVILLIER
D180	AWL, SADDLER'S	ALENE DE SELLIER
D180	AWL, SADDLER'S STITCHING	ALENE A COUDRE POUR SELLIER
D180	AWL, SCRATCH	GRIFFE A TRACER
D180	AWL, SEAT	ALENE A PREMIERE SEMELLE
D180	AWL, SEWING	ALENE A COUTURE
D320	AWL, SQUARE	POINTE A PERCER CARREE
D320	AX	HACHE
D140	AX, BARKING	PELLE A ECORCER
E080	AX, BOARDING	HACHE D'ABORDAGE
D200	AX, BRICK	MARTELET
D320	AX, COOPER'S	HACHE DE TONNELIER
D140	AX, FELLING	HACHE D'ABATTAGE
E480	AX, FIRE	HACHE A INCENDIE

Class. Code	Object, suffix	Objet, suffixe
D140	AX, MARKING	HACHE A MARQUER
E080	AX, MILITARY BOARDING	HACHE D'ABORDAGE MILITAIRE
D320	AX, MORTISING	HACHE A MORTAISER
D320	AX, SHIPWRIGHT'S	HACHE DE CHARPENTIER NAVAL
D320	AX, SIDE	HACHE A EQUARRIR
D100	AX, SLAUGHTERING	HACHE D'ABATTOIR
D200	AX, TOOTH	HACHE D'ARDOISIER A PIC TRANSVERSAL
D140	AX BLADE, FELLING	LAME DE HACHE D'ABATTAGE
D140	AX HANDLE	MANCHE DE HACHE
D140	AX HANDLE, MILITARY	MANCHE DE HACHE MILITAIRE
D320	AX HANDLE, SIDE	MANCHE DE HACHE A EQUARRIR
C160	BACKPACK	SAC A DOS A ARMATURE
C160	BACKPACK, MILITARY	SAC A DOS A ARMATURE MILITAIRE
E160	BACKPLATE	DOSSIERE
E080	BACKSWORD, MILITARY	EPEE A UN TRANCHANT MILITAIRE
H120	BADGE, CAP	INSIGNE DE CALOT
H120	BADGE, FIREMAN"S	INSIGNE DE POMPIER
H120	BADGE, MILITARY	INSIGNE MILITAIRE
H120	BADGE, MILITARY BONNET	INSIGNE DE BONNET MILITAIRE
H120	BADGE, MILITARY CAP	INSIGNE DE CALOT MILITAIRE
H120	BADGE, MILITARY SHOULDER BELT	INSIGNE DE BAUDRIER MILITAIRE
H120	BADGE, POLICE	INSIGNE DE POLICE
G020	BAG	SAC
E480	BAG, BALLOT	SAC ELECTORAL
E400	BAG, BEAN	SAC A FEVES
D300	BAG, BUTTON	SAC A BOUTONS
E400	BAG, CEMENT	SAC A CIMENT
E400	BAG, CEREAL	SAC A CEREALES
H060	BAG, CEREMONIAL	SAC CEREMONIEL
F080	BAG, CHANGING	SAC POUR CHANGEMENT DE FILM
E400	BAG, COAL	SAC A CHARBON
E400	BAG, COFFEE	SAC A CAFE
C160	BAG, DITTY	NECESSAIRE DE MARIN
C160	BAG, DUFFLE	SAC DE VOYAGE
E400	BAG, DYE	SAC A TEINTURE
E400	BAG, FEED	SAC A FOURRAGE
E400	BAG, FLOUR	SAC A FARINE
C160	BAG, GARMENT	HOUSSE A VETEMENTS
E400	BAG, GLOVE	SAC A GANTS
E400	BAG, GLUE	SAC A COLLE
I080	BAG, GOLF CLUB	SAC DE GOLF
E400	BAG, GRAIN	SAC A GRAINS
E400	BAG, GUNPOWDER	SAC A POUDRE A CANON
E180	BAG, HUNTING	GIBECIERE
E400	BAG, JEWELRY	SAC A BIJOUX
E340	BAG, LAUNDRY	SAC A LESSIVE
E340	BAG, LAUNDRY BLUEING	SAC A BLEU DE LESSIVE
E400	BAG, LEAD SHOT	SAC A PLOMBS
I020	BAG, MARBLE	SAC DE BILLES
C160	BAG, MILITARY DUFFLE	SAC DE VOYAGE MILITAIRE
E400	BAG, NAIL	SAC A CLOUS
D300	BAG, NEEDLEWORK	SAC DE TRAVAIL A L'AIGUILLE
D240	BAG, ORE	SAC A MINERAI
C160	BAG, PIPE	POCHETTE A PIPE
C160	BAG, POLICE DUFFLE	SAC DE VOYAGE DE POLICE
B020	BAG, POLICE SLEEPING	SAC DE COUCHAGE DE POLICE
E400	BAG, POTATO	SAC A PATATES
E400	BAG, RICE	SAC A RIZ
E400	BAG, SALT	SAC A SEL
E400	BAG, SAND	SAC A SABLE
C160	BAG, SCHOOL	SAC D'ECOLE

Class. Code	Object, suffix	Objet, suffixe
E400	BAG, SEED	SAC A SEMENCES
C160	BAG, SHOE	POCHETTE A SOULIERS
I080	BAG, SKATE	SAC A PATINS
B020	BAG, SLEEPING	SAC DE COUCHAGE
E400	BAG, STOCKING	SAC A BAS
E400	BAG, SUGAR	SAC A SUCRE
B080	BAG, TABLE LEAF	COUVRE-ABATTANT
E400	BAG, TANKAGE	SAC A FARINE DE VIANDE
E400	BAG, TOBACCO	SAC A TABAC
E400	BAG, TRADE	SAC A ARTICLES DE COMMERCE
H020	BAG, TRADE	SAC PUBLICITAIRE
D060	BAG, WHALER'S	SAC DE BALEINIER
F060	BAGPIPE, MILITARY	CORNEMUSE MILITAIRE
G300	BAILER	ECOPE
D100	BAKEBOARD	PLANCHE A PATE
H060	BALDACHIN	BALDAQUIN
G020	BALE	BALLOT
E400	BALE, BLANKET	BALLOT DE COUVERTURES
E400	BALE, CARPET	BALLOT DE MOQUETTE
E400	BALE, CLOTH BOLT	BALLOT DE PIECES DE TISSU
E400	BALE, PANTS	BALLOT DE PANTALONS
E400	BALE, PELT	BALLOT DE FOURRURES
E400	BALE, ROPE	BALLOT DE CORDE
I100	BALL	BALLE
I080	BALL, BILLIARD	BILLE DE BILLARD
I080	BALL, BOWLING	BOULE DE JEU DE QUILLES
I080	BALL, CARPET	BOULE DE JEU DE SALON
I080	BALL, CROQUET	BOULE DE CROQUET
E140	BALL, MUSKET	BALLE DE MOUSQUET
I080	BALL, TENNIS	BALLE DE TENNIS
C080	BALMORAL	BERET ECOSSAIS
A040	BALUSTER	BALUSTRE
A020	BALUSTRADE	BALUSTRADE
E540	BAND, WRISTWATCH	BRACELET DE MONTRE
E380	BANDAGE	BANDAGE
C160	BANDBOX	BOITE DE RANGEMENT CYLINDRIQUE
F060	BANJO	BANJO
B080	BANK, COIN	TIRELIRE
I100	BANK, STILL	TIRELIRE
H060	BANNER	BANNIERE
H020	BANNER	BANNIERE
H080	BANNER, COMMEMORATIVE	BANNIERE COMMEMORATIVE
A040	BAR	BARRE
D220	BAR, COPPER	LINGOT DE CUIVRE
D220	BAR, GRAPHITE	LINGOT DE GRAPHITE
D240	BAR, MINER'S	BARRE A MINE
A060	BARBWIRE	BARBELE
E420	BAROMETER	BAROMETRE
E420	BAROMETER, ANEROID	BAROMETRE ANEROIDE
E420	BAROMETER, MERCURY	BAROMETRE AU MERCURE
E400	BARRIER, DISPLAY	CORDON PROTECTEUR D'ETALAGE
G140	BARROW	BARD
A040	BASEBOARD	PLINTHE
C180	BASIN	CUVETTE
C180	BASIN, MILITARY	CUVETTE MILITAIRE
G020	BASKET	PANIER
D120	BASKET, BREAD	CORBEILLE A PAIN
D120	BASKET, CAKE	CORBEILLE A GATEAUX
D100	BASKET, COOKING	PANIER A FRITURE
D100	BASKET, DOUGH-RISING	PANIER DE FERMENTATION
D120	BASKET, FRUIT	CORBEILLE A FRUITS

Class. Code	Object, suffix	Objet, suffixe
D020	BASKET, GATHERING	*PANIER A CUEILLIR*
E340	BASKET, LAUNDRY	*CORBEILLE A LESSIVE*
D300	BASKET, NEEDLEWORK	*PANIER DE TRAVAIL A L'AIGUILLE*
D220	BASKET, ORE	*PANIER A MINERAI*
D060	BASKET, OYSTER	*PANIER A HUITRES*
D040	BASKET, PET	*PANIER POUR ANIMAL FAMILIER*
D120	BASKET, PICNIC	*PANIER POUR PIQUE-NIQUE*
G300	BASKET, ROPE	*CORBEILLE A CORDE*
D100	BASKET, STORAGE	*PANIER D'ENTREPOSAGE*
C160	BASKET, TRINKET	*PANIER A COLIFICHETS*
D120	BASKET, WINE	*PANIER VERSEUR A VIN*
D020	BASKET, WINNOWING	*VAN*
F060	BASSOON	*BASSON*
I080	BAT, BASEBALL	*BATON DE BASEBALL*
I080	BAT, CRICKET	*BATTE DE CRICKET*
I100	BATEAU	*BATEAU*
G280	BATEAU, EXHIBITION MODEL	*BATEAU MODELE D'EXPOSITION*
G280	BATEAU, MINIATURE	*BATEAU MINIATURE*
B080	BATHTUB	*BAIGNOIRE*
I100	BATHTUB	*BAIGNOIRE*
B120	BATHTUB	*BAIGNOIRE*
E280	BATTERY, DRY-CELL	*BATTERIE DE PILES SECHES*
E280	BATTERY, WET-CELL	*PILE HYDRO-ELECTRIQUE*
E080	BAYONET	*BAIONNETTE*
E080	BAYONET, HILTED SWORD	*BAIONNETTE-EPEE A POIGNEE*
E080	BAYONET, MILITARY HILTED KNIFE	*BAIONNETTE-COUTEAU A POIGNEE MILITAIRE*
E080	BAYONET, MILITARY HILTED SWORD	*BAIONNETTE-EPEE A POIGNEE MILITAIRE*
E080	BAYONET, MILITARY HILTED TRIANGULAR	*BAIONNETTE A POIGNEE ET A TRANCHE TRIANGULAIRE MILITAIRE*
E080	BAYONET, MILITARY PLUG KNIFE	*BAIONNETTE-COUTEAU A MANCHE MILITAIRE*
E080	BAYONET, MILITARY PLUG SWORD	*BAIONNETTE-EPEE A MANCHE MILITAIRE*
E080	BAYONET, MILITARY SOCKET CRUCIFORM	*BAIONNETTE A DOUILLE ET A TRANCHE CRUCIFORME MILITAIRE*
E080	BAYONET, MILITARY SOCKET KNIFE	*BAIONNETTE-COUTEAU A DOUILLE MILITAIRE*
E080	BAYONET, MILITARY SOCKET SPIKE	*BAIONNETTE-CLOU A DOUILLE MILITAIRE*
E080	BAYONET, MILITARY SOCKET SWORD	*BAIONNETTE-EPEE A DOUILLE MILITAIRE*
E080	BAYONET, MILITARY SOCKET TRIANGULAR	*BAIONNETTE A DOUILLE ET A TRANCHE TRIANGULAIRE MILITAIRE*
E080	BAYONET, SOCKET	*BAIONNETTE A DOUILLE*
E080	BAYONET MOUNT SPRING	*MONTURE DE BAIONNETTE A RESSORT*
C020	BEAD	*PERLE*
D220	BEAD-TOOL, BOILER TUBE	*OUTIL A EMBOUTIR LES TUBES DE CHAUDIERE*
H120	BEADS, ROSARY	*CHAPELET*
E240	BEAKER	*BECHER*
A020	BEAM, TRUSS	*SABLIERE*
E300	BEARING	*ROULEMENT*
F060	BEATER, DRUM	*BAGUETTE*
E340	BEATER, LAUNDRY	*BATTOIR A LESSIVE*
E340	BEATER, RUG	*BATTOIR A TAPIS*
B060	BED	*LIT*
I100	BED	*LIT*
B060	BED, CHILD'S	*LIT D'ENFANT*
B060	BED, FOLDING	*LIT PLIANT*
B060	BED, FOUR-POSTER	*LIT A COLONNES*
I100	BED, FOUR-POSTER	*LIT A COLONNES*
B060	BED, MILITARY	*LIT DE CAMP MILITAIRE*
B060	BED, MINIATURE CHILD'S	*LIT D'ENFANT MINIATURE*
B060	BED, MINIATURE FOUR-POSTER	*LIT A COLONNES MINIATURE*
B060	BED, POLICE	*LIT DE POLICE*
B060	BED, SOFA	*DIVAN-LIT*
B060	BED LEG	*PIED DE LIT*
B060	BED HEADBOARD	*TETE DE LIT*
B060	BED POST	*COLONNE DE LIT*
B060	BED POST FINIAL	*POMMEAU DE LIT*

Class. Code	Object, suffix	Objet, suffixe
B060	BED RAIL	TRAVERSE DE LIT
B080	BEDKEY	SERRE-ECROU DE CHALIT
C180	BEDPAN	BASSIN DE LIT
B020	BEDSPREAD	COUVRE-LIT
I100	BEDSPREAD	COUVRE-LIT
B020	BEDSPRINGS	SOMMIER A RESSORTS
D040	BEEHIVE	RUCHE
D320	BEETLE	MASSE
F060	BELL	CLOCHE
F120	BELL	CLOCHE
H060	BELL, ALTAR	CLOCHETTE LITURGIQUE
G180	BELL, BICYCLE	CLOCHETTE DE BICYCLETTE
F120	BELL, CHURCH	CLOCHE D'EGLISE
F120	BELL, COUNTER	SONNETTE DE COMPTOIR
G240	BELL, LOCOMOTIVE	CLOCHE DE LOCOMOTIVE
F120	BELL, SCHOOL	CLOCHE D'ECOLE
F120	BELL, SERVICE	CLOCHETTE DE SERVICE
G300	BELL, SHIP'S	CLOCHE DE NAVIRE
G180	BELL, SLEIGH	GRELOT
B140	BELLOWS	SOUFFLET
J060	BELLOWS	SOUFFLET
D220	BELLOWS, BLACKSMITH'S	SOUFFLET DE FORGE
B080	BELLPULL	CORDON DE SONNETTE
C140	BELT	CEINTURE
H120	BELT	CEINTURE
E300	BELT	COURROIE
E180	BELT, CARTRIDGE	CEINTURE A CARTOUCHES
H060	BELT, CEREMONIAL	CEINTURE DE CEREMONIE
C120	BELT, GARTER	PORTE-JARRETELLES
C140	BELT, MILITARY	CEINTURE MILITAIRE
C160	BELT, MILITARY BACKPACK	COURROIE DE SAC A DOS A ARMATURE MILITAIRE
E180	BELT, MILITARY BAYONET	BAUDRIER PORTE-BAIONNETTE MILITAIRE
B020	BELT, MILITARY BEDDING	COURROIE DE MATELAS MILITAIRE
C160	BELT, MILITARY BLANKET	COURROIE DE COUVERTURE MILITAIRE
C160	BELT, MILITARY CANTEEN	COURROIE DE GOURDE MILITAIRE
E180	BELT, MILITARY CARTRIDGE	CEINTURE A CARTOUCHES MILITAIRE
E180	BELT, MILITARY CARTRIDGE-BOX	BAUDRIER DE GIBERNE MILITAIRE
C160	BELT, MILITARY DRUM	COURROIE DE TAMBOUR MILITAIRE
C160	BELT, MILITARY MESS TIN	COURROIE DE GAMELLE MILITAIRE
C160	BELT, MILITARY MONEY	CEINTURE A ARGENT MILITAIRE
C160	BELT, MILITARY POUCH	BANDEROLE DE GIBERNE MILITAIRE
E180	BELT, MILITARY POWDER HORN	BANDEROLE DE CORNET A POUDRE MILITAIRE
H120	BELT, MILITARY PRESENTATION SWORD	CEINTURE PORTE-EPEE D'HONNEUR MILITAIRE
C160	BELT, MILITARY SABRETACHE	COURROIE DE SABRETACHE MILITAIRE
C140	BELT, MILITARY SAM BROWNE	CEINTURE SAM BROWNE MILITAIRE
C140	BELT, MILITARY SHOULDER	BAUDRIER MILITAIRE
E180	BELT, MILITARY SWORD	CEINTURE PORTE-EPEE MILITAIRE
C160	BELT, MONEY	CEINTURE A ARGENT
C140	BELT, POLICE	CEINTURE DE POLICE
E180	BELT, POLICE CARTRIDGE	CEINTURON DE POLICE
E180	BELT, POLICE HOLSTER	CEINTURE D'ETUI A PISTOLET DE POLICE
C160	BELT, POLICE POUCH	BANDEROLE DE GIBERNE DE POLICE
C140	BELT, POLICE SAM BROWNE	CEINTURE SAM BROWNE DE POLICE
B060	BENCH	BANC
B060	BENCH, BUCKET	BANC A BAQUET
D320	BENCH, CARPENTER'S	ETABLI DE MENUISIER
D180	BENCH, COBBLER'S	ETABLI DE CORDONNIER
B060	BENCH, GARDEN	BANC DE JARDIN
D180	BENCH, HARNESS MAKER'S	BANC DE SELLIER
E340	BENCH, LAUNDRY	BANC A LESSIVE
B060	BENCH LEG	PIED DE BANC

Class. Code	Object, suffix	Objet, suffixe
B060	BENCH, MILITARY	BANC MILITAIRE
B060	BENCH, MINIATURE	BANC MINIATURE
F060	BENCH, ORGAN	BANC D'HARMONIUM
F060	BENCH, PIANO	BANC DE PIANO
D100	BENCH, SLAUGHTERING	TABLE D'ABATTAGE
D300	BENCH, WEAVER'S	BANC DE TISSERAND
D320	BENCH, WHEELWRIGHT'S	ETABLI DE CHARRON
D220	BENDER, PIPE	CINTREUSE DE TUYAUX
D240	BENDER, POINT	OUTIL A CINTRER LES POINTES
D240	BENDER, RAIL	CINTREUSE DE RAIL
C080	BERET	BERET
D180	BEVELER, EDGE	BISEAU DE BORDURE
C140	BIB	BAVETTE
G140	BICYCLE, ORDINARY	BICYCLE
C180	BIDET	BIDET
E080	BILL	SERPE
H080	BILL-OF-LADING	CONNAISSEMENT
H080	BILL-OF-SALE	FACTURE
A080	BILLBOARD	PANNEAU D'AFFICHAGE
D020	BILLHOOK	SERPE
B140	BIN, COAL	BOITE A CHARBON
D220	BIN, MILITARY CHARCOAL	BOITE A CHARBON MILITAIRE
E400	BIN, STORAGE	COFFRE DE STOCKAGE
C120	BINDER	BANDE OMBILICALE
F180	BINDER	CLASSEUR
F180	BINDER, RING	CLASSEUR A ANNEAUX
I080	BINDING, SNOW SKI	FIXATION DE SKI
E460	BINOCULARS	JUMELLES
B080	BIRDCAGE	CAGE A OISEAUX
A060	BIRDHOUSE	MAISON D'OISEAUX
C080	BIRETTA	BARRETTE
D100	BISCUIT	BISCUIT
D320	BIT	MECHE
G180	BIT	MORS
D320	BIT, CENTER	MECHE ANGLAISE
D320	BIT, COUNTERSINK	FRAISE CONIQUE
D220	BIT, FLAT	MECHE PLATE
D320	BIT, GIMLET	TARIERE A VRILLE
D220	BIT, LATHE	MECHE DE TOUR
D320	BIT, MORTISE	MECHE A MORTAISES
D200	BIT, SCUTCH	CISEAU A FENDRE
D320	BIT, SHELL	MECHE A GOUGE
D320	BIT, SPOKE-TRIMMER	TETE A EFFILER LES POINTES DE RAIES
D320	BIT, SPOON	MECHE EN CUILLERE
D320	BIT, TAPER	MECHE CONIQUE POINTUE
D320	BIT, TWIST	MECHE A VRILLE
D220	BIT, TWIST	MECHE HELICOIDALE
E100	BLACKJACK	GARCETTE
C180	BLADE, RAZOR	LAME DE RASOIR
B020	BLANKET	COUVERTURE
D040	BLANKET	COUVERTURE
I100	BLANKET	COUVERTURE
H060	BLANKET, DANCE	COUVERTURE DE DANSE
B020	BLANKET, MILITARY	COUVERTURE MILITAIRE
B020	BLANKET, MINIATURE	COUVERTURE MINIATURE
B020	BLANKET, POLICE	COUVERTURE DE POLICE
H120	BLANKET, SHOULDER	COUVERTURE-CHALE
B020	BLANKET/SHEET	COUVERTURE/DRAP
D100	BLENDER, PASTRY	MALAXEUR A PATISSERIE
B160	BLIND, VENETIAN	STORE VENITIEN
G180	BLINDER	LUNETTES

Class. Code	Object, suffix	Objet, suffixe
I100	BLOCK	BLOC
G300	BLOCK	POULIE
D320	BLOCK, BEVEL	CALE EN V POUR FACONNAGE
D100	BLOCK, CHOPPING	HACHOIR
D040	BLOCK, CLINCHING	BLOC A RIVER
D300	BLOCK, HAT	FORME A CHAPEAUX
I100	BLOCK, PARQUETRY	BLOC DE PARQUETERIE
D320	BLOCK, SANDING	CALE A PONCER
D220	BLOCK, SWAGE	ENCLUME-ETAMPE
D320	BLOCK, WHEELWRIGHT'S CHOPPING	BILLOT DE CHARRON
D300	BLOCK, WOOD	ETAMPE DE BOIS
A020	BLOCKHOUSE, MODEL	REDOUTE MODELE REDUIT
F180	BLOTTER	BUVARD
H020	BLOTTER	BUVARD
C100	BLOUSE	BLOUSE
C100	BLOUSE, CHILD'S	BLOUSE D'ENFANT
C100	BLOUSE, MILITARY	VAREUSE MILITAIRE
E360	BLOWER	SOUFFLERIE
H080	BLUEPRINT	PLAN
H080	BLUEPRINT, MILITARY	PLAN MILITAIRE
E060	BLUNDERBUSS	TROMBLON
C140	BOA	BOA
A040	BOARD	PLANCHE
I020	BOARD, ALPHABET GAME	TABLIER DU JEU DE L'ALPHABET
H020	BOARD, BULLETIN	TABLEAU D'AFFICHAGE
I020	BOARD, CHECKER	DAMIER
I020	BOARD, CRIBBAGE	TABLIER DU JEU DE CRIBBAGE
D100	BOARD, CUTTING	PLANCHE A DECOUPER
I020	BOARD, GAME	TABLIER DE JEU
E340	BOARD, IRONING	PLANCHE A REPASSER
F100	BOARD, MATRIX	CARTON A MATRICE
H020	BOARD, MILITARY BULLETIN	TABLEAU D'AFFICHAGE MILITAIRE
B140	BOARD, MILITARY STOVE	PLAQUE DE POELE MILITAIRE
G300	BOARD, NAME	TABLEAU DE NAVIRE
D300	BOARD, SCUTCHING	PLANCHE A TEILLER
B140	BOARD, STOVE	PLAQUE DE POELE
H060	BOARD, TOBACCO CUTTING	PLANCHE A DECOUPER LE TABAC
E500	BOARD, TRAVERSE	RENARD
G280	BOAT, DESIGN MODEL	BATEAU MODELE DE PROJET
G280	BOAT, DESIGN MODEL PADDLE	NAVIRE A AUBES MODELE DE PROJET
G280	BOAT HULL, DESIGN MODEL	COQUE DE BATEAU MODELE DE PROJET
G280	BOAT, LOBSTER	HOMARDIER
G280	BOAT WHEEL, DESIGN MODEL PADDLE	ROUE A AUBES DE NAVIRE MODELE DE PROJET
C080	BOATER	CANOTIER
J060	BOB, MILITARY PLUMB	FIL A PLOMB MILITAIRE
J060	BOB, PLUMB	FIL A PLOMB
D300	BOBBIN	BOBINE
B100	BOBECHE	BOBECHE
I080	BOBSLED	BOBSLEIGH
C100	BODICE	CORSAGE
D300	BODKIN	PASSE-LACET
D240	BOILER	CHAUDIERE
D320	BOILER, BOATBUILDER'S	ETUVE A BOIS
D100	BOILER, DOUBLE	BAIN-MARIE DOUBLE
E300	BOILER, STEAM	GENERATEUR DE VAPEUR
C100	BOLERO	BOLERO
G300	BOLLARD	BITTE
E080	BOLO	MACHETTE
B020	BOLSTER	TRAVERSIN
I100	BOLSTER	TRAVERSIN
B020	BOLSTER, MILITARY	TRAVERSIN MILITAIRE

Class. Code	Object, suffix	Objet, suffixe
D320	BOLT	*BOULON*
D220	BOLT	*BOULON*
D300	BOLT, CLOTH	*PIÈCE DE TISSU*
D300	BOLT, MILITARY CLOTH	*PIÈCE DE TISSU MILITAIRE*
J060	BOLT, U	*BOULON EN U*
H080	BOND	*TITRE*
J020	BONE FRAGMENT	*FRAGMENT D'OS*
H120	BONNET	*BONNET*
I100	BONNET	*BONNET*
C080	BONNET	*CAPOTE*
C080	BONNET, INDOOR	*BONNET*
C080	BONNET, INFANT'S	*BEGUIN*
C080	BONNET, MILITARY	*BONNET ECOSSAIS MILITAIRE*
H080	BOOK	*LIVRE*
H080	BOOK, ACCOUNT	*LIVRE DE COMPTES*
F180	BOOK, ACCOUNT	*LIVRE DE COMPTES*
H080	BOOK, ADDRESS	*CARNET D'ADRESSES*
H080	BOOK, CHILD'S	*LIVRE POUR ENFANTS*
I100	BOOK, DRAWING	*CAHIER DE DESSIN*
H080	BOOK, MILITARY	*LIVRE MILITAIRE*
H080	BOOK, MILITARY ACCOUNT	*LIVRE DE COMPTES MILITAIRE*
H080	BOOK, POLICE ACCOUNT	*LIVRE DE COMPTES DE POLICE*
B060	BOOKCASE	*BIBLIOTHEQUE*
B060	BOOKCASE, MILITARY	*BIBLIOTHEQUE MILITAIRE*
B080	BOOKEND	*SERRE-LIVRES*
H080	BOOKLET	*LIVRET*
H020	BOOKLET	*LIVRET*
H080	BOOKLET, MILITARY	*LIVRET MILITAIRE*
F180	BOOKMARK	*SIGNET*
C060	BOOT	*BOTTE*
I100	BOOT	*BOTTE*
D040	BOOT, ANKLE	*GUETRE DE CHEVILLE*
C060	BOOT, HIP	*CUISSARDE*
C060	BOOT, MILITARY	*BOTTE MILITAIRE*
C060	BOOT, POLICE	*BOTTE DE POLICE*
C060	BOOT, RIDING	*BOTTE A L'ECUYERE*
C060	BOOT, WELLINGTON	*BOTTE WELLINGTON*
C060	BOOTEE	*CHAUSSON*
B080	BOOTJACK	*TIRE-BOTTE*
C060	BOTTE SAUVAGE	*BOTTE SAUVAGE*
G020	BOTTLE	*BOUTEILLE*
E400	BOTTLE, ALCOHOLIC BEVERAGE	*BOUTEILLE A BOISSON ALCOOLISEE*
E400	BOTTLE, AMMONIA	*BOUTEILLE A AMMONIAC*
E400	BOTTLE, ANALGESIC	*BOUTEILLE A ANALGESIQUES*
E400	BOTTLE, ANTACID	*BOUTEILLE A ANTI-ACIDE*
E400	BOTTLE, ANTISEPTIC	*BOUTEILLE POUR ANTISEPTIQUE*
E400	BOTTLE, APOTHECARY	*BOUTEILLE D'APOTHICAIRE*
E400	BOTTLE, ASTRINGENT	*BOUTEILLE A ASTRINGENT*
E400	BOTTLE, BEER	*BOUTEILLE A BIERE*
E400	BOTTLE, BEVERAGE	*BOUTEILLE A BOISSON*
E400	BOTTLE, BITTERS	*BOUTEILLE A BITTER*
E400	BOTTLE, BOOT POLISH	*BOUTEILLE A CIRAGE A CHAUSSURES*
E400	BOTTLE, BORACIC ACID	*BOUTEILLE POUR ACIDE BORIQUE*
E400	BOTTLE, BRANDY	*BOUTEILLE A BRANDY*
E400	BOTTLE, CANDLE	*BOUTEILLE A BOUGIE*
E400	BOTTLE, CARBOLIC ACID	*BOUTEILLE A PHENOL*
E400	BOTTLE, CASTOR OIL	*BOUTEILLE A HUILE DE CASTOR*
E400	BOTTLE, CHEMICAL	*BOUTEILLE A PRODUIT CHIMIQUE*
E400	BOTTLE, CLEANING FLUID	*BOUTEILLE A NETTOYANT LIQUIDE*
E400	BOTTLE, CLOVE	*BOUTEILLE A CLOUS DE GIROFLE*
E400	BOTTLE, COD LIVER OIL	*BOUTEILLE A HUILE DE FOIE DE MORUE*

Class. Code	Object, suffix	Objet, suffixe
E400	BOTTLE, COFFEE SYRUP	BOUTEILLE A SIROP DE CAFE
E400	BOTTLE, COGNAC	BOUTEILLE A COGNAC
E400	BOTTLE, CONDIMENT SAUCE	BOUTEILLE A SAUCE AUX CONDIMENTS
E400	BOTTLE, CONFECTION	BOUTEILLE A CONFISERIES
E400	BOTTLE, CORN OIL	BOUTEILLE A HUILE DE MAIS
E400	BOTTLE, COSMETIC	BOUTEILLE A PRODUIT COSMETIQUE
E400	BOTTLE, COTTON SEED OIL	BOUTEILLE A HUILE DE COTON
E400	BOTTLE, COUGH DROP	BOUTEILLE A PASTILLES CONTRE LA TOUX
E400	BOTTLE, CREAM	BOUTEILLE A CREME
E400	BOTTLE, CURRY	BOUTEILLE A CARI
E400	BOTTLE, DECONGESTANT	BOUTEILLE A DECONGESTIF
E400	BOTTLE, DISH SOAP	BOUTEILLE A SAVON A VAISSELLE
E400	BOTTLE, DYE	BOUTEILLE A TEINTURE
E400	BOTTLE, EMBALMING FLUID	BOUTEILLE A LIQUIDE D'EMBAUMEMENT
E400	BOTTLE, EYEWASH	BOUTEILLE A COLLYRE
E400	BOTTLE, FLAVORING	BOUTEILLE A ESSENCE
E400	BOTTLE, FOOD COLORING	BOUTEILLE A COLORANT ALIMENTAIRE
E400	BOTTLE, FORMALDEHYDE	BOUTEILLE A FORMALDEHYDE
E400	BOTTLE, FRUIT JUICE	BOUTEILLE A JUS DE FRUITS
E400	BOTTLE, GIN	BOUTEILLE A GIN
E400	BOTTLE, GINGER	BOUTEILLE A GINGEMBRE
E400	BOTTLE, GINGER ALE	BOUTEILLE A SODA DE GINGEMBRE
E400	BOTTLE, GINGER BEER	BOUTEILLE A BIERE DE GINGEMBRE
E400	BOTTLE, GLUE	BOUTEILLE A COLLE
E400	BOTTLE, GLYCERIN	BOUTEILLE A GLYCERINE
E400	BOTTLE, GRAPE JUICE	BOUTEILLE A JUS DE RAISIN
E400	BOTTLE, GUN BLUEING	BOUTEILLE A BRONZAGE DE CANON
E400	BOTTLE, HAIR TONIC	BOUTEILLE A TONIQUE CAPILLAIRE
H060	BOTTLE, HOLY WATER	BOUTEILLE A EAU BENITE
E400	BOTTLE, HORSERADISH	BOUTEILLE A RAIFORT
B080	BOTTLE, HOT-WATER	BOUILLOTTE
E400	BOTTLE, HYDROGEN PEROXIDE	BOUTEILLE A PEROXIDE D'HYDROGENE
E400	BOTTLE, INK	BOUTEILLE A ENCRE
E400	BOTTLE, INSECT REPELLANT	BOUTEILLE POUR INSECTIFUGE
E400	BOTTLE, INSECTICIDE	BOUTEILLE A INSECTICIDE
E400	BOTTLE, IODINE	BOUTEILLE A IODE
E400	BOTTLE, KETCHUP	BOUTEILLE A KETCHUP
E400	BOTTLE, LAUNDRY BLEACH	BOUTEILLE A BLANCHIMENT
E400	BOTTLE, LAUNDRY BLUEING	BOUTEILLE A BLEU DE LESSIVE
E400	BOTTLE, LAXATIVE	BOUTEILLE A LAXATIF
E400	BOTTLE, LEATHER DRESSING	BOUTEILLE POUR APPRET A CUIR
E400	BOTTLE, LEMON JUICE	BOUTEILLE A JUS DE CITRON
E400	BOTTLE, LEMONADE	BOUTEILLE A LIMONADE
E400	BOTTLE, LIME JUICE	BOUTEILLE A JUS DE LIMETTE
E400	BOTTLE, LINIMENT	BOUTEILLE A LINIMENT
E400	BOTTLE, LIQUEUR	BOUTEILLE A LIQUEUR
E400	BOTTLE, LUBRICATING OIL	BOUTEILLE A HUILE LUBRIFIANTE
E400	BOTTLE, MALT EXTRACT	BOUTEILLE A EXTRAIT DE MALT
E400	BOTTLE, MANDRAKE	BOUTEILLE A MANDRAGORE
E400	BOTTLE, MEAT EXTRACT	BOUTEILLE A EXTRAIT DE VIANDE
E400	BOTTLE, MEDICINAL	BOUTEILLE A PRODUIT PHARMACEUTIQUE
E400	BOTTLE, MEDICINAL SYRUP	BOUTEILLE A SIROP PHARMACEUTIQUE
C160	BOTTLE, MEDICINE	FLACON A MEDICAMENT
E400	BOTTLE, MILK	BOUTEILLE A LAIT
E400	BOTTLE, MINERAL OIL	BOUTEILLE A HUILE MINERALE
E400	BOTTLE, MINERAL WATER	BOUTEILLE A EAU MINERALE
G020	BOTTLE, MINIATURE	BOUTEILLE MINIATURE
E400	BOTTLE, MOUTHWASH	BOUTEILLE A GARGARISME
E400	BOTTLE, MUSTARD	BOUTEILLE A MOUTARDE
E400	BOTTLE, NAIL POLISH	BOUTEILLE A VERNIS A ONGLES
E400	BOTTLE, NON-ALCOHOLIC BEVERAGE	BOUTEILLE A BOISSON NON-ALCOOLISEE

Class. Code	Object, suffix	Objet, suffixe
D120	BOTTLE, NURSING	BIBERON
E400	BOTTLE, OINTMENT	BOUTEILLE A ONGUENT
E400	BOTTLE, OLIVE	BOUTEILLE A OLIVES
E400	BOTTLE, OLIVE OIL	BOUTEILLE A HUILE D'OLIVE
E400	BOTTLE, OPIUM	BOUTEILLE POUR OPIUM
C160	BOTTLE, OPIUM	FLACON A OPIUM
E400	BOTTLE, PAINT	BOUTEILLE A PEINTURE
E400	BOTTLE, PECTIN	BOUTEILLE A PECTINE
E400	BOTTLE, PHOTOGRAPHIC DEVELOPER	BOUTEILLE POUR REVELATEUR
E400	BOTTLE, PICKLE	BOUTEILLE A CORNICHONS
E400	BOTTLE, PIGMENT	BOUTEILLE A PIGMENTS
E400	BOTTLE, PILL	BOUTEILLE A PILULES
E400	BOTTLE, POISON	BOUTEILLE A POISON
E400	BOTTLE, SALT	BOUTEILLE A SEL
E400	BOTTLE, SAVORY	BOUTEILLE A SARRIETTE
E400	BOTTLE, SCOTCH	BOUTEILLE A SCOTCH
D120	BOTTLE, SELTZER	SIPHON
E400	BOTTLE, SHAMPOO	BOUTEILLE A SHAMPOOING
E400	BOTTLE, SHELLAC	BOUTEILLE A SHELLAC
E400	BOTTLE, SKIN LOTION	BOUTEILLE A LOTION POUR LA PEAU
C160	BOTTLE, SMELLING	FLACON DE SELS
E400	BOTTLE, SMELLING SALTS	BOUTEILLE A SELS AMMONIACAUX
E400	BOTTLE, SNUFF	BOUTEILLE A TABAC A PRISER
C160	BOTTLE, SNUFF	FLACON A TABAC A PRISER
E400	BOTTLE, SODA WATER	BOUTEILLE A EAU DE SELTZ
E400	BOTTLE, SPICE	BOUTEILLE A EPICES
E400	BOTTLE, STIMULANT	BOUTEILLE A STIMULANT
E400	BOTTLE, STOVE POLISH	BOUTEILLE A PATE A POLIR LE POELE
E400	BOTTLE, THYME	BOUTEILLE A THYM
E400	BOTTLE, TOILET	BOUTEILLE DE TOILETTE
C180	BOTTLE, TOILET	FLACON DE TOILETTE
E400	BOTTLE, TOOTHPASTE	BOUTEILLE A PATE DENTIFRICE
E400	BOTTLE, TRANQUILIZER	BOUTEILLE A CALMANTS
E400	BOTTLE, TURPENTINE	BOUTEILLE A TEREBENTHINE
D120	BOTTLE, VACUUM	BOUTEILLE ISOLANTE
E400	BOTTLE, VARNISH	BOUTEILLE A VERNIS
E400	BOTTLE, VERMIFUGE	BOUTEILLE A VERMIFUGE
E400	BOTTLE, VINEGAR	BOUTEILLE A VINAIGRE
D120	BOTTLE, WATER	BOUTEILLE A EAU
E400	BOTTLE, WHISKEY	BOUTEILLE A WHISKY
E400	BOTTLE, WINE	BOUTEILLE A VIN
E400	BOTTLE, WOOD POLISH	BOUTEILLE A LIQUIDE A POLIR LE BOIS
E400	BOTTLE, YEAST	BOUTEILLE A LEVURE
D100	BOULOIR	BOULOIR
H040	BOUQUET, FLORAL	BOUQUET DE FLEURS
E080	BOW	ARC
F060	BOW, VIOLIN	ARCHET DE VIOLON
F060	BOW, VIOLONCELLO	ARCHET DE VIOLONCELLE
D100	BOWL	BOL
D120	BOWL	BOL
G020	BOWL	BOL
C180	BOWL, BARBER'S	BOL DE RASAGE
E380	BOWL, BLEEDING	PLATEAU POUR LA SAIGNEE
D100	BOWL, BUTTER-WORKING	TERRINE A BEURRE
D120	BOWL, CEREAL	BOL A CEREALES
D100	BOWL, CHOPPING	BOL A HACHER
H080	BOWL, COMMEMORATIVE	BOL COMMEMORATIF
D120	BOWL, CREAM	POT A CREME
D120	BOWL, FINGER	RINCE-DOIGTS
B080	BOWL, FLOWER	BOL A FLEURS
D120	BOWL, FRUIT	BOL A FRUITS

Class. Code	Object, suffix	Objet, suffixe
D120	BOWL LID	COUVERCLE DE BOL
D120	BOWL, MILITARY	BOL MILITAIRE
D100	BOWL, MINIATURE BUTTER-WORKING	TERRINE A BEURRE MINIATURE
D100	BOWL, MIXING	BOL A MELANGER
D040	BOWL, PET	BOL POUR ANIMAL FAMILIER
D120	BOWL, PUNCH	BOL A PUNCH
D120	BOWL, SALAD	SALADIER
E400	BOWL, SHAVING SOAP	BOL A SAVON A BARBE
D120	BOWL, SOUP	BOL A SOUPE
D120	BOWL, SUGAR	BOL A SUCRE
I100	BOWL, SUGAR	SUCRIER
G020	BOX	BOITE
E400	BOX, ABSORBENT COTTON	BOITE A COTON HYDROPHILE
E400	BOX, AIR FRESHENER	BOITE A DESODORISANT D'AIR
E400	BOX, AMMONIA	BOITE A AMMONIAQUE
E180	BOX, AMMUNITION	BOITE DE MUNITIONS
E400	BOX, ANALGESIC	BOITE A ANALGESIQUES
E400	BOX, ANTACID	BOITE A ANTI-ACIDE
E400	BOX, ANTISEPTIC	BOITE POUR ANTISEPTIQUE
E400	BOX, ARMBAND	BOITE A BRASSARDS
D260	BOX, ARTIST'S	COFFRE D'ARTISTE-PEINTRE
B140	BOX, ASH	BOITE A CENDRES
E400	BOX, ASTRINGENT	BOITE A ASTRINGENT
E400	BOX, ATOMIZER	BOITE A PULVERISATEUR
E400	BOX, AXLE WASHER	BOITE A RONDELLES D'ESSIEU
D060	BOX, BAIT	BOITE A APPATS
E400	BOX, BAKING SODA	BOITE A BICARBONATE DE SOUDE
E480	BOX, BALLOT	URNE ELECTORALE
E400	BOX, BANDAGE	BOITE A BANDAGES
E400	BOX, BEAD	BOITE A PERLES
E400	BOX, BELT	BOITE A CEINTURE
B080	BOX, BIBLE	COFFRET A BIBLE
E400	BOX, BISCUIT	BOITE A BISCUITS
E400	BOX, BONING KNIFE	BOITE A COUTEAU A DESOSSER
E400	BOX, BOOT POLISH	BOITE A CIRAGE A CHAUSSURES
C140	BOX, BOOTBLACKING	BOITE A CIRAGE
E400	BOX, BORACIC ACID	BOITE A ACIDE BORIQUE
D100	BOX, BREAD	BOITE A PAIN
E400	BOX, BREATH FRESHENER	BOITE A PURIFICATEUR D'HALEINE
E400	BOX, BUTTER	BOITE A BEURRE
E400	BOX, BUTTON	BOITE A BOUTONS
E400	BOX, BUTTON CARD	BOITE A CARTES DE BOUTONS
D100	BOX, CAKE	BOITE A GATEAU
E400	BOX, CAKE DECORATOR	BOITE A PISTON A DECORER
E400	BOX, CAKE MOLD	BOITE A MOULES A GATEAU
B100	BOX, CANDLE	BOITE A BOUGIES
E400	BOX, CANDLE	BOITE A BOUGIES
E400	BOX, CARD DECK	BOITE A JEU DE CARTES
D320	BOX, CARPENTER'S TOOL	BOITE A OUTILS DE MENUISIER
E400	BOX, CARTRIDGE	BOITE A CARTOUCHES
E180	BOX, CARTRIDGE	CARTOUCHIERE
E400	BOX, CARTRIDGE LOADING TOOL	BOITE A SERTISSEUR
E400	BOX, CARVING SET	BOITE A SERVICE A DECOUPER
F100	BOX, CASTING	CHASSIS DE MOULAGE
E400	BOX, CELERY SEED	BOITE A GRAINES DE CELERI
E400	BOX, CEREAL	BOITE A CEREALES
E400	BOX, CHALK	BOITE A CRAIES
F180	BOX, CHALK	BOITE A CRAIES
D100	BOX, CHEESE	BOITE A FROMAGE
E400	BOX, CHEESECLOTH	BOITE A ETAMINE
E400	BOX, CHEMICAL	BOITE A PRODUIT CHIMIQUE

Class. Code	Object, suffix	Objet, suffixe
E400	BOX, CHEWING GUM	BOITE A GOMMES A MACHER
E400	BOX, CIGAR	BOITE A CIGARES
E400	BOX, CIGARETTE	BOITE A CIGARETTES
B080	BOX, CIGARETTE	BOITE A CIGARETTES
E400	BOX, CIGARETTE PAPER	BOITE A PAPIER A CIGARETTES
E400	BOX, CINNAMON	BOITE A CANNELLE
E400	BOX, CITRIC ACID	BOITE A ACIDE CITRIQUE
E400	BOX, CLASP	BOITE A FERMOIRS
E400	BOX, CLEANSER	BOITE A POUDRE A NETTOYER
E400	BOX, CLOTHING	BOITE A VETEMENTS
E400	BOX, CLOTHING FASTENER	BOITE A AGRAFES POUR VETEMENTS
E400	BOX, CLOVE	BOITE A CLOUS DE GIROFLE
E400	BOX, COCOA	BOITE A CACAO
E400	BOX, COD LIVER OIL	BOITE A HUILE DE FOIE DE MORUE
E400	BOX, COFFEE	BOITE A CAFE
E400	BOX, COFFIN PLATE	BOITE A PLAQUES DE CERCUEIL
E400	BOX, COIN ENVELOPE	BOITE POUR ENVELOPPES A MONNAIE
E400	BOX, COLLAR	BOITE A COLS
E400	BOX, COLLAR & CUFF	BOITE A COL ET MANCHETTES
E400	BOX, COMB	BOITE A PEIGNES
H080	BOX, COMMEMORATIVE	COFFRET COMMEMORATIF
E400	BOX, CONFECTION	BOITE A CONFISERIES
E280	BOX, CONTROL	BOITE DE COMMANDE
E400	BOX, CORN STARCH	BOITE A FECULE DE MAIS
E400	BOX, CORSET	BOITE A CORSET
E400	BOX, COSMETIC	BOITE A COSMETIQUES
E400	BOX, COUGH DROP	BOITE A PASTILLES CONTRE LA TOUX
E400	BOX, CRAYON	BOITE A CRAYONS
E400	BOX, CREAM OF TARTAR	BOITE A CREME DE TARTRE
E400	BOX, CREAM SKIMMER	BOITE POUR ECUMOIRE A CREME
E400	BOX, CUFF	BOITE A MANCHETTES
E400	BOX, CURLER	BOITE A BIGOUDIS
E400	BOX, CURTAIN RING	BOITE A ANNEAUX DE RIDEAU
E400	BOX, CUSTARD	BOITE A CREME-DESSERT
E400	BOX, DANCE FLOOR WAX	BOITE POUR CIRE A PLANCHER DE DANSE
E400	BOX, DECONGESTANT	BOITE A DECONGESTIF
B080	BOX, DEED	COFFRET A DOCUMENTS
F120	BOX, DICTAPHONE CYLINDER	BOITE A CYLINDRE DE DICTAPHONE
E400	BOX, DINNER MIX	BOITE A PREPARATION POUR PLAT MINUTE
D100	BOX, DOUGH-RISING	BOITE DE FERMENTATION
E400	BOX, DRILL	BOITE A PERCEUSE
E400	BOX, DRILL BIT	BOITE A MECHES DE PERCEUSE
E400	BOX, DYE	BOITE A TEINTURE
E400	BOX, EMBALMING FLUID	BOITE A LIQUIDE D'EMBAUMEMENT
E400	BOX, ERASER	BOITE A GOMMES A EFFACER
E400	BOX, EYE CAP	BOITE A OEILLETON
E400	BOX, EYECUP	BOITE A OEILLERE
E400	BOX, EYEGLASSES	BOITE A LUNETTES
E400	BOX, EYEWASH	BOITE A COLLYRE
D040	BOX, FARRIER'S NAIL	BOITE A CLOUS DE MARECHAL-FERRANT
E400	BOX, FILE	BOITE A LIMES
F180	BOX, FILE	BOITE DE CLASSEMENT
E400	BOX, FILM	BOITE POUR FILM
E400	BOX, FISHHOOK	BOITE A HAMECONS
E400	BOX, FLASHLIGHT	BOITE A TORCHE ELECTRIQUE
E400	BOX, FLATWARE	BOITE A COUTELLERIE
E400	BOX, FLAVORING	BOITE A ESSENCE
E400	BOX, FLOUR	BOITE A FARINE
E400	BOX, FLYPAPER	BOITE A PAPIER ATTRAPE-MOUCHES
E400	BOX, FOOD COLORING	BOITE A COLORANT ALIMENTAIRE
D100	BOX, FOOD-STORAGE	BOITE D'ENTREPOSAGE DE NOURRITURE

THESAURUS – ALPHABETICAL

Class. Code	Object, suffix	Objet, suffixe
E400	BOX, FUNNEL	BOITE A ENTONNOIR
E400	BOX, GAITER	BOITE A GUETRES
I020	BOX, GAME	BOITE DE JEU
E400	BOX, GARTER	BOITE A JARRETIERES
E400	BOX, GELATIN	BOITE A GELATINE
E400	BOX, GINGER	BOITE A GINGEMBRE
E400	BOX, GLOVE	BOITE A GANTS
E400	BOX, GLUE	BOITE A COLLE
E400	BOX, GOGGLES FILTER	BOITE A FILTRE POUR LUNETTES DE PROTECTION
E400	BOX, GRAVY MIX	BOITE A PREPARATION POUR SAUCE BRUNE
E400	BOX, GREETING CARD	BOITE A CARTES DE VOEUX
E400	BOX, GUN GREASE	BOITE A GRAISSE DE FUSIL
E400	BOX, GUN WAD	BOITE A BOURRES DE FUSIL
E400	BOX, GUNPOWDER	BOITE A POUDRE A CANON
E400	BOX, HAIR CLIPPERS	BOITE A TONDEUSE A CHEVEUX
E400	BOX, HAIR TONIC	BOITE A TONIQUE CAPILLAIRE
E400	BOX, HAIRPIN	BOITE A EPINGLES A CHEVEUX
E400	BOX, HANDKERCHIEF	BOITE A MOUCHOIRS
E400	BOX, HARMONICA	BOITE A HARMONICA
E400	BOX, HAT	BOITE A CHAPEAU
E400	BOX, HOOK	BOITE A CROCHETS
E400	BOX, HOPS	BOITE A HOUBLON
E400	BOX, ICE CREAM MIX	BOITE POUR MELANGE A CREME GLACEE
E400	BOX, INK	BOITE POUR ENCRE
E400	BOX, INSECTICIDE	BOITE A INSECTICIDE
E400	BOX, INSTANT POTATO	BOITE A POMMES DE TERRE DESHYDRATEES
E400	BOX, JELLY	BOITE A GELEE
E400	BOX, JEWELRY	BOITE A BIJOUX
B080	BOX, JEWELRY	COFFRET A BIJOUX
D120	BOX, KNIFE	BOITE A COUTEAUX
E400	BOX, LABEL	BOITE A ETIQUETTES
E400	BOX, LAMP CHIMNEY	BOITE A VERRE DE LAMPE
E400	BOX, LAMP GLOBE	BOITE A GLOBE DE LAMPE
E400	BOX, LAMP MANTLE	BOITE A MANCHON DE LAMPE
E400	BOX, LANTERN	BOITE A LANTERNE
E400	BOX, LARD	BOITE A LARD
E400	BOX, LAUNDRY BLUEING	BOITE A BLEU DE LESSIVE
E400	BOX, LAUNDRY SOAP	BOITE A SAVON A LESSIVE
E400	BOX, LAXATIVE	BOITE A LAXATIF
E400	BOX, LEATHER DRESSING	BOITE POUR APPRET A CUIR
E400	BOX, LEMONADE	BOITE A LIMONADE
D100	BOX LID, CHEESE	COUVERCLE DE BOITE A FROMAGE
E400	BOX, LIGHT SOCKET	BOITE A DOUILLES
E400	BOX, LIGHTER FLINT	BOITE A PIERRES A BRIQUET
E400	BOX, LINEN MARKING SET	BOITE A TROUSSE DE MARQUAGE DU LINGE
E400	BOX, LINIMENT	BOITE A LINIMENT
D060	BOX, LOBSTER PEG	BOITE A CHEVILLES A HOMARD
E400	BOX, LUBRICATING GREASE	BOITE A GRAISSE LUBRIFIANTE
E400	BOX, LUBRICATING OIL	BOITE A HUILE LUBRIFIANTE
E400	BOX, LUGGAGE/SHAWL CARRIER	BOITE A PORTE-BAGAGES
H060	BOX, LUNULA	BOITE A LUNULE
F180	BOX, MARKING STAMP	BOITE A TAMPONS A ENCRER
D200	BOX, MASON'S TOOL	BOITE A OUTILS DE MACON
E400	BOX, MATCH	BOITE A ALLUMETTES
E400	BOX, MEAT EXTRACT	BOITE POUR EXTRAIT DE VIANDE
E400	BOX, MEAT TENDERIZER	BOITE POUR ATTENDRISSEUR A VIANDE
E400	BOX, MEDICINAL	BOITE A PRODUIT PHARMACEUTIQUE
E400	BOX, MEDICINAL SYRUP	BOITE A SIROP PHARMACEUTIQUE
E400	BOX, METAL POLISH	BOITE A PRODUIT A POLIR LE METAL
E180	BOX, MILITARY AMMUNITION	BOITE DE MUNITIONS MILITAIRE
B140	BOX, MILITARY ASH	BOITE A CENDRES MILITAIRE

138

Class. Code	Object, suffix	Objet, suffixe
E180	BOX, MILITARY CARTRIDGE	CARTOUCHIERE MILITAIRE
H080	BOX, MILITARY COMMEMORATIVE	COFFRET COMMEMORATIF MILITAIRE
E400	BOX, MILITARY FRICTION TUBE	BOITE A TUBES DE FRICTION MILITAIRE
E180	BOX, MILITARY FUSE	BOITE A FUSEE MILITAIRE
E400	BOX, MILITARY SIGHT	BOITE A MIRES MILITAIRE
E400	BOX, MILK	BOITE A LAIT
E400	BOX, MILK POWDER	BOITE A LAIT EN POUDRE
D100	BOX, MINIATURE SALT	BOITE A SEL MINIATURE
B080	BOX, MISSAL	COFFRET A MISSEL
D320	BOX, MITRE	BOITE A ONGLETS
E400	BOX, MITT	BOITE A MITAINES
E400	BOX, MONEY	COFFRET-CAISSE
E400	BOX, MOP	BOITE A VADROUILLE
E400	BOX, MUSTARD	BOITE A MOUTARDE
E400	BOX, NAIL	BOITE A CLOUS
E400	BOX, NAIL POLISH	BOITE A VERNIS A ONGLES
E400	BOX, NAPKIN	BOITE A SERVIETTES
E400	BOX, NASAL DOUCHE	BOITE POUR DOUCHE NASALE
E400	BOX, NECKTIE	BOITE A CRAVATES ETROITES
D300	BOX, NEEDLEWORK	COFFRET DE TRAVAIL A L'AIGUILLE
E400	BOX, NEWSPAPER CLIP	BOITE A PINCES A JOURNAL
E400	BOX, NOISEMAKER	BOITE A CRECELLES
E400	BOX, NURSING BOTTLE	BOITE A BIBERON
E400	BOX, NURSING BOTTLE NIPPLE	BOITE A TETINES DE BIBERON
E400	BOX, NUTMEG	BOITE A MUSCADE
E400	BOX, OINTMENT	BOITE A ONGUENT
E300	BOX, OUTLET	BOITE DE SORTIE
E400	BOX, PAINT	BOITE A PEINTURE
E400	BOX, PAPER CLIP	BOITE A PINCES A PAPIERS
E400	BOX, PASTA	BOITE A PATES ALIMENTAIRES
E400	BOX, PEANUT	BOITE A ARACHIDES
E400	BOX, PEN	BOITE A PLUMES
E400	BOX, PENCIL	BOITE A CRAYONS A MINE DE PLOMB
E400	BOX, PENCIL SHARPENER	BOITE POUR TAILLE-CRAYONS
E400	BOX, PEPPER	BOITE A POIVRE
E400	BOX, PERCUSSION CAP	BOITE A AMORCES
E400	BOX, PHONOGRAPH NEEDLE	BOITE A AIGUILLES DE PHONOGRAPHE
E400	BOX, PHOTOGRAPHIC DEVELOPER	BOITE POUR REVELATEUR
E400	BOX, PHOTOGRAPHIC FILM	BOITE A PELLICULES PHOTOGRAPHIQUE
E400	BOX, PHOTOGRAPHIC FIXER	BOITE POUR FIXATEUR
E400	BOX, PICTURE FRAME HANGER	BOITE A CROCHETS A CADRE
E400	BOX, PIGMENT	BOITE A PIGMENTS
E400	BOX, PILL	BOITE A PILULES
E400	BOX, PIPE FILTER	BOITE A FILTRES DE PIPE
E400	BOX, POCKET KNIFE	BOITE A COUTEAU DE POCHE
E180	BOX, POLICE CARTRIDGE	CARTOUCHIERE DE POLICE
E400	BOX, POPCORN	BOITE A MAIS SOUFFLE
E400	BOX, PORTABLE STOVE	BOITE A CUISINIERE PORTATIVE
E400	BOX, POULTRY GRIT	BOITE A GRAVIER POUR VOLAILLE
F180	BOX, POUNCE	POUDRIER
E400	BOX, PRESERVING JAR LINER	BOITE A DISQUES DE BOCAL A CONSERVE
E400	BOX, PRESERVING JAR SEAL	BOITE A JOINTS DE BOCAL A CONSERVE
E400	BOX, PRINTER'S LEADS	BOITE A PLOMBS D'IMPRIMERIE
E400	BOX, PRINTER'S TYPE	BOITE A CARACTERES D'IMPRIMERIE
C180	BOX, PUFF	BOITE A POUDRE
E400	BOX, RAISIN	BOITE A RAISINS SECS
E400	BOX, RAZOR	BOITE A RASOIRS
C180	BOX, RAZOR	ETUI A RASOIR
E400	BOX, RAZOR BLADE	BOITE A LAMES DE RASOIR
E400	BOX, RAZOR BLADE SHARPENER	BOITE A AFFILOIR DE LAMES DE RASOIR
H060	BOX, RELIGIOUS STATUE	COFFRE A STATUE RELIGIEUSE

Class. Code	Object, suffix	Objet, suffixe
E400	BOX, RESPIRATOR FILTER	BOITE A FILTRE DE MASQUE RESPIRATOIRE
E400	BOX, ROSIN	BOITE A COLOPHANE
E400	BOX, RUBBER BOOT	BOITE A COUVRE-CHAUSSURES
E400	BOX, SADIRON	BOITE A FER A REPASSER AVEC POIGNEE AMOVIBLE
D100	BOX, SALT	BOITE A SEL
E400	BOX, SALT	BOITE A SEL
E400	BOX, SAW JOINTER	BOITE A DRESSEUSE
E400	BOX, SAW-SET	BOITE A TOURNE-A-GAUCHE POUR SCIE
D320	BOX, SCREW	FILIERE A BOIS
E400	BOX, SCRUBBER	BOITE A LAVETTE METALLIQUE
E400	BOX, SEALING WAX	BOITE A CIRE A CACHETER
E400	BOX, SEED	BOITE A SEMENCES
E400	BOX, SELENIUM	BOITE A SELENIUM
A080	BOX, SENTRY	GUERITE
E400	BOX, SERUM	BOITE A SERUM
E400	BOX, SEWING SUPPLIES	BOITE A FOURNITURES DE COUTURE
H040	BOX, SHADOW	BOITE-CADRE
E400	BOX, SHAMPOO	BOITE A SHAMPOOING
E400	BOX, SHAVING SOAP	BOITE A SAVON A BARBE
G300	BOX, SHIP'S LOG	BOITE A JOURNAL DE BORD
E400	BOX, SHIRT	BOITE A CHEMISES
E400	BOX, SHOE	BOITE A SOULIERS
D040	BOX, SHOEING	BOITE DE CONTENTION
E400	BOX, SHROUD	BOITE A LINCEUL
E400	BOX, SHUTTLECOCK	BOITE A VOLANTS
F180	BOX, SIGNET	BOITE A SCEAUX
E400	BOX, SKATE	BOITE A PATINS A GLACE
E400	BOX, SKATE BLADE	BOITE A LAMES DE PATIN A GLACE
E400	BOX, SKIN LOTION	BOITE A LOTION POUR LA PEAU
D240	BOX, SLUICE	SLUICE
E400	BOX, SNUFF	BOITE A TABAC A PRISER
E400	BOX, SODA BISCUIT	BOITE A CRAQUELINS
E400	BOX, SOLDER FLUX	BOITE A FONDANT DE SOUDURE TENDRE
E400	BOX, SPARK PLUG	BOITE A BOUGIES D'ALLUMAGE
E400	BOX, SPICE	BOITE A EPICES
D100	BOX, SPICE	BOITE A EPICES
F180	BOX, STAMP	BOITE POUR TIMBRES-POSTE
E400	BOX, STAPLER	BOITE POUR AGRAFES
E400	BOX, STARCH	BOITE A EMPOIS
E400	BOX, STATIONERY	BOITE A PAPETERIE
E400	BOX, STOCKING	BOITE A BAS
E400	BOX, STORAGE	BOITE DE RANGEMENT
E400	BOX, STOVE MICA	BOITE A MICA DE POELE
E400	BOX, STOVE POLISH	BOITE A PATE A POLIR LE POELE
E400	BOX, STOVEPIPE COLLAR	BOITE A COLLETS DE TUYAU DE POELE
E400	BOX, STRAIGHT PIN	BOITE A EPINGLES DROITES
E400	BOX, STROP	BOITE POUR CUIR A RASOIR
E400	BOX, SUGAR	BOITE A SUCRE
E400	BOX, SUPPOSITORY	BOITE A SUPPOSITOIRES
E400	BOX, SUSPENDER	BOITE A BRETELLES
E400	BOX, SYRINGE	BOITE A SERINGUES
D060	BOX, TACKLE	BOITE A MOUCHES
E400	BOX, TALCUM POWDER	BOITE A POUDRE DE TALC
E400	BOX, TAPER	BOITE A BOUGIES FINES
E400	BOX, TEA	BOITE A THE
E400	BOX, TEAT DILATOR	BOITE A DILATANT DE TRAYON
E400	BOX, TEST TUBE	BOITE A TUBES A ESSAI
E400	BOX, THIMBLE	BOITE A DES
E400	BOX, THREAD	BOITE A FILS
E400	BOX, TISSUE	BOITE A MOUCHOIRS DE PAPIER
C160	BOX, TOBACCO	BOITE A TABAC

Class. Code	Object, suffix	Objet, suffixe
E400	BOX, TOBACCO	*BOITE A TABAC*
E400	BOX, TOILET BOTTLE	*BOITE A FLACON DE TOILETTE*
E400	BOX, TOILET SOAP	*BOITE A SAVON DE TOILETTE*
E400	BOX, TOILETRY SET	*BOITE POUR ENSEMBLE D'ARTICLES DE TOILETTE*
E400	BOX, TONIC	*BOITE A TONIQUE*
J060	BOX, TOOL	*BOITE A OUTILS*
E400	BOX, TOOTHBRUSH	*BOITE A BROSSE A DENTS*
E400	BOX, TOOTHPASTE	*BOITE A PATE DENTRIFICE*
E400	BOX, TOOTHPICK	*BOITE A CURE-DENTS*
B080	BOX, TRINKET	*COFFRET A COLIFICHETS*
I100	BOX, TRINKET	*COFFRET A COLIFICHETS*
E400	BOX, TYPEWRITER RIBBON	*BOITE A RUBAN DE MACHINE A ECRIRE*
E400	BOX, UNDERWEAR	*BOITE A SOUS-VETEMENTS*
E400	BOX, VALVE	*BOITE A VALVES*
E400	BOX, VAPORIZER	*BOITE A VAPORISATEUR*
E400	BOX, VARNISH	*BOITE A VERNIS*
E400	BOX, VEHICLE LIGHT SWITCH	*BOITE A COMMUTATEUR DE PHARE DE VEHICULE*
E400	BOX, VERMIFUGE	*BOITE A VERMIFUGE*
E400	BOX, VIOLIN STRING	*BOITE A CORDES DE VIOLON*
B080	BOX, WALL	*BOITE MURALE*
E400	BOX, WATCH	*BOITE A MONTRE*
E400	BOX, WELDING FLUX	*BOITE A FONDANT DE SOUDURE AUTOGENE*
E400	BOX, WHETSTONE	*BOITE A PIERRE A AIGUISER*
E400	BOX, WHITEWASH	*BOITE A BLANC DE CHAUX*
E400	BOX, WICK	*BOITE A MECHES DE LAMPE*
E400	BOX, WINDOW LIFT	*BOITE A GACHETTES DE FENETRE*
E400	BOX, WINE GLASS	*BOITE A VERRE A VIN*
E400	BOX, YEAST	*BOITE A LEVURE*
D320	BRACE	*VILEBREQUIN*
D220	BRACE	*VILEBREQUIN*
C020	BRACELET	*BRACELET*
A040	BRACKET	*SUPPORT*
B140	BRACKET, FIRESET	*CROCHET D'ENSEMBLE DE FOYER*
A040	BRACKET, MILITARY	*SUPPORT MILITAIRE*
B080	BRACKET, PICTURE FRAME	*SUPPORT DE CADRE*
B160	BRACKET, ROD	*SUPPORT DE TRINGLE A RIDEAU*
B160	BRACKET, SHADE	*SUPPORT DE STORE*
G300	BRACKET, SHIP'S BELL	*SUPPORT DE CLOCHE DE NAVIRE*
D100	BRACKET, TEAKETTLE	*CHEVRETTE*
D320	BRADAWL	*ALENE PLATE*
D220	BRAKE	*PLIEUSE*
C120	BRASSIERE	*SOUTIEN-GORGE*
F100	BRAYER	*BRAYON*
D100	BRAZIER	*BRASERO*
D300	BREAKER, FLAX	*BROIE POUR CHANVRE*
J060	BREAKER, ICE	*FOURCHE CASSE-GLACE*
D180	BREAKER, SEAT	*REDRESSEUR DE SIEGE DE TALONS*
E160	BREASTPLATE	*PLASTRON*
C100	BREECHES	*CULOTTE*
C100	BREECHES, CHILD'S	*CULOTTE D'ENFANT*
C100	BREECHES, MILITARY	*CULOTTE MILITAIRE*
C100	BREECHES, MILITARY RIDING	*CULOTTE D'EQUITATION MILITAIRE*
C100	BREECHES, POLICE RIDING	*CULOTTE D'EQUITATION DE POLICE*
G180	BREECHING	*AVALOIRE*
C020	BRELOQUE	*BRELOQUE*
H040	BRIC-A-BRAC	*BIBELOT*
A040	BRICK	*BRIQUE*
G180	BRIDLE	*BRIDE*
C160	BRIEFCASE	*SERVIETTE*
B140	BRIQUETTE	*BRIQUETTE*
D180	BRISTLE, SEWING	*SOIE*

Class. Code	Object, suffix	Objet, suffixe
D320	BROADAX	*DOLOIRE*
D320	BROADAX BLADE	*LAME DE DOLOIRE*
E080	BROADSWORD	*FORTE-EPEE*
E080	BROADSWORD, MILITARY	*FORTE-EPEE MILITAIRE*
E080	BROADSWORD TASSEL	*FRANGE DE FORTE-EPEE*
D100	BROILER	*GRIL*
C020	BROOCH	*BROCHE*
D040	BROODER, POULTRY	*ELEVEUSE POUR VOLAILLE*
E340	BROOM	*BALAI*
B140	BROOM, FIREPLACE	*BALAI DE FOYER*
E340	BROOM, MINIATURE	*BALAI MINIATURE*
E340	BROOM, WHISK	*EPOUSSETTE*
E340	BRUSH	*BROSSE*
J060	BRUSH	*BROSSE*
F100	BRUSH	*PINCEAU*
F180	BRUSH	*PINCEAU*
D040	BRUSH, ANIMAL	*BROSSE D'ANIMAL*
C140	BRUSH, CLOTHES	*BROSSE A VETEMENTS*
D220	BRUSH, FILE	*CARDE*
E340	BRUSH, FLUE	*HERISSON*
D100	BRUSH, FOOD	*BROSSE POUR NOURRITURE*
J060	BRUSH, GLUE	*PINCEAU A COLLE*
D260	BRUSH, GRAINING	*VEINETTE*
C180	BRUSH HANDLE, SHAVING	*MANCHE DE BLAIREAU*
C140	BRUSH, HAT	*BROSSE A CHAPEAUX*
D260	BRUSH, LETTERING	*PINCEAU A LETTRAGE*
D200	BRUSH, MASON'S	*BROSSE DE MACON*
D220	BRUSH, METAL	*BROSSE A METAL*
E180	BRUSH, MILITARY CANNON	*BROSSE A CHAMBRE DE CANON*
E180	BRUSH, MILITARY GUNNER'S	*FAUBERT MILITAIRE*
E340	BRUSH, MILITARY SCRUB	*BROSSE A RECURAGE MILITAIRE*
C180	BRUSH, NAIL	*BROSSE A ONGLES*
D260	BRUSH, PAINT	*PINCEAU*
D100	BRUSH, PASTRY	*PINCEAU A PATISSERIE*
E340	BRUSH, POLISH	*BROSSE A POLIR*
E340	BRUSH, SCRUB	*BROSSE A RECURAGE*
C180	BRUSH, SHAVING	*BLAIREAU*
C140	BRUSH, SHOE	*BROSSE A CHAUSSURES*
E380	BRUSH, TREPANNING	*BROSSE POUR TREPANATION*
D260	BRUSH, WALLPAPER	*PINCEAU A ENCOLLER*
J060	BRUSH, WIRE	*BROSSE A METAL*
G120	BUCKBOARD	*CHARIOT AMERICAIN*
D060	BUCKET, BAIT	*SEAU A APPATS*
D240	BUCKET, DRAGLINE	*BENNE A TRACTION*
E480	BUCKET, FIRE	*SEAU A INCENDIE*
E180	BUCKET, MILITARY	*BAQUET MILITAIRE*
E180	BUCKET, MILITARY LANCE	*BOTTE DE LANCE MILITAIRE*
E180	BUCKET, MILITARY SADDLE	*ETUI A CARABINE DE CAVALERIE MILITAIRE*
E180	BUCKET, MINIATURE MILITARY	*BAQUET MILITAIRE MINIATURE*
E180	BUCKET, POLICE SADDLE	*ETUI A CARABINE DE POLICE*
D140	BUCKET, SAP	*SEAU A SEVE*
G020	BUCKET, WELL	*SEAU DE PUITS*
D240	BUCKETLINE	*CORDE DE GODET AVEC CROCHET*
C140	BUCKLE	*BOUCLE*
G180	BUCKLE, COMMON-ROLLER	*BOUCLE A ROULEAU ET ARDILLON*
G180	BUCKLE, CONWAY	*BOUCLE DE SANGLE CAMBREE*
G180	BUCKLE, HALTER	*BOUCLE DE LICOU A BARRETTE*
G180	BUCKLE, LOOP	*BOUCLE DE SANGLE A BARRETTE SURELEVEE*
H120	BUCKLE, MILITARY	*BOUCLE MILITAIRE*
H120	BUCKLE, POLICE	*BOUCLE DE POLICE*
G180	BUCKLE, ROLLER-AND-LOOP	*BOUCLE DOUBLE CAMBREE A ROULEAU ET ARDILLON*

Class. Code	Object, suffix	Objet, suffixe
D140	BUCKSAW	SCIE DE LONG
C180	BUFFER	POLISSOIR
C140	BUFFER, BUTTON	POLISSOIR A BOUTONS
D040	BUFFER, HOOF	COUPE-RIVET DE MARECHAL-FERRANT
C140	BUFFER, SHOE	POLISSOIR A CHAUSSURES
F060	BUGLE	CLAIRON
F060	BUGLE, MILITARY	CLAIRON MILITAIRE
F060	BUGLE MOUTHPIECE	EMBOUCHURE DE CLAIRON
F060	BUGLE, POLICE	CLAIRON DE POLICE
A020	BUILDING, MODEL OFFICE	IMMEUBLE A BUREAUX MODELE REDUIT
B100	BULB, LIGHT	AMPOULE ELECTRIQUE
E140	BULLET	BALLE
H060	BUNDLE, MEDICINE	SAC A MEDECINE
D320	BUNGSTART	TAPETTE
C100	BUNTING	NID D'ANGE
D060	BUOY, LOSBTER POT	BOUEE DE CASIER A HOMARD
G300	BUOY, MOORING	BOUEE D'AMARRAGE
F160	BUOY, SIGNAL	BOUEE DE SIGNALISATION
E240	BURNER, BUNSEN	BRULEUR BUNSEN
B080	BURNER, INCENSE	CASSOLETTE
D220	BURNISHER	POLISSOIR
D180	BURNISHER, STRIP	BRUNISSOIR DE BANDE
H060	BURSE	BOURSE
D200	BUSHHAMMER	BOUCHARDE
H040	BUST	BUSTE
H080	BUST, COMMEMORATIVE	BUSTE COMMEMORATIF
C120	BUSTLE	TOURNURE
E340	BUTLER, SILENT	RAMASSE-MIETTES
C140	BUTTON	BOUTON
H120	BUTTON	BOUTON
H120	BUTTON, MILITARY	BOUTON MILITAIRE
H120	BUTTON, POLICE	BOUTON DE POLICE
C140	BUTTONHOOK	TIRE-BOUTON
B060	CABINET	MEUBLE DE RANGEMENT
B060	CABINET, CHINA	ARMOIRE A PORCELAINE
B060	CABINET, CORNER	ENCOIGNURE
B060	CABINET, DISPLAY	ARMOIRE-VITRINE
B060	CABINET, FILING	CLASSEUR
D100	CABINET, FOOD-STORAGE	GARDE-MANGER
B060	CABINET, HANGING	ARMOIRE MURALE
B060	CABINET, KEY	ARMOIRE A CLES
A040	CABINET, MEDICINE	ARMOIRE A PHARMACIE
B060	CABINET, PHONOGRAPH	BOITIER DE PHONOGRAPHE
B060	CABINET, PHONOGRAPH/RADIO	BOITIER DE PHONOGRAPHE/RADIO
B060	CABINET, POLICE HANGING	MEUBLE FIXE DE RANGEMENT DE POLICE
B060	CABINET, RADIO	COFFRE DE RADIO
F100	CABINET, TYPE CASE	RANG
E280	CABLE, ELECTRICAL	CABLE ELECTRIQUE
F140	CABLE, SUBMARINE	CABLE SOUS-MARIN
F140	CABLE, SUBMARINE INSTRUCTIONAL MODEL	CABLE SOUS-MARIN MODELE D'INSTRUCTION
B080	CACHEPOT	CACHE-POT
D100	CADDY	BOITE A THE
H080	CADDY, COMMEMORATIVE	BOITE A THE COMMEMORATIVE
I100	CAGE, ANIMAL	CAGE A ANIMAL
F020	CALCULATOR	CALCULATRICE
D100	CALDRON	CHAUDRON
D100	CALDRON, MINIATURE	CHAUDRON MINIATURE
D680	CALDRON, POTASH	CHAUDRON A POTASSE
D100	CALDRON HANDLE	POIGNEE DE CHAUDRON
H080	CALENDAR	CALENDRIER
E560	CALIPERS, DOUBLE	COMPAS A DOUBLE FONCTION

Class. Code	Object, suffix	Objet, suffixe
E560	CALIPERS, INSIDE	COMPAS D'INTERIEUR
E180	CALIPERS, MILITARY GUNNER'S	CALIBRE D'ARTILLEUR MILITAIRE
E560	CALIPERS, OUTSIDE	COMPAS D'EPAISSEUR
D140	CALIPERS, TIMBER	COMPAS FORESTIER
E180	CALL, GAME	CORNE DE CHASSE
E180	CALTROP	CHAUSSE-TRAPPE
H060	CALUMET	CALUMET
F080	CAMERA	APPAREIL-PHOTO
F080	CAMERA, BOX	APPAREIL-PHOTO RIGIDE
F080	CAMERA, FOLDING	APPAREIL-PHOTO PLIANT
F080	CAMERA, OBSCURA	CHAMBRE NOIRE
C120	CAMISOLE	CAMISOLE
G020	CAN	BOITE A CONSERVE
E400	CAN, ANCHOVY	BOITE DE CONSERVE A ANCHOIS
E400	CAN, APPLE	BOITE DE CONSERVE A POMMES
E400	CAN, APPLESAUCE	BOITE DE CONSERVE A COMPOTE DE POMMES
E400	CAN, APRICOT	BOITE DE CONSERVE A ABRICOTS
E400	CAN, ARTICHOKE	BOITE DE CONSERVE A ARTICHAUTS
E400	CAN, ASBESTOS	BOITE DE CONSERVE A ASBESTE
E400	CAN, ASPARAGUS	BOITE DE CONSERVE A ASPERGES
E400	CAN, BEAN	BOITE DE CONSERVE A FEVES
E400	CAN, BEEF	BOITE DE CONSERVE A BOEUF
E400	CAN, BEET	BOITE DE CONSERVE A BETTERAVES
E400	CAN, BELT DRESSING	BOITE DE CONSERVE D'APPRET DE COURROIE
E400	CAN, CABBAGE	BOITE DE CONSERVE A CHOUX
E400	CAN, CARROT	BOITE DE CONSERVE A CAROTTES
E400	CAN, CAULIFLOWER	BOITE DE CONSERVE A CHOUX-FLEURS
E400	CAN, CAUSTIC SODA	BOITE DE CONSERVE A SOUDE CAUSTIQUE
E400	CAN, CHERRY	BOITE DE CONSERVE A CERISES
E400	CAN, CHICKEN	BOITE DE CONSERVE A POULET
E400	CAN, CHILI CON CARNE	BOITE DE CONSERVE A CHILI CON CARNE
E400	CAN, COFFEE	BOITE DE CONSERVE A CAFE
E400	CAN, CONDENSED MILK	BOITE DE CONSERVE A LAIT CONDENSE
E400	CAN, CORN	BOITE DE CONSERVE A MAIS
D100	CAN, CREAM	BIDON A CREME
E400	CAN, CREAM	BOITE DE CONSERVE A CREME
E400	CAN, EVAPORATED MILK	BOITE DE CONSERVE A LAIT EVAPORE
E400	CAN, FRUIT	BOITE DE CONSERVE A FRUITS
E400	CAN, GOULASH	BOITE DE CONSERVE A GOULASCH
E400	CAN, GRAPE	BOITE DE CONSERVE A RAISINS
E400	CAN, HAM	BOITE DE CONSERVE A JAMBON
E400	CAN, JAM	BOITE DE CONSERVE A CONFITURE
E340	CAN, KEROSENE	BIDON A PETROLE
E400	CAN, LOBSTER	BOITE DE CONSERVE A HOMARDS
E400	CAN, LUBRICATING GREASE	BOITE DE CONSERVE A GRAISSE LUBRIFIANTE
E400	CAN, LUNCHEON MEAT	BOITE DE CONSERVE A PAIN DE VIANDE
E400	CAN, MEAT BALL	BOITE DE CONSERVE A BOULETTES DE VIANDE
G180	CAN, MILITARY FUEL	BIDON A COMBUSTIBLE MILITAIRE
D100	CAN, MILK	BIDON A LAIT
E400	CAN, MILK POWDER	BOITE DE CONSERVE A LAIT EN POUDRE
E400	CAN, MIXED VEGETABLES	BOITE DE CONSERVE A MACEDOINE DE LEGUMES
E400	CAN, NUT	BOITE DE CONSERVE A NOIX
E400	CAN, ONION FLAKE	BOITE DE CONSERVE A FLOCONS D'OIGNON
E400	CAN, PAINT	BOITE DE CONSERVE A PEINTURE
E400	CAN, PEA	BOITE DE CONSERVE A POIS
E400	CAN, PEACH	BOITE DE CONSERVE A PECHES
E400	CAN, PEAR	BOITE DE CONSERVE A POIRES
E400	CAN, PINEAPPLE	BOITE DE CONSERVE A ANANAS
E400	CAN, PLUM	BOITE DE CONSERVE A PRUNEAUX
E400	CAN, PORK	BOITE DE CONSERVE A PORC
E400	CAN, POTATO	BOITE DE CONSERVE A POMMES DE TERRE

Class. Code	Object, suffix	Objet, suffixe
E400	CAN, RASPBERRY	*BOITE DE CONSERVE A FRAMBOISES*
E400	CAN, SALMON	*BOITE DE CONSERVE A SAUMON*
E400	CAN, SARDINE	*BOITE DE CONSERVE A SARDINES*
E400	CAN, SAUERKRAUT	*BOITE DE CONSERVE A CHOUCROUTE*
E400	CAN, SOUP	*BOITE DE CONSERVE A SOUPE*
E400	CAN, SPAGHETTI SAUCE	*BOITE DE CONSERVE A SAUCE A SPAGHETTI*
E400	CAN, SPINACH	*BOITE DE CONSERVE A EPINARDS*
E400	CAN, STRAWBERRY	*BOITE DE CONSERVE A FRAISES*
E400	CAN, TOMATO	*BOITE DE CONSERVE A TOMATES*
E400	CAN, TOMATO JUICE	*BOITE DE CONSERVE A JUS DE TOMATE*
E340	CAN, TRASH	*POUBELLE*
E400	CAN, TURNIP	*BOITE DE CONSERVE A NAVETS*
E400	CAN, VARNISH	*BOITE DE CONSERVE A VERNIS*
D020	CAN, WATERING	*ARROSOIR*
B080	CAN, WATERING	*ARROSOIR*
B100	CANDELABRUM	*CANDELABRE*
H060	CANDELABRUM	*CANDELABRE*
B100	CANDLE	*BOUGIE*
H060	CANDLE, BIRTHDAY CAKE	*BOUGIE A GATEAU*
H060	CANDLE, RELIGIOUS	*CIERGE*
B100	CANDLESNUFFER	*MOUCHETTES*
B100	CANDLESNUFFER & TRAY	*MOUCHETTES ET PLATEAU*
B060	CANDLESTAND	*TABLE DE SUPPORT A BOUGIES*
B100	CANDLESTICK	*CHANDELIER*
H060	CANDLESTICK	*CHANDELIER*
B100	CANDLESTICK, MILITARY	*CHANDELIER MILITAIRE*
B100	CANDLESTICK, MINER'S	*BOUGEOIR DE MINEUR*
B100	CANDLESTICK, MINIATURE	*CHANDELIER MINIATURE*
C160	CANE	*CANNE*
D100	CANISTER	*BOITE DE RANGEMENT*
D100	CANISTER, BAKING POWDER	*BOITE DE RANGEMENT A LEVURE CHIMIQUE*
D100	CANISTER, BARLEY	*BOITE DE RANGEMENT A ORGE*
D100	CANISTER, COCOA	*BOITE DE RANGEMENT A CACAO*
D100	CANISTER, COFFEE	*BOITE DE RANGEMENT A CAFE*
D100	CANISTER, FLOUR	*BOITE DE RANGEMENT A FARINE*
D100	CANISTER, MILK POWDER	*BOITE DE RANGEMENT A LAIT EN POUDRE*
D100	CANISTER, NUT	*BOITE DE RANGEMENT A NOIX*
D100	CANISTER, RICE	*BOITE DE RANGEMENT A RIZ*
D100	CANISTER, SUGAR	*BOITE DE RANGEMENT A SUCRE*
D100	CANISTER, TEA	*BOITE DE RANGEMENT A THE*
I100	CANNON	*CANON*
E120	CANNON	*CANON*
E140	CANNONBALL	*BOULET DE CANON*
E140	CANNONBALL, MILITARY	*BOULET DE CANON MILITAIRE*
G280	CANOE	*CANOT*
I100	CANOE	*CANOT*
G280	CANOE, DUGOUT	*PIROGUE*
G280	CANOE, ICE	*CANOT A GLACE*
G280	CANOE, MINIATURE	*CANOT MINIATURE*
G280	CANOE, MODEL	*CANOT MODELE REDUIT*
G280	CANOE, MODEL DUGOUT	*PIROGUE MODELE REDUIT*
G280	CANOE, MODEL ICE	*CANOT A GLACE MODELE REDUIT*
B020	CANOPY	*BALDAQUIN*
C160	CANTEEN	*GOURDE*
C160	CANTEEN, MILITARY	*GOURDE MILITAIRE*
B060	CANTERBURY	*CASIER A MUSIQUE*
D140	CANTHOOK HANDLE	*MANCHE DE TOURNE-BILLES*
C080	CAP	*CASQUETTE*
I100	CAP	*CASQUETTE*
C080	CAP, BATHING	*BONNET DE BAIN*
B080	CAP, BOTTLE	*CAPSULE DE BOUTEILLE*

Class. Code	Object, suffix	Objet, suffixe
C080	CAP, BOUDOIR	BONNET DE LINGERIE
C080	CAP, FORAGE	KEPI
C080	CAP, MILITARY	CALOT MILITAIRE
E140	CAP, MILITARY FUSE	COIFFE DE FUSEE MILITAIRE
E180	CAP, PERCUSSION	AMORCE
C080	CAP, POLICE	CALOT DE POLICE
D100	CAP, PRESERVING JAR	COUVERCLE DE BOCAL A CONSERVE
C080	CAP, SMOKING	CALOTTE GRECQUE
E180	CAP, SNAP	AMORCE A PRESSION
E280	CAPACITOR, ELECTROLYTIC	CONDENSATEUR ELECTROMAGNETIQUE
C100	CAPE	CAPE
H120	CAPE	CAPE
C100	CAPE, MILITARY	CAPE MILITAIRE
C100	CAPOTE	CAPOTE
D100	CAPPER, BOTTLE	CAPSULATEUR
G300	CAPSTAN	CABESTAN
D060	CAPSTAN	CABESTAN
G300	CAPSTAN, MINIATURE	CABESTAN MINIATURE
D240	CAR, MINE	BERLINE
D240	CAR WHEEL, MINE	ROUE DE BERLINE
D120	CARAFE	CARAFE
E060	CARBINE	MOUSQUETON
E060	CARBINE, MILITARY BREECHLOAD	MOUSQUETON A CHARGEMENT PAR LA CULASSE MILITAIRE
E060	CARBINE, MILITARY CENTER-FIRE	MOUSQUETON A PERCUSSION CENTRALE MILITAIRE
E060	CARBINE, MILITARY FLINTLOCK	MOUSQUETON A SILEX MILITAIRE
E060	CARBINE, MILITARY PERCUSSION	MOUSQUETON A PERCUSSION MILITAIRE
E060	CARBINE, MILITARY RIM-FIRE	MOUSQUETON A PERCUSSION ANNULAIRE MILITAIRE
E060	CARBINE BREECH MECHANISM	BLOC DE CULASSE DE MOUSQUETON
G020	CARBOY	BONBONNE
E400	CARBOY, LUBRICATING OIL	BONBONNE A HUILE LUBRIFIANTE
H060	CARD, ALTAR	CANON D'AUTEL
H080	CARD, BASEBALL	CARTE DE BASEBALL
E400	CARD, BUCKLE	CARTE DE BOUCLES
E400	CARD, BUTTON	CARTE DE BOUTONS
H080	CARD, CALLING	CARTE D'ADRESSE
E400	CARD, CLOTHING FASTENER	CARTE D'AGRAFES POUR VETEMENTS
H080	CARD, COMMUNION	CARTE DE PREMIERE COMMUNION
H080	CARD, DANCE	CARNET DE BAL
E400	CARD, FISHHOOK	CARTE D'HAMECONS
I020	CARD, GAME	CARTE DE JEU
H080	CARD, GREETING	CARTE DE VOEUX
F180	CARD, GREETING	CARTE DE VOEUX
E400	CARD, HAIRPIN	CARTE D'EPINGLES A CHEVEUX
D300	CARD, HAND	CARDE
E400	CARD, HANDKERCHIEF	CARTE DE MOUCHOIRS
E400	CARD, HATPIN	CARTE D'EPINGLES A CHAPEAU
H080	CARD, IDENTIFICATION	CARTE D'IDENTITE
H080	CARD, INDEX	FICHE
H080	CARD, MEMBERSHIP	CARTE DE MEMBRE
H080	CARD, MOURNING	FAIRE-PART DE DECES
E400	CARD, PEN	CARTE DE PLUMES
H060	CARD, PRAYER	CARTE DE PRIERES
E400	CARD, RIBBON	CARTE DE RUBANS
E400	CARD, SEWING SUPPLIES	CARTE DE FOURNITURES DE COUTURE
E400	CARD, STRAIGHT PIN	CARTE D'EPINGLES DROITES
F180	CARD, SYMPATHY	CARTE DE CONDOLEANCES
H080	CARD, TALLY	CARTE DE POINTAGE
F180	CARD, TIME CLOCK	CARTE D'HORODATEUR
H020	CARD, TRADE	CARTE PROFESSIONNELLE
B040	CARPET	MOQUETTE
G120	CARRIAGE	VOITURE

Class. Code	Object, suffix	Objet, suffixe
I100	CARRIAGE	*VOITURE*
E180	CARRIAGE, ARTILLERY SLING	*TRIQUEBALLE D'ARTILLERIE*
E120	CARRIAGE AXLE PIN, CANNON	*AXE D'AFFUT DE CANON*
E120	CARRIAGE AXLE WASHER, CANNON	*RONDELLE D'ESSIEU D'AFFUT DE CANON*
G140	CARRIAGE, BABY	*LANDAU DE BEBE*
I100	CARRIAGE, DOLL	*CAROSSE DE POUPEE*
E120	CARRIAGE, MILITARY CANNON	*AFFUT DE CANON MILITAIRE*
G120	CARRIAGE STEP	*MARCHEPIED DE VOITURE*
E120	CARRIAGE WHEEL, MILITARY CANNON	*ROUE D'AFFUT DE CANON MILITAIRE*
D100	CARRIER, BOTTLE	*PORTE-BOUTEILLES*
B140	CARRIER, EMBER	*PORTE-BRAISE*
B140	CARRIER, LOG	*PORTE-BUCHES*
C160	CARRIER, LUGGAGE/SHAWL	*PORTE-BAGAGES*
E400	CARRIER, MONEY	*PORTE-MONNAIE*
D220	CARRIER, WHETSTONE	*COFFIN*
E120	CARRONADE	*CARONADE*
E120	CARRONADE, MINIATURE	*CARONADE MINIATURE*
I100	CART	*CHARRETTE*
G120	CART	*CHARRETTE*
G120	CART, DOG	*CHARRETTE A CHIEN*
G120	CART, TIP	*CHARIOT A BASCULE*
G120	CART SHAFT	*LIMON DE CHARRETTE*
H080	CARTE-DE-VISITE	*CARTE DE VISITE*
H080	CARTE-DE-VISITE, MILITARY	*CARTE DE VISITE MILITAIRE*
G020	CARTON	*CARTON*
E400	CARTON, ANALGESIC	*CARTON A ANALGESIQUE*
E400	CARTON, BUTTER	*CARTON A BEURRE*
E400	CARTON, CANNED FOOD	*CARTON A ALIMENTS EN CONSERVE*
E400	CARTON, CHALK	*CARTON A CRAIES*
E400	CARTON, CIGARETTE	*CARTON A CIGARETTES*
E400	CARTON, CIGARETTE PAPER	*CARTON A PAPIER A CIGARETTES*
E400	CARTON, COFFEE	*CARTON A CAFE*
E400	CARTON, COLLAR STAY	*CARTON A SUPPORTS A COL*
E400	CARTON, CONDENSED MILK	*CARTON A LAIT CONDENSE*
E400	CARTON, CONFECTION	*CARTON A CONFISERIES*
E400	CARTON, EGG	*CARTON A OEUFS*
E400	CARTON, EVAPORATED MILK	*CARTON A LAIT EVAPORE*
E400	CARTON, HOOPS	*CARTON A HOUBLON*
E400	CARTON, KETCHUP	*CARTON A KETCHUP*
E400	CARTON, LIGHTER FLINT	*CARTON A PIERRES A BRIQUET*
E400	CARTON, LIME JUICE	*CARTON A JUS DE LIMETTE*
E400	CARTON, MILK POWDER	*CARTON A LAIT EN POUDRE*
E400	CARTON PANEL, EVAPORATED MILK	*PANNEAU DE CARTON A LAIT EVAPORE*
E400	CARTON, PASTA	*CARTON A PATES ALIMENTAIRES*
E400	CARTON, PEPPER	*CARTON A POIVRE*
E400	CARTON, RENNET	*CARTON A PRESURE*
E400	CARTON, SKIN LOTION	*CARTON A LOTION POUR LA PEAU*
E400	CARTON, SPONGE	*CARTON A EPONGES*
E400	CARTON, STOVE POLISH	*CARTON A PATE A POLIR LE POELE*
E400	CARTON, TOILET SOAP	*CARTON A SAVONS DE TOILETTE*
E400	CARTON, TOOTHPASTE	*CARTON A PATE DENTIFRICE*
E400	CARTON, VACUUM BOTTLE	*CARTON A BOUTEILLE ISOLANTE*
E140	CARTRIDGE	*CARTOUCHE*
E140	CARTRIDGE, BAG	*GARGOUSSE*
E140	CARTRIDGE CASE	*DOUILLE DE CARTOUCHE*
E140	CARTRIDGE, CASELESS	*CARTOUCHE SANS DOUILLE*
E140	CARTRIDGE, CENTER-FIRE	*CARTOUCHE A PERCUSSION CENTRALE*
E140	CARTRIDGE, MINIATURE BAG	*GARGOUSSE MINIATURE*
G020	CASE	*ETUI*
E080	CASE, ARROW	*ETUI A FLECHES*
E180	CASE, ARTILLERY CARTRIDGE	*GARGOUSSIER D'ARTILLERIE*

Class. Code	Object, suffix	Objet, suffixe
E500	CASE, ASTROLABE	*ETUI A ASTROLABE DE MARIN*
F060	CASE, BASS VIOL	*BOITE A CONTREBASSE*
E460	CASE, BINOCULARS	*ETUI A JUMELLES*
D320	CASE, BIT	*ETUI A MECHES*
D140	CASE, BUCKSAW	*COFFRE A SCIE DE LONG*
H060	CASE, CALUMET	*ETUI A CALUMET*
F080	CASE, CAMERA	*ETUI A APPAREIL-PHOTO*
C160	CASE, CARD	*PORTE-CARTES*
H060	CASE, CHALICE	*BOITE A CALICE*
H060	CASE, CIBORIUM	*BOITE A CIBOIRE*
C160	CASE, CIGAR	*PORTE-CIGARES*
C160	CASE, CIGAR HOLDER	*ETUI A FUME-CIGARE*
C160	CASE, CIGARETTE	*PORTE-CIGARETTES*
C160	CASE, CLOTHES BRUSH	*ETUI A BROSSE A VETEMENTS*
C160	CASE, COLLAR	*BOITE A COLS*
E400	CASE, COLLAR	*ETUI A COLS*
E400	CASE, COLLAR & CUFF	*ETUI A COL ET MANCHETTES*
C180	CASE, COMPACT	*ETUI A POUDRIER*
D300	CASE, CROCHET HOOK	*ETUI DE CROCHETS POUR TRAVAIL AU CROCHET*
E400	CASE, CUFF	*ETUI A MANCHETTES*
H080	CASE, DAGUERREOTYPE	*ETUI A DAGUERREOTYPE*
E400	CASE, DISPLAY	*MONTRE D'ETALAGE*
B080	CASE, DISPLAY	*VITRINE D'EXPOSITION*
F180	CASE, DOCUMENT	*PORTE-DOCUMENTS*
E400	CASE, DOILY	*ETUI A NAPPERONS*
B080	CASE, DOILY	*POCHETTE A NAPPERONS*
B060	CASE, DRESSING	*NECESSAIRE DE VOYAGE*
C160	CASE, EAR TRUMPET	*ETUI A CORNET ACOUSTIQUE*
B100	CASE, ELECTRIC LAMP	*ETUI A LAMPE ELECTRIQUE*
C160	CASE, EYEGLASSES	*ETUI A LUNETTES*
F100	CASE, FILLET	*CASSEAU A FILETS*
D060	CASE, FISHING ROD	*ETUI A CANNE A PECHE*
D120	CASE, FLATWARE	*ETUI A COUTELLERIE*
C160	CASE, GLOVE	*ETUI A GANTS*
E180	CASE, GUN	*ETUI A FUSIL*
E180	CASE, GUNPOWDER	*BOITE DE POUDRE A CANON*
C160	CASE, HANDKERCHIEF	*POCHETTE A MOUCHOIRS DE POCHE*
F120	CASE, INTERCOM	*BOITE A INTERPHONE*
C160	CASE, JEWELRY	*ETUI A BIJOUX*
E400	CASE, JEWELRY	*ETUI A BIJOUX*
C160	CASE, KEY	*ETUI A PORTE-CLEFS*
D300	CASE, KNITTING NEEDLE	*ETUI A AIGUILLES A TRICOTER*
H080	CASE, MAP	*PORTE-CARTES*
H120	CASE, MEDAL	*COFFRET A MEDAILLES*
C160	CASE, MEDICINE	*TROUSSE DE SOINS MEDICAUX*
C160	CASE, MEDICINE BOTTLE	*ETUI A FLACON DE MEDICAMENT*
E460	CASE, MILITARY BINOCULARS	*ETUI A JUMELLES MILITAIRE*
E400	CASE, MILITARY CARTRIDGE	*CAISSETTE A CARTOUCHES MILITAIRE*
H120	CASE, MILITARY EPAULET	*BOITE D'EPAULETTE MILITAIRE*
F060	CASE, MILITARY FIFE	*ETUI A FIFRE MILITAIRE*
E180	CASE, MILITARY GUN	*ETUI A FUSIL MILITAIRE*
E180	CASE, MILITARY GUNNER'S QUADRANT	*ETUI A NIVEAU DE POINTAGE D'ARTILLEUR MILITAIRE*
D300	CASE, MILITARY NEEDLEWORK	*ETUI DE COUTURE MILITAIRE*
H120	CASE, MILITARY PRESENTATION SWORD	*ETUI A EPEE D'HONNEUR MILITAIRE*
C160	CASE, MILITARY SABRETACHE	*BOITE A SABRETACHE MILITAIRE*
H120	CASE, MILITARY SHAKO PLUME	*ETUI A PLUMETS DE SHAKO MILITAIRE*
E080	CASE, MILITARY SWORD	*ETUI A EPEE MILITAIRE*
C160	CASE, MIRROR	*ETUI A MIROIR*
H060	CASE, MONSTRANCE	*BOITE A OSTENSOIR*
D120	CASE, NAPKIN	*HOUSSE A SERVIETTES DE TABLE*
D300	CASE, NEEDLE	*ETUI A AIGUILLES*

Class. Code	Object, suffix	Objet, suffixe
E400	CASE, NEEDLE	ETUI A AIGUILLES
D300	CASE, NEEDLEWORK	ETUI DE TRAVAIL A L'AIGUILLE
C160	CASE, NIGHTGOWN	POCHETTE A ROBE DE NUIT
F180	CASE, PEN	PLUMIER
F180	CASE, PENCIL	PORTE-CRAYONS
F180	CASE, PENCIL LEAD	ETUI A MINES DE PLOMB
C160	CASE, PHOTOGRAPH	PORTE-PHOTOS
D300	CASE, PIN	ETUI A EPINGLES
C160	CASE, PIPE	ETUI A PIPE
E380	CASE, PNEUMOTHORAX APPARATUS	ETUI D'APPAREIL PNEUMOTHORAX
H120	CASE, POLICE HELMET PLUME	ETUI A PLUMETS DE CASQUE DE POLICE
D180	CASE, PUNCH	ETUI A POINCONS
H120	CASE, ROSARY BEADS	ETUI A CHAPELET
D300	CASE, SCISSORS	ETUI A CISEAUX
F180	CASE, SEALING WAX	ETUI A CIRE A CACHETER
E500	CASE, SEXTANT	ETUI A SEXTANT
C180	CASE, SHAVING BRUSH	ETUI A BLAIREAU
E400	CASE, SHOELACE SALES-SAMPLE	BOITE D'ECHANTILLONS DE LACETS DE SOULIER
F020	CASE, SLIDE RULE	ETUI A REGLE A CALCUL
C160	CASE, SLIPPER	ETUI A PANTOUFLES
C180	CASE, SOAP	ETUI A SAVON
E380	CASE, SPECIMEN	BOITE POUR ECHANTILLONS D'ANALYSES
C160	CASE, STOCKING	POCHETTE A BAS
E400	CASE, STOVE POLISH	ETUI A PATE A POLIR LE POELE
C160	CASE, STUD	BOITE A BOUTONS DE COL
E380	CASE, SURGICAL INSTRUMENT	BOITE A INSTRUMENTS DE CHIRURGIE
F140	CASE, TELEPHONE BATTERY	BOITE A BATTERIES DE TELEPHONE
C160	CASE, THERMOMETER	ETUI A THERMOMETRE
D300	CASE, THREAD	ETUI A FILS
C160	CASE, TIE	POCHETTE A CRAVATES
C180	CASE, TOILET BOTTLE	ETUI A FLACON DE TOILETTE
C180	CASE, TOOTHBRUSH	ETUI A BROSSE A DENTS
E500	CASE, TRANSIT	ETUI DE CERCLE D'ARPENTEUR
F100	CASE, TYPE	CASE
F180	CASE, TYPEWRITER	MALLETTE DE MACHINE A ECRIRE
C160	CASE, VACUUM BOTTLE	PORTE-BOUTEILLE ISOLANTE
F060	CASE, VIOLIN	BOITE A VIOLON
E560	CASE, WEIGHT	BOITE A POIDS
F180	CASE, WRITING	NECESSAIRE POUR ECRIRE
G020	CASK	BARIL
D240	CASK	CAQUE
E400	CASK, APPLE	BARIL A POMMES
E400	CASK, BEER	BARIL A BIERE
E400	CASK, BISCUIT	BARIL A BISCUITS
E400	CASK, BUTTER	BARIL A BEURRE
E400	CASK, COFFEE	BARIL A CAFE
E400	CASK, COGNAC	BARIL A COGNAC
G020	CASK, DRY-TIGHT	BARIL ETANCHE A SEC
E400	CASK, FIG	BARIL A FIGUES
D100	CASK, FISH DRESSER'S	BARIL POUR PREPARATION DU POISSON
E400	CASK, FLOOR CLEANER	BARIL A PRODUIT DE NETTOYAGE POUR PLANCHER
E400	CASK, FLOUR	BARIL A FARINE
E400	CASK, GUNPOWDER	BARIL DE POUDRE A CANON
E180	CASK, GUNPOWDER	BARIL DE POUDRE A CANON
E400	CASK, KEROSINE	BARIL A PETROLE
E400	CASK, LEAD SHOT	BARIL A PLOMBS
E400	CASK, LIME	BARIL A BLANC DE CHAUX
E400	CASK, MADEIRA	BARIL A MADERE
E400	CASK, MEAT	BARIL A VIANDE
E400	CASK, MILITARY GUNPOWDER	BARIL A POUDRE A CANON MILITAIRE
E180	CASK, MILITARY GUNPOWDER	BARIL DE POUDRE A CANON MILITAIRE

Class. Code	Object, suffix	Objet, suffixe
G020	CASK, MINIATURE	*BARIL MINIATURE*
E400	CASK, MOLASSES	*BARIL A MELASSE*
E400	CASK, NAIL	*BARIL A CLOUS*
E400	CASK, OYSTER SHELL	*BARIL A ECAILLES D'HUITRES*
E400	CASK, PAINT	*BARIL A PEINTURE*
E400	CASK, PICKLE	*BARIL A CORNICHONS*
E400	CASK, PIGMENT	*BARIL A PIGMENTS*
E400	CASK, PINE TAR	*BARIL A GOUDRON DE BOIS*
E400	CASK, PLASTER	*BARIL A PLATRE*
E400	CASK, POISON	*BARIL A POISON*
E400	CASK, PORK	*BARIL A LARD*
E400	CASK, POTASH	*BARIL A POTASSE*
E400	CASK, RICE	*BARIL A RIZ*
D100	CASK, RUM	*BARIL A RHUM*
E400	CASK, RUM	*BARIL A RHUM*
E400	CASK, SALMON	*BARIL A SAUMON*
G020	CASK, SLACK	*BARIL NON ETANCHE*
E400	CASK, SULFUR	*BARIL A SOUFRE*
E400	CASK, TABLEWARE	*BARIL A SERVICE DE VAISSELLE*
E400	CASK, VINEGAR	*BARIL A VINAIGRE*
E400	CASK, WATER	*BARIL A EAU*
G020	CASK, WET-TIGHT	*BARIL ETANCHE*
E400	CASK, WHISKEY	*BARIL A WHISKY*
D100	CASK, WINE	*BARIL A VIN*
E400	CASK, WINE	*BARIL A VIN*
G020	CASK BUNG	*BONDE DE BARIL*
G020	CASK HEAD	*FOND DE BARIL*
E400	CASK HEAD, PORK	*FOND DE BARIL A PORC*
E400	CASK HEAD, WINE	*FOND DE BARIL A VIN*
G020	CASK HOOP	*CERCEAU DE BARIL*
G020	CASK STAVE	*DOUVE DE BARIL*
D100	CASSEROLE	*COCOTTE*
C100	CASSOCK	*SOUTANE*
D120	CASTER	*PORTE-CARAFE*
B080	CASTER	*ROULETTE DE FAUTEUIL*
H060	CATAFALQUE	*CATAFALQUE*
H020	CATALOG	*CATALOGUE*
G280	CATAMARAN, MODEL	*CATAMARAN MODELE DE PROJET*
E120	CATAPULT, MINIATURE	*CATAPULTE MINIATURE*
J060	CAULKING	*ETOUPE*
A020	CEILING	*PLAFOND*
E360	CELL, TETRAHEDRAL	*CELLULE TETRAEDRIQUE*
B060	CELLARETTE	*CABINET-CELLIER*
H060	CENSER	*ENCENSOIR*
H080	CERTIFICATE, ACHIEVEMENT	*CERTIFICAT D'HONNEUR*
H080	CERTIFICATE, APPOINTMENT	*CERTIFICAT DE NOMINATION*
H080	CERTIFICATE, BAPTISMAL	*BAPTISTAIRE*
H080	CERTIFICATE, BIRTH	*EXTRAIT DE NAISSANCE*
H080	CERTIFICATE, BURIAL	*EXTRAIT D'INHUMATION*
H080	CERTIFICATE, DISCHARGE	*CERTIFICAT DE LICENCIEMENT*
H080	CERTIFICATE, FIRST COMMUNION	*CERTIFICAT DE PREMIERE COMMUNION*
H080	CERTIFICATE, FREE MINER	*DROIT AUX MINERAUX*
H080	CERTIFICATE, MARRIAGE	*CONTRAT DE MARIAGE*
H080	CERTIFICATE, MEMBERSHIP	*CERTIFICAT DE MEMBRE*
H080	CERTIFICATE, MILITARY	*BREVET MILITAIRE*
H080	CERTIFICATE, MILITARY COMMISSION	*COMMISSION MILITAIRE*
H080	CERTIFICATE, MILITARY DISCHARGE	*CERTIFICAT DE LICENCIEMENT MILITAIRE*
H080	CERTIFICATE, MILITARY ENLISTMENT	*ACTE D'ENGAGEMENT MILITAIRE*
H080	CERTIFICATE, PAROLE	*CERTIFICAT DE LIBERATION CONDITIONNELLE*
H080	CERTIFICATE, PENSION	*CERTIFICAT DE RETRAITE*
H080	CERTIFICATE, POLICE DISCHARGE	*CERTIFICAT DE LICENCIEMENT DE POLICE*

Class. Code	Object, suffix	Objet, suffixe
H080	CERTIFICATE, SIGNATURE	SPECIMEN DE SIGNATURE
H080	CERTIFICATE, STOCK	CERTIFICAT D'ACTION
H080	CERTIFICATE, TESTIMONIAL	LETTRE TESTIMONIALE
J060	CHAIN	CHAINE
G300	CHAIN	CHAINE
J060	CHAIN, BUCKET	CHAINE DE PUITS
G180	CHAIN, HAME	CHAINE D'ATTELLE
C160	CHAIN, KEY	CHAINETTE DE PORTE-CLEFS
B080	CHAIN, PICTURE FRAME	CHAINE DE CADRE
G180	CHAIN, STAY	CHAINE DE TRAIT
E500	CHAIN, SURVEYOR'S	CHAINE D'ARPENTEUR
C160	CHAIN, WATCH	CHAINE DE MONTRE
G180	CHAIN, WHIFFLETREE	CHAINE DE PALONNIER
B060	CHAIR	CHAISE
I100	CHAIR	CHAISE
B060	CHAIR, BARBER'S	FAUTEUIL DE BARBIER
G300	CHAIR, BOATSWAIN'S	CHAISE DE MAITRE D'EQUIPAGE
B060	CHAIR, CHILD'S	CHAISE D'ENFANT
B060	CHAIR, CHILD'S ROCKING	BERCEUSE D'ENFANT
B060	CHAIR, DESK	CHAISE DE BUREAU
B060	CHAIR, DINING	CHAISE DE SALLE A MANGER
B060	CHAIR, EASY	FAUTEUIL
B060	CHAIR, FOLDING	CHAISE PLIANTE
B060	CHAIR, GARDEN	CHAISE DE JARDIN
B060	CHAIR, HALL	CHAISE D'ENTREE
B060	CHAIR, INVALID	FAUTEUIL ROULANT
B060	CHAIR, MILITARY	CHAISE MILITAIRE
B060	CHAIR, MILITARY FOLDING	CHAISE DE CAMP MILITAIRE
B060	CHAIR, MINIATURE	CHAISE MINIATURE
B060	CHAIR, OCCASIONAL	CHAISE D'APPOINT
B060	CHAIR, PILOT'S	CHAISE DE PILOTE
B060	CHAIR, PLATFORM ROCKING	CHAISE A PLATE-FORME
B060	CHAIR, POLICE DESK	CHAISE DE BUREAU DE POLICE
B060	CHAIR, POTTY	MEUBLE D'AISANCES D'ENFANT
B060	CHAIR, RECLINING	CHAISE A DOSSIER INCLINABLE
I100	CHAIR, ROCKING	BERCEUSE
B060	CHAIR, ROCKING	BERCEUSE
B060	CHAIR, SPEAKER'S	FAUTEUIL DE PRESIDENT
B060	CHAIR BACK	DOSSIER DE CHAISE
B060	CHAIR SEAT	SIEGE DE CHAISE
B060	CHAIR/TABLE	FAUTEUIL-TABLE
H060	CHALICE	CALICE
F180	CHALK	CRAIE
I080	CHALK, BILLIARD CUE	CRAIE DE QUEUE DE BILLARD
D320	CHALK, CARPENTER'S	CRAIE DE MENUISIER
D300	CHALK, TAILOR'S	CRAIE DE TAILLEUR
F180	CHALKBOARD	TABLEAU
B100	CHANDELIER	LUSTRE
B100	CHANDELIER, CANDLE	LUSTRE A BOUGIES
B100	CHANDELIER, ELECTRIC	LUSTRE ELECTRIQUE
B100	CHANDELIER, GAS	LUSTRE A GAZ
B100	CHANDELIER, KEROSINE	LUSTRE A PETROLE
D180	CHANNELER	COUTEAU A CANNELER
C100	CHAPS	CHAPARAJOS
H060	CHARCOAL, CENSER	CHARBON DE BOIS POUR ENCENSOIR
D120	CHARGER	GRAND PLAT
H080	CHART	CARTE
H080	CHART, MILITARY NAVIGATIONAL	CARTE DE NAVIGATION MILITAIRE
H080	CHART, NAVIGATIONAL	CARTE DE NAVIGATION
H080	CHART, POLICE NAVIGATIONAL	CARTE DE NAVIGATION DE POLICE
F180	CHART, THERMOGRAPH	FEUILLE DE THERMOGRAPHE

Class. Code	Object, suffix	Objet, suffixe
E380	CHART, VISUAL-ACUITY	*TABLEAU D'ACUITE VISUELLE*
F100	CHASE	*CHASSIS*
C100	CHASUBLE	*CHASUBLE*
C020	CHATELAINE	*CHATELAINE*
H080	CHECK, BANK	*CHEQUE BANCAIRE*
B060	CHEST	*COFFRE*
I100	CHEST	*COFFRE*
C160	CHEST	*COFFRET*
B060	CHEST, BLANKET	*COFFRE A COUVERTURES*
I100	CHEST, BLANKET	*COFFRE A COUVERTURES*
G300	CHEST, CHART	*COFFRE A CARTES DE NAVIGATION*
D060	CHEST, FISHING	*COFFRE DE PECHE*
B060	CHEST HANDLE	*POIGNEE DE COFFRE*
B060	CHEST, MILITARY	*COFFRE MILITAIRE*
B060	CHEST, MINIATURE	*COFFRE MINIATURE*
C160	CHEST, MINIATURE	*COFFRET MINIATURE*
B060	CHEST OF DRAWERS	*MEUBLE A TIROIRS*
I100	CHEST OF DRAWERS	*MEUBLE A TIROIRS*
B060	CHEST OF DRAWERS, CHILD'S	*MEUBLE A TIROIRS D'ENFANT*
B060	CHEST ON FRAME	*COFFRE-BAHUT*
C160	CHEST, SEA	*COFFRE DE MARIN*
B080	CHEST, SILVER	*COFFRET A ARGENTERIE*
E500	CHEST, SURVEYOR'S	*COFFRE D'ARPENTEUR*
J060	CHEST, TOOL	*COFFRE A OUTILS*
D180	CHEST, TOOL SADDLER'S	*COFFRE A OUTILS DE SELLIER*
B060	CHIFFOROBE	*ARMOIRE-CHIFFONNIER*
F120	CHIME	*CARILLON*
I020	CHIP, POKER	*JETON DE POKER*
D320	CHISEL	*CISEAU*
D200	CHISEL	*GRAIN DE MACON*
D320	CHISEL, CARVING	*CISEAU DE SCULPTEUR*
D220	CHISEL, COLD	*TRANCHE A FROID*
D320	CHISEL, CORNER	*CISEAU TRIANGULAIRE*
D200	CHISEL, CUTTING	*CISEAU DE MACON*
D320	CHISEL, FIRMER	*CISEAU A BISEAU*
D040	CHISEL, HOOF	*CISEAU A SABOT*
D220	CHISEL, HOT	*TRANCHE A CHAUD*
D100	CHISEL, ICE	*CISEAU A GLACE*
D220	CHISEL, MILITARY COLD	*TRANCHE A FROID MILITAIRE*
D320	CHISEL, MORTISE	*CISEAU A MORTAISER*
D320	CHISEL, PARTING	*CISEAU A TRONCONNER*
D200	CHISEL, PITCHING	*CISEAU A ARETES*
D200	CHISEL, POINT	*CISEAU POINTU*
D020	CHISEL, PRUNING	*CISEAU D'ELAGAGE*
D320	CHISEL, RIPPING	*CISEAU A PLANCHES*
D200	CHISEL, STRAIGHT	*CISEAU DROIT*
D180	CHISEL, THONGING	*CISEAU A LANIERES*
D200	CHISEL, TOOTH	*CISEAU A DENTS*
E380	CHISEL, TREPANNING	*TREPAN*
D320	CHISEL, TURNING	*FERMOIR DE TOUR*
D320	CHISEL HANDLE	*MANCHE DE CISEAU*
G300	CHOCK	*CHAUMARD*
G180	CHOCK, WHEEL	*CALE DE ROUE*
D020	CHOPPER, FEED	*HACHOIR A NOURRITURE DE BETAIL*
D100	CHOPPER, FOOD	*HACHOIR A LAME*
D120	CHOPSTICK	*BAGUETTE A RIZ*
D220	CHUCK, LATHE	*MANDRIN DE TOUR*
D100	CHURN	*BARATTE*
D100	CHURN, BUTTER	*BARATTE A BEURRE*
D100	CHURN LID, BUTTER	*COUVERCLE DE BARATTE A BEURRE*
D100	CHURN, MINIATURE	*BARATTE MINIATURE*

Class. Code	Object, suffix	Objet, suffixe
H060	CIBORIUM	CIBOIRE
G180	CINCH	SANGLE
E500	CIRCUMFERENTOR	GRAPHOMETRE
A060	CISTERN	CITERNE
H080	CITATION, MILITARY	CITATION MILITAIRE
D180	CLAMP	PINCE
D320	CLAMP	SERRE-JOINT
F100	CLAMP, BOOKBINDING	VIS DE SERRAGE DE PRESSE
D320	CLAMP, C	SERRE-JOINT EN C
D320	CLAMP, FURNITURE	SERRE-JOINT DE MENUISIER
E240	CLAMP, HOSECOCK	PINCE A VIS
D320	CLAMP, JOINER'S	SERRE-JOINT A BARRE
F180	CLAMP, MAILBAG	FERMETURE DE SAC POSTAL
D300	CLAMP, QUILTING-FRAME	PINCE DE METIER A COURTEPOINTE
D320	CLAMP, SAW	ETAU D'AFFUTAGE POUR SCIES
D300	CLAMP, SEWING	PINCE A COUTURE
E280	CLAMP, SPLICING	PINCE A COSSES
E300	CLAMP, STEAM HOSE	COLLIER DE TUYAU A VAPEUR
D180	CLAMP, STRETCHING	PINCE A TENDRE
D060	CLAMP, TRAP SETTING	BRIDE DE POSE A PIEGE
F120	CLAPPER	CLAQUETTE
F060	CLARINET	CLARINETTE
C140	CLASP	FERMOIR
D240	CLASSIFIER	CLASSIFICATEUR
E340	CLEANER, LAMP CHIMNEY	CURETTE DE VERRE DE LAMPE
C160	CLEANER, PIPE	NETTOIE-PIPE
E340	CLEANER, VACUUM	ASPIRATEUR
E340	CLEANSER	PIERRE A NETTOYER
G300	CLEAT	TAQUET
B160	CLEAT, AWNING	TAQUET DE VELUM
D100	CLEAVER	COUPERET
G180	CLEVIS	MANILLE
J060	CLEVIS	OEILLET DE SUSPENSION
E180	CLINOMETER, MILITARY GUNNER'S	CLINOMETRE D'ARTILLERIE MILITAIRE
E180	CLIP, CARTRIDGE	LAME-CHARGEUR
E180	CLIP, MILITARY CARTRIDGE	LAME-CHARGEUR MILITAIRE
C160	CLIP, MONEY	PINCE A BILLETS DE BANQUE
E400	CLIP, NEWSPAPER	PINCE A JOURNAL
F180	CLIP, PAPER	PINCE A PAPIERS
C140	CLIP, TIE	FIXE CRAVATE
F180	CLIPBOARD	PLANCHETTE A PINCES
D040	CLIPPER, ANIMAL	TONDEUSE POUR ANIMAL
D040	CLIPPER PLATE, ANIMAL	PLAQUE DE TONDEUSE POUR ANIMAL
C180	CLIPPERS, HAIR	TONDEUSE A CHEVEUX
H080	CLIPPING, MAGAZINE	COUPURE DE REVUE
H080	CLIPPING, NEWSPAPER	COUPURE DE PRESSE
C100	CLOAK	MANTE
H120	CLOAK	MANTE
E540	CLOCK	HORLOGE
E540	CLOCK, CASE	COFFRE D'HORLOGE
E540	CLOCK, SHELF	PENDULE DE CHEMINEE
E540	CLOCK, TALL CASE	GRAND COFFRE D'HORLOGE
E540	CLOCK, TIMERECORDING	HORODATEUR
E540	CLOCK, TRAVEL	REVEIL DE VOYAGE
E540	CLOCK, WALL	PENDULE MURALE
E540	CLOCK PENDULUM	PENDULE D'HORLOGE
E540	CLOCK WEIGHT	POIDS D'HORLOGE
E540	CLOCKWORK	ROUAGE D'HORLOGE
C060	CLOG	GALOCHE
H060	CLOTH, ALTAR	NAPPE D'AUTEL
E340	CLOTH, CLEANING	TORCHON

Class. Code	Object, suffix	Objet, suffixe
D220	CLOTH, EMERY	TOILE D'EMERI
F080	CLOTH, FOCUSING	VOILE DE MISE AU POINT
D120	CLOTH, KNIFE BOX	TOILE DE BOITE A COUTEAUX
E340	CLOTHESLINE	CORDE A LINGE
E340	CLOTHESPIN	EPINGLE A LINGE
E100	CLUB	MASSUE
D060	CLUB, FISH	MATRAQUE A POISSON
D320	CLUB, FROE	MAILLET DE DEPARTOIR
I080	CLUB, GOLF	BATON DE GOLF
I080	CLUB, INDIAN	MIL
D120	COASTER	DESSOUS DE BOUTEILLE
B080	COASTER, FURNITURE	DESSOUS DE PIED DE MEUBLE
C100	COAT	MANTEAU
I100	COAT	MANTEAU
C100	COAT, AUTOMOBILE	CACHE-POUSSIERE
C100	COAT, CUTAWAY	JAQUETTE
C100	COAT, FROCK	REDINGOTE
C100	COAT, LABORATORY	VESTE DE LABORATOIRE
C100	COAT, MILITARY	HABIT MILITAIRE
C100	COAT, MILITARY FROCK	REDINGOTE MILITAIRE
B060	COAT-TREE	PORTEMANTEAU
C100	COATEE, MILITARY	HABIT-VESTE MILITAIRE
B080	COATHANGER	CINTRE
B080	COATHANGER, MILITARY	CINTRE MILITAIRE
B060	COATRACK	PORTEMANTEAU MURAL
B060	COATRACK, MILITARY	PORTEMANTEAU MURAL MILITAIRE
H120	COCKADE, MILITARY	COCARDE MILITAIRE
G180	COCKEYE, SCREW	ANNEAU DE TRAIT A ROULEAU
D120	COFFEEPOT	CAFETIERE
D120	COFFEEPOT LID	COUVERCLE DE CAFETIERE
H060	COFFIN	CERCUEIL
H060	COFFIN HANDLE	POIGNEE DE CERCUEIL
H060	COFFIN LOCK	SERRURE DE CERCUEIL
F140	COHERER	COHEREUR
H100	COIN	PIECE DE MONNAIE
H080	COIN, COMMEMORATIVE	MONNAIE COMMEMORATIVE
D100	COLANDER	PASSOIRE
D100	COLANDER, MILITARY	PASSOIRE MILITAIRE
H040	COLLAGE	COLLAGE
C140	COLLAR	COL
G180	COLLAR, DOG	COLLIER DE CHIEN
G180	COLLAR, HORSE	BOURRELET DE CHEVAL
D040	COLLAR, PET	COLLIER D'ANIMAL FAMILIER
C140	COLLAR, POLICE	FAUX COL DE POLICE
C140	COLLAR, ROMAN	COL ROMAIN
H120	COLLECTION, BADGE	COLLECTION D'INSIGNES
H080	COLLECTION, COIN	COLLECTION DE PIECES DE MONNAIE
H120	COLLECTION, MILITARY BADGE	COLLECTION D'INSIGNES MILITAIRES
H120	COLLECTION, MILITARY BUTTON	COLLECTION DE BOUTONS MILITAIRES
H080	COLLECTION, STAMP	COLLECTION DE TIMBRES
A040	COLUMN	COLONNE
C180	COMB	PEIGNE
D040	COMB, ANIMAL	PEIGNE POUR ANIMAL
D260	COMB, GRAINING	PEIGNE A VEINER
D300	COMB, HAND	PEIGNE A MAIN
C120	COMBINATION	COMBINAISON
C120	COMBINATION, CHILD'S	COMBINAISON D'ENFANT
E480	COME-ALONG	CHAINE-ENTRAVE
B020	COMFORTER	EDREDON
I100	COMFORTER	EDREDON
B060	COMMODE	MEUBLE D'AISANCES

Class. Code	Object, suffix	Objet, suffixe
C180	COMPACT	POUDRIER
E500	COMPASS	BOUSSOLE
F040	COMPASS	COMPAS
F040	COMPASS, BEAM	COMPAS A TRUSQUIN
D320	COMPASS, BEAM	COMPAS A VERGE
F040	COMPASS, BOW	COMPAS COURBE
D320	COMPASS, COOPER'S WING	COMPAS DE TONNELIER
F040	COMPASS POINT	POINTE DE COMPAS
E500	COMPASS, SURVEYOR'S	COMPAS D'ARPENTEUR
D120	COMPOTE	COMPOTIER
E300	COMPRESSOR, DUPLEX AIR	COMPRESSEUR DOUBLE D'AIR
F060	CONCERTINA	CONCERTINA
E240	CONDENSER	CONDENSEUR
C160	CONDOM	PRESERVATIF
B060	CONFESSIONAL	CONFESSIONNAL
E360	CONNECTOR, MULTIPLE	JOINT MULTIPLE
G180	CONNECTOR, TRACE	FERRURE DE TRAIT
E180	CONTAINER, GREASE	CONTENANT DE GRAISSE
H080	CONTRACT	CONTRAT
D120	COOLER, WATER	RAFRAICHISSOIR A EAU
D120	COOLER, WINE	RAFRAICHISSOIR A VIN
D040	COOP, POULTRY-SHIPPING	CAGE A POULES
E300	CORD, ELECTRICAL	CORDON ELECTRIQUE
J020	CORDAGE FRAGMENT	FRAGMENT DE CORDAGE
H060	CORDELIERE, FLAGPOLE	CORDELIERE DE HAMPE DE DRAPEAU
D220	COREBOX, ANVIL	BOITE A NOYAUX D'ENCLUME
D220	COREBOX, CALDRON	BOITE A NOYAUX DE CHAUDRON
D220	COREBOX, CANNON CARRIAGE	BOITE A NOYAUX D'AFFUT DE CANON
D220	COREBOX, CANNON CARRIAGE TRUCK LEVER	BOITE A NOYAUX DE LEVIER D'AFFUT DE CANON
D220	COREBOX, GUN	BOITE A NOYAUX DE CANON
D220	COREBOX, LATCH ASSEMBLY	BOITE A NOYAUX D'ASSEMBLAGE DE LOQUET
D220	COREBOX, MILITARY CARRONADE	BOITE A NOYAUX DE CARONADE MILITAIRE
D220	COREBOX, MORTAR	BOITE A NOYAUX DE MORTIER
D220	COREBOX, RACK	BOITE A NOYAUX DE RATELIER
D220	COREBOX, SHELL	BOITE A NOYAUX DE BOMBE
D220	COREBOX, STOVE LID	BOITE A NOYAUX DE ROND DE POELE
D220	COREBOX, SWIVEL GUN	BOITE A NOYAUX DE CANON SUR PIVOT
D100	CORER, FRUIT	VIDE-POMME
D100	CORKER, BOTTLE	BOUCHE-BOUTEILLES
D100	CORKSCREW	TIRE-BOUCHON
A040	CORNERSTONE	PIERRE ANGULAIRE
D020	CORNHUSKER, HAND	EFFEUILLEUSE A MAIS
A040	CORNICE	CORNICHE
H060	CORPORAL	CORPORAL
C020	CORSAGE	BOUTONNIERE
C120	CORSET	CORSET
C120	CORSET, CHILD'S	CORSET D'ENFANT
G280	CORVETTE, MODEL	CORVETTE MODELE REDUIT
C100	COSTUME, SEASONAL	COSTUME DES FETES
E400	COUNTER	COMPTOIR
E280	COUNTER	DISPOSITIF D'AFFICHAGE POUR COMPTEUR
E300	COUNTERSHAFT	ARBRE DE RENVOI
J060	COUPLING, PNEUMATIC HOSE	RACCORD POUR TUYAU SOUPLE A AIR COMPRIME
G180	COUPLING, WHIFFLETREE	DISPOSITIF D'ACCOUPLEMENT DE PALONNIER
H020	COUPON	BON
H100	COUPON	COUPON
E240	COVER, BEAKER	COUVERCLE DE BECHER
B020	COVER, BOLSTER	HOUSSE DE TRAVERSIN
H080	COVER, BOOK	COUVERTURE DE LIVRE
E400	COVER, BOTTLE STOPPER	ENVELOPPE DE BOUCHON DE BOUTEILLE
B080	COVER, CHAIR SEAT	COUVRE-SIEGE DE CHAISE

Class. Code	Object, suffix	Objet, suffixe
C180	COVER, CHAMBER POT	COUVRE-POT DE CHAMBRE
C120	COVER, CORSET	CACHE-CORSET
B080	COVER, CUSHION	HOUSSE DE COUSSIN
A040	COVER, FLUE	CAPUCHON DE TUYAU DE POELE
D100	COVER, FOOD	COUVRE-PLAT
B060	COVER, FOOTSTOOL	DESSUS DE MARCHEPIED
E340	COVER, IRONING BOARD	HOUSSE DE PLANCHE A REPASSER
B100	COVER, LAMP ROSETTE	COUVERCLE DE SOCLE DE LAMPE
F180	COVER, LEDGER	COUVERTURE DE GRAND LIVRE
B100	COVER, LIGHTHOUSE LENS	COUVRE-LENTILLE DE PHARE
B020	COVER, MATTRESS	ENVELOPPE DE MATELAS
B020	COVER, MILITARY BOLSTER	HOUSSE DE TRAVERSIN MILITAIRE
C160	COVER, MILITARY CANTEEN	HOUSSE DE GOURDE MILITAIRE
E180	COVER, MILITARY CARTRIDGE-BOX	ETUI A CARTOUCHIERE MILITAIRE
B020	COVER, MILITARY MATTRESS	ENVELOPPE DE MATELAS MILITAIRE
D120	COVER, MILITARY MESS TIN	HOUSSE DE GAMELLE MILITAIRE
C160	COVER, MILITARY POUCH	ETUI DE GIBERNE MILITAIRE
C160	COVER, MILITARY SABRETACHE	HOUSSE DE SABRETACHE MILITAIRE
G300	COVER, MOTOR	BACHE DE MOTEUR
E280	COVER, OUTLET BOX	COUVERCLE DE BOITE ELECTRIQUE
C160	COVER, PARASOL	TOILE D'OMBRELLE
H080	COVER, PHOTOGRAPH	ETUI A PHOTOS
B020	COVER, PILLOW	HOUSSE D'OREILLER
D300	COVER, PINCUSHION	DESSUS DE PELOTE A EPINGLES
H080	COVER, POLICE BOOK	COUVERTURE DE LIVRE DE POLICE
E180	COVER, POLICE CARTRIDGE-BOX	ETUI A CARTOUCHIERE DE POLICE
C160	COVER, POLICE POUCH	ETUI DE GIBERNE DE POLICE
B020	COVER, POLICE SLEEPING BAG	HOUSSE DE SAC DE COUCHAGE DE POLICE
D100	COVER, ROLLING PIN	HOUSSE DE ROULEAU A PATISSERIE
C160	COVER, SHOE	HOUSSE A SOULIER
B020	COVER, SLEEPING BAG	HOUSSE DE SAC DE COUCHAGE
B040	COVER, STAIR	DESSUS D'ESCALIER
E300	COVER, STEAM BOILER INSPECTION	JUDAS DE CHAUDIERE A VAPEUR
I080	COVER, TENNIS RACKET	HOUSSE DE RAQUETTE DE TENNIS
A020	COVER, TEPEE	ENVELOPPE DE TIPI
C100	COVERALLS	COMBINAISON DE TRAVAIL
D040	COWBELL	CLOCHETTE
D120	COZY	COUVRE-THEIERE
B060	CRADLE	MOISE
I100	CRADLE	MOISE
G140	CRADLE, BOARD	PLANCHE PORTE-BEBE
G300	CRADLE, DESIGN MODEL BOAT	CHANTIER D'EMBARCATION MODELE DE PROJET
G140	CRADLE, SLAT	PORTE-BEBE EN LATTES
B060	CRADLE/ROCKER	BERCEAU
I080	CRAMPON	CRAMPON
D100	CRANE	POTENCE DE CHEMINEE
G020	CRATE	CAISSE
E400	CRATE, ANALGESIC	CAISSE POUR ANALGESIQUES
E400	CRATE, APPLE	CAISSE A POMMES
E400	CRATE, ART OBJECT	BOITE A OBJET D'ART
E400	CRATE, AX BLADE	CAISSE A LAMES DE HACHE
E400	CRATE, BAKING POWDER	CAISSE A LEVURE CHIMIQUE
E400	CRATE, BANANA	CAISSE A BANANES
E400	CRATE, BEAN	CAISSE A FEVES
E400	CRATE, BISCUIT	CAISSE A BISCUITS
E400	CRATE, BITTERS	CAISSE A BITTER
E400	CRATE, BOOT	CAISSE A BOTTES
E400	CRATE, BOOT POLISH	CAISSE A CIRAGE A CHAUSSURES
E400	CRATE, BOTTLE STOPPER	CAISSE A BOUCHONS DE BOUTEILLE
E400	CRATE, BUTTER	CAISSE A BEURRE
E400	CRATE, CANDLE	CAISSE A BOUGIES

Class. Code	Object, suffix	Objet, suffixe
E400	CRATE, CARTRIDGE	CAISSE A CARTOUCHES
E400	CRATE, CEREAL	CAISSE A CEREALES
E400	CRATE, CHALK	CAISSE A CRAIES
E400	CRATE, CHEESE	CAISSE A FROMAGES
E400	CRATE, CHOCOLATE	CAISSE A CHOCOLATS
E400	CRATE, CLEANSER	CAISSE A POUDRE A NETTOYER
E400	CRATE, CLOTH BOLT	CAISSE A PIECES DE TISSU
E400	CRATE, COCOA	CAISSE A CACAO
E400	CRATE, COD	CAISSE A MORUES
E400	CRATE, COFFEE	CAISSE A CAFE
E400	CRATE, COGNAC	CAISSE A COGNAC
E400	CRATE, CONDENSED MILK	CAISSE A LAIT CONDENSE
E400	CRATE, CONDIMENT SAUCE	CAISSE A SAUCE AUX CONDIMENTS
E400	CRATE, CONFECTION	CAISSE A CONFISERIES
E400	CRATE, CORN	CAISSE A MAIS
E400	CRATE, CRAYON	CAISSE A CRAYONS DE COULEUR
E400	CRATE, DATE	CAISSE A DATTES
E400	CRATE, DRIED APPLE	CAISSE A POMMES SECHEES
E400	CRATE, DRIED FRUIT	CAISSE A FRUITS SECHES
E400	CRATE, EGG	CAISSE A OEUFS
E400	CRATE, EMBALMING FLUID	CAISSE A LIQUIDE D'EMBAUMEMENT
E400	CRATE, EVAPORATED CREAM	CAISSE A CREME EVAPOREE
E400	CRATE, EVAPORATED MILK	CAISSE A LAIT EVAPORE
E400	CRATE, FAN	CAISSE A EVENTAILS
E400	CRATE, FISH	CAISSE A POISSONS
E400	CRATE, FLAVORING	CAISSE A ESSENCE
E400	CRATE, FOOD SYRUP	CAISSE A SIROP ALIMENTAIRE
E400	CRATE, FOOTWEAR	CAISSE A CHAUSSURES
E400	CRATE, FRUIT	CAISSE A FRUITS
E400	CRATE, GASOLINE	CAISSE A GAZOLINE
E400	CRATE, GIN	CAISSE A GIN
E400	CRATE, GLUE	CAISSE A COLLE
E400	CRATE, GRAPEFRUIT	CAISSE A PAMPLEMOUSSES
E400	CRATE, HAIR TONIC	CAISSE A TONIQUES CAPILLAIRES
E400	CRATE, HARDWARE	CAISSE A QUINCAILLERIE
E400	CRATE, HATCHET	CAISSE A HACHETTES
E400	CRATE, INK	CAISSE A ENCRE
E400	CRATE, JIG	CAISSE A TURLUTTES
E400	CRATE, KEROSENE	CAISSE A PETROLE
E400	CRATE, KETCHUP	CAISSE A KETCHUP
E400	CRATE, LARD	CAISSE A LARD
E400	CRATE, LAUNDRY BLUEING	CAISSE A BLEU DE LESSIVE
E400	CRATE, LAUNDRY SOAP	CAISSE A SAVON A LESSIVE
E400	CRATE, LEMON	CAISSE A CITRONS
E400	CRATE, LEMON PEEL	CAISSE A ZESTE DE CITRON
E400	CRATE, LIME JUICE	CAISSE A JUS DE LIMETTE
E400	CRATE, LIQUEUR	CAISSE A LIQUEUR
E400	CRATE, LOBSTER	CAISSE A HOMARDS
E400	CRATE, LUBRICATING GREASE	CAISSE A GRAISSE LUBRIFIANTE
E400	CRATE, LUBRICATING OIL	CAISSE A HUILE LUBRIFIANTE
E400	CRATE, MATCH	CAISSE A ALLUMETTES
E400	CRATE, MEAT	CAISSE A VIANDE
E400	CRATE, MEDICINAL	CAISSE A PRODUITS PHARMACEUTIQUES
E400	CRATE, MILK	CAISSE A LAIT
E400	CRATE, MILKPOWDER	CAISSE A LAIT EN POUDRE
E400	CRATE, MUSTARD	CAISSE A MOUTARDE
E400	CRATE, NAIL	CAISSE A CLOUS
E400	CRATE, NON-ALCOHOLIC BEVERAGE	CAISSE A BOISSONS NON-ALCOOLISEES
E400	CRATE, NUT	CAISSE A NOIX
E400	CRATE, ORANGE	CAISSE A ORANGES
E400	CRATE, OYSTER	CAISSE A HUITRES

Class. Code	Object, suffix	Objet, suffixe
E400	CRATE, PEA	CAISSE A POIS
E400	CRATE, PEAR	CAISSE A POIRES
E400	CRATE, PENCIL	CAISSE A CRAYONS A MINE DE PLOMB
E400	CRATE, PHONOGRAPH RECORD	CAISSE A DISQUES DE PHONOGRAPHE
E400	CRATE, PORT	CAISSE A PORTO
E400	CRATE, PRUNE	CAISSE A PRUNEAUX
E400	CRATE, RADIO	CAISSE A RADIO
E400	CRATE, RAISIN	CAISSE A RAISINS
E400	CRATE, RIFLE	CAISSE A FUSILS
E400	CRATE, RUM	CAISSE A RHUM
E400	CRATE, SALMON	CAISSE A SAUMON
E400	CRATE, SALT	CAISSE A SEL
E400	CRATE, SARDINE	CAISSE A SARDINES
E400	CRATE, SAW	CAISSE A SCIE
E400	CRATE, SAW BLADE	CAISSE A LAMES DE SCIE
E400	CRATE, SEED	CAISSE A SEMENCES
E400	CRATE, SHELLAC	CAISSE A SHELLAC
E400	CRATE, SKIN LOTION	CAISSE A LOTION POUR LA PEAU
E400	CRATE, SODA BISCUIT	CAISSE A CRAQUELINS
E400	CRATE, SOFT DRINK	CAISSE A BOISSONS GAZEUSES
E400	CRATE, SPICE	CAISSE A EPICES
E400	CRATE, STARCH	CAISSE A EMPOIS
E400	CRATE, STEAM GAUGE	CAISSE A INDICATEUR DE PRESSION
E400	CRATE, STOVE POLISH	CAISSE A PATE A POLIR LE POELE
E400	CRATE, STOVEPIPE	CAISSE A TUYAUX DE POELE
E400	CRATE, SUGAR	CAISSE A SUCRE
E400	CRATE, TEA	CAISSE A THE
E400	CRATE, TOBACCO	CAISSE A TABAC
E400	CRATE, TOILET	CAISSE DE TOILETTE
E400	CRATE, TOILET SOAP	CAISSE A SAVONS DE TOILETTE
E400	CRATE, TOMATO	CAISSE A TOMATES
E400	CRATE, TONIC	CAISSE A TONIQUES
E400	CRATE, VARNISH	CAISSE A VERNIS
E400	CRATE, VEGETABLE	CAISSE A LEGUMES
E400	CRATE, VERMIFUGE	CAISSE A VERMIFUGE
E400	CRATE, VINEGAR	CAISSE A VINAIGRE
E400	CRATE, WELDING FLUX	CAISSE A FONDANT DE SOUDURE AUTOGENE
E400	CRATE, WELDING ROD	CAISSE A BAGUETTES DE SOUDURE
E400	CRATE, WHISKEY	CAISSE A WHISKY
E400	CRATE, WINDOWPANE	CAISSE A CARREAUX
E400	CRATE, WINE	CAISSE A VINS
E400	CRATE, YEAST	CAISSE A LEVURE
E400	CRATE PANEL, GASOLINE	PANNEAU DE CAISSE A GAZOLINE
E400	CRATE PANEL, OYSTER	PANNEAU DE CAISSE A HUITRES
C140	CRAVAT	CRAVATE
H120	CRAVAT, MAGISTRATE	RABAT DE MAGISTRAT
C140	CRAVAT, MILITARY	CRAVATE MILITAIRE
D260	CRAYON	CRAYON A DESSINER
I100	CRAYON	CRAYON DE COULEUR
D320	CRAYON, LUMBER	CRAYON DE MESUREUR DE BOIS
D180	CREASER	PLISSEUR
D180	CREASER, BEVEL	PLISSEUR CONIQUE
D180	CREASER, EDGE	PLISSEUR DE BORD
D220	CREASER, HOT	MARTEAU A CANNELER A CHAUD
D180	CREASER, SCREW	PLISSEUR A ECROU
D180	CREASER, SINGLE	PLISSEUR SIMPLE
H060	CRECHE	CRECHE
D060	CREEL	PANIER DE PECHE
C060	CREEPER	CRAMPON
C060	CREEPER, MILITARY	CRAMPON MILITAIRE
B100	CRESSET	BRASERO

Class. Code	Object, suffix	Objet, suffixe
D320	CRESSET	BRASERO
B060	CRIB	LIT DE BEBE
B060	CRIB, MINIATURE	LIT DE BEBE MINIATURE
J060	CRIMPER, SEAL	PRESSE-PLOMB
D100	CROCK	POT
D100	CROCK LID	COUVERCLE DE POT
D100	CROCK, MINIATURE	POT MINIATURE
G180	CROP, MILITARY RIDING	CRAVACHE MILITAIRE
G180	CROP, POLICE RIDING	CRAVACHE DE POLICE
G180	CROP, RIDING	CRAVACHE
H060	CROSS	CROIX
A040	CROSS	CROIX
D120	CROSS, DISH	RECHAUD
E500	CROSS-STAFF	EQUERRE D'ARPENTEUR
E080	CROSSBOW	ARBALETE
G240	CROSSTIE	TRAVERSE DE VOIE COURANTE
D320	CROWBAR	PINCE A LEVIER
D320	CROZE	JABLOIR
D220	CRUCIBLE	CREUSET
E240	CRUCIBLE	CREUSET
D220	CRUCIBLE LID	COUVERCLE DE CREUSET
H060	CRUCIFIX	CRUCIFIX
D120	CRUET	BURETTE
D120	CRUET STOPPER	BOUCHON DE BURETTE
G280	CRUISER, MODEL STEAM	NAVIRE DE CROISIERE A VAPEUR MODELE REDUIT
G180	CRUPPER	CROUPIERE
C160	CRUTCH	BEQUILLE
I100	CUE, BILLIARD	QUEUE DE BILLARD
I080	CUE, BILLIARD	QUEUE DE BILLARD
C140	CUFF	MANCHETTE
D020	CULTIVATOR, GARDEN	CULTIVATEUR DE JARDIN
D020	CULTIVATOR, HAND	CULTIVATEUR A MAIN
D020	CULTIVATOR, WALKING	CULTIVATEUR A TRACTION ANIMALE
D020	CULTIVATOR HANDLE	MANCHE DE CULTIVATEUR
D120	CUP	TASSE
I100	CUP & BALL	BILBOQUET
H060	CUP, BRIDE'S	COUPE DE LA MARIEE
D120	CUP, COFFEE	TASSE A CAFE
H080	CUP, COMMEMORATIVE	COUPE COMMEMORATIVE
D120	CUP, DEMITASSE	TASSE A MOKA
I020	CUP, DICE	CORNET A DES
D120	CUP, INVALID'S	TASSE D'INVALIDE
H120	CUP, LOVING	COUPE D'AMITIE
D100	CUP, MEASURING	TASSE A MESURER
D120	CUP, MILITARY	TASSE MILITAIRE
D120	CUP, MUSTACHE	TASSE MOUSTACHE
D120	CUP & SAUCER	TASSE ET SOUCOUPE
D120	CUP & SAUCER, DEMITASSE	TASSE ET SOUCOUPE A MOKA
D120	CUP & SAUCER, MINIATURE	TASSE ET SOUCOUPE MINIATURE
D120	CUP, WATER	VERRE A EAU
B060	CUPBOARD	PLACARD
B060	CUPBOARD, HANGING	PENDERIE
B060	CUPBOARD, MILITARY HANGING	PENDERIE MILITAIRE
B060	CUPBOARD, MINIATURE	PLACARD MINIATURE
B060	CUPBOARD, PRESS	MEUBLE A LINGE
D220	CUPEL	COUPELLE
E380	CURETTE	CURETTE
C180	CURLER	BIGOUDI
H100	CURRENCY	MONNAIE
D040	CURRYCOMB	ETRILLE-PEIGNE
B160	CURTAIN	RIDEAU

Class. Code	Object, suffix	Objet, suffixe
B020	CURTAIN, BED	RIDEAU DE LIT
B160	CURTAIN, DOOR	PORTIERE
B080	CURTAIN, SPLASH	RIDEAU ANTI-ECLABOUSSURES
D300	CURVE/SQUARE, PATTERN DRAFTING	PISTOLET/EQUERRE DE DESSIN DE PATRONS
B080	CUSHION	COUSSIN
G180	CUSHION, CARRIAGE	COUSSIN DE VOITURE
D300	CUSHION, EMERY	PELOTE D'EPINGLES A POUDRE D'EMERI
E080	CUTLASS	SABRE D'ABORDAGE
E080	CUTLASS, MILITARY	SABRE D'ABORDAGE MILITAIRE
I100	CUTTER	COUPE-BOULON
G120	CUTTER	TRAINEAU AMERICAIN
D220	CUTTER, BOILER SHEET	CISAILLE A TOLE DE CHAUDIERE
D220	CUTTER, BOILER TUBE	CISAILLE A CONDUIT DE CHAUDIERE
D220	CUTTER, BOLT	COUPE-BOULON
D100	CUTTER, CABBAGE	COUPE-CHOUX
B080	CUTTER, CIGAR	COUPE-CIGARE
C160	CUTTER, CIGAR	COUPE-CIGARE
D100	CUTTER, COOKIE	COUPE-PATE
D320	CUTTER, COOPER'S	COUTEAU DE TONNELIER
D100	CUTTER, DOUGHNUT	COUPE-BEIGNE
D180	CUTTER, EDGE	COUPE-BORDURE
D020	CUTTER, ENSILAGE	ENSILEUSE
D220	CUTTER, FLUE	CISAILLES A CONDUIT DE CHEMINEE
D160	CUTTER, GLASS	COUPE-VERRE
F180	CUTTER, PAPER	TRANCHE-PAPIER
D100	CUTTER, PASTRY	EMPORTE-PIECE
D320	CUTTER, PEG	COUTEAU A CHEVILLE
D220	CUTTER, PIPE	COUPE-TUBE
D180	CUTTER, REVOLVING-WHEEL	COUTEAU A ROULETTE
D220	CUTTER, RIVET	CISAILLE A RIVETS
G120	CUTTER RUNNER	PATIN DE TRAINEAU AMERICAIN
F100	CUTTER, SLUG	COUPOIR A LIGNE-BLOCS
E400	CUTTER, STRING	COUPE-FICELLE
D100	CUTTER, SUGAR	CASSE-SUCRE
E400	CUTTER, TOBACCO	HACHOIR A TABAC
E180	CUTTER, WAD	COUPE-BOURRE
D180	CUTTER, WASHER	COUPE-RONDELLE
D180	CUTTER, WELT	BISEAUTEUR DE TREPOINTE
D220	CUTTER, WIRE	TENAILLE COUPE-FILS
D180	CUTTER BLADE	LAME D'OUTIL A COUPER
F120	CYLINDER, DICTAPHONE	CYLINDRE DE DICTAPHONE
F120	CYLINDER, MUSIC-BOX	CYLINDRE DE BOITE A MUSIQUE
F120	CYLINDER, ORGANETTE	CYLINDRE D'ORGUE DE BARBARIE
E080	DAGGER	DAGUE
E080	DAGGER, MILITARY	DAGUE MILITAIRE
E080	DAGGER HANDLE	MANCHE DE DAGUE
H080	DAGUERREOTYPE	DAGUERREOTYPE
C100	DALMATIC	DALMATIQUE
D100	DASHER	BATTE-BEURRE
G300	DEADEYE	MOQUE
F100	DECAL	PAPIER A DECALCOMANIE
D120	DECANTER	CARAFE AVEC BOUCHON
D120	DECANTER STOPPER	BOUCHON DE CARAFE EN VERRE
I020	DECK, CARD	JEU DE CARTES
D100	DECORATOR, CAKE	PISTON A DECORER
E180	DECOY	APPELANT
E180	DECOY, MINIATURE	APPELANT MINIATURE
H080	DEED	ACTE NOTARIE
G020	DEMIJOHN	DAME-JEANNE
E400	DEMIJOHN, WINE	DAME-JEANNE A VIN
E380	DEPRESSOR, TONGUE	ABAISSE-LANGUE

Class. Code	Object, suffix	Objet, suffixe
C080	DERBY	CHAPEAU MELON
E060	DERRINGER	DERRINGER
B060	DESK	BUREAU
B060	DESK, DROP-FRONT	BUREAU A BATTANT
B060	DESK, MILITARY	BUREAU MILITAIRE
B060	DESK, MILITARY CAMPAIGN	BUREAU DE CAMPAGNE MILITAIRE
F180	DESK, MILITARY PORTABLE	SECRETAIRE PORTATIF MILITAIRE
F180	DESK, PORTABLE	SECRETAIRE PORTATIF
B060	DESK, ROLLTOP	BUREAU A CYLINDRE
B060	DESK, SCHOOL	PUPITRE D'ECOLIER
B060	DESK, SLANT-TOP	BUREAU A COUVERCLE INCLINE
E480	DETECTOR, METAL	DETECTEUR DE METAUX
H080	DIAGRAM, MILITARY	DIAGRAMME MILITAIRE
C120	DIAPER	COUCHE
H080	DIARY	JOURNAL PERSONNEL
D020	DIBBLE	PLANTOIR
I020	DICE	DES A JOUER
C140	DICKEY	PLASTRON
F120	DICTAPHONE, EDISON	DICTAPHONE
I020	DIE	DE A JOUER
D220	DIE	FILIERE
D220	DIE, FISHHOOK	MATRICE A HAMECON
D220	DIE, MILITARY BUTTON	MATRICE A BOUTON MILITAIRE
D220	DIE, MILITARY MESS PLATE	MATRICE A ASSIETTE DE CANTINE MILITAIRE
D220	DIE, MILITARY SHAKO PLATE	MATRICE A PLAQUE DE SHAKO MILITAIRE
D220	DIE, STAMP	MATRICE A TIMBRE A ENCRER
D220	DIE, TOE-CALK WELDING	MACHOIRE DE SOUDAGE DE CRAMPON DE PINCE
J060	DIGGER, POST-HOLE	BECHE A POTEAU
D020	DIGGER, POTATO	FOURCHE A POMMES DE TERRE
H080	DIORAMA	DIORAMA
H040	DIORAMA	DIORAMA
H080	DIPLOMA	DIPLOME
D100	DIPPER	POCHON
E380	DIRECTOR	SONDE CANNELEE
H080	DIRECTORY, TELEPHONE	ANNUAIRE DE TELEPHONE
E080	DIRK, MILITARY	POIGNARD MILITAIRE
D120	DISH	PLAT
E380	DISH	PLAT
I100	DISH	PLAT
D100	DISH, BAKING	PLAT A CUISSON
D120	DISH, BONBON	BONBONNIERE
D120	DISH, BONE	PLAT A DECHETS
I100	DISH, BUTTER	BEURRIER
D120	DISH, BUTTER	BEURRIER
D120	DISH, CANDY	PLAT A BONBONS
H060	DISH, CEREMONIAL	PLAT DE CEREMONIE
D100	DISH, CHAFING	CHAUFFE-PLATS
D120	DISH, CHEESE	PLAT A FROMAGE
E240	DISH, EVAPORATING	CAPSULE D'EVAPORATION
D120	DISH, FISH	PLAT A POISSON
D120	DISH, HONEY	POT A MIEL
D120	DISH, HOT-WATER	BOL A EAU CHAUDE
D120	DISH LID, BUTTER	COUVERCLE DE BEURRIER
C180	DISH LID, SOAP	COUVERCLE DE PORTE-SAVON
E220	DISH, PETRI	BOITE A CULTURES
D120	DISH, RELISH	PLAT A CONDIMENTS
C180	DISH, SOAP	PORTE-SAVON
D120	DISH, VEGETABLE	PLAT A LEGUMES
D120	DISH, WASTE	VIDE-TASSE
E340	DISHPAN	BASSINE A VAISSELLE
J060	DISPENSER, TAPE	DEVIDOIR A RUBAN ADHESIF

Class. Code	Object, suffix	Objet, suffixe
B080	DISPENSER, TOWEL	DISTRIBUTEUR D'ESSUIE-MAINS
E400	DISPENSER, WRAPPING PAPER	DEVIDOIR DE PAPIER D'EMBALLAGE
D300	DISTAFF	QUENOUILLE
E340	DIVIDER, CLOTHESLINE	SEPARATEUR DE CORDE A LINGE
F040	DIVIDERS	COMPAS A POINTES SECHES
D040	DOCKER	COUPE-QUEUE
G300	DODGER	TOILE DE PASSERELLE DE COMMANDEMENT
D320	DOG, HOOPING	TIRETOIRE
D140	DOG, LOG	HAPPE
D200	DOG, RING	CROCHET A ANNEAU
D140	DOG, RING	CROCHET A ANNEAU
D140	DOG, SPAN	CROCHET DE HALAGE
D320	DOG, SPOKE	SERRE-RAIES
I100	DOGSLED	TRAINEAU A CHIENS
G120	DOGSLED	TRAINEAU A CHIENS
G120	DOGSLED SEAT	SIEGE DE TRAINEAU A CHIENS
B080	DOILY	NAPPERON
I100	DOLL	POUPEE
I100	DOLL HEAD	TETE DE POUPEE
I100	DOLL, PAPER	POUPEE EN PAPIER
I100	DOLLHOUSE	MAISON DE POUPEE
G140	DOLLY	DIABLE
E340	DOLLY, WASH	AGITATEUR A LESSIVE
D120	DOME, FOOD	CLOCHE
I020	DOMINOES	DOMINOS
A040	DOOR	PORTE
A040	DOOR, BAKEOVEN	PORTE DE FOUR A PAIN
A040	DOOR, FIREPLACE	PORTE DE FOYER
A040	DOORBELL	SONNETTE
A040	DOORFRAME	DORMANT DE PORTE
A040	DOORKNOB	POIGNEE DE PORTE
B040	DOORMAT	PAILLASSON
A040	DOORPLATE	PLAQUE DE PORTE
A040	DOORSPRING	RESSORT DE PORTE
B080	DOORSTOP	BUTOIR DE PORTE
G280	DORY	DORIS
G280	DORY, MODEL	DORIS MODELE REDUIT
C100	DOUBLET, MILITARY	DOUBLET ECOSSAIS MILITAIRE
G180	DOUBLETREE	PALONNIER DOUBLE
G180	DOUBLETREE, LOGGER'S	PALONNIER DOUBLE DE BUCHERON
E380	DOUCHE, NASAL	DOUCHE NASALE
D320	DOWNSHAVE, COOPER'S	RABOT D'EXTERIEUR DE TONNELIER
B160	DRAPERY	DRAPERIE
C120	DRAWERS	CALECON
C120	DRAWERS, CHILD'S	CALECON D'ENFANT
H040	DRAWING	DESSIN
H080	DRAWING, MILITARY TECHNICAL	DESSIN TECHNIQUE MILITAIRE
H080	DRAWING, TECHNICAL	DESSIN TECHNIQUE
D320	DRAWKNIFE	PLANE
D320	DRAWKNIFE, BOXING	VASTRINGUE
D320	DRAWKNIFE, COOPER'S	PLANE DE TONNELIER
D320	DRAWKNIFE, COOPER'S CHAMFERING	PLANE A CHANFREINER DE TONNELIER
D320	DRAWKNIFE, COOPER'S HEADING	PLANE DE FONCAGE
D320	DRAWKNIFE, COOPER'S HOLLOWING	PLANE CREUSE DE TONNELIER
G120	DRAY	FARDIER
D240	DREDGE	DRAGUE
D060	DREDGE, SHRIMP	DRAGUE A CREVETTES
D100	DREDGER	SAUPOUDROIR
C100	DRESS	ROBE
I100	DRESS	ROBE
C100	DRESS, CHILD'S	ROBE D'ENFANT

Class. Code	Object, suffix	Objet, suffixe
C100	DRESS, INSTRUCTIONAL MODEL	ROBE MODELE D'INSTRUCTION
D220	DRESSER, GRINDING WHEEL	REDRESSEUR DE MEULE
D320	DRILL	PERCEUSE
D320	DRILL, BOW	EMBOUCHURE DE FORET A ARCHET
B140	DRILL, FIREMAKING	ARCHET A FEU
D240	DRILL, PERCUSSIVE AIR	PERFORATRICE PNEUMATIQUE A PERCUSSION
D240	DRILL, PLACER	PERFORATRICE A EXPLOITATION DE PLACERS
D240	DRILL, ROTARY	PERFORATRICE ROTATIVE
D200	DRILL, ROUND	FORET CYLINDRIQUE
D320	DRIVER, HOOP	CHASSE
D240	DRIVER, POINT	MASSE
F060	DRUM	TAMBOUR
H060	DRUM, CEREMONIAL	TAMBOUR DE CEREMONIE
E400	DRUM, DIESEL OIL	BIDON A CARBURANT DIESEL
E400	DRUM, GASOLINE	BIDON A GAZOLINE
F060	DRUM HEAD	PEAU DE TAMBOUR
E400	DRUM, KEROSINE	BIDON A PETROLE
F060	DRUM, MILITARY	TAMBOUR MILITAIRE
F060	DRUMSTICK	BAGUETTE DE TAMBOUR
F060	DRUMSTICK, MILITARY	BAGUETTE DE TAMBOUR MILITAIRE
E340	DRYER	SECHEUSE
D100	DRYER, CORN	SECHOIR A EPIS DE MAIS
D100	DRYER, HERB	SECHOIR POUR FINES HERBES
D300	DRYER, YARN	SECHOIR POUR FIL DE LAINE
I080	DUMBBELL	HALTERE
A040	DUMBWAITER	MONTE-PLATS
E340	DUSTER	PLUMEAU
C180	DUSTER, BARBER'S	EPOUSSETTE DE COIFFEUR
D020	DUSTER, DRY-POWDER	PULVERISATEUR
E340	DUSTPAN	RAMASSE-POUSSIERE
I100	DUSTPAN	RAMASSE-POUSSIERE
E300	DYNAMOTOR	DYNAMOTEUR
F120	EARPHONE	ECOUTEUR
C020	EARRING	BOUCLE D'OREILLE
B060	EASEL	CHEVALET
D020	EDGER, TURF	COUPE-BORDURE
D300	EGG, DARNING	BOULE A REPRISER
D100	EGGBEATER	BATTEUR A OEUFS
D120	EGGCUP	COQUETIER
E380	ELEVATOR, MALAR	ELEVATOIRE MOLAIRE
E380	ELEVATOR, TREPANNING	ELEVATEUR POUR TREPANATION
F100	ENDPAPER	PAGE DE GARDE
H080	ENDPAPER, BOOK	PAGE DE GARDE
G080	ENGINE	MOTEUR
E300	ENGINE, DESIGN MODEL	MOTEUR MODELE DE PROJET
E300	ENGINE, GASOLINE	MOTEUR A ESSENCE
E300	ENGINE, STEAM	MACHINE A VAPEUR
I100	ENGINE, STEAM	MACHINE A VAPEUR
H080	ENVELOPE	ENVELOPPE
H080	ENVELOPE, COMMEMORATIVE	ENVELOPPE COMMEMORATIVE
H120	EPAULET	EPAULETTE
H120	EPAULET, MILITARY	EPAULETTE MILITAIRE
H120	EPAULET, POLICE	EPAULETTE DE POLICE
D120	EPERGNE	SURTOUT DE TABLE
F180	ERASER	GOMME A EFFACER
A040	ESCUTCHEON	ECUSSON
B060	ETAGERE	ETAGERE
C160	ETUI	ETUI
H080	EXERCISE, SCHOOL	CAHIER D'EXERCICES
I100	EXPLODER, CAP	DETONATEUR
B100	EXTINGUISHER, CANDLE	ETEIGNOIR DE BOUGIE

Class. Code	Object, suffix	Objet, suffixe
E480	EXTINGUISHER, FIRE	EXTINCTEUR D'INCENDIE
D320	EXTRACTOR, BUNG	TIRE-BONDE
E380	EXTRACTOR, LITHOTOMY	LITHOTRITEUR
C180	EYECUP	OEILLERE
E240	EYEDROPPER	COMPTE-GOUTTES
C160	EYEGLASSES	LUNETTES
E120	FALCONET	FALCONET
C160	FAN	EVENTAIL
H020	FAN	EVENTAIL
I100	FAN	EVENTAIL
B080	FAN, FLY	VENTILATEUR CHASSE-MOUCHES
D240	FAN, VENTILATION	VENTILATEUR D'AERAGE
B120	FAUCET	ROBINET
H060	FAVOR, POTLATCH	CADEAU DE POTLATCH
D200	FEATHER	AIGUILLE
C080	FEDORA	FEDORA
D040	FEEDBAG	SAC A MOUTURE
D040	FEEDER, LIVESTOCK	NOURRISSEUR A BETAIL
D040	FEEDER, POULTRY	NOURRISSEUR A VOLAILLE
A060	FENCE	CLOTURE
G300	FENDER	AMORTISSEUR
B060	FENDER	GARDE-FEU
G280	FERRY, MODEL	TRAVERSIER MODELEREDUIT
C140	FICHU	FICHU
D180	FID	EPISSOIR
D300	FID	EPISSOIR A CABLE
G300	FIDDLE, MESS TABLE	VIOLONS DE MER
F060	FIFE	FIFRE
F060	FIFE, MILITARY	FIFRE MILITAIRE
I100	FIGURE	FIGURE
H080	FIGURE	MANNEQUIN
H080	FIGURE, INSTRUCTIONAL MODEL	FIGURE MODELE D'INSTRUCTION
G300	FIGUREHEAD	FIGURE DE PROUE
H040	FIGURINE	FIGURINE
H080	FIGURINE	FIGURINE
H080	FIGURINE, MILITARY	FIGURINE MILITAIRE
H040	FIGURINE, MILITARY	FIGURINE MILITAIRE
H060	FIGURINE, RELIGIOUS	FIGURINE RELIGIEUSE
D320	FILE	LIME
D220	FILE, FLAT	LIME PLATE
D220	FILE, MILL	LIME A PARER
C180	FILE, NAIL	LIME A ONGLES
F180	FILE, PORTABLE	CLASSEUR PORTATIF
D220	FILE, ROUND	LIME RONDE
D220	FILE, SAW	LIME A SCIE
D220	FILE, TRIANGULAR	TIERS-POINT
D220	FILE HANDLE	MANCHE DE LIME
H080	FILM	FILM
F080	FILTER	FILTRE
B080	FILTER, WATER	FILTRE A EAU
E500	FINDER, RANGE	TELEMETRE
E180	FINDER, RANGE	TELEMETRE
D180	FINGERSTALL	DOIGTIER
A040	FINIAL	EPI DE FAITAGE
B140	FIREBACK	CONTRE-FEU
B140	FIREBOARD	ECRAN DE CHEMINEE
A020	FIREPLACE	FOYER
A020	FIREPLACE FACADE	FACADE DE CHEMINEE
B140	FIRESET	ENSEMBLE DE FOYER
B140	FIRESET, MILITARY	ENSEMBLE DE FOYER MILITAIRE
D100	FIRKIN	BARILLET

Class. Code	Object, suffix	Objet, suffixe
H040	FISH, ARTIFICIAL	POISSON ARTIFICIEL
G280	FISHERMAN	CHALOUPE DE PECHE
G280	FISHERMAN, MINIATURE	CHALOUPE DE PECHE MINIATURE
G280	FISHERMAN, MODEL	CHALOUPE DE PECHE MODELE REDUIT
G280	FISHERMAN, MODEL SCHOONER	GOELETTE DE PECHE MODELE REDUIT
D060	FISHHOOK	HAMECON
H060	FLABELLUM	PLUME
H060	FLAG	DRAPEAU
H060	FLAG, MILITARY	DRAPEAU MILITAIRE
F160	FLAG, SIGNAL	PAVILLON
F060	FLAGEOLET	FLAGEOLET
I100	FLAGEOLET	FLAGEOLET
F060	FLAGEOLET, MILITARY	FLAGEOLET MILITAIRE
D120	FLAGON	POT A ANSE A VIN
H060	FLAGPOLE	HAMPE DE DRAPEAU
A060	FLAGPOLE	MAT DE DRAPEAU
H060	FLAGPOLE FINIAL	POMMEAU DE HAMPE DE DRAPEAU
D020	FLAIL	FLEAU
B100	FLASHLIGHT	TORCHE ELECTRIQUE
E240	FLASK	BALLON
D220	FLASK, MOLDING	BOITE A MOULER
C160	FLASK, POCKET	FLASQUE DE POCHE
E180	FLASK, POWDER	FLASQUE A POUDRE
E180	FLASK, PRIMING	PULVERIN
E180	FLASK, SHOT	FOURNIMENT
D220	FLATTER	APLATISSOIR
B140	FLINT	PIERRE A FEU
E180	FLINT	PIERRE A FEU
E060	FLINTLOCK MECHANISM	PLATINE A SILEX
D200	FLOAT	RIPE
D060	FLOAT	FLOTTEUR
D040	FLOAT, DENTAL	RAPE A DENTS
G300	FLOAT, LIFE	FLOTTEUR DE SAUVETAGE
E180	FLOAT, MINIATURE	FLOTTEUR DE HARPON MINIATURE
A020	FLOOR	PLANCHER
B040	FLOORCLOTH	SERPILLIERE
H040	FLOWER, ARTIFICIAL	FLEUR ARTIFICIELLE
B080	FLOWERPOT	POT A FLEURS
B080	FLOWERPOT, MINIATURE	POT A FLEURS MINIATURE
A040	FLUE	CONDUIT DE CHEMINEE
F060	FLUTE	FLUTE
B080	FLYPAPER	PAPIER ATTRAPE-MOUCHES
B080	FLYTRAP	PIEGE A MOUCHES
E360	FLYWHEEL	VOLANT
C020	FOB	BRELOQUE DE CHAINE DE MONTRE
F120	FOGHORN	CORNE DE BRUME
E080	FOIL	FLEURET
F180	FOLDER, FILE	CHEMISE
H060	FONT, BAPTISMAL	FONTS BAPTISMAUX
H060	FONT, HOLY WATER	BENITIER
H040	FOOD, MISCELLANEOUS ARTIFICIAL	PRODUITS ALIMENTAIRES ARTIFICIELS
B060	FOOTSTOOL	MARCHEPIED
E380	FORCEPS	FORCEPS
E380	FORCEPS, ASSALINI	PINCE ASSALINI
E380	FORCEPS, BONE-CUTTING	OSTEOTOME
E380	FORCEPS, DENTAL	FORCEPS DE DENTISTE
I100	FORGE	FORGE
D220	FORGE, BLACKSMITH'S	FORGE DE FORGERON
D020	FORK	FOURCHE
D120	FORK	FOURCHETTE
D020	FORK, ALFALFA	FOURCHE A LUZERNE

Class. Code	Object, suffix	Objet, suffixe
D220	FORK, BENDING	FOURCHE A CINTRER
D120	FORK, CARVING	FOURCHETTE A DECOUPER
D120	FORK, COLD-MEAT	FOURCHETTE A VIANDES FROIDES
D120	FORK, DESSERT	FOURCHETTE A DESSERT
D120	FORK, DINNER	FOURCHETTE A DINER
B140	FORK, FIREPLACE	FOURCHE DE FOYER
D100	FORK, FISH	FOURCHE A POISSON
D120	FORK, FISH	FOURCHETTE A POISSON
D120	FORK, FISH-SERVING	FOURCHETTE DE SERVICE A POISSON
D120	FORK, FRUIT	FOURCHETTE A FRUITS
D020	FORK, HAY-LIFTING	FOURCHE A FANER
E340	FORK, LAUNDRY	FOURCHE A LESSIVE
D120	FORK, LUNCHEON	FOURCHETTE A COLLATION
D020	FORK, MANURE	FOURCHE A FUMIER
D100	FORK, MILITARY TOASTING	FOURCHETTE A GRIL MILITAIRE
D120	FORK, MINIATURE	FOURCHETTE MINIATURE
D120	FORK, OYSTER	FOURCHETTE A HUITRES
D120	FORK, PICKLE	FOURCHETTE A CORNICHONS
D120	FORK, SALAD	FOURCHETTE A SALADE
D240	FORK, SLUICE	FOURCHE A AUGE
D020	FORK, SPADING	FOURCHE A BECHER
D180	FORK, STRAINING	FOURCHETTE DE TENSION DE SANGLE
D550	FORK, THATCHING	FOURCHE A CHAUME
D100	FORK, TOASTING	FOURCHETTE A GRIL
E020	FORK, TUNING	DIAPASON
D020	FORK, VEGETABLE SCOOP	FOURCHE-PELLE A LEGUMES
F180	FORM, ACCOUNT STATEMENT	ETAT DE COMPTE
F180	FORM, BANK DEPOSIT	BORDERAU DE DEPOT
H080	FORM, BANK DEPOSIT	BORDEREAU DE DEPOT
F180	FORM, BANK WITHDRAWAL	BORDEREAU DE RETRAIT
F180	FORM, DEATH CERTIFICATE	FORMULAIRE D'ACTE DE DECES
F180	FORM, DEATH REGISTRATION	FORMULE D'INSCRIPTION POUR ACTE DE DECES
D300	FORM, DRESS	MANNEQUIN
F180	FORM, EMPLOYMENT	FORMULAIRE DE DEMANDE D'EMPLOI
F180	FORM, FUNERAL RECORD	FORMULAIRE D'EXTRAIT MORTUAIRE
F180	FORM, GOLD RECOVERY	FORMULAIRE DE RECUPERATION D'OR
F180	FORM, MEDICAL	FORMULAIRE DE DOSSIER MEDICAL
F180	FORM, ORDER	BON DE COMMANDE
F180	FORM, POLICE ISSUE	FORMULAIRE DE DISTRIBUTION DE POLICE
F180	FORM, PROMISSORY NOTE	FORMULAIRE DE BILLET A ORDRE
F180	FORM, SHIPPING	FORMULAIRE D'EXPEDITION
F180	FORM, TIME SHEET	FORMULAIRE DE FEUILLE DE PRESENCE
H080	FORM, WILL	FORMULAIRE DE TESTAMENT
A020	FORT, MODEL	FORT MODELE REDUIT
H060	FOUNTAIN, HOLY WATER	FONTAINE A EAU BENITE
A060	FOUNTAIN, WATER	
D040	FRAME, OX-SHOEING	CHUTE DE CONTENTION POUR BOVINS
C160	FRAME, PACK	SUPPORT DE SAC A DOS
B080	FRAME, PICTURE	CADRE
H040	FRAME, PICTURE	CADRE
D300	FRAME, QUILTING	METIER A COURTEPOINTE
D300	FRAME, TENTER	RAME DE METIER
D300	FRAME, WARPING	OURDISSOIR
D320	FRAME, WHEELWRIGHT'S WHEEL	CADRE D'ASSEMBLAGE DE ROUE
A040	FRAME, WINDOW	DORMANT DE FENETRE
D100	FREEZER, ICE-CREAM	SORBETIERE
D320	FROE	DEPARTOIR
B080	FROG	PORTE-FLEURS
E180	FROG, MILITARY BAYONET	PORTE-BAIONNETTE MILITAIRE
E180	FROG, MILITARY SWORD	PENDANT PORTE-EPEE MILITAIRE
E180	FROG STUD, MILITARY	BOUTON DE PENDANT PORTE-BAIONNETTE MILITAIRE

Class. Code	Object, suffix	Objet, suffixe
H060	FRONTAL	DEVANT D'AUTEL
H040	FRUIT, ARTIFICIAL	FRUIT ARTIFICIEL
D220	FULLER, BOTTOM	MATOIR INFERIEUR
D220	FULLER, TOP	MATOIR SUPERIEUR
D100	FUNNEL	ENTONNOIR
E240	FUNNEL	ENTONNOIR
J060	FUNNEL	ENTONNOIR
E240	FUNNEL, FILTER	ENTONNOIR DE FILTRATION
D160	FUNNEL, WAX	ENTONNOIR A CIRE
D100	FUNNEL, WINE	ENTONNOIR A VIN
J020	FUR FRAGMENT	FRAGMENT DE FOURRURE
F100	FURNACE, SMELT	FONDEUSE
F100	FURNITURE	GARNITURE
E140	FUSE, MILITARY DETONATING	DETONATEUR MILITAIRE
E280	FUSEBOARD	PORTE-FUSIBLES
D060	GAFF, FISH	GAFFE A POISSON
D060	GAFF, MINIATURE SEALING	GAFFE DE CHASSE AU PHOQUE MINIATURE
D040	GAG, HORSE'S MOUTH	MUSEROLLE DE CHEVAL
C060	GAITER	GUETRE
C060	GAITER, MILITARY	GUETRE MILITAIRE
F100	GALLEY	GALEE
G280	GALLEY, MODEL VIKING	GALERE DE VIKING MODELE REDUIT
E380	GALLIPOT	GALIPOT
D100	GAMBREL	JAMBIER
G300	GANGPLANK	PASSERELLE D'EMBARQUEMENT
E180	GARLAND, MILITARY SHOT	CADRE A PILE DE PROJECTILES MILITAIRE
C140	GARTER	JARRETIERE
E560	GAUGE	JAUGE
E360	GAUGE, AIR-PRESSURE	CONTROLEUR DE PRESSION D'AIR
D220	GAUGE, BOILER TUBE DIAMETER	CALIBRE POUR CONDUIT DE CHAUDIERE
D320	GAUGE, CLAPBOARD	JAUGE A PLANCHES
D320	GAUGE, CUTTING	TRUSQUIN A MARQUER
D180	GAUGE, DRAW	TRUSQUIN A MARQUER
D220	GAUGE, FLUE DIAMETER	CALIBRE POUR CONDUIT DE CHEMINEE
D060	GAUGE, LOBSTER	JAUGE A HOMARD
D320	GAUGE, MARKING	TRUSQUIN
D300	GAUGE, NET	JAUGE A FILET
E560	GAUGE, PRESSURE	MANOMETRE
E560	GAUGE, SNOW	SONDE A NEIGE
E360	GAUGE, STEAM-PRESSURE	MANOMETRE A VAPEUR
E560	GAUGE, WATER	NIVEAU D'EAU
I100	GAUNTLET	GANTELET
E360	GEAR	ROUE D'ENGRENAGE
E300	GENERATOR	GENERATEUR
D320	GIMLET	VRILLE
E180	GIN, ARTILLERY	CHEVRE D'ARTILLERIE
B100	GIRANDOLE	GIRANDOLE
C120	GIRDLE	GAINE
G180	GIRTH	SOUS-VENTRIERE
E080	GLADIUS, MILITARY	GLAIVE MILITAIRE
D120	GLASS	VERRE
D120	GLASS, CHAMPAGNE	VERRE A CHAMPAGNE
D120	GLASS, COCKTAIL	VERRE A COCKTAIL
D120	GLASS, CORDIAL	VERRE A LIQUEUR
J020	GLASS FRAGMENT	FRAGMENT DE VERRE
E460	GLASS, MAGNIFYING	LOUPE
D120	GLASS, MALT-BEVERAGE	VERRE A BIERE
B080	GLASS, PICTURE FRAME	VERRE POUR ENCADREMENT
D120	GLASS, SHERBET	COUPE A DESSERT
D120	GLASS, SHOT	VERRE DE MESURE A ALCOOL
D120	GLASS, SWEETMEAT	VERRE A DESSERT

Class. Code	Object, suffix	Objet, suffixe
D120	GLASS, WINE	VERRE A VIN
E460	GLASSES, FIELD	JUMELLES D'OBSERVATION
D180	GLAZER	GLACEUR
C080	GLENGARRY	GLENGARRY
C080	GLENGARRY, MILITARY	GLENGARRY MILITAIRE
G060	GLIDER, DESIGN MODEL	PLANEUR MODELE DE PROJET
H080	GLOBE	GLOBE
D300	GLOBE, LACEMAKER'S	BALLON DE PASSEMENTIER
C140	GLOVE	GANT
I080	GLOVE, BOXING	GANT DE BOXE
C140	GLOVE, FISHERMAN'S	GANT DE PECHEUR
C140	GLOVE, POLICE	GANT DE POLICE
D320	GLUEPOT	POT A COLLE
D120	GOBLET	GOBELET
D120	GOBLET, MINIATURE	GOBELET MINIATURE
C160	GOGGLES	LUNETTES DE PROTECTION
C160	GOGGLES, SNOW	LUNETTES DE NEIGE
C160	GOGGLES FILTER	FILTRE POUR LUNETTES DE PROTECTION
F120	GONG	GONG
F060	GONG	GONG
H120	GORGET, MILITARY	HAUSSE-COL MILITAIRE
D180	GOUGE	GOUGE
D320	GOUGE	GOUGE
D320	GOUGE, CARVING	GOUGE A SCULPTER
D320	GOUGE, FIRMER	CISEAU A GOUGE
D320	GOUGE, PARING	CISEAU LONG
D320	GOUGE, TURNING	GOUGE DE TOURNAGE
D180	GOUGE, V	GOUGE EN V
E300	GOVERNOR	REGULATEUR
G240	GOVERNOR, STEAM LOCOMOTIVE	REGULATEUR DE LOCOMOTIVE A VAPEUR
H120	GOWN, ACADEMIC	ROBE ACADEMIQUE
C100	GOWN, BAPTISMAL	ROBE DE BAPTEME
C100	GOWN, DRESSING	ROBE DE CHAMBRE
C100	GOWN, WEDDING	ROBE DE MARIEE
E240	GRADUATE	RECIPIENT GRADUE
E140	GRAPESHOT	MITRAILLE EN GRAPPE
E140	GRAPESHOT, MILITARY	MITRAILLE EN GRAPPE MILITAIRE
E140	GRAPESHOT, MINIATURE	MITRAILLE EN GRAPPE MINIATURE
B140	GRATE, FIREPLACE	GRILLE DE FOYER
D100	GRATER	RAPE
E340	GRATER, SOAP	RAPE A SAVON
D100	GRATER, SPICE	RAPE A EPICES
C160	GRATER, TOBACCO	RAPE A TABAC
D180	GRAVER	BURIN
C100	GREATCOAT, MILITARY	CAPOTE MILITAIRE
E140	GRENADE	GRENADE
E140	GRENADE, ANTIPERSONNEL	GRENADE ANTIPERSONNEL
D100	GRIDDLE	POELE A CREPES
A040	GRILL, VENTILATOR	GRILLE DE VENTILATEUR
A040	GRILL, WINDOW	GRILLE DE FENETRE
D220	GRINDER	RECTIFIEUSE
D100	GRINDER, BONE	BROYEUR A OS
D020	GRINDER, FEED	BROYEUR A NOURRITURE DE BETAIL
D100	GRINDER, MEAT	HACHOIR A VIANDE
D220	GRINDSTONE	MEULE A AIGUISER
E300	GRIP, SERVICE CABLE	TIRE-CABLE DE SERVICE
J060	GRIPPER, BARREL	SERRE-TONNEAU
B100	GRISETTE	GRISETTE
J060	GROMMET	OEILLET
D220	GROOVER, HAND	FRAISE A CANNELER A MAIN
D180	GROOVER, MARTINGALE	GRAVOIR A MARTINGALE

Class. Code	Object, suffix	Objet, suffixe
D180	GROOVER, STITCHING	*POINTE A TRACER*
D180	GROOVER BLADE	*LAME DE GOUGE A RAINURER*
H040	GROUP, FIGURINE	*GROUPE DE FIGURINES*
I080	GUARD, ICE SKATE	*PROTECTEUR DE LAME DE PATIN*
D020	GUARD, MOWER SICKLE BAR	*PROTECTEUR DE BARRE DE COUPE DE FAUCHEUSE*
A040	GUDGEON	*CHEVILLE DE CHARNIERE*
F060	GUITAR	*GUITARE*
I100	GUN	*FUSIL*
I100	GUN, AIR	*CARABINE A AIR*
E120	GUN, ANTITANK	*CANON ANTICHAR*
E120	GUN, GATLING	*MITRAILLEUSE GATLING*
J060	GUN, GREASE	*POMPE DE GRAISSAGE*
E060	GUN, MACHINE	*MITRAILLEUSE*
E120	GUN, MILITARY	*CANON MILITAIRE*
E120	GUN, MILITARY ANTIAIRCRAFT	*CANON ANTIAERIEN MILITAIRE*
E120	GUN, MILITARY FIELD	*CANON DE CAMPAGNE MILITAIRE*
E120	GUN, MILITARY GARRISON	*CANON DE GARNISON MILITAIRE*
E120	GUN, MILITARY SEA-COAST	*CANON DE DEFENSE COTIERE*
E120	GUN, SWIVEL	*CANON SUR PIVOT*
E360	GYROSCOPE	*GYROSCOPE*
C100	HABIT, RELIGIOUS	*HABIT RELIGIEUX*
C100	HABIT, RIDING	*AMAZONE*
A020	HABITATION, MODEL	*HABITATION MODELE REDUIT*
D220	HACKSAW	*SCIE A METAUX*
D220	HACKSAW BLADE	*LAME DE SCIE A METAUX*
D180	HAFT, AWL	*MANCHE D'ALENE*
D180	HAFT, PEGGING AWL	*MANCHE DE BROCHE*
D180	HAFT, SEWING AWL	*MANCHE DE CARRELET DE COORDONNIER*
C180	HAIRBAG, MILITARY	*BOURSE A CHEVEUX MILITAIRE*
C180	HAIRBRUSH	*BROSSE A CHEVEUX*
C080	HAIRNET	*RESILLE*
C020	HAIRPIECE	*POSTICHE*
C180	HAIRPIN	*EPINGLE A CHEVEUX*
E080	HALBERD	*HALLEBARDE*
E080	HALBERD, MILITARY	*HALLEBARDE MILITAIRE*
B060	HALLSTAND	*PORTEMANTEAU D'ENTREE*
I020	HALMA	*JEU DE HALMA*
G180	HALTER	*LICOU*
G180	HAME	*ATTELLE*
J060	HAMMER	*MARTEAU*
I100	HAMMER	*MARTEAU*
D220	HAMMER	*MARTEAU*
D320	HAMMER	*MARTEAU*
D200	HAMMER	*MARTEAU*
D220	HAMMER, BALL-PEEN	*MARTEAU A PANNE RONDE*
D320	HAMMER, CLAW	*MARTEAU A DENT*
D180	HAMMER, COBBLER'S	*MARTEAU DE CORDONNIER*
D320	HAMMER, COOPER'S	*MARTEAU DE TONNELIER*
D220	HAMMER, CROSS-PEEN	*MARTEAU A PANNE TRANSVERSALE*
D200	HAMMER, FACE	*MARTEAU A PANNE*
D040	HAMMER, FARRIER'S DRIVING	*BROCHOIR*
D040	HAMMER, FARRIER'S FITTING	*FERRATIER*
D240	HAMMER, HAND	*MARTEAU-PERFORATEUR A MAIN*
D320	HAMMER, JOINER'S	*MARTEAU DE MENUISIER*
E180	HAMMER, MAGAZINE COOPER'S	*MARTEAU DE TONNELIER DE POUDRIERE*
D140	HAMMER, MARKING	*MARTEAU A MARQUER*
D200	HAMMER, PATENT	*MARTEAU A PIERRE*
D220	HAMMER, RAISING	*MARTEAU A REHAUSSER*
D220	HAMMER, RIVETING	*RIVOIR*
D180	HAMMER, SADDLER'S	*MARTEAU DE SELLIER*
D220	HAMMER, SET	*PAROIR*

Class. Code	Object, suffix	Objet, suffixe
D220	HAMMER, SETTING	*MARTEAU A RESTREINDRE*
D320	HAMMER, SETTING	*MARTEAU A RESTREINDRE*
G300	HAMMER, SHACKLE PIN	*MARTEAU D'EXTRACTION DE GOUPILLE DE MANILLE*
D220	HAMMER, SHIPWRIGHT'S COPPERING	*MARTEAU A CUIVRAGE DE CHARPENTIER NAVAL*
D200	HAMMER, SLATER'S	*MARTEAU A ARDOISE*
D200	HAMMER, SPALLING	*MARTEAU A DEGROSSIR*
D220	HAMMER, STRAIGHT-PEEN	*MARTEAU A PANNE DROIT*
D100	HAMMER, SUGAR	*MARTEAU A SUCRE*
D320	HAMMER, TACK	*MARTEAU DE TAPISSIER*
J060	HAMMER HANDLE	*MANCHE DE MARTEAU*
D140	HAMMER HEAD, MARKING	*TETE DE MARTEAU A MARQUER*
J060	HAMMERSTONE	*PIERRE-MARTEAU*
B020	HAMMOCK	*HAMAC*
E340	HAMPER	*PANIER A LINGE*
D100	HAND, SCOTCH	*PALETTE A BEURRE*
G140	HANDBARROW	*CIVIERE*
H080	HANDBILL	*FEUILLET*
H020	HANDBILL	*PROSPECTUS*
G220	HANDCAR	*CHARIOT*
E480	HANDCUFFS	*MENOTTES*
E480	HANDCUFFS, MILITARY	*MENOTTES MILITAIRE*
C160	HANDKERCHIEF	*MOUCHOIR*
H080	HANDKERCHIEF, COMMEMORATIVE	*MOUCHOIR COMMEMORATIF*
F100	HANDPRESS	*PRESSE A BRAS*
I100	HANDPRESS	*PRESSE A BRAS*
A020	HANDRAIL	*RAMPE*
E180	HANDSPIKE, MILITARY	*LEVIER DE POINTAGE*
E080	HANGER, MILITARY	*SABRE COURT MILITAIRE*
D180	HANGER, PELT	*CROCHET A PEAUX*
B080	HANGER, PICTURE FRAME	*CROCHET DE CADRE*
A040	HANGER, PIPE	*ETRIER DE SUSPENSION*
H040	HANGING	*TENTURE*
D220	HARDY	*TRANCHET*
D220	HARDY, HALF-ROUND	*TRANCHET DEMI-LUNE*
D220	HARDY, STRAIGHT	*TRANCHET DROIT*
F060	HARMONICA	*HARMONICA*
G180	HARNESS	*HARNAIS*
I100	HARNESS	*HARNAIS*
G180	HARNESS, DOG	*HARNAIS DE CHIEN*
G180	HARNESS, FARM	*HARNAIS DE FERME*
F060	HARP, JEW'S	*GUIMBARDE*
E080	HARPOON	*HARPON*
E080	HARPOON, MINIATURE	*HARPON MINIATURE*
E080	HARPOON HEAD	*HARPOISE*
F060	HARPSICHORD	*CLAVECIN*
E060	HARQUEBUS	*ARQUEBUSE*
D020	HARROW, DISK	*HERSE A DISQUES*
D020	HARROW, SPIKE-TOOTH	*HERSE A DENTS RIGIDES*
A040	HASP	*MORAILLON*
C080	HAT	*CHAPEAU*
H120	HAT	*CHAPEAU*
C080	HAT, HARD	*CASQUE DE SECURITE*
C080	HAT, MILITARY BICORN	*BICORNE MILITAIRE*
C080	HAT, MILITARY TRICORN	*TRICORNE MILITAIRE*
C080	HAT, PANAMA	*PANAMA*
C080	HAT, POLICE	*CHAPEAU DE POLICE*
C080	HAT, RAIN	*SUROIT*
C080	HAT, TOP	*HAUT-DE-FORME*
C080	HAT, TRICORN	*TRICORNE*
C080	HAT BODY	*CALOTTE DE CHAPEAU*
C080	HATBAND	*BOURDALOU*

Class. Code	Object, suffix	Objet, suffixe
C080	HATBAND, MILITARY	*BOURDALOU MILITAIRE*
C080	HATBAND, POLICE	*BOURDALOU DE POLICE*
C160	HATBOX	*BOITE A CHAPEAU*
C160	HATBOX, MILITARY	*BOITE A CHAPEAU MILITAIRE*
C160	HATBOX, POLICE	*BOITE A CHAPEAU DE POLICE*
D300	HATCHEL	*SERANCOIR*
D320	HATCHET	*HACHETTE*
D320	HATCHET, LATHING	*HACHETTE DE LATTAGE*
I100	HATCHET, SHINGLING	*HACHETTE A BARDEAUX*
D320	HATCHET, SHINGLING	*HACHETTE A BARDEAUX*
D320	HATCHET, SIDE	*HACHETTE A BISEAU*
C140	HATPIN	*EPINGLE A CHAPEAU*
C080	HAVELOCK, MILITARY	*COUVRE-NUQUE MILITAIRE*
C160	HAVERSACK	*HAVRESAC*
C160	HAVERSACK, MILITARY	*HAVRESAC MILITAIRE*
C160	HAVERSACK, POLICE	*HAVRESAC DE POLICE*
D200	HAWK	*TALOCHE*
D020	HAYFORK	*FOURCHE A FOIN*
C080	HEADBAND	*BANDEAU*
H120	HEADDRESS	*COIFFURE*
B140	HEATER	*APPAREIL DE CHAUFFAGE*
B140	HEATER, ALCOHOL	*RADIATEUR A ALCOOL*
B140	HEATER, BURNING-FLUID	*RADIATEUR A CARBURANT LIQUIDE*
B140	HEATER, COAL	*APPAREIL DE CHAUFFAGE AU CHARBON*
C180	HEATER, CURLING IRON	*CHAUFFE-FER A FRISER*
B140	HEATER, LAMP	*RADIATEUR DE LAMPE*
D100	HEATER, MILK	*CHAUFFE-LAIT*
B120	HEATER, WATER	*CHAUFFE-EAU*
B140	HEATER, WOOD	*APPAREIL DE CHAUFFAGE AU BOIS*
F160	HELIOGRAPH	*HELIOGRAPHE*
E160	HELMET	*CASQUE*
C080	HELMET, AVIATOR'S	*CASQUE D'AVIATEUR*
C080	HELMET, FIREMAN'S	*CASQUE DE POMPIER*
C080	HELMET, MILITARY	*CASQUE MILITAIRE*
E160	HELMET, MILITARY	*CASQUE MILITAIRE*
C080	HELMET, MILITARY PITH	*CASQUE COLONIAL MILITAIRE*
C080	HELMET, MINER'S	*CASQUE DE MINEUR*
C080	HELMET, POLICE PITH	*CASQUE COLONIAL DE POLICE*
B060	HIGHCHAIR	*CHAISE HAUTE*
I100	HIGHCHAIR	*CHAISE HAUTE*
A040	HINGE	*CHARNIERE*
B160	HINGE, AWNING	*CHARNIERE DE VELUM*
D040	HOBBLE	*ENTRAVE*
I100	HOBBYHORSE	*DADA*
D200	HOD	*HOTTE DE MACON*
I100	HOE	*HOUE*
D020	HOE	*HOUE*
D060	HOE, CLAMMING	*HOUE A PALOURDES*
D020	HOE, GARDEN	*HOUE DE JARDINAGE*
D020	HOE, GRUB	*HOUE*
D200	HOE, MILITARY MORTAR	*HOUE A MORTIER MILITAIRE*
D200	HOE, MORTAR	*HOUE A MORTIER*
D020	HOE, TURNIP	*HOUE A BETTERAVES*
D020	HOE BLADE	*LAME DE HOUE*
E360	HOIST	*PALAN*
D240	HOIST, MINE	*TREUIL DE MINE*
G180	HOLDBACK	*RETENUE*
E400	HOLDER, BAG	*SUPPORT A SACS*
H060	HOLDER, BIRTHDAY CANDLE	*PORTE-BOUGIE A GATEAU*
F180	HOLDER, CALENDAR	*SUPPORT DE CALENDRIER*
F180	HOLDER, CARD	*PORTE-ETIQUETTE*

Class. Code	Object, suffix	Objet, suffixe
D320	HOLDER, CAULKING IRON	POCHETTE A CISEAU DE CALFAT
C160	HOLDER, CIGAR	FUME-CIGARE
C160	HOLDER, CIGARETTE	FUME-CIGARETTE
E340	HOLDER, CLOTHESPIN	POCHETTE A EPINGLES A LINGE
C160	HOLDER, COIN	PORTE-MONNAIE
D120	HOLDER, CORNCOB	PORTE-EPI DE MAIS
F180	HOLDER, DESK-BLOTTER	SOUS-MAIN
D220	HOLDER, DIE	PORTE-MATRICE
E340	HOLDER, DUSTER	PORTE-PLUMEAU
E480	HOLDER, FIRE HOSE	SUPPORT A MANCHE A INCENDIE
A040	HOLDER, FLAG	SUPPORT A DRAPEAU
C140	HOLDER, HATPIN	PORTE-EPINGLES A CHAPEAU
B100	HOLDER, LAMP	SUPPORT A LAMPE
H060	HOLDER, LAMPION	SUPPORT A LAMPIONS
B100	HOLDER, LANTERN	SUPPORT A LANTERNE
C020	HOLDER, LAPEL PIN	PROTEGE-POINTE D'EPINGLE DE REVERS
B080	HOLDER, MATCH	SUPPORT A BOITE A ALLUMETTES
B100	HOLDER, MILITARY LAMP	SUPPORT A LAMPE MILITAIRE
C160	HOLDER, NOSEGAY	PORTE-BOUQUET
F180	HOLDER, PAPER CLIP	SEBILE A PINCES A PAPIERS
F180	HOLDER, PEN	PORTE-PLUME
F180	HOLDER, PENCIL	SUPPORT A CRAYONS
D120	HOLDER, PLACECARD	PORTE-NOM
B080	HOLDER, PLATE	PORTE-PLAT
B080	HOLDER, RING	BAGUIER
F080	HOLDER, ROLL-FILM	PORTE-ROULEAU DE FILM
B100	HOLDER, RUSHLIGHT	SUPPORT DE CHANDELLE A MECHE DE JONC
B100	HOLDER, SHADE	SUPPORT D'ABAT-JOUR
C160	HOLDER, SHOE	PORTE-CHAUSSURES
E400	HOLDER, SIGN	PORTE-AFFICHE
B080	HOLDER, SPILL	PORTE-ALLUME-FEU
B100	HOLDER, SPLINT	SUPPORT D'ALLUME-FEU
D300	HOLDER, SPOOL	PORTE-BOBINES
F180	HOLDER, STAMP	ETUI A TIMBRES-POSTE
D180	HOLDER, STRAP	DISPOSITIF DE SOUTIEN DE COURROIE
E400	HOLDER, STRING	DISTRIBUTEUR DE FICELLE
B100	HOLDER, TAPER	SUPPORT DE BOUGIE FILEE
B080	HOLDER, TISSUE	PORTE-MOUCHOIRS DE PAPIER
B080	HOLDER, TOILET PAPER	SUPPORT A PAPIER HYGIENIQUE
C180	HOLDER, TOOTHBRUSH	RECEPTACLE DE BROSSE A DENTS
D120	HOLDER, TOOTHPICK	PORTE-CURE-DENTS
B080	HOLDER, TREE	PIED D'ARBRE
B080	HOLDER, UMBRELLA	PORTE-PARAPLUIES
B080	HOLDER, WATCH	ECRIN DE MONTRE
E340	HOLDER, WHISK BROOM	PORTE-EPOUSSETTE
D320	HOLDFAST	PRESSE A MAIN
E180	HOLSTER	ETUI A PISTOLET
I100	HOLSTER	ETUI A REVOLVER
E180	HOLSTER, MILITARY	ETUI A PISTOLET MILITAIRE
E180	HOLSTER, POLICE	ETUI A PISTOLET DE POLICE
G300	HOLYSTONE	PIERRE PONCEUSE
C080	HOMBERG	HOMBERG
C080	HOOD	CHAPERON
J060	HOOK	CROCHET
D320	HOOK, BENCH	MENTONNET
B080	HOOK, BIRDCAGE	CROCHET A CAGE D'OISEAUX
G300	HOOK, BOAT	CROC DE MARINIER
C140	HOOK, BOOT	TIRE-BOTTE
D020	HOOK, BRUSH	SERPE A BROUSSAILLE
J060	HOOK, BUCKET	CROCHET DE PUITS
D140	HOOK, CANT	TOURNE-BILLES

Class. Code	Object, suffix	Objet, suffixe
J060	HOOK, CARGO	CROC DE CHARGE
G180	HOOK, CARRIAGE CLOTHES	PATERE DE VOITURE
D320	HOOK, CAULKING SHIPWRIGHT'S	CROCHET DE CALFAT
A040	HOOK, CEILING	CROCHET DE PLAFOND
B080	HOOK, COAT	PATERE
D320	HOOK, COOPER'S BLOCK	CROCHET DE BILLOT DE TONNELIER
D020	HOOK, CORN	SERPE A MAIS
D300	HOOK, CROCHET	CROCHET DE TRAVAIL AU CROCHET
J060	HOOK, CUP	CLOU A CROCHET
B160	HOOK, CURTAIN	CROCHET DE RIDEAU
D020	HOOK, GRASS	FAUCILLE A HERBE
G180	HOOK, HAME	CROCHET D'ATTELLE
J060	HOOK, HARNESS	CROCHET A HARNAIS
D020	HOOK, HAY-BALE	CROC A BALLES DE FOIN
J060	HOOK, JAMB	CROCHET SUR BOIS
D180	HOOK, LAST	CROCHET A DEFORMER
D020	HOOK, MANURE	CROC A FUMIER
D100	HOOK, MEAT	CROC DE BOUCHERIE
D220	HOOK, PLATE BENDING	CROCHET DE CINTRAGE DE TOLES
D020	HOOK, POTATO	FOURCHE-ARRACHEUSE DE POMMES DE TERRE
D300	HOOK, RUG	CROCHET A TAPIS
D300	HOOK, SAILMAKER'S	CROCHET A VOILES
G180	HOOK, WHIFFLETREE	CROCHET DE PALONNIER
I100	HOOP	CERCEAU
D300	HOOP, EMBROIDERY	CERCEAU A BRODERIE
G300	HOOP, MAST	CERCLE DE MAT
D320	HOOP, TRUSS	CERCLE RENFORCE DE MONTAGE DE TONNEAU
E500	HORIZON, ARTIFICIAL	HORIZON ARTIFICIEL
G180	HORN	AVERTISSEUR SONORE
I100	HORN	CORNET
F060	HORN, ALTO	COR ANGLAIS
F060	HORN, COACH	BUCCIN DE LA MAIL-COACH
D120	HORN, DRINKING	CORNE A BOIRE
F060	HORN, HUNTING	TROMPE DE CHASSE
E180	HORN, MILITARY POWDER	CORNET A POUDRE MILITAIRE
F120	HORN, PHONOGRAPH	PAVILLON DE PHONOGRAPHE
F060	HORN, POST	TROMPE DE LA MALLE-POSTE
E180	HORN, POWDER	CORNET A POUDRE
D220	HORN, SPRUE MOLDER'S	TROU DE COULEE EN FORME DE COR
I100	HORSE, ROCKING	CHEVAL A BASCULE
D320	HORSE, SHAVING	BANC DE CHARPENTIER
D180	HORSE, STITCHING	CHEVALET A PIQUAGE
D040	HORSESHOE	FER A CHEVAL
D040	HORSESHOE PAD	PATIN DE FER A CHEVAL
D040	HORSESHOE TOE-CALK	CRAMPON DE PINCE A FER A CHEVAL
G300	HOSE, FIRE	MANCHE A INCENDIE
H060	HOST	HOSTIE
E540	HOURGLASS	SABLIER
A020	HOUSE	MAISON
A020	HOUSE, MINIATURE	MAISON MINIATURE
C100	HOUSECOAT	ROBE-TABLIER
B080	HUMIDOR	HUMIDIFICATEUR
F060	HURDY-GURDY	VIELLE
A080	HYDRANT	BORNE-FONTAINE
G300	HYDROFOIL	HYDROFOIL
G300	HYDROFOIL, DESIGN MODEL	HYDROFOIL MODELE DE PROJET
E360	HYDROMETER	HYDROMETRE
G280	HYDROPLANE	HYDROPLANE
G280	HYDROPLANE, DESIGN MODEL	HYDROPLANE MODELE DE PROJET
G280	HYDROPLANE, MODEL	HYDROPLANE MODELE REDUIT
H060	HYMNAL	HYMNAIRE

Class. Code	Object, suffix	Objet, suffixe
D100	ICEBOX	GLACIERE
C120	IMPROVER, BUST	POSTICHE DE BUSTE
H060	INCENSE	ENCENS
E340	INCINERATOR	INCINERATEUR
D040	INCUBATOR, FISH	INCUBATEUR A POISSONS
G300	INDICATOR, MODEL ENGINE-ROOM TELEGRAPH	TRANSMETTEUR D'ORDRE DE COMPARTIMENT DE MACHINES MODELE
D100	INFUSER, MILITARY TEA	PASSE-THE MILITAIRE
D100	INFUSER, TEA	PASSE-THE
D220	INGOT	LINGOT
E300	INJECTOR, LUBRICATING OIL	INJECTEUR A HUILE LUBRIFIANTE
F180	INKPAD	TAMPON ENCREUR
F180	INKSTAND	ECRITOIRE
F180	INKWELL	ENCRIER
E280	INSULATOR	ISOLATEUR
E300	INSULATOR	ISOLATEUR
H080	INSURANCE POLICY	POLICE D'ASSURANCE
F120	INTERCOM	INTERPHONE
H080	INVENTORY	INVENTAIRE
H080	INVENTORY, MILITARY	INVENTAIRE MILITAIRE
H080	INVITATION	INVITATION
E340	IRON	FER A REPASSER
D040	IRON, BRANDING	FER A MARQUER
F180	IRON, BRANDING	MARQUE A BRULER
C180	IRON, CURLING	FER A FRISER
D180	IRON, EDGE	FER A LISSER
D320	IRON, FLAGGING	FER A TASSER LA FIBRE DE MASSETTE
E340	IRON, FLUTING	FER A TUYAUTER
E340	IRON HANDLE	POIGNEE DE FER A REPASSER
D300	IRON, HATTER'S	FER DE CHAPELIER
D040	IRON, HOOF-SEARING	FER POUR PARURE DE SABOT
D040	IRON, HORSE'S MOUTH	MORS DE CHEVAL
E480	IRON, MILITARY BRANDING	FER A MARQUER MILITAIRE
F180	IRON, MILITARY BRANDING	MARQUE A BRULER MILITAIRE
D220	IRON, PIG	GUEUSE
D320	IRON, SHIPWRIGHT'S CAULKING	CISEAU DE CALFAT
D220	IRON, SMOOTHING	LISSOIR
D220	IRON, SOLDERING	FER A SOUDER
C180	IRON, STRAIGHTENING	FER A DEFRISER
G240	IRON, SWITCH	TRIANGLE D'ACCOUPLEMENT
D320	IRON, VENEERING	FER A PLAQUER
D100	IRON, WAFER	FER A GAUFRETTE
D100	IRON, WAFFLE	GAUFRIER
D320	IRON, WHEELWRIGHT'S BURNING	TIGE DE BRULAGE DE CHARRON
J020	IVORY, WORKED	IVOIRE OUVRE
C140	JABOT	JABOT
D100	JACK, BOTTLE	MECANISME CYLINDRIQUE DE ROTISSAGE
I100	JACK, JUMPING	PANTIN
E360	JACK, LIFTING	CRIC DE LEVAGE
E360	JACK, PULLING	CRIC DE TRACTION
G180	JACK, WAGON	CHEVRE
C100	JACKET	VESTE
C100	JACKET, BED	LISEUSE
H080	JACKET, BOOK	LISEUSE
C100	JACKET, CHILD'S	VESTE D'ENFANT
G300	JACKET, LIFE	GILET DE SAUVETAGE
C100	JACKET, MILITARY	GILET MILITAIRE
C100	JACKET, MILITARY FATIGUE	VESTE DE CORVEE MILITAIRE
C100	JACKET, MILITARY MESS	VESTE DE MESS MILITAIRE
C100	JACKET, MOURNING	VESTE DE DEUIL
C100	JACKET, PEA	CABAN

Class. Code	Object, suffix	Objet, suffixe
C100	JACKET, POLICE PEA	*CABAN DE POLICE*
C100	JACKET, PRISONER	*VESTE DE PRISONNIER*
C100	JACKET, SMOKING	*VESTE D'INTERIEUR*
C100	JACKET, SUIT	*VESTON*
C100	JACKET, WAITER	*VESTE DE GARCON*
E180	JAG, MILITARY	*BAGUETTE DE NETTOYAGE DE FUSIL MILITAIRE*
G020	JAR	*BOCAL*
D120	JAR	*BOCAL*
E400	JAR, ANTACID	*BOCAL A ANTI-ACIDE*
E400	JAR, ANTISEPTIC	*BOCAL A ANTISEPTIQUE*
E400	JAR, APOTHECARY	*BOCAL D'APOTHICAIRE*
E400	JAR, BAKING POWDER	*BOCAL A LEVURE CHIMIQUE*
E400	JAR, BANDAGE	*BOCAL A BANDAGES*
B080	JAR, BELL	*CLOCHE DE VERRE*
E400	JAR, BLACKCURRANT JAM	*BOCAL A CONFITURE DE CASSIS*
E400	JAR, CAPER	*BOCAL A CAPRES*
E400	JAR, CELERY SALT	*BOCAL A SEL DE CELERI*
E400	JAR, CHEESE	*BOCAL A FROMAGE*
E400	JAR, CHEMICAL	*BOCAL A PRODUIT CHIMIQUE*
E400	JAR, CINNAMON	*BOCAL A CANNELLE*
E400	JAR, COFFEE	*BOCAL A CAFE*
E400	JAR, COLA SEED	*BOCAL A GRAINES DE KOLA*
E400	JAR, COLD CREAM	*BOCAL A COLD-CREAM*
E400	JAR, CONFECTION	*BOCAL A CONFISERIES*
E400	JAR, CONFECTIONER'S	*POT DE CONFISEUR*
D100	JAR, COOKIE	*BOCAL A BISCUITS*
E400	JAR, COSMETIC	*BOCAL A COSMETIQUES*
C180	JAR, COSMETIC	*BOCAL A COSMETIQUE*
E400	JAR, CURRY	*BOCAL A CARI*
E400	JAR, DECONGESTANT	*BOCAL A DECONGESTIF*
E400	JAR, DEODORANT	*BOCAL A DESODORISANT*
E400	JAR, FISH PASTE	*BOCAL A PATE DE POISSON*
E400	JAR, FLAVORING	*BOCAL A ESSENCE*
D100	JAR, FOOD-STORAGE	*BOCAL D'ENTREPOSAGE DE NOURRITURE*
E400	JAR, GELATINE	*BOCAL A GELATINE*
D120	JAR, GINGER	*BOCAL A GINGEMBRE*
E400	JAR, GOOSEBERRY JAM	*BOCAL A CONFITURE DE GROSEILLES*
E400	JAR, HAIR TONIC	*BOCAL A TONIQUE CAPILLAIRE*
E400	JAR, HONEY	*BOCAL A MIEL*
E400	JAR, JAM	*BOCAL A CONFITURE*
E400	JAR, KETCHUP	*BOCAL A KETCHUP*
E400	JAR, MARJORAM	*BOCAL A MARJOLAINE*
E400	JAR, MARMALADE	*BOCAL A MARMELADE*
E400	JAR, MEAT PASTE	*BOCAL A PATE DE VIANDE*
E400	JAR, MEDICINAL	*BOCAL A PRODUIT PHARMACEUTIQUE*
E400	JAR, METAL POLISH	*BOCAL A PRODUIT A POLIR LE METAL*
E400	JAR, MUSTARD	*BOCAL A MOUTARDE*
E400	JAR, MUSTARD PLASTER MIX	*BOCAL A PREPARATION POUR CATAPLASME SINAPISE*
E400	JAR, OINTMENT	*BOCAL A ONGUENT*
E400	JAR, OLIVE	*BOCAL A OLIVES*
E400	JAR, OLIVE OIL	*BOCAL A HUILE D'OLIVE*
E400	JAR, PEANUT	*BOCAL A ARACHIDES*
E400	JAR, PEANUT BUTTER	*BOCAL A BEURRE D'ARACHIDES*
E400	JAR, PETROLEUM JELLY	*BOCAL A VASELINE*
D120	JAR, PICKLE	*BOCAL A CORNICHONS*
E400	JAR, PICKLE	*BOCAL A CORNICHONS*
E400	JAR, PICKLE SPICE	*BOCAL POUR EPICES A MARINADES*
E400	JAR, PIGMENT	*BOCAL A PIGMENTS*
E400	JAR, POISON	*BOCAL A POISON*
B080	JAR, POTPOURRI	*POT-POURRI*
E400	JAR, POULTRY SPICE	*BOCAL A EPICES A VOLAILLE*

Class. Code	Object, suffix	Objet, suffixe
D100	JAR, PRESERVING	BOCAL A CONSERVE
E400	JAR, SALAD DRESSING	BOCAL A VINAIGRETTE
E400	JAR, SALT	BOCAL A SEL
E400	JAR, SHAMPOO	BOCAL A SHAMPOOING
E400	JAR, SHAVING SOAP	BOCAL A SAVON A BARBE
E400	JAR, SKIN LOTION	BOCAL A LOTION POUR LA PEAU
B080	JAR, SLOP	SEAU DE TOILETTE
E400	JAR, SNUFF	BOCAL A TABAC A PRISER
E400	JAR, SPICE	BOCAL A EPICES
E400	JAR, STRAWBERRY JAM	BOCAL A CONFITURE DE FRAISES
E400	JAR, SYRUP	BOCAL A SIROP
E400	JAR, TALCUM POWDER	BOCAL A POUDRE DE TALC
E400	JAR, THYME	BOCAL A THYM
E400	JAR, TOILET	BOCAL DE TOILETTE
E400	JAR, TOOTHPASTE	BOCAL A PATE DENTIFRICE
B080	JARDINIERE	JARDINIERE
D120	JAR LID	COUVERCLE DE BOCAL
G020	JAR LID	COUVERCLE DE BOCAL
E400	JAR LID, ANTISEPTIC	COUVERCLE DE BOCAL POUR ANTISEPTIQUE
E400	JAR LID, COLD CREAM	COUVERCLE DE BOCAL A COLD-CREAM
E400	JAR LID, COSMETIC	COUVERCLE DE BOCAL A COSMETIQUES
E400	JAR LID, TOOTHPASTE	COUVERCLE DE BOCAL A PATE DENTIFRICE
C100	JERKIN	POURPOINT
D320	JIG	GABARIT
D060	JIG	TURLUTTE
D220	JIG, ASSEMBLING	GABARIT D'ASSEMBLAGE
D320	JIG, BASKETMAKER'S	GABARIT DE VANNIER
D220	JIG, CUTTING	GABARIT DE COUPE
D220	JIG, DRILLING	GABARIT DE PERCAGE
D320	JIGSAW	SCIE SAUTEUSE
D200	JOINTER	MIRETTE
D220	JOINTER, SAW	DRESSEUSE
D320	JOINTER-PLANER	DRESSEUSE
H080	JOURNAL	LIVRE-JOURNAL
F180	JOURNAL	LIVRE-JOURNAL
H080	JOURNAL, POLICE	LIVRE-JOURNAL DE POLICE
D100	JUG	CRUCHE
G020	JUG	CRUCHE
E400	JUG, ALCOHOLIC BEVERAGE	CRUCHE A BOISSON ALCOOLISEE
E400	JUG, MUSTARD	CRUCHE A MOUTARDE
E400	JUG, VARNISH	CRUCHE A VERNIS
E400	JUG, VINEGAR	CRUCHE A VINAIGRE
E400	JUG, WHISKEY	CRUCHE A WHISKY
F120	JUKEBOX	JUKE-BOX
C100	JUSTAUCORPS, MILITARY	JUSTEAUCORPS MILITAIRE
I020	KAKEE	KAKEE
G280	KAYAK, MODEL	KAYAC MODELE REDUIT
C080	KERCHIEF	FOULARD DE TETE
D100	KETTLE	MARMITE
B080	KEY	CLE
E540	KEY, CLOCK	REMONTOIR D'HORLOGE
H080	KEY, COMMEMORATIVE	CLE COMMEMORATIVE
E180	KEY, MILITARY TRUNNION	CLE DE TOURILLON MILITAIRE
E540	KEY, POCKET WATCH	CLE DE MONTRE DE POCHE
F100	KEY, QUOIN	CLE DE SERRAGE
F140	KEY, TELEGRAPH	MANIPULATEUR TELEGRAPHIQUE
E540	KEY, TIME CLOCK	CLE D'HORODATEUR
F180	KEY, WRITING CASE	CLE DE NECESSAIRE POUR ECRIRE
D240	KIBBLE	CUFAT
G300	KILLICK	PETITE ANCRE
C100	KILT	KILT

Class. Code	Object, suffix	Objet, suffixe
C100	KIMONO	*KIMONO*
G180	KIT, AUTOMOBILE TOOL	*TROUSSE D'OUTILS D'AUTOMOBILE*
G300	KIT, CANOE REPAIR	*TROUSSE DE REPARATION DE CANOT*
E380	KIT, FIRST-AID	*TROUSSE DE SECOURS*
D060	KIT, FISHING	*ATTIRAIL DE PECHE*
E180	KIT, GUN-CLEANING	*ACCESSOIRES DE FUSIL*
E380	KIT, INSTRUCTIONAL MODEL ACUPUCTURE	*TROUSSE D'ACUPUNCTURE MODELE D'INSTRUCTION*
E140	KIT, INSTRUCTIONAL MODEL AMMUNITION	*TROUSSE DE MUNITIONS MODELE D'INSTRUCTION*
F180	KIT, LAUNDRY MARKING	*TROUSSE DE MARQUAGE DE LESSIVE*
C140	KIT, MILITARY BUTTON POLISHING	*TROUSSE D'ASTIQUAGE DE BOUTONS MILITAIRE*
C140	KIT, SHOESHINE	*TROUSSE DE CIRAGE A CHAUSSURES*
C160	KIT, SHOESHINE	*TROUSSE DE CIRAGE A CHAUSSURES*
H060	KIT, SICK CALL	*TROUSSE DE VISITE AUX MALADES*
D040	KIT, SYRINGE	*TROUSSE DE SERINGUES*
J060	KIT, TOOL	*TROUSSE D'OUTILS*
G060	KITE	*CERF-VOLANT*
C160	KNAPSACK	*SAC A DOS*
B060	KNEELER	*AGENOUILLOIR*
C100	KNICKERS	*CULOTTE DE GOLF*
E080	KNIFE	*COUTEAU*
D100	KNIFE	*COUTEAU*
D120	KNIFE	*COUTEAU*
D180	KNIFE	*COUTEAU*
D260	KNIFE	*COUTEAU*
D180	KNIFE, BEAMING	*COUTEAU A DOLER LES PEAUX*
D180	KNIFE, BEVEL-POINT SKIVING	*DOLOIR A POINTE BISEAUTE*
D320	KNIFE, BLOCK	*PAROIR*
D100	KNIFE, BONING	*COUTEAU A DESOSSER*
E080	KNIFE, BOWIE	*COUTEAU BOWIE*
D100	KNIFE, BREAD	*COUTEAU A PAIN*
D100	KNIFE, BUTCHER	*COUTEAU DE BOUCHER*
D120	KNIFE, BUTTER	*COUTEAU A BEURRE*
D120	KNIFE, CAKE	*COUTEAU A GATEAU*
D320	KNIFE, CARVING	*COUTEAU A DECOUPER*
D120	KNIFE, CARVING	*COUTEAU A DECOUPER*
D100	KNIFE, CHEESE	*COUTEAU A FROMAGE*
D100	KNIFE, CHEF'S	*COUTEAU DE CHEF*
D100	KNIFE, CHOPPING	*COUTEAU A HACHER*
D180	KNIFE, CURRIER'S	*COUTEAU-GRATTOIR DE CORROYEUR*
C180	KNIFE, CUTICLE	*COUPE-CUTICULES*
D120	KNIFE, DESSERT	*COUTEAU A DESSERT*
D120	KNIFE, DINNER	*COUTEAU DE TABLE*
D120	KNIFE, FISH	*COUTEAU A POISSON*
D180	KNIFE, FLESHING	*GRATTOIR A ECHARNAGE*
D120	KNIFE, FRUIT	*COUTEAU A FRUITS*
D260	KNIFE, GRAINING	*COUTEAU A DECOR*
D300	KNIFE, HATTER'S	*COUTEAU DE CHAPELIER*
D020	KNIFE, HAY	*COUPE-PAILLE*
D180	KNIFE, HEAD	*COUTEAU A LAME RONDE*
D180	KNIFE, HEEL	*TRANCHET DE TALON*
D040	KNIFE, HOOF	*COUTEAU A SABOT*
J060	KNIFE, LINOLEUM	*COUTEAU A LINOLEUM*
D120	KNIFE, LUNCHEON	*COUTEAU A LUNCH*
D060	KNIFE, MINCING	*COUTEAU A APPATS*
D120	KNIFE, MINIATURE TABLE	*COUTEAU DE TABLE MINIATURE*
D100	KNIFE, OYSTER	*COUTEAU A HUITRES*
D260	KNIFE, PALETTE	*COUTEAU A PALETTE*
F180	KNIFE, PAPER	*COUPE-PAPIER*
D100	KNIFE, PARING	*COUTEAU A EPLUCHER*
D180	KNIFE, PEG	*PAROIR A CHEVILLES*
C160	KNIFE, PIPE	*CURE-PIPE*

Class. Code	Object, suffix	Objet, suffixe
C160	KNIFE, POCKET	COUTEAU DE POCHE
D020	KNIFE, PRUNING	EMONDOIR
D260	KNIFE, PUTTY	COUTEAU A MASTIQUER
D180	KNIFE, ROUND-HEAD	COUTEAU A LAME DEMI-CIRCULAIRE
D300	KNIFE, SCUTCHING	COUTEAU A TEILLER
D100	KNIFE, SKINNING	COUTEAU A ECORCHER
D180	KNIFE, SKIVING	DOLOIR
D060	KNIFE, SNOW	COUTEAU A NEIGE
D100	KNIFE, SPLITTING	COUTEAU A FENDRE
D180	KNIFE, SQUARE-POINT	COUTEAU A BOUT DE LAME CARREE
D100	KNIFE, THROATING	COUTEAU A EGORGER
D020	KNIFE, TOBACCO	COUPE-TABAC
J060	KNIFE, UTILITY	COUTEAU TOUT USAGE
D260	KNIFE, WALLPAPER	COUTEAU A PAPIER PEINT
D120	KNIFE HANDLE	MANCHE DE COUTEAU
D100	KNIFEBOARD	PLANCHE A COUTEAUX
A040	KNOCKER	HEURTOIR
E340	KNOCKER, SNOW	CASSE-GLACE POUR SABOTS
H120	KNOT, MILITARY PRESENTATION SWORD	DRAGONNE D'HONNEUR MILITAIRE
E100	KNUCKLES, BRASS	COUP-DE-POING
E400	LABEL, ANAESTHETIC	ETIQUETTE D'ANESTHESIQUE
E400	LABEL, ANALGESIC	ETIQUETTE D'ANALGESIQUES
E400	LABEL, ANTACID	ETIQUETTE D'ANTI-ACIDE
E400	LABEL, ANTISEPTIC	ETIQUETTE D'ANTISEPTIQUE
E400	LABEL, APPLE	ETIQUETTE DE POMMES
E400	LABEL, APRICOT	ETIQUETTE D'ABRICOTS
E400	LABEL, APRICOT JAM	ETIQUETTE DE CONFITURE D'ABRICOTS
E400	LABEL, ARTICHOKE	ETIQUETTE D'ARTICHAUTS
E400	LABEL, ASPARAGUS	ETIQUETTE D'ASPERGES
E400	LABEL, ASTRINGENT	ETIQUETTE D'ASTRINGENT
E400	LABEL, AXLE CLIP	ETIQUETTE D'ATTACHES D'ESSIEUX
E400	LABEL, BACON	ETIQUETTE DE BACON
E400	LABEL, BAKING POWDER	ETIQUETTE DE LEVURE CHIMIQUE
E400	LABEL, BAKING SODA	ETIQUETTE DE BICARBONATE DE SOUDE
E400	LABEL, BANDAGE	ETIQUETTE DE BANDAGES
E400	LABEL, BEAN	ETIQUETTE DE FEVES
E400	LABEL, BEEF	ETIQUETTE DE BOEUF
E400	LABEL, BEER	ETIQUETTE DE BIERE
E400	LABEL, BEET	ETIQUETTE DE BETTERAVES
E400	LABEL, BISCUIT	ETIQUETTE DE BISCUITS
E400	LABEL, BITTERS	ETIQUETTE DE BITTER
E400	LABEL, BITUMINIZED PAPER	ETIQUETTE DE PAPIER BITUME
E400	LABEL, BLACKBERRY	ETIQUETTE DE MURES
E400	LABEL, BLACKBERRY JAM	ETIQUETTE DE CONFITURE DE MURES
E400	LABEL, BLACKCURRANT	ETIQUETTE DE CASSIS
E400	LABEL, BLUEBERRY	ETIQUETTE DE BLEUETS
E400	LABEL, BOLOGNA	ETIQUETTE DE SAUCISSES DE BOLOGNE
E400	LABEL, BOLT	ETIQUETTE DE BOULONS
E400	LABEL, BOOT POLISH	ETIQUETTE DE CIRAGE A CHAUSSURES
E400	LABEL, BRANDY	ETIQUETTE DE BRANDY
E400	LABEL, BUTTER	ETIQUETTE DE BEURRE
E400	LABEL, BUTTON	ETIQUETTE DE BOUTONS
E400	LABEL, CALK	ETIQUETTE DE CRAMPON DE FER A CHEVAL
E400	LABEL, CANDLE	ETIQUETTE DE BOUGIES
E400	LABEL, CARROT	ETIQUETTE DE CAROTTES
E400	LABEL, CARTRIDGE	ETIQUETTE DE CARTOUCHE
E400	LABEL, CARTRIDGE LOADING TOOL	ETIQUETTE DE SERTISSEUR
E400	LABEL, CASTER	ETIQUETTE DE ROULETTE DE FAUTEUIL
E400	LABEL, CASTOR OIL	ETIQUETTE D'HUILE DE CASTOR
E400	LABEL, CEILING HOOK	ETIQUETTE DE CROCHET DE PLAFOND
E400	LABEL, CEREAL	ETIQUETTE DE CEREALES

Class. Code	Object, suffix	Objet, suffixe
E400	LABEL, CHEESE	ETIQUETTE DE FROMAGE
E400	LABEL, CHEMICAL	ETIQUETTE DE PRODUIT CHIMIQUE
E400	LABEL, CHERRY	ETIQUETTE DE CERISES
E400	LABEL, CHEWING GUM	ETIQUETTE DE GOMMES A MACHER
E400	LABEL, CHICKEN	ETIQUETTE DE POULET
E400	LABEL, CHILI CON CARNE	ETIQUETTE DE CHILI CON CARNE
E400	LABEL, CHOP SUEY	ETIQUETTE DE CHOP SUEY
E400	LABEL, CIGAR	ETIQUETTE DE CIGARES
E400	LABEL, CIGARETTE	ETIQUETTE DE CIGARETTE
E400	LABEL, CINNAMON	ETIQUETTE DE CANNELLE
E400	LABEL, CITRUS FRUIT	ETIQUETTE D'AGRUMES
E400	LABEL, CLAM	ETIQUETTE DE PALOURDE
E400	LABEL, CLOTH BOLT	ETIQUETTE DE PIECE DE TOILE
E400	LABEL, CLOTHING	ETIQUETTE DE VETEMENT
E400	LABEL, COCOA	ETIQUETTE DE CACAO
E400	LABEL, COD LIVER OIL	ETIQUETTE D'HUILE DE FOIE DE MORUE
E400	LABEL, COFFEE	ETIQUETTE DE CAFE
E400	LABEL, COGNAC	ETIQUETTE DE COGNAC
E400	LABEL, COLD CREAM	ETIQUETTE DE COLD-CREAM
E400	LABEL, CONDENSED MILK	ETIQUETTE DE LAIT CONDENSE
E400	LABEL, CONDIMENT SAUCE	ETIQUETTE DE SAUCE AUX CONDIMENTS
E400	LABEL, CONFECTION	ETIQUETTE DE CONFISERIES
E400	LABEL, CORN	ETIQUETTE DE MAIS
E400	LABEL, COSMETIC	ETIQUETTE DE PRODUIT COSMETIQUE
E400	LABEL, COUGH DROP	ETIQUETTE DE PASTILLES CONTRE LA TOUX
E400	LABEL, CRAB	ETIQUETTE DE CRABES
E400	LABEL, CUSTARD	ETIQUETTE DE CREME-DESSERT
D120	LABEL, DECANTER	ETIQUETTE DE CARAFE AVEC BOUCHON
E400	LABEL, DISINFECTANT	ETIQUETTE DE DESINFECTANT
E400	LABEL, DOOR/DRAWER PULL	ETIQUETTE DE GACHETTE DE PORTE/TIROIR
E400	LABEL, DRILL BIT	ETIQUETTE DE MECHE DE PERCEUSE
E400	LABEL, EGG	ETIQUETTE D'OEUFS
E400	LABEL, EMBALMING FLUID	ETIQUETTE DE LIQUIDE D'EMBAUMEMENT
E400	LABEL, EVAPORATED MILK	ETIQUETTE DE LAIT EVAPORE
E400	LABEL, EXPLOSIVE	ETIQUETTE D'EXPLOSIFS
E400	LABEL, FLAVORING	ETIQUETTE D'ESSENCE
E400	LABEL, FOOD	ETIQUETTE DE NOURRITURE
E400	LABEL, FRUIT	ETIQUETTE DE FRUITS
E400	LABEL, GAME	ETIQUETTE DE JEU
E400	LABEL, GIN	ETIQUETTE DE GIN
E400	LABEL, GINGER	ETIQUETTE DE GINGEMBRE
E400	LABEL, GINGER BEER	ETIQUETTE DE BIERE DE GINGEMBRE
E400	LABEL, GLUE	ETIQUETTE DE COLLE
E400	LABEL, GOOSEBERRY	ETIQUETTE DE GROSEILLES
E400	LABEL, GRAPE	ETIQUETTE DE RAISINS
E400	LABEL, GRAPEFRUIT	ETIQUETTE DE PAMPLEMOUSSE
E400	LABEL, GUNPOWDER	ETIQUETTE DE POUDRE A CANON
E400	LABEL, HAIR TONIC	ETIQUETTE DE TONIQUE CAPILLAIRE
E400	LABEL, HAM	ETIQUETTE DE JAMBON
E400	LABEL, HORSESHOE NAIL	ETIQUETTE DE CLOUS DE FER A CHEVAL
E400	LABEL, INK	ETIQUETTE D'ENCRE
E400	LABEL, JELLY	ETIQUETTE DE GELEE
E400	LABEL, KETCHUP	ETIQUETTE DE KETCHUP
E400	LABEL, LAMP BURNER	ETIQUETTE DE BEC DE LAMPE
E400	LABEL, LARD	ETIQUETTE DE LARD
E400	LABEL, LAUNDRY BLUEING	ETIQUETTE DE BLEU DE LESSIVE
E400	LABEL, LAUNDRY SOAP	ETIQUETTE DE SAVON A LESSIVE
E400	LABEL, LAXATIVE	ETIQUETTE DE LAXATIF
E400	LABEL, LEMON	ETIQUETTE DE CITRON
E400	LABEL, LETTUCE	ETIQUETTE DE LAITUE
E400	LABEL, LIME JUICE	ETIQUETTE DE JUS DE LIMETTE

Class. Code	Object, suffix	Objet, suffixe
E400	LABEL, LINIMENT	*ETIQUETTE DE LINIMENT*
E400	LABEL, LOBSTER	*ETIQUETTE DE HOMARD*
E400	LABEL, LOGANBERRY JAM	*ETIQUETTE DE CONFITURE DE FRAMBOISES DE LOGAN*
E400	LABEL, LUBRICATING OIL	*ETIQUETTE D'HUILE LUBRIFIANTE*
E400	LABEL, MARMALADE	*ETIQUETTE DE MARMELADE*
E400	LABEL, MATCH	*ETIQUETTE D'ALLUMETTE*
E400	LABEL, MEAT PASTE	*ETIQUETTE DE PATE DE VIANDE*
E400	LABEL, MEDICINAL	*ETIQUETTE DE PRODUIT PHARMACEUTIQUE*
E400	LABEL, METAL POLISH	*ETIQUETTE DE PRODUIT A POLIR LE METAL*
E400	LABEL, MILITARY FRICTION TUBE	*ETIQUETTE DE TUBE A FRICTION MILITAIRE*
E400	LABEL, MUSTARD	*ETIQUETTE DE MOUTARDE*
E400	LABEL, NAIL	*ETIQUETTE DE CLOUS*
E400	LABEL, NUT	*ETIQUETTE DE NOIX*
E400	LABEL, NUTMEG	*ETIQUETTE DE MUSCADE*
E400	LABEL, OINTMENT	*ETIQUETTE D'ONGUENT*
E400	LABEL, OLIVE	*ETIQUETTE D'OLIVES*
E400	LABEL, OLIVE OIL	*ETIQUETTE D'HUILE D'OLIVE*
E400	LABEL, ORANGE	*ETIQUETTE D'ORANGES*
E400	LABEL, PAINT	*ETIQUETTE DE PEINTURE*
E400	LABEL, PANCAKE MIX	*ETIQUETTE DE PREPARATION A CREPES*
E400	LABEL, PASTA	*ETIQUETTE DE PATES ALIMENTAIRES*
E400	LABEL, PEA	*ETIQUETTE DE POIS*
E400	LABEL, PEACH	*ETIQUETTE DE PECHES*
E400	LABEL, PEAR	*ETIQUETTE DE POIRES*
E400	LABEL, PEN	*ETIQUETTE DE PLUMES*
E400	LABEL, PENCIL	*ETIQUETTE DE CRAYONS A MINE DE PLOMB*
E400	LABEL, PEPPER	*ETIQUETTE DE POIVRE*
E400	LABEL, PICKLE	*ETIQUETTE DE CORNICHONS*
E400	LABEL, PILL	*ETIQUETTE DE PILULES*
E400	LABEL, PINEAPPLE	*ETIQUETTE D'ANANAS*
E400	LABEL, PLUM	*ETIQUETTE DE PRUNES*
E400	LABEL, PLUM JAM	*ETIQUETTE DE CONFITURE DE PRUNES*
E400	LABEL, POPCORN	*ETIQUETTE DE MAIS SOUFFLE*
E400	LABEL, PRUNE	*ETIQUETTE DE PRUNEAUX*
E400	LABEL, PUMPKIN	*ETIQUETTE DE CITROUILLE*
E400	LABEL, QUINCE	*ETIQUETTE DE COINGS*
E400	LABEL, RASPBERRY	*ETIQUETTE DE FRAMBOISES*
E400	LABEL, ROOF SHEATHING	*ETIQUETTE DE REVETEMENT DE TOIT*
E400	LABEL, RUM	*ETIQUETTE DE RHUM*
E400	LABEL, SALAD DRESSING	*ETIQUETTE DE VINAIGRETTE*
E400	LABEL, SALMON	*ETIQUETTE DE SAUMON*
E400	LABEL, SANDWICH SPREAD	*ETIQUETTE DE GARNITURE A SANDWICH*
E400	LABEL, SARDINE	*ETIQUETTE DE SARDINES*
E400	LABEL, SAUERKRAUT	*ETIQUETTE DE CHOUCROUTE*
E400	LABEL, SEALING WAX	*ETIQUETTE DE CIRE A CACHETER*
E400	LABEL, SEDATIVE	*ETIQUETTE DE CALMANT*
E400	LABEL, SEWING NEEDLE	*ETIQUETTE D'AIGUILLES A COUDRE*
E400	LABEL, SHAFT SEAL	*ETIQUETTE DE DISPOSITIF D'ETANCHEITE POUR LIMON*
E400	LABEL, SHOE	*ETIQUETTE DE CHAUSSURE*
E400	LABEL, SHOE BRUSH	*ETIQUETTE DE BROSSE A CHAUSSURES*
E400	LABEL, SHORTENING	*ETIQUETTE DE GRAISSE ALIMENTAIRE*
E400	LABEL, SKIN LOTION	*ETIQUETTE DE LOTION POUR LA PEAU*
E400	LABEL, SODA BISCUIT	*ETIQUETTE DE CRAQUELINS*
E400	LABEL, SOLVENT	*ETIQUETTE DE SOLVANT*
E400	LABEL, SOUP	*ETIQUETTE DE SOUPE*
E400	LABEL, SPAGHETTI SAUCE	*ETIQUETTE DE SAUCE A SPAGHETTI*
E400	LABEL, SPICE	*ETIQUETTE DE EPICES*
E400	LABEL, SPINACH	*ETIQUETTE DE EPINARDS*
E400	LABEL, STARCH	*ETIQUETTE D'EMPOIS*
E400	LABEL, STATIONERY	*ETIQUETTE DE PAPETERIE*
E400	LABEL, STOVE POLISH	*ETIQUETTE DE PATE A POLIR LE POELE*

Class. Code	Object, suffix	Objet, suffixe
E400	LABEL, STRAIGHT PIN	*ETIQUETTE D'EPINGLES DROITES*
E400	LABEL, STRAWBERRY	*ETIQUETTE DE FRAISES*
E400	LABEL, STRAWBERRY JAM	*ETIQUETTE DE CONFITURE DE FRAISES*
E400	LABEL, SUGAR	*ETIQUETTE DE SUCRE*
E400	LABEL, SYRUP	*ETIQUETTE DE SIROP*
E400	LABEL, TEA	*ETIQUETTE DE THE*
E400	LABEL, TEAKETTLE	*ETIQUETTE DE BOUILLOIRE*
E400	LABEL, THREAD	*ETIQUETTE DE FIL DE COTON*
E400	LABEL, TOBACCO	*ETIQUETTE DE TABAC*
E400	LABEL, TOILET BOTTLE	*ETIQUETTE DE FLACON DE TOILETTE*
E400	LABEL, TOILET PAPER	*ETIQUETTE DE PAPIER HYGIENIQUE*
E400	LABEL, TOILET SOAP	*ETIQUETTE DE SAVON DE TOILETTE*
E400	LABEL, TOMATO	*ETIQUETTE DE TOMATES*
E400	LABEL, TOMATO JUICE	*ETIQUETTE DE JUS DE TOMATE*
E400	LABEL, TOMATO SAUCE	*ETIQUETTE DE SAUCE TOMATE*
E400	LABEL, TONIC	*ETIQUETTE DE TONIQUE*
E400	LABEL, TOOL HANDLE	*ETIQUETTE DE MANCHE D'OUTILS*
E400	LABEL, TOOTHPASTE	*ETIQUETTE DE PATE DENTIFRICE*
H020	LABEL, TRADE	*ETIQUETTE D'AFFAIRES*
E400	LABEL, VARNISH	*ETIQUETTE DE VERNIS*
E400	LABEL, VEGETABLE	*ETIQUETTE DE LEGUMES*
E400	LABEL, VINEGAR	*ETIQUETTE DE VINAIGRE*
E400	LABEL, WHISKEY	*ETIQUETTE DE WHISKY*
E400	LABEL, WINE	*ETIQUETTE DE VIN*
E400	LABEL, WOOD POLISH	*ETIQUETTE DE LIQUIDE A POLIR LES BOIS*
E400	LABEL, WOODSCREW	*ETIQUETTE DE VIS A BOIS*
E400	LABEL, YARN	*ETIQUETTE DE FIL*
E400	LABEL, YEAST	*ETIQUETTE DE LEVURE*
C020	LABRET	*LABRET*
C120	LACE, CORSET	*LACET DE CORSET*
B080	LADDER	*ECHELLE*
B080	LADDER, MILITARY	*ECHELLE MILITAIRE*
D100	LADLE	*LOUCHE*
D120	LADLE	*LOUCHE*
D220	LADLE, HOT-METAL	*POCHE A FONTE*
E180	LADLE, HOT-SHOT	*CUILLERE A BOULET ROUGE*
E180	LADLE, MILITARY ARTILLERY	*LANTERNE A CHARGEMENT MILITAIRE*
D240	LADLE, PITCH	*LOUCHE A ETOUPE*
B080	LAMBREQUIN	*LAMBREQUIN*
B100	LAMP	*LAMPE*
B100	LAMP, BURNING-FLUID	*LAMPE A CARBURANT LIQUIDE*
B100	LAMP, CAMPHENE	*LAMPE A CAMPHENE*
B100	LAMP, CANDLE	*LAMPE A BOUGIE*
G180	LAMP, CARRIAGE	*LAMPE DE VOITURE*
H060	LAMP, CEREMONIAL	*LAMPE DE CEREMONIE*
B100	LAMP, ELECTRIC	*LAMPE ELECTRIQUE*
B100	LAMP, ELECTRIC MINER'S	*LAMPE ELECTRIQUE DE MINEUR*
B100	LAMP, GAS	*LAMPE A GAZ*
B100	LAMP, GASOLINE	*LAMPE A GAZOLINE*
B100	LAMP, KEROSINE	*LAMPE A PETROLE*
B100	LAMP, MILITARY OIL	*LAMPE A HUILE MILITAIRE*
B100	LAMP, MINER'S CARBIDE	*LAMPE A CARBURE DE MINEUR*
B100	LAMP, MINER'S OIL	*LAMPE A HUILE DE MINEUR*
B100	LAMP, MINIATURE SEMILIQUID	*LAMPE A COMBUSTION SEMI-LIQUIDE MINIATURE*
B100	LAMP, OIL	*LAMPE A HUILE*
B100	LAMP, SEMILIQUID	*LAMPE A COMBUSTION SEMI-LIQUIDE*
D040	LAMP, SINGEING	*LAMPE A FLAMBER*
B100	LAMP BASE	*PIED DE LAMPE*
B100	LAMP BURNER	*BEC DE LAMPE*
B100	LAMP BURNER DEFLECTOR	*DEFLECTEUR DE BEC DE LAMPE*
B100	LAMP BURNER, LIGHTHOUSE	*BEC DE LAMPE DE PHARE*

Class. Code	Object, suffix	Objet, suffixe
B100	LAMP CHIMNEY	VERRE DE LAMPE
B100	LAMP COUNTERWEIGHT	CONTREPOIDS DE LAMPE
B100	LAMP FONT	RESERVOIR DE LAMPE
B100	LAMP GLOBE	GLOBE DE LAMPE
B100	LAMP GLOBE GALLERY	GRIFFE DE VERRE DE LAMPE
B100	LAMP MANTLE	MANCHON DE LAMPE
B100	LAMP PENDANT	PENDELOQUE DE LAMPE
B100	LAMP REFLECTOR	REFLECTEUR DE LAMPE
B100	LAMP SHADE	ABAT-JOUR
B100	LAMP SHADE, MILITARY	ABAT-JOUR MILITAIRE
H060	LAMPION	LAMPION
E080	LANCE	LANCE
E080	LANCE, MILITARY	LANCE MILITAIRE
E080	LANCE, MINIATURE WHALE	LANCE DE BALEINE MINIATURE
E080	LANCE, POLICE	LANCE DE POLICE
E080	LANCE, WHALE	LANCE DE BALEINE
E080	LANCE BARB, MINIATURE	BARBELURE DE LANCE MINIATURE
D040	LANCET	BISTOURI
E380	LANCET, BLOOD	BISTOURI A SAIGNEE
B100	LANTERN	LANTERNE
I100	LANTERN	LANTERNE
B100	LANTERN, CANDLE	LANTERNE A BOUGIE
B100	LANTERN, CARBIDE	LANTERNE A CARBURE
H060	LANTERN, CEREMONIAL	LANTERNE DE CEREMONIE
B100	LANTERN, ELECTRIC	LANTERNE ELECTRIQUE
B100	LANTERN, FISHERMAN'S	FANAL DE PECHE
B100	LANTERN, GAS	LANTERNE A GAZ
B100	LANTERN GLOBE	GLOBE DE LANTERNE
B100	LANTERN, KEROSINE	LANTERNE A PETROLE
I100	LANTERN, MAGIC	LANTERNE MAGIQUE
B100	LANTERN, MILITARY	LANTERNE MILITAIRE
B100	LANTERN, MINIATURE CANDLE	LANTERNE A BOUGIE MINIATURE
B100	LANTERN, OIL	LANTERNE A HUILE
B080	LANTERN, PAPER	LANTERNE VENITIENNE
F160	LANTERN, RAILROAD	FANAL DE CHEMIN DE FER
B100	LANTERN, SHIP'S	LANTERNE DE NAVIRE
F160	LANTERN, SIGNAL	FANAL DE SIGNALISATION
B100	LANTERN FONT, MILITARY	RESERVOIR DE LANTERNE MILITAIRE
E180	LANYARD, MILITARY	FOURRAGERE MILITAIRE
E180	LANYARD, POLICE REVOLVER	CORDON DE REVOLVER DE POLICE
C080	LAPPET	BARBE
G180	LARIAT	CORDE A PIQUET
D180	LAST	FORME A CHAUSSURE
D180	LAST, COBBLER'S	FORME DE CORDONNIER
A040	LATCH	LOQUET
D320	LATHE	TOUR
D220	LATHE, HAND	TOUR A MAIN
D320	LATHE SPUR CENTER	TOUR PARALLELE
E060	LAUNCHER, GRENADE	LANCE-GRENADES
G080	LAUNCHER, KITE	LANCE CERF-VOLANT
E120	LAUNCHER, MISSILE	LANCE-FUSEES
E360	LAUNCHER, PROPELLER	LANCE-HELICE
B080	LAVABO	LAVABO
G300	LEAD, SOUNDING	PLOMB DE SONDE
D040	LEADER, LIVESTOCK	GUIDE A BETAIL
D040	LEASH	LAISSE
D180	LEATHER	CUIR
J020	LEATHER FRAGMENT	FRAGMENT DE CUIR
H080	LEDGER	GRAND LIVRE
F180	LEDGER	GRAND LIVRE
C100	LEGGING	JAMBIERES

Class. Code	Object, suffix	Objet, suffixe
F080	LENS	*LENTILLE*
E460	LENS, MICROSCOPE	*LENTILLE DE MICROSCOPE*
H080	LETTER	*LETTRE*
H080	LETTER, POLICE	*LETTRE DE POLICE*
H080	LETTER, TESTMONIAL	*ATTESTATION*
F100	LETTERPRESS	*PRESSE A IMPRIMER*
H080	LETTERS PATENT	*LETTRES PATENTES*
D320	LEVEL	*NIVEAU*
D200	LEVEL, MASON'S	*NIVEAU DE MACON*
D200	LEVEL, MILLSTONE	*NIVEAU DE MEULE DE MOULIN*
D320	LEVEL, PLUMB	*NIVEAU A PLOMB*
E500	LEVEL, SURVEYOR'S	*NIVEAU A LUNETTE D'ARPENTEUR*
E360	LEVER	*LEVIER*
E180	LEVER, CANNON CARRIAGE TRUCK	*LEVIER D'AFFUT DE CANON*
E180	LEVER, MINIATURE CANNON CARRIAGE TRUCK	*LEVIER D'AFFUT DE CANON MINIATURE*
H080	LICENSE	*LICENCE*
H080	LICENSE, MARRIAGE	*PERMIS DE MARIAGE*
H080	LICENSE, OCCUPATIONAL	*CARTE DE COMMERCE*
H080	LICENSE, RADIO	*PERMIS D'OPERATEUR DE RADIO*
D100	LICORICE	*REGLISSE*
A040	LIFT, WINDOW	*GACHETTE DE FENETRE*
D220	LIFTER	*CROCHET A RAMASSER*
D100	LIFTER, PIE	*PORTE-MOULE A TARTE*
D100	LIFTER, STOVE	*POIGNEE DE POELE*
G300	LIGHT, RUNNING	*FEU DE ROUTE*
B100	LIGHT SOCKET	*DOUILLE*
C160	LIGHTER	*BRIQUET*
B100	LIGHTER, GAS LAMP	*ALLUMEUR DE LAMPE A GAZ*
E180	LIMBER, MILITARY	*AVANT-TRAIN DE CAISSON MILITAIRE*
E180	LINCHPIN, MILITARY	*CHEVILLE A TETE PLATE MILITAIRE*
D320	LINE, CHALK	*CORDE A LIGNER*
D200	LINE, CHALK	*CORDEAU A CRAIE*
D060	LINE, FISH	*LIGNE A PECHE*
E080	LINER, BROADSWORD HILT	*DOUBLURE DE POIGNEE DE FORTE-EPEE*
F180	LINER, INKWELL	*MANCHON D'ENCRIER*
D120	LINER, PLATTER	*PLAT-EGOUTTOIR*
D100	LINER, PRESERVING JAR	*JOINT DE BOCAL A CONSERVE*
C140	LINK, CUFF	*BOUTON DE MANCHETTE*
A040	LINOLEUM	*LINOLEUM*
E180	LINSTOCK, MILITARY	*BOUTEFEU MILITAIRE*
H080	LIST, MILITARY	*ETAT MILITAIRE*
H080	LIST, POLICE	*ETAT DE POLICE*
J020	LITHIC FRAGMENT	*FRAGMENT LITHIQUE*
A040	LOCK	*SERRURE*
A040	LOCK, DOOR	*SERRURE DE PORTE*
F180	LOCK, MAILBAG	*VERROU DE SAC POSTAL*
A040	LOCK, MILITARY DOOR	*SERRURE DE PORTE MILITAIRE*
C160	LOCK, TRUNK	*SERRURE DE MALLE*
A040	LOCK, WINDOW	*FERMETURE DE FENETRE*
F160	LOCKER, FLAG	*COFFRE A PAVILLONS*
C020	LOCKET	*MEDAILLON*
I100	LOCOMOTIVE	*LOCOMOTIVE*
D240	LOCOMOTIVE, MINE	*LOCOMOTIVE DE MINE*
G220	LOCOMOTIVE, MINIATURE	*LOCOMOTIVE MINIATURE*
H080	LOG	*CARNET DE ROUTE*
G300	LOG	*LOCH*
B140	LOG, ARTIFICIAL	*BUCHE ARTIFICIELLE*
H080	LOG, POLICE SHIP'S	*JOURNAL DE BORD DE POLICE*
H080	LOG, SHIP'S	*JOURNAL DE BORD*
D100	LOGGERHEAD	*CHAUFFE-VIN*
C100	LOINCLOTH	*PAGNE*

Class. Code	Object, suffix	Objet, suffixe
G280	LONGSHIP, MODEL VIKING	DRAKKAR MODELE REDUIT
D300	LOOM	METIER
D300	LOOM, BEAD	METIER A PERLES
D300	LOOM, CARPET	METIER A TAPIS
D300	LOOM, HAND	METIER A TISSER A LA MAIN
D300	LOOM, RIGID HEDDLE	METIER A LISSE RIGIDE
D300	LOOM, TABLET	METIER A TISSER A CARTONS
D300	LOOM, TAPE	METIER A RUBANS
B160	LOOP, CURTAIN	ATTACHE A RIDEAU
G180	LOOP, HARNESS	BOUCLE SIMPLE DE HARNAIS
H060	LOOP, MARRIAGE	NOEUD DE MARIAGE
H120	LOOP, SHOULDER	AIGUILLETTE
I020	LOTTO	JEU DE LOTO
B060	LOUNGE	CHAISE LONGUE
I080	LUGE	LUGE
I100	LUGE	LUGE
I080	LUGE, CHILD'S	LUGE D'ENFANT
D060	LURE	LEURRE
F060	LYRE	LYRE
H120	MACE	MASSE
D020	MACHETE	MACHETTE
F020	MACHINE, ADDING	MACHINE A ADDITIONNER
D320	MACHINE, BORING	ALESEUSE
D220	MACHINE, BURRING	MACHINE A BORDER
C160	MACHINE, CIGARETTE	MACHINE A CIGARETTES
D300	MACHINE, CRIMPING	MACHINE A CREPER
D220	MACHINE, DIE-CUTTING	DECOUPEUSE A L'EMPORTE-PIECE
D180	MACHINE, DIE-CUTTING	DECOUPEUSE A L'EMPORTE-PIECE
F100	MACHINE, FOLDING	PLIEUSE
D220	MACHINE, FORMING	MACHINE A EMBOUTIR
D220	MACHINE, GROOVING	BOUVETEUSE
D300	MACHINE, KNITTING	TRICOTEUSE
D320	MACHINE, MORTISING	MORTAISEUSE
E380	MACHINE, PILL	PILULIER
D220	MACHINE, PIPE THREADING	MACHINE A TARAUDER LES TUBES
D300	MACHINE, PLEATING	PLISSEUSE
D220	MACHINE, RIVETING	RIVETEUSE
D320	MACHINE, SAW SHARPENING	MACHINE A AFFUTER LES SCIES
D220	MACHINE, SETTING-DOWN	APPAREIL DE POSITIONNEMENT
D300	MACHINE, SEWING	MACHINE A COUDRE
I100	MACHINE, SEWING	MACHINE A COUDRE
D220	MACHINE, SHEARING	CISAILLE MECANIQUE
I020	MACHINE, SLOT	MACHINE A SOUS
D180	MACHINE, SPLITTING	MACHINE A REFENDRE
F020	MACHINE, TEACHING	MACHINE A ENSEIGNER
D020	MACHINE, THRESHING	BATTEUSE
D220	MACHINE, TIRE-BENDING	MACHINE A CINTRER LES BANDAGES DE ROUE
D220	MACHINE, TURNING	TOUR
E400	MACHINE, VENDING	DISTRIBUTEUR AUTOMATIQUE
E340	MACHINE, WASHING	LAVEUSE MECANIQUE
E180	MAGAZINE	CHARGEUR
H080	MAGAZINE	REVUE
H080	MAGAZINE, POLICE	REVUE DE POLICE
E280	MAGNET	AIMANT
E300	MAGNETO	MAGNETO
E160	MAIL	MAILLES
F180	MAILBAG	SAC POSTAL
F180	MAILBOX	BOITE AUX LETTRES
D100	MAKER, COFFEE	PERCOLATEUR
F180	MAKER, LABEL	POCHOIR A ETIQUETAGE
I100	MALLET	MAILLET

Class. Code	Object, suffix	Objet, suffixe
D320	MALLET	MAILLET
D320	MALLET, CARPENTER'S	MAILLET DE CHARPENTIER
D320	MALLET, CARVER'S	MAILLET DE SCULPTEUR
F120	MALLET, CHIME	MAILLET DE CARILLON
E180	MALLET, MAGAZINE	MAILLET DE POUDRIERE
D200	MALLET, MASON'S	MAILLET DE MACON
D300	MALLET, SERVING	MAILLET A CORDER
D320	MALLET, SHIPWRIGHT'S CAULKING	MAILLET DE CALFAT
D220	MANDREL	MANDRIN
E340	MANGLE	REPASSEUSE
E400	MANIKIN	MANNEQUIN
C100	MANIPLE	MANIPULE
E300	MANOMETER, STEAM BOILER	MANOMETRE DE CHAUDIERE A VAPEUR
A040	MANTEL	MANTEAU DE CHEMINEE
H080	MANUSCRIPT	MANUSCRIT
H080	MANUSCRIPT, MILITARY	MANUSCRIT MILITAIRE
H060	MANUTERGIUM	MANUTERGE
H080	MAP	CARTE GEOGRAPHIQUE
H080	MAP, ROAD	CARTE ROUTIERE
H040	MAQUETTE	MAQUETTE
I020	MARBLE	BILLE
E500	MARKER, CONCRETE	BORNE
D300	MARKER, HEM	MARQUEUR D'OURLET
D300	MARLINSPIKE	EPISSOIR A MERLIN
D100	MASHER	PILON A CLAIRE-VOIE
D100	MASHER, POTATO	PILON A PATATES
H060	MASK	MASQUE
E380	MASK, ANAESTHESIA	MASQUE D'ANESTHESIE
I080	MASK, FENCING	MASQUE D'ESCRIMEUR
E480	MASK, MILITARY GAS	MASQUE A GAZ MILITAIRE
G300	MAST	MAT
B040	MAT	TAPIS TRESSE
B040	MAT, BATH	TAPIS DE BAIN
G300	MAT, CANOE	PAILLET DE CANOT
D240	MAT, GOLD	TAPIS RAMASSE-OR
D120	MAT, PLACE	NAPPERON
B020	MAT, SLEEPING	NATTE
B080	MAT, TABLE	DESSUS DE TABLE
B140	MATCH	ALLUMETTE
F100	MATRIX	MATRICE
D020	MATTOCK	PIOCHE PIEMONTAISE
D020	MATTOCK HANDLE	MANCHE DE PIOCHE
B020	MATTRESS	MATELAS
I100	MATTRESS	MATELAS
B020	MATTRESS, MILITARY	MATELAS MILITAIRE
D320	MAUL, CLEAVING	MASSE A REFENDRE
D100	MAUL, MEAT	MAILLET A VIANDE
D320	MAUL, POST	MASSE A PIEU
G300	MAUL, SHACKLE PIN	MASSE D'EXTRACTION DE GOUPILLE DE MANILLE
A020	MAUSOLEUM, MODEL	MAUSOLEE MODELE REDUIT
E560	MEASURE, DRY	MESURE A MATIERES SECHES
E560	MEASURE, FATHOM	MESURE A BRASSE
E560	MEASURE, LIQUID	MESURE A LIQUIDES
E560	MEASURE, MILITARY LIQUID	MESURE A LIQUIDES MILITAIRE
E180	MEASURE, POWDER	MESURE A POUDRE
E560	MEASURE, TAPE	RUBAN A MESURER
H020	MEASURE, TAPE	RUBAN A MESURER
H040	MEAT, ARTIFICIAL	VIANDE ARTIFICIELLE
H120	MEDAL	MEDAILLE
H120	MEDAL, ACHIEVEMENT	MEDAILLE D'HONNEUR
H080	MEDAL, COMMEMORATIVE	MEDAILLE COMMEMORATIVE

Class. Code	Object, suffix	Objet, suffixe
H120	MEDAL, FRATERNAL	MEDAILLE D'ASSOCIATION
H120	MEDAL, MILITARY	MEDAILLE MILITAIRE
H120	MEDAL, MILITARY CAMPAIGN	MEDAILLE DE CAMPAGNE MILITAIRE
H120	MEDAL, MILITARY GOOD CONDUCT	MEDAILLE DE BONNE CONDUITE MILITAIRE
H120	MEDAL, MILITARY SERVICE	MEDAILLE DE SERVICE MILITAIRE
H120	MEDAL, MILITARY SERVICE & GOOD CONDUCT	MEDAILLE DE SERVICE ET DE BONNE CONDUITE
H120	MEDAL, MILITARY VALOR	MEDAILLE DE COURAGE MILITAIRE
H120	MEDAL, RELIGIOUS	MEDAILLE RELIGIEUSE
H120	MEDAL, SERVICE	MEDAILLE DE SERVICE
F120	MEGAPHONE	MEGAPHONE
H080	MEMORANDUM	MEMORANDUM
H080	MEMORANDUM, MILITARY	MEMORANDUM MILITAIRE
H080	MEMORANDUM, POLICE	MEMORANDUM DE POLICE
H080	MENU	MENU
J020	METAL FRAGMENT	FRAGMENT DE METAL
F080	METER, LIGHT	POSEMETRE
E540	METRONOME	METRONOME
H080	MICROFILM	MICROFILM
F120	MICROPHONE	MICROPHONE
E460	MICROSCOPE	MICROSCOPE
D100	MILL, BUHR	PIERRE MEULIERE
D100	MILL, COFFEE	MOULIN A CAFE
D020	MILL, FANNING	CRIBLE
D100	MILL, FLOUR	MOULIN A FARINE
D100	MILL, NUT	MOULIN A NOIX
D120	MILL, PEPPER	MOULIN A POIVRE
D260	MILL, ROLLER	LAMINOIR A COULEURS
D100	MILL, SPICE	MOULIN A EPICES
D300	MILL, STRAW ROLLING	DEVIDOIR A PAILLE
D300	MILL, WARPING	METIER A OURDIR
D240	MINER, CONTINUOUS	MINEUR CONTINU
B060	MIRROR	MIROIR
B060	MIRROR, CHEVAL	PSYCHE
B060	MIRROR, DRESSER	MIROIR DE TABLE
C180	MIRROR, HAND	MIROIR A MAIN
E380	MIRROR, HEAD	GLACE FRONTALE
E380	MIRROR, ORAL EXAMINING	MIROIR POUR EXAMEN BUCAL
B060	MIRROR, WALL	MIROIR MURAL
H060	MISSAL	MISSEL
E140	MISSILE, DESIGN MODEL	FUSEE MODELE DE PROJET
C140	MITT	MITAINE
C140	MITTEN	MOUFLE
C140	MITTEN, POLICE	MOUFLE DE POLICE
D100	MIXER, DOUGH	MELANGEUSE A PATE
C060	MOCCASIN	MOCASSIN
I100	MOCCASIN	MOCASSIN
E380	MODEL, ANATOMICAL	REPRESENTATION ANATOMIQUE
H080	MODEL, TOPOGRAPHIC	MAQUETTE TOPOGRAPHIQUE
D100	MOLD	MOULE
D220	MOLD	MOULE
E180	MOLD, BALL	MOULE A BALLES DE MOUSQUET
D220	MOLD, BELL CLAPPER	MOULE A BATTANT DE CLOCHE
D220	MOLD, BOILER	MOULE A BAC
D160	MOLD, BOTTLE	MOULE A BOUTEILLE
E180	MOLD, BULLET	MOULE A BALLES
D100	MOLD, BUTTER	MOULE A BEURRE
D160	MOLD, CANDLE	MOULE A BOUGIE
D100	MOLD, CHEESE	MOULE A FROMAGE
D100	MOLD, CONFECTION	MOULE A CONFISERIES
D100	MOLD, COOKIE	MOULE A BISCUIT
D160	MOLD, DICTAPHONE CYLINDER	MOULE A CYLINDRE DE DICTAPHONE

186

Class. Code	Object, suffix	Objet, suffixe
D100	MOLD, GELATIN	MOULE A GELATINE
D220	MOLD, GOLD BULLION	MOULE A LINGOT D'OR
D160	MOLD, GUNPOWDER TIN	MOULE A BOITE A POUDRE A CANON
D100	MOLD, JELLY	MOULE A GELEE
D180	MOLD, LEATHER	MOULE A CUIR
D220	MOLD, LURE	MOULE A LEURRE
E180	MOLD, MILITARY BALL	MOULE A BALLES DE MOUSQUET MILITAIRE
D220	MOLD, MILITARY CAP BADGE	MOULE A INSIGNE DE CALOT MILITAIRE
D220	MOLD, MILITARY SHOULDER BELT PLATE	MOULE A PLAQUE DE BAUDRIER MILITAIRE
D160	MOLD, MINIATURE CANDLE	MOULE A BOUGIE MINIATURE
D220	MOLD, MULTIPLE CONNECTOR	MOULE A JOINT MULTIPLE
D220	MOLD, NET WEIGHT	MOULE A LEST
D220	MOLD, POLICE CREST	MOULE A ECUSSON DE POLICE
D220	MOLD, PROPELLER	MOULE A HELICE
D100	MOLD, PUDDING	MOULE A ENTREMETS
D300	MOLD, PURSE	MOULE A BOURSE
D160	MOLD, SOAP	MOULE A SAVON
D220	MOLD, SPOON	MOULE A CUILLERE
D220	MOLD, STEERING WHEEL	MOULE A VOLANT D'ORIENTATION
A040	MOLDING	MOULURE
D240	MONITOR, HYDRAULIC	LANCE GEANTE A EAU
C160	MONOCLE	MONOCLE
H060	MONSTRANCE	OSTENSOIR
H060	MONUMENT	MONUMENT
H060	MONUMENT, MODEL	MONUMENT MODELE REDUIT
E340	MOP	VADROUILLE
D320	MOP, PITCH	BROSSE A GOUDRONNER
E240	MORTAR	MORTIER
D100	MORTAR	MORTIER
E120	MORTAR	MORTIER
D100	MORTAR AND PESTLE	MORTIER ET PILON
E120	MORTAR, MODEL	MORTIER MODELE REDUIT
E240	MORTAR & PESTLE	MORTIER ET PILON
E380	MORTAR & PESTLE	MORTIER ET PILON
E300	MOTOR, ELECTRIC	MOTEUR ELECTRIQUE
G300	MOTOR, OUTBOARD	HORS-BORD
G180	MOUNT, BRIDLE	MONTURE DE BRIDE
B080	MOUSETRAP	SOURICIERE
D020	MOWER	FAUCHEUSE
D020	MOWER, LAWN	TONDEUSE A GAZON
D020	MOWER BLADE	LAME DE FAUCHEUSE
D020	MOWER HANDLE	MANCHERON DE FAUCHEUSE
C140	MUFF	MANCHON
C140	MUFFLER	CACHE-COL
D120	MUG	GROSSE TASSE
I100	MUG	GROSSE TASSE
D120	MUG, CHILD'S	GROSSE TASSE D'ENFANT
H080	MUG, COMMEMORATIVE	GROSSE TASSE COMMEMORATIVE
D120	MUG, MILITARY	GROSSE TASSE MILITAIRE
C180	MUG, SHAVING	TASSE A RASER
C060	MUKLUK	MUKLUK
A020	MUSEUM, MODEL	MUSEE MODELE REDUIT
H080	MUSIC, SHEET	PARTITION DE MUSIQUE
E060	MUSKET	FUSIL
E060	MUSKET, FLINTLOCK	FUSIL A SILEX
E060	MUSKET, MILITARY FLINTLOCK	FUSIL A SILEX MILITAIRE
E060	MUSKET, MILITARY MATCHLOCK	MOUSQUET A MECHE MILITAIRE
E060	MUSKET, MILITARY PERCUSSION	FUSIL A PERCUSSION MILITAIRE
E060	MUSKET, PERCUSSION	FUSIL A PERCUSSION
E060	MUSKET BARREL	CANON DE FUSIL
E060	MUSKET BUTT PLATE	PLAQUE DE COUCHE DE FUSIL

Class. Code	Object, suffix	Objet, suffixe
E060	MUSKET STOCK	MONTURE DE FUSIL
E060	MUSKET TRIGGER	DETENTE DE FUSIL
E060	MUSKET TRIGGER GUARD	SOUS-GARDE DE MOUSQUET
E060	MUSKETOON, MILITARY	MOUSQUETON MILITAIRE
I060	MUTASCOPE	STEREOSCOPE
D040	MUZZLE	MUSELIERE
I020	NABAHON	JEU DE NABAHON
D320	NAIL	CLOU
D040	NAIL, HORSESHOE	CLOU DE FER A CHEVAL
B080	NAIL, PICTURE FRAME	CLOU DE CADRE
D180	NAIL, SHOE	CLOU DE CHAUSSURE
B080	NAILHEAD, PICTURE FRAME	TETE DE CLOU DE CADRE
H080	NAMEPLATE	MEDAILLON
H080	NAMEPLATE, MILITARY	MEDAILLON MILITAIRE
D120	NAPKIN	SERVIETTE
D120	NAPKIN, BREAD BASKET	SERVIETTE DE CORBEILLE A PAIN
D120	NAPPY	COUPE A DESSERT
H060	NAVETTE	NAVETTE
C140	NECKERCHIEF	MOUCHOIR DE COU
C020	NECKLACE	COLLIER
H120	NECKLACE, RELIGIOUS	CHAINE RELIGIEUSE
C140	NECKTIE	CRAVATE ETROITE
C140	NECKTIE, POLICE	CRAVATE ETROITE DE POLICE
D180	NEEDLE	AIGUILLE
D020	NEEDLE, BAGGER'S	ALENE D'ENSACHAGE
D300	NEEDLE, DARNING	AIGUILLE A REPRISER
D180	NEEDLE, GLOVER'S	AIGUILLE DE GANTIER
D180	NEEDLE, HARNESS	AIGUILLE DE SELLIER
D300	NEEDLE, KNITTING	AIGUILLE A TRICOTER
D300	NEEDLE, NETMAKING	AIGUILLE A FILET
F120	NEEDLE, PHONOGRAPH	AIGUILLE DE PHONOGRAPHE
D300	NEEDLE, RUGMAKING	AIGUILLE A TAPIS
D300	NEEDLE, SAILMAKER'S	CARRELET A VOILES
D300	NEEDLE, SEWING	AIGUILLE A COUDRE
D300	NEEDLE, SNOWSHOEMAKING	AIGUILLE A RAQUETTES
E380	NEEDLE, SUTERING	AIGUILLE A SUTURE
D300	NEEDLE, UPHOLSTERER'S	AIGUILLE A DEUX POINTES
H080	NEGATIVE, FILM	NEGATIF DE FILM
H080	NEGATIVE, MILITARY FILM	NEGATIF DE FILM MILITAIRES
D040	NEST, EGG	NICHET
D060	NET	FILET
D040	NET, ANIMAL	FILET A ANIMAUX
D060	NET, DIP	EPUISETTE
D060	NET, DRIFT	FILET DERIVANT
E160	NET, MILITARY HELMET CAMOUFLAGE	FILET DE CAMOUFLAGE DE CASQUE MILITAIRE
D060	NET, POUND	FILET DE BORDIGUE
I080	NET, TENNIS	FILET DE TENNIS
E180	NET, TORPEDO	PARE-TORPILLES
A040	NEWEL CAP	POMMEAU D'ESCALIER
H080	NEWSPAPER	JOURNAL
H060	NICHE, RELIGIOUS STATUE	NICHE DE STATUE RELIGIEUSE
D300	NIDDY NODDY	DEVIDOIR PRIMITIF
C080	NIGHTCAP	BONNET DE NUIT
C100	NIGHTGOWN	CHEMISE DE NUIT
I100	NIGHTGOWN	CHEMISE DE NUIT
E480	NIGHTSTICK	MATRAQUE
D220	NIPPERS, NAIL	PINCE COUPE-CLOU
E400	NIPPERS, TICKET	PINCE A CONTROLE
D120	NIPPLE, NURSING BOTTLE	TETINE DE BIBERON
I100	NOISEMAKER	CRECELLE

Class. Code	Object, suffix	Objet, suffixe
E480	NOOSE, HANGMAN'S	CORDE DE POTENCE
H080	NOTE	NOTE
H080	NOTE, MILITARY	NOTE MILITAIRE
H080	NOTE, PROMISSORY	BILLET A ORDRE
H080	NOTEBOOK	CARNET
H020	NOTEBOOK	CARNET
F180	NOTEBOOK	CARNET
H080	NOTEBOOK, MILITARY	CARNET MILITAIRE
H080	NOTEBOOK, POLICE	CARNET DE POLICE
E480	NOZZLE, FIRE HOSE	AJUTAGE DE MANCHE A INCENDIE
D020	NOZZLE, GARDEN HOSE	AJUTAGE DE TUYAU D'ARROSAGE
D240	NOZZLE, HYDRAULIC	AJUTAGE
H080	NUMBERPLATE	PLAQUE NUMERIQUE
E360	NUT	ECROU
E360	NUT, TETRAHEDRAL	ECROU TETRAEDRIQUE
D120	NUTCRACKER	CASSE-NOISETTES
D120	NUTPICK	PIC A NOIX
G300	OAR	RAME
G300	OARLOCK	DAME DE MAGE
F060	OBOE	HAUTBOIS
E500	OCTANT	OCTANT
E180	OILCAN	BURETTE A HUILE
J060	OILCAN	HUILIER
C180	OINTMENT CONTAINER	RECIPIENT A POMMADE
D100	OPENER, BOTTLE	DECAPSULEUR
D100	OPENER, CAN	OUVRE-BOITES
H080	ORDERS, MILITARY	ORDRES MILITAIRE
H080	ORDERS, POLICE	ORDRES DE POLICE
F060	ORGAN, PIPE	GRAND ORGUE
F060	ORGAN, REED	HARMONIUM
F060	ORGANETTE	ORGUE DE BARBARIE
G180	ORNAMENT, AUTOMOBILE HOOD	ORNEMENT DE CAPOT D'AUTOMOBILE
H040	ORNAMENT, CHRISTMAS TREE	ORNEMENT D'ARBRE DE NOEL
H040	ORNAMENT, EASTER	ORNEMENT DE PAQUES
C020	ORNAMENT, HAIR	ORNEMENT POUR CHEVEUX
G180	ORNAMENT, HARNESS	ORNEMENT DE HARNAIS
E200	ORRERY	PLANETAIRE
F140	OSCILLATOR, FREQUENCY	OSCILLATEUR
B060	OTTOMAN	OTTOMANE
D220	OVEN, AMALGAM DRYING	FOUR DE SECHAGE POUR AMALGAME
D100	OVEN, REFLECTOR	FOUR
C100	OVERCOAT	PARDESSUS
C100	OVERCOAT, MILITARY	PARDESSUS MILITAIRE
C100	OVERCOAT, POLICE	PARDESSUS DE POLICE
G120	OXCART	CHAR A BOEUF
D040	OXSHOE	FER A BOVIN
E400	PACKAGE, ADDRESS LABEL	EMBALLAGE POUR ETIQUETTES D'ADRESSES
E400	PACKAGE, ALLSPICE	EMBALLAGE A POIVRE DE LA JAMAIQUE
E400	PACKAGE, ANALGESIC	EMBALLAGE A ANALGESIQUES
E400	PACKAGE, ANTACID	EMBALLAGE A ANTI-ACIDE
E400	PACKAGE, ASTRINGENT	EMBALLAGE A ASTRINGENT
E400	PACKAGE, BAKING SODA	EMBALLAGE A BICARBONATE DE SOUDE
E400	PACKAGE, BANDAGE	EMBALLAGE A BANDAGES
E400	PACKAGE, BOOT POLISH	EMBALLAGE A CIRAGE A CHAUSSURES
E400	PACKAGE, BREAD	EMBALLAGE A PAIN
E400	PACKAGE, BUTTER	EMBALLAGE A BEURRE
E400	PACKAGE, CARD DECK	EMBALLAGE A JEU DE CARTES
E400	PACKAGE, CARTRIDGE	EMBALLAGE A CARTOUCHES
E400	PACKAGE, CHEMICAL FILTER	EMBALLAGE A FILTRE CHIMIQUE
E400	PACKAGE, CHESTNUT LEAF	EMBALLAGE A FEUILLES DE MARRONNIER
E400	PACKAGE, CHEWING GUM	EMBALLAGE A GOMMES A MACHER

Class. Code	Object, suffix	Objet, suffixe
E400	PACKAGE, CIGARETTE	EMBALLAGE A CIGARETTES
E400	PACKAGE, CIGARETTE PAPER	EMBALLAGE A PAPIER A CIGARETTES
E400	PACKAGE, CLASP	EMBALLAGE A FERMOIRS
E400	PACKAGE, CLEANSER	EMBALLAGE A POUDRE A NETTOYER
E400	PACKAGE, CLOTH BOLT	EMBALLAGE A PIECES DE TISSU
E400	PACKAGE, COD LIVER OIL	EMBALLAGE A HUILE DE FOIE DE MORUE
E400	PACKAGE, COFFEE	EMBALLAGE A CAFE
E400	PACKAGE, COLLAR	EMBALLAGE A COLS
E400	PACKAGE, CONDIMENT SAUCE	EMBALLAGE A SAUCE AUX CONDIMENTS
E400	PACKAGE, COSMETIC	EMBALLAGE A COSMETIQUES
E400	PACKAGE, COUGH DROP	EMBALLAGE A PASTILLES CONTRE LA TOUX
E400	PACKAGE, DECAL	EMBALLAGE A PAPIER A DECALCOMANIE
E400	PACKAGE, DYE	EMBALLAGE A TEINTURE
E400	PACKAGE, EGG SUBSTITUTE	EMBALLAGE A SUCCEDANE D'OEUF
E400	PACKAGE, FISH LINE	EMBALLAGE A LIGNES A PECHE
E400	PACKAGE, FISHHOOK	EMBALLAGE A HAMECONS
E400	PACKAGE, FRUIT	EMBALLAGE A FRUITS
E400	PACKAGE, GAUGE PIN	EMBALLAGE DE POINTES DE REGISTRES
E400	PACKAGE, GLAZIER'S POINT	EMBALLAGE A POINTES DE VITRIER
E400	PACKAGE, GUN WAD	EMBALLAGE A BOURRE DE FUSIL
E400	PACKAGE, HAIRPIN	EMBALLAGE A EPINGLES A CHEVEUX
E400	PACKAGE, HATPIN	EMBALLAGE A EPINGLES A CHAPEAU
E400	PACKAGE, JELLY	EMBALLAGE A GELEE
E400	PACKAGE, LACE	EMBALLAGE A DENTELLE
E400	PACKAGE, LAMP WICK	EMBALLAGE A MECHES DE LAMPE
E400	PACKAGE, LAUNDRY BLUEING	EMBALLAGE A BLEU DE LESSIVE
E400	PACKAGE, LAUNDRY SOAP	EMBALLAGE A SAVON A LESSIVE
E400	PACKAGE, LEMONADE	EMBALLAGE A LIMONADE
E400	PACKAGE, LIGHT BULB	EMBALLAGE A AMPOULES ELECTRIQUES
E400	PACKAGE, LINIMENT	EMBALLAGE A LINIMENT
E400	PACKAGE, MACE	EMBALLAGE A MACIS
E400	PACKAGE, MARJORAM	EMBALLAGE A MARJOLAINE
E400	PACKAGE, MASTERWORT ROOT	EMBALLAGE A RACINES DE BERCE LAINEUSE
E400	PACKAGE, MATCH	EMBALLAGE A ALLUMETTES
E400	PACKAGE, MEDICINAL	EMBALLAGE A PRODUIT PHARMACEUTIQUE
E400	PACKAGE, MEDICINAL SYRUP	EMBALLAGE A SIROP PHARMACEUTIQUE
E400	PACKAGE, METAL POLISH	EMBALLAGE A PRODUIT A POLIR LE METAL
E400	PACKAGE, MUSTARD	EMBALLAGE A MOUTARDE
E400	PACKAGE, MUSTARD PLASTER MIX	EMBALLAGE A PRÈPARATION POUR CATAPLASME SINAPISE
E400	PACKAGE, NAIL	EMBALLAGE A CLOUS
E400	PACKAGE, PAINT	EMBALLAGE A PEINTURE
E400	PACKAGE, PEN	EMBALLAGE A PLUMES
E400	PACKAGE, PENCIL	EMBALLAGE A CRAYONS A MINE DE PLOMB
E400	PACKAGE, PEPPER	EMBALLAGE A POIVRE
E400	PACKAGE, PHONOGRAPH NEEDLE	EMBALLAGE D'AIGUILLES DE PHONOGRAPHE
E400	PACKAGE, PHOTOGRAPHIC FILM	EMBALLAGE A PELLICULE PHOTOGRAPHIQUE
E400	PACKAGE, PILL	EMBALLAGE A PILULES
E400	PACKAGE, PIPE CLEANER	EMBALLAGE A NETTOIE-PIPES
E400	PACKAGE, POUNCE	EMBALLAGE A POUDRE A PONCER
E400	PACKAGE, PRESERVING JAR SEAL	EMBALLAGE A RONDELLES DE BOCAL DE CONSERVE
E400	PACKAGE, PROMISSORY NOTE	EMBALLAGE DE BILLETS A ORDRE
E400	PACKAGE, RAZOR BLADE	EMBALLAGE A LAMES DE RASOIR
E400	PACKAGE, RENNET	EMBALLAGE A PRESURE
E400	PACKAGE, ROSIN	EMBALLAGE A COLOPHANE
E400	PACKAGE, SAFFRON	EMBALLAGE A SAFRAN
E400	PACKAGE, SEED	EMBALLAGE A SEMENCES
E400	PACKAGE, SEWING NEEDLE	EMBALLAGE A AIGUILLES A COUDRE
E400	PACKAGE, SEWING SUPPLIES	EMBALLAGE A FOURNITURES DE COUTURE
E400	PACKAGE, SHAMPOO	EMBALLAGE A SHAMPOOING
E400	PACKAGE, SHOELACE	EMBALLAGE A LACETS DE SOULIER
E400	PACKAGE, SLEEVE GARTER	EMBALLAGE A BRACELET POUR MANCHE

Class. Code	Object, suffix	Objet, suffixe
E400	PACKAGE, SPICE	EMBALLAGE A EPICES
E400	PACKAGE, STARCH	EMBALLAGE A EMPOIS
E400	PACKAGE, STATIONERY	EMBALLAGE A PAPETERIE
E400	PACKAGE, STOVE MICA	EMBALLAGE A MICA DE POELE
E400	PACKAGE, STOVE POLISH	EMBALLAGE A PATE A POLIR LE POELE
E400	PACKAGE, STRAIGHT PIN	EMBALLAGE A EPINGLES DROITES
E400	PACKAGE, STRING	EMBALLAGE A FICELLE
E400	PACKAGE, TEA	EMBALLAGE A THE
E400	PACKAGE, THREAD	EMBALLAGE A FILS
E400	PACKAGE, THYME	EMBALLAGE A THYM
E400	PACKAGE, TISSUE	EMBALLAGE A MOUCHOIRS DE PAPIER
E400	PACKAGE, TOBACCO	EMBALLAGE A TABAC
E400	PACKAGE, TOILET PAPER	EMBALLAGE A PAPIER HYGIENIQUE
E400	PACKAGE, TOILET SOAP	EMBALLAGE A SAVON DE TOILETTE
E400	PACKAGE, TOILETRY SET	EMBALLAGE POUR ENSEMBLE D'ARTICLES DE TOILETTE
E400	PACKAGE, TONIC	EMBALLAGE A TONIQUE
E400	PACKAGE, VERMIFUGE	EMBALLAGE A VERMIFUGE
E400	PACKAGE, VIOLIN STRING	EMBALLAGE A CORDES DE VIOLON
E400	PACKAGE, WAX PAPER	EMBALLAGE A PAPIER CIRE
E380	PAD, HEATING	COUSSIN CHAUFFANT
G180	PAD, HORSE COLLAR	COUSSIN DE BOURRELET DE CHEVAL
E240	PAD, HOT	DESSOUS PROTECTEUR
G180	PAD, SADDLE	TAPIS DE SELLE
D120	PAD, TABLE	SOUS-NAPPE
D100	PADDLE	PALETTE
D300	PADDLE	PLANCHE A TROUS
G300	PADDLE, CANOE	AVIRON DE CANOT
H080	PADDLE, COMMEMORATIVE	AVIRON COMMEMORATIF
E340	PADDLE, LAUNDRY	PALETTE A LESSIVE
G300	PADDLE, MINIATURE	AVIRON MINIATURE
D320	PADDLE, PITCH	PALETTE A GOUDRON
B080	PADLOCK	CADENAS
B080	PADLOCK, MILITARY	CADENAS MILITAIRE
H080	PAGE, ACCOUNT BOOK	PAGE DE LIVRE DE COMPTES
H080	PAGE, BOOK	PAGE DE LIVRE
H080	PAGE, LEDGER	PAGE DE GRAND LIVRE
F180	PAGE, LEDGER	PAGE DE GRAND LIVRE
H080	PAGE, MAGAZINE	PAGE DE REVUE
H080	PAGE, MILITARY BOOK	PAGE DE LIVRE MILITAIRE
E340	PAIL	SEAU
D120	PAIL, DINNER	BOITE A LUNCH
D100	PAIL, LARD	SEAU A SAINDOUX
E180	PAIL, MAGAZINE WATER	SEAU A EAU DE POUDRIERE
E340	PAIL, MILITARY	SEAU MILITAIRE
D120	PAIL, MILITARY SOUP	SEAU A SOUPE MILITAIRE
D100	PAIL, MILKING	SEAU A LAIT
D120	PAIL, MINIATURE WATER	SEAU A EAU MINIATURE
D120	PAIL, WATER	SEAU A EAU
E340	PAIL & WRINGER	SEAU ET ESSOREUSE
D260	PAINT	PEINTURE
A040	PAINT FRAGMENT	FRAGMENT DE PEINTURE
H040	PAINTING	PEINTURE
C100	PAJAMAS	PYJAMA
D260	PALETTE	PALETTE
H060	PALL	PALE
J060	PALLET, CARGO	PALETTE DE CHARGE
H060	PALM	RAMEAU
D200	PALM, MASON'S	PAUMELLE DE MACON
D300	PALM, SAILMAKER'S	PAUMELLE DE VOILIER
D180	PALMIRON	POUSSE-ALENE
E560	PAN, BALANCE	BASSIN DE BALANCE

Class. Code	Object, suffix	Objet, suffixe
D100	PAN, BREAD	MOULE A PAIN
D100	PAN, CAKE	MOULE A GATEAU
D100	PAN, DOUGH	MOULE DE FERMENTATION
D100	PAN, FRYING	POELE A FRIRE
D100	PAN, MILK	JATTE A LAIT
D240	PAN, MINER'S	PELLE DE MINEUR
D100	PAN, MINIATURE FRYING	POELE A FRIRE MINIATURE
D100	PAN, MUFFIN	MOULE A MUFFINS
D100	PAN, PIE	MOULE A TARTE
D100	PAN, PUDDING	MOULE A POUDING
D100	PAN, ROASTING	ROTISSOIRE
D100	PAN, TUBE	MOULE EN FORME DE TUBE
A040	PANELING	PANNEAU
C120	PANTALETTES	PANTALON DE LINGERIE
F040	PANTOGRAPH	PANTOGRAPHE
C100	PANTS	PANTALON
I100	PANTS	PANTALON
C100	PANTS, INSTRUCTIONAL MODEL	PANTALON MODELE D'INSTRUCTION
C100	PANTS, MILITARY	PANTALON MILITAIRE
C100	PANTS, POLICE	PANTALON DE POLICE
F180	PAPER, CARBON	PAPIER CARBONE
E240	PAPER, FILTER	PAPIER FILTRE
J020	PAPER FRAGMENT	FRAGMENT DE PAPIER
E340	PAPER, SHELF	PAPIER A ETAGERE
J060	PAPER, WAX	PAPIER CIRE
E400	PAPER, WRAPPING	PAPIER D'EMBALLAGE
H080	PAPERS	ECRITURES
F180	PAPERWEIGHT	PRESSE-PAPIERS
C160	PARASOL	OMBRELLE
G180	PARASOL, CARRIAGE	PARASOL DE VOITURE
C160	PARASOL HANDLE	POIGNEE D'OMBRELLE
D100	PARER, FRUIT	EPLUCHEUR A FRUITS
D040	PARER, HOOF	ROGNE-PIED
C160	PARFLECHE	PARFLECHE
C100	PARKA	PARKA
E080	PARTISAN	PERTUISANE
H080	PASSPORT	PASSEPORT
H120	PATCH	APPLIQUE
H120	PATCH, MILITARY	APPLIQUE MILITAIRE
H060	PATEN	PATENE
H080	PATENT	BREVET
D300	PATTERN	PATRON
D320	PATTERN	PATRON
D220	PATTERN, ANVIL	MODELE D'ENCLUME
D220	PATTERN, ASHPAN	MODELE DE GARDE-CENDRES
D220	PATTERN, BOILER	MODELE DE BAC
D220	PATTERN, CANNON CARRIAGE	MODELE D'AFFUT DE CANON
D220	PATTERN, CANNON CARRIAGE TRUCK LEVER	MODELE DE LEVIER D'AFFUT DE CANON
D220	PATTERN, CANNONBALL	MODELE DE BOULET DE CANON
D220	PATTERN, CARD HOLDER	MODELE DE PORTE-ETIQUETTE
D220	PATTERN, CLOTHES HOOK	MODELE DE PATERE
D160	PATTERN, DICTAPHONE CYLINDER	MODELE DE CYLINDRE DE DICTAPHONE
D220	PATTERN, GEAR	MODELE DE ROUE D'ENGRENAGE
D220	PATTERN, GRAPESHOT	MODELE DE MITRAILLE
D220	PATTERN, GUN	MODELE DE CANON
D220	PATTERN, GUN WHEEL	MODELE DE ROUE DE CANON
D220	PATTERN, HEATER	MODELE D'APPAREIL DE CHAUFFAGE
D220	PATTERN, HORSESHOE	MODELE DE FER A CHEVAL
D220	PATTERN, KETTLE	MODELE DE MARMITE
D220	PATTERN, KNIFE	MODELE DE COUTEAU
D220	PATTERN, LATCH ASSEMBLY	MODELE D'ASSEMBLAGE DE LOQUET

Class. Code	Object, suffix	Objet, suffixe
D220	PATTERN, MILITARY BASIN	MODELE DE CUVETTE MILITAIRE
D220	PATTERN, MILITARY CARRONADE	MODELE DE CARONADE MILITAIRE
D220	PATTERN, MILITARY SHELL VISE	MODELE D'ETAU A OBUS MILITAIRE
D220	PATTERN, MORTAR	MODELE DE MORTIER
D220	PATTERN, MULTIPLE CONNECTOR	MODELE DE JOINT MULTIPLE
D220	PATTERN, PIE PAN	MODELE DE MOULE A TARTE
D220	PATTERN, RACK	MODELE DE RATELIER
D220	PATTERN, SADIRON	MODELE DE FER A REPASSER
D220	PATTERN, SHELL	MODELE DE BOMBE
D220	PATTERN, SHOT GARLAND	MODELE DE CADRE DE PILE A PROJECTILES
D220	PATTERN, SPONTOON	MODELE D'ESPONTON
D220	PATTERN, STEERING WHEEL	MODELE DE VOLANT D'ORIENTATION DU TRAIN AVANT
D220	PATTERN, STOVE	MODELE DE POELE
D220	PATTERN, STOVE DOOR	MODELE DE PORTE DE POELE
D220	PATTERN, STOVE LID REDUCER	MODELE D'ANNEAU DE ROND DE POELE
D220	PATTERN, STOVE PLATE CENTER	MODELE DE CENTRE DE PLAQUE DE POELE
D220	PATTERN, STOVEPIPE COLLAR	MODELE DE COLLET DE TUYAU DE POELE
D220	PATTERN, SWIVEL GUN	MODELE DE CANON SUR PIVOT
D220	PATTERN, TEAKETTLE LID	MODELE DE COUVERCLE DE BOUILLOIRE
D220	PATTERN, TRAP	MODELE DE PIEGE
H080	PAYROLL	FEUILLE DE PAIE
D140	PEAVY	TOURNE-BILLES A EPERON
B060	PEDESTAL	PIEDESTAL
D100	PEEL	PELLE EN ENFOURNER
D100	PEELER, VEGETABLE	EPLUCHEUR A LEGUMES
D320	PEG	CHEVILLE
D060	PEG, LOBSTER	CHEVILLE A HOMARD
D180	PEG, SHOE	CHEVILLE A CHAUSSURE
F180	PEN	PLUME
F180	PEN, FOUNTAIN	PLUME A RESERVOIR
F040	PEN, RULING	TIRE-LIGNE
F180	PENCIL	CRAYON A MINE DE CRAYON
D320	PENCIL, CARPENTER'S	CRAYON DE CHARPENTIER
C180	PENCIL, EYEBROW	CRAYON A SOURCILS
C020	PENDANT	PENDENTIF
H120	PENDANT, MINIATURE RELIGIOUS	PENDENTIF RELIGIEUX MINIATURE
H120	PENDANT, RELIGIOUS	PENDENTIF RELIGIEUX
H080	PENNANT	FANION
H060	PENNANT	FANION
H080	PENNANT, COMMEMORATIVE	FANION COMMEMORATIF
H060	PENNON	BANDEROLE
E060	PEPPERBOX	PISTOLET A CANONS MULTIPLES
E060	PERCUSSION LOCK MECHANISM	PLATINE A PERCUSSION
F100	PERFORATOR	PERFOREUSE
E380	PERFORATOR, TREPANNING	PERFORATEUR POUR TREPANATION
E460	PERISCOPE	PERISCOPE
H080	PERMIT	PERMIS
E240	PESTLE	PILON
D100	PESTLE	PILON
D260	PESTLE	PILON
E140	PETARD	PETARD
H080	PETITION	PETITION
H080	PETITION, MILITARY	PETITION MILITAIRE
C120	PETTICOAT	JUPON
I100	PETTICOAT	JUPON
C120	PETTICOAT, CHILD'S	JUPON D'ENFANT
C120	PETTICOAT, HOOP	JUPON A CERCEAUX
B060	PEW	BANC D'EGLISE
D100	PEW	GAFFE A POISSON
B060	PEW HEADBOARD	TETE DE BANC D'EGLISE
F120	PHONOGRAPH	PHONOGRAPHE

Class. Code	Object, suffix	Objet, suffixe
F140	PHOTOPHONE	PHOTOPHONE
F140	PHOTOPHONE, DESIGN MODEL	PHOTOPHONE MODELE DE PROJET
F060	PIANO	PIANO
F060	PIANO, GRAND	PIANO A QUEUE
F060	PIANO, SQUARE	PIANO CARRE
D240	PICK	PIC
D200	PICK	PIC
J060	PICK	PIOCHE
D240	PICK, DOUBLE-POINTED	PIC A DEUX POINTES
D200	PICK, FLINTING	PICOT
D040	PICK, HOOF	CURE-PIED
D100	PICK, ICE	PIC A GLACE
D200	PICK, MASON'S	PIC DE MACON
D240	PICK, MILITARY	PIC MILITAIRE
D200	PICK, MILL	HERMINETTE A MEULE
D200	PICK, SLATE	PIC D'ARDOISIER
D200	PICK HANDLE	MANCHE DE PIC
D240	PICK HEAD	TETE DE PIC
D240	PICKAROON	CROC A LEVIER
D140	PICKAROON	CROC A LEVIER
D020	PICKER, FRUIT	CUEILLE-FRUITS
H080	PICTURE	IMAGE
H040	PICTURE	TABLEAU
H040	PICTURE, BARK	TABLEAU EN ECORCE
H040	PICTURE, CUT-PAPER	TABLEAU EN PAPIER DECOUPE
H040	PICTURE, FLORA	TABLEAU EN FLEURS
H040	PICTURE, HAIR	TABLEAU EN CHEVEUX
H040	PICTURE, LEAF	TABLEAU EN FEUILLES
H080	PICTURE, MILITARY	IMAGE MILITAIRE
H040	PICTURE, NEEDLEWORK	TABLEAU DE TRAVAIL A L'AIGUILLE
H080	PICTURE, POLICE	IMAGE DE POLICE
H060	PICTURE, RELIGIOUS	IMAGE RELIGIEUSE
H040	PICTURE, RIBBON	TABLEAU EN RUBAN
H040	PICTURE, SHELL	TABLEAU EN COQUILLAGES
H040	PICTURE, SILK	TABLEAU SUR SOIE
H040	PICTURE, WAX	TABLEAU A L'ENCAUSTIQUE
I020	PIECE, CHESS	PIECE DE JEU D'ECHECS
I020	PIECE, GAME	PIECE DE JEU
D300	PIECE, QUILT	COURTEPOINTE
E080	PIKE	PIQUE
E080	PIKE, BOARDING	PIQUE D'ABORDAGE
D140	PIKE, FORK	FOURCHE
E080	PIKE, MILITARY	PIQUE MILITAIRE
E080	PIKE, MILITARY BOARDING	PIQUE D'ABORDAGE MILITAIRE
D140	PIKE, POLE	GAFFE
A040	PILLAR	PILIER
C160	PILLBOX	BOITE A PILULES
C080	PILLBOX	PILLBOX
C080	PILLBOX, MILITARY	PILLBOX MILITAIRE
C080	PILLBOX, POLICE	PILLBOX DE POLICE
B020	PILLOW	OREILLER
I100	PILLOW	OREILLER
H060	PILLOW, COFFIN	OREILLER DE CERCUEIL
E300	PILLOWBLOCK	PALIER A CHAPEAU
B020	PILLOWCASE	TAIE D'OREILLER
I100	PILLOWCASE	TAIE D'OREILLER
H080	PIN	EPINGLE
H120	PIN	PETITE BROCHE
G300	PIN, BELAYING	CABILLOT
C180	PIN, BOBBY	PINCE A CHEVEUX
I080	PIN, BOWLING	QUILLE

Class.
Code Object, suffix   Objet, suffixe

Code	Object, suffix	Objet, suffixe
H080	PIN, COMMEMORATIVE	EPINGLE COMMEMORATIVE
G240	PIN, COUPLING	GOUPILLE D'ATTELAGE
D240	PIN, DREDGE BUCKET	AXE DE FIXATION DE GODET DE DRAGUE
D220	PIN, DRIFT	BROCHES D'ASSEMBLAGE
H120	PIN, FRATERNAL	PETITE BROCHE DE MEMBRE
F100	PIN, GAUGE	ARDILLON
D300	PIN, HATTER'S	ROULEAU DE CHAPELIER
C020	PIN, LAPEL	EPINGLE DE REVERS
D220	PIN, LIFTING	CRAMPON
D200	PIN, LINE	PIQUET DE CORDEAU
D040	PIN, PICKET	PIQUET D'ATTACHE
D100	PIN, ROLLING	ROULEAU A PATISSERIE
D300	PIN, SAFETY	EPINGLE DE SURETE
D300	PIN, STRAIGHT	EPINGLE DROITE
G300	PIN, THOLE	TOLET
E380	PIN, TREPHINE	MECHE A TREPHINE
G180	PIN, YOKE	CLE DE JOUG
C100	PINAFORE	TABLIER D'ECOLE
D040	PINCERS, FARRIER'S	PINCES DE MARECHAL-FERRANT
D020	PINCERS, GARDEN	PINCES DE JARDIN
D180	PINCERS, LASTING	TENAILLE A FORMER
D300	PINCUSHION	PELOTE A EPINGLES
A040	PINTLE	RIVURE
G300	PINTLE, RUDDER	AIGUILLOT DE GOUVERNAIL
C160	PIPE	PIPE
A040	PIPE	TUYAU
I100	PIPE, BUBBLE	PIPE A BULLES DE SAVON
F060	PIPE, PITCH	DIAPASON A BOUCHE
E180	PIPE, RAMROD	PORTE-BAGUETTE
E060	PISTOL	PISTOLET
E060	PISTOL, AUTOMATIC	PISTOLET AUTOMATIQUE
I100	PISTOL, CAP	PISTOLET A DETONATEUR
E060	PISTOL, DUELLING	PISTOLET DE DUEL
E060	PISTOL, FLINTLOCK	PISTOLET A SILEX
E060	PISTOL, HORSEMAN'S	PISTOLET DE CAVALIER
E060	PISTOL, MILITARY AUTOMATIC	PISTOLET AUTOMATIQUE MILITAIRE
E060	PISTOL, MILITARY FLINTLOCK	PISTOLET A SILEX MILITAIRE
E060	PISTOL, MILITARY PERCUSSION	PISTOLET A PERCUSSION MILITAIRE
F160	PISTOL, MILITARY SIGNAL	PISTOLET DE SIGNALISATION MILITAIRE
E060	PISTOL, PERCUSSION	PISTOLET A PERCUSSION
E060	PISTOL, POCKET	PISTOLET DE POCHE
E060	PISTOL, POCKET CENTER-FIRE	PISTOLET DE POCHE A PERCUSSION CENTRALE
F160	PISTOL, SIGNAL	PISTOLET DE SIGNALISATION
D180	PITCH	BRAI
E260	PITCH	ETOUPE
C180	PITCHER	CRUCHE
D120	PITCHER	PICHET
I100	PITCHER	POT
D120	PITCHER, CREAM	PICHET A CREME
D120	PITCHER, MILK	PICHET A LAIT
D120	PITCHER, MINIATURE	PICHET MINIATURE
D120	PITCHER, SYRUP	PICHET A SIROP
D120	PITCHER, WATER	PICHET A EAU
D120	PITCHER, WINE	PICHET A VIN
D100	PITTER, FRUIT	DENOYAUTEUR DE FRUITS
C100	PLAID, MILITARY FLY	PLAID VOLANT MILITAIRE
D320	PLANE	RABOT
D320	PLANE, ASTRAGAL	BOUVET A ASTRAGALE
D320	PLANE, BLOCK	RABOT DE COUPE
D320	PLANE, BOX-SCRAPER	RABOT A EFFACER
D320	PLANE, CHAMFERING	RABOT A CHANFREINER

Class. Code	Object, suffix	Objet, suffixe
D320	PLANE, COMPASS	RABOT CINTRE
D320	PLANE, DADO	BOUVET A TARABISCOT
D320	PLANE, EDGE	RABOT A ECORNER
D320	PLANE, FILLISTER	FEUILLERET
D320	PLANE, FLOOR	RABOT A PLANCHER
D320	PLANE, FORKSTAFF	RABOT A MANCHE DE FOURCHE
D320	PLANE, GROOVING	BOUVET A RAINURES
D320	PLANE, GUTTERING	VARLOPE A ONGLETS
D320	PLANE, HOLLOW	GORGET
D320	PLANE, JACK	DEMIE-VARLOPE
D320	PLANE, LONG-JOINTER	GRANDE VARLOPE
D320	PLANE, MAST-AND-SPAR	RABOT A MAT ET EPART
D320	PLANE, MITER	RABOT A ONGLET
D320	PLANE, MOLDING	RABOT A MOULURES
D320	PLANE, NOSING	RABOT A BOUDINS
D320	PLANE, PANEL	RABOT A PANNEAU
D320	PLANE, PLOW	BOUVET
D320	PLANE, RABBET	GUILLAUME
D320	PLANE, ROUND	RABOT ROND
D320	PLANE, ROUNDER	RABOT CIRCULAIRE
D320	PLANE, ROUTER	GUIMBARDE
D320	PLANE, SASH	RABOT A CHASSIS
D320	PLANE, SHORT-JOINTER	RIFLARD
D320	PLANE, SMOOTHING	RABOT A REPASSER
D320	PLANE, SPILL	RABOT A COPEAUX
D320	PLANE, SUN	COLOMBE DE TONNELIER
D320	PLANE, TONGUE-AND-GROOVE	BOUVET A RAINURE ET A LANGUETTE
D320	PLANE, TONGUEING	BOUVET A LANGUETTES
D320	PLANE, TOOTHING	RABOT DENTE
D320	PLANE, TRYING	VARLOPE
D320	PLANE BLADE	LAME DE RABOT
D320	PLANE FENCE, CHAMFERING	GUIDE DE RABOT A CHANFREINER
D320	PLANE HANDLE	MANCHE DE RABOT
D320	PLANE WEDGE	COIN DE RABOT
F100	PLANER	TAQUOIR
F100	PLANER, LINOTYPE	TAQUOIR LINOTYPE
A020	PLANT, MODEL INDUSTRIAL	INSTALLATION INDUSTRIELLE MODELE REDUIT
C180	PLANTER	JARDINIERE SUSPENDUE
H120	PLAQUE	PLAQUE
H040	PLAQUE	PLAQUE
H080	PLAQUE	PLAQUE
H060	PLAQUE	PLAQUE
H080	PLAQUE, COMMEMORATIVE	PLAQUE COMMEMORATIVE
H120	PLAQUE, MILITARY	PLAQUE MILITAIRE
H060	PLAQUE, POLICE	PLAQUE DE POLICE
H060	PLAQUE, RELIGIOUS	PLAQUE RELIGIEUSE
H120	PLAQUE, RELIGIOUS	PLAQUE RELIGIEUSE
E380	PLASTER, COUGH	CATAPLASME
D120	PLATE	ASSIETTE
I100	PLATE	ASSIETTE
D220	PLATE, BENCH	TABLE D'ETABLI
D120	PLATE, BUTTER	ASSIETTE A BEURRE
G300	PLATE, CHAIN	CADENE DE HAUBANS
D120	PLATE, CHILD'S	ASSIETTE D'ENFANT
H060	PLATE, COFFIN	PLAQUE DE CERCUEIL
H080	PLATE, COMMEMORATIVE	ASSIETTE COMMEMORATIVE
D120	PLATE, CUP	ASSIETTE A TASSE
D120	PLATE, DESSERT	ASSIETTE A DESSERT
D120	PLATE, DINNER	ASSIETTE A DINER
F100	PLATE, ENGRAVING	CLICHE
F080	PLATE, FILM	PLAQUE PHOTOGRAPHIQUE

Class. Code	Object, suffix	Objet, suffixe
D100	PLATE, HOT	PLAQUE CHAUFFANTE
G180	PLATE, LICENSE	PLAQUE D'IMMATRICULATION
D120	PLATE, LUNCHEON	ASSIETTE A COLLATION
D120	PLATE, MILITARY	ASSIETTE MILITAIRE
H120	PLATE, MILITARY BACKPACK	PLAQUE DE SAC A DOS A ARMATURE MILITAIRE
H120	PLATE, MILITARY CARTRIDGE-BOX	PLAQUE DE CARTOUCHIERE MILITAIRE
D120	PLATE, MILITARY DESSERT	ASSIETTE A DESSERT MILITAIRE
H120	PLATE, MILITARY HELMET	PLAQUE DE CASQUE MILITAIRE
D120	PLATE, MILITARY SERVING	ASSIETTE A SERVIR MILITAIRE
H120	PLATE, MILITARY SHAKO	PLAQUE DE SHAKO MILITAIRE
H120	PLATE, MILITARY SHOULDER BELT	PLAQUE DE BAUDRIER MILITAIRE
D120	PLATE, MINIATURE	ASSIETTE MINIATURE
H060	PLATE, OFFERING	PLATEAU A OFFRANDES
D120	PLATE, SALAD	ASSIETTE A SALADE
D120	PLATE, SAUCEBOAT	SOUCOUPE DE SAUCIERE
D120	PLATE, SERVING	ASSIETTE A SERVIR
D120	PLATE, SOUP	ASSIETTE A SOUPE
F080	PLATEHOLDER	PORTE-PLAQUES
E120	PLATFORM PINTLE, TRAVERSING	PIVOT DE CHASSIS D'AFFUT
D120	PLATTER	PLAT DE SERVICE
D120	PLATTER, MILITARY	PLAT MILITAIRE
J060	PLIERS	PINCE
D300	PLIERS, BUTTON	PINCE A BOUTON
E260	PLIERS, FENCING	PINCE COUPE-FIL
E280	PLIERS, NEEDLENOSE	PINCE A BECS DEMI-RONDS
D180	PLIERS, PAD-SCREW	PINCE D'ECROU A COUSSINET
D180	PLIERS, SETTING	PINCE A ATTACHE DE BOUTON
J060	PLIERS, VISE-GRIP	PINCE-ETAU
D020	PLOW	CHARRUE
D060	PLOW	CHARRUE
D020	PLOW, BOG-CUTTER	CHARRUE A TOURBIERE
D020	PLOW, MOLDBOARD	CHARRUE A VERSOIRS
D020	PLOW, SALES MODEL	CHARRUE MODELE DE VENTE
D020	PLOW BEAM	AGE DE CHARRUE
D020	PLOW COULTER	COUTRE DE CHARRUE
D020	PLOW GAUGE WHEEL	ROUE DE JAUGE DE CHARRUE
D020	PLOW HANDLE	MANCHERON DE CHARRUE
D020	PLOWSHARE	SOC DE CHARRUE
D200	PLUG	COIN
E300	PLUG	FICHE
E300	PLUG, SPARK	BOUGIE D'ALLUMAGE
H120	PLUME, MILITARY	PLUMET MILITAIRE
H120	PLUME, MILITARY BICORN HAT	PLUMET DE BICORNE MILITAIRE
H120	PLUME, MILITARY BONNET	PLUMET DE BONNET MILITAIRE
H120	PLUME, MILITARY CAP	PLUMET DE CALOT MILITAIRE
H120	PLUME, MILITARY SHAKO	PLUMET DE SHAKO MILITAIRE
H120	PLUME, POLICE HELMET	PLUMET DE CASQUE DE POLICE
E340	PLUNGER	DEBOUCHOIR A VENTOUSE
E340	PLUNGER, WASH	AGITATEUR CONIQUE
D100	POACHER	POCHEUSE
D100	POACHER, FISH	POISSONNIERE
C160	POCKET	POCHE
B080	POCKET, WALL	FOURRE-TOUT
B060	PODIUM	PODIUM
H080	POEM	POEME
D180	POINT, AWL	POINTE D'ALENE
D240	POINT, COLD WATER THAWING	POINTE DE DECONGELATION A EAU FROIDE
D160	POINT, GLAZIER'S	POINTE DE VITRIER
E080	POINT, PROJECTILE	POINTE DE PROJECTILE
D240	POINT, STEAM THAWING	POINTE DE DECONGELATION A VAPEUR
F160	POINTER	BAGUETTE

Class. Code	Object, suffix	Objet, suffixe
D040	POKE	TRIBART
D220	POKER	PIQUE-FEU
B140	POKER	TISONNIER
D200	POKER, KILN	TISONNIER DE FOUR A BRIQUES
B140	POKER, MINIATURE	TISONNIER MINIATURE
D240	POLE, GIN	FLECHE DE LEVAGE
D140	POLE HANDLE, PIKE	MANCHE DE GAFFE
I080	POLE, SNOW SKI	BATON DE SKI
A080	POLE, UTILITY	POTEAU DE LIGNES DE TRANSMISSION
E340	POLISHER, FLOOR	CIREUSE
C180	POMANDER	POMME D'AMBRE
G280	PONTOON	FLOTTEUR
G280	PONTOON, DESIGN MODEL	FLOTTEUR MODELE DE PROJET
I100	POPGUN	PISTOLET
D100	POPPER, CORN	ECLATEUR DE MAIS
D120	PORRINGER	ECUELLE
F180	PORTFOLIO	SERVIETTE A DOCUMENTS
A060	POST, HITCHING	POTEAU D'ATTACHE DES CHEVAUX
E180	POST, MILITARY AIMING	JALON DE MIRE MILITAIRE
D220	POST, MILITARY BEAKIRON	SOCLE DE BIGORNE MILITAIRE
B060	POST, MILITARY CURTAIN	POTEAU DE RIDEAU MILITAIRE
A060	POST RING, HITCHING	ANNEAU DE POTEAU D'ATTACHE
I080	POST, TENNIS	POTEAU DE FILET DE TENNIS
H080	POSTCARD	CARTE POSTALE
F180	POSTCARD	CARTE POSTALE
H020	POSTER	AFFICHE
H080	POSTER, COMMEMORATIVE	AFFICHE COMMEMORATIVE
H080	POSTER, INSTRUCTIONAL	AFFICHE EDUCATIVE
H020	POSTER, MILITARY	AFFICHE MILITAIRE
H020	POSTER, POLITICAL	AFFICHE POLITIQUE
D160	POT	POT
C180	POT, CHAMBER	POT DE CHAMBRE
A040	POT, CHIMNEY	MITRON DE CHEMINEE
D120	POT, CHOCOLATE	CHOCOLATIER
D100	POT, CROCK	JARRE
F100	POT, GLUE	POT DE COLLE
D320	POT, GREASE	POT A GRAISSE
C180	POT LID, CHAMBER	COUVERCLE DE POT DE CHAMBRE
D060	POT, LOBSTER	CASIER A HOMARD
C180	POT, MINIATURE CHAMBER	POT DE CHAMBRE MINIATURE
D100	POT, MINIATURE CROCK	JARRE MINIATURE
D120	POT, MUSTARD	MOUTARDIER
D320	POT, PITCH	POT A GOUDRON
D100	POTHOLDER	POIGNEE
H120	POUCH	POCHETTE
E180	POUCH, BALL	SACOCHE A BALLES DE MOUSQUET
D240	POUCH, BLASTING CAP	SACOCHE POUR DETONATEUR
C160	POUCH, FIRE	POCHETTE-TROUSSE A FEU
D240	POUCH, GOLD	SACOCHE POUR CHERCHEUR D'OR
C160	POUCH, MILITARY	GIBERNE MILITAIRE
E180	POUCH, MILITARY BALL	SACOCHE A BALLES DE MOUSQUET MILITAIRE
E180	POUCH, MILITARY CAP	SACOCHE A AMORCES MILITAIRES
E180	POUCH, MILITARY MAGAZINE	SACOCHE A MAGAZINES MILITAIRE
E180	POUCH, MILITARY SHOT	SACOCHE A PROJECTILES MILITAIRE
D320	POUCH, NAIL	POCHETTE A CLOUS
C160	POUCH, POLICE	GIBERNE DE POLICE
E180	POUCH, SHOT	SACOCHE A PROJECTILES
C160	POUCH, TOBACCO	BLAGUE A TABAC
H080	POWER OF APPOINTMENT	POUVOIR DE DESIGNATION
H080	POWER OF ATTORNEY	PROCURATION
J060	PRESS, BARREL	PRESSE-BARIL

Class. Code	Object, suffix	Objet, suffixe
F100	PRESS, BLOCKING	*PRESSE A DORER*
D100	PRESS, BUTTER	*PRESSE A BEURRE*
E180	PRESS, CARTRIDGE-CASE	*PRESSE A DOUILLE DE CARTOUCHE*
D100	PRESS, CHEESE	*PRESSE A FROMAGE*
D320	PRESS, CORK	*PRESSE-BOUCHON*
F100	PRESS, CYLINDER	*PRESSE A CYLINDRE*
D220	PRESS, DRILL	*PERCEUSE A COLONNE*
D100	PRESS, FRUIT	*PRESSE-FRUITS*
D180	PRESS, FUR	*PRESSE A FOURRURES*
D100	PRESS, LARD	*PRESSE-SAINDOUX*
E340	PRESS, LINEN	*PRESSE A LINGE*
C140	PRESS, PANTS	*PRESSE-PANTALON*
F100	PRESS, PLATEN	*PRESSE A PLATINE*
E180	PRESS, PRIMING	*PRESSE A AMORCAGE DE CARTOUCHE*
D180	PRICK, SINGLE STITCH	*SEPARATEUR DE COUTURE*
D240	PRICKER	*LANCE DE SONDE*
E180	PRICKER, MILITARY	*EPINGLETTE MILITAIRE*
E180	PRICKER, MINIATURE MILITARY	*EPINGLETTE A MITRAILLE MILITAIRE MINIATURE*
D180	PRICKER, SINGLE-STITCH	*TIRE-POINT*
D180	PRICKER, WHEEL	*MARQUE-POINTS A ROULETTE*
B060	PRIE-DIEU	*PRIE-DIEU*
E140	PRIMER	*AMORCE*
H040	PRINT	*GRAVURE*
H080	PRINT, MILITARY PHOTOGRAPHIC	*EPREUVE PHOTOGRAPHIQUE MILITAIRE*
H040	PRINT, MINIATURE	*GRAVURE MINIATURE*
H080	PRINT, PHOTOGRAPHIC	*EPREUVE PHOTOGRAPHIQUE*
H040	PRINT, PHOTOGRAPHIC	*EPREUVE PHOTOGRAPHIQUE*
H080	PRINT, POLICE PHOTOGRAPHIC	*EPREUVE PHOTOGRAPHIQUE DE POLICE*
H080	PRINT, SOLAR	*EPREUVE INSOLEE*
E380	PROBE	*SONDE*
J040	PROBLEMATICAL	*PROBLEMATIQUE*
H080	PROGRAM	*PROGRAMME*
F160	PROJECTOR, LANTERN-SLIDE	*LANTERNE DE PROJECTION*
F160	PROJECTOR, MOTION-PICTURE	*PROJECTEUR DE CINEMA*
F160	PROJECTOR, SLIDE	*PROJECTEUR DE DIAPOSITIVES*
G300	PROPELLER	*HELICE*
G080	PROPELLER, ADJUSTABLE-PITCH	*HELICE A PAS REGLABLE*
G080	PROPELLER, DESIGN MODEL	*HELICE MODELE DE PROJET*
G080	PROPELLER, DESIGN MODEL ADJUSTABLE-PITCH	*HELICE A PAS REGLABLE MODELE DE PROJET*
G080	PROPELLER, DESIGN MODEL FIXED-PITCH	*HELICE A PAS FIXE MODELE DE PROJET*
G080	PROPELLER, FIXED-PITCH	*HELICE A PAS FIXE*
G080	PROPELLER HUB	*MOYEU D'HELICE*
E180	PROTECTOR, MILITARY NIPPLE	*COUVERCLE DE CHEMINEE MILITAIRE*
C160	PROTHESIS	*PROTHESE*
F040	PROTRACTOR	*RAPPORTEUR*
C180	PUFF, POWDER	*HOUPPE A POUDRE*
B060	PULL, DOOR/DRAWER	*GACHETTE DE PORTE/TIROIR*
B160	PULL, SHADE	*CORDON DE STORE*
E180	PULLER, BULLET	*EXTRACTEUR DE BALLE*
E180	PULLER, GUN WHEEL	*EXTRACTEUR DE ROUE DE CANON*
D320	PULLER, NAIL	*ARRACHE-CLOU*
D020	PULLER, STUMP	*EXTRACTEUR*
D320	PULLER, TACK	*ARRACHE-BROQUETTE*
E360	PULLEY	*POULIE*
B160	PULLEY, CURTAIN	*POULIE DE RIDEAU*
A040	PULPIT	*CHAIRE*
D240	PUMP	*POMPE*
G300	PUMP	*POMPE*
J060	PUMP, BARREL	*CORPS DE POMPE*
G300	PUMP, BILGE	*POMPE DE CALE*
E380	PUMP, BREAST	*POMPE TIRE-LAIT*

Class. Code	Object, suffix	Objet, suffixe
E380	PUMP, EMBALMING	POMPE D'EMBAUMEMENT
E360	PUMP, HYDROSTATIC TEST	POMPE A ESSAI HYDROSTATIQUE
D100	PUMP, LIQUID	POMPE A LIQUIDES
D240	PUMP, SINGLE-ACTION	POMPE A SIMPLE EFFET
E300	PUMP, STEAM BOILER	POMPE DE CHAUDIERE A VAPEUR
G180	PUMP, TIRE	POMPE DE PNEU DE BICYCLETTE
B120	PUMP, WATER	POMPE A EAU
E260	PUMP, WATER	POMPE A EAU
G300	PUMP WHEEL, BILGE	TURBINE DE POMPE DE CALE
G120	PUMPER, HAND	POMPE MANUELLE A INCENDIE
G120	PUMPER, STEAM	POMPE A VAPEUR
D220	PUNCH	POINCON
D320	PUNCH	POINCON
D180	PUNCH, ASYMMETRIC OBLONG	POINCON ASYMETRIQUE ET OBLONG
D180	PUNCH, BUTTON-HOLE	POINCON A BOUTONNIERE
D320	PUNCH, CARVER'S	POINCON DE SCULPTEUR SUR BOIS
D220	PUNCH, CENTRE	CENTREUR
D320	PUNCH, COOPER'S	POINCON DE TONNELIER
D220	PUNCH, DRIFT	CHASSE-GOUPILLE
D300	PUNCH, GROMMET	POINCON A VOILES
D180	PUNCH, HAND	POINCON A MAIN
D180	PUNCH, HEEL LIFT	POINCON A TALON
D220	PUNCH, HOLLOW	EMPORTE-PIECE
D180	PUNCH, LINE	POINCON A TRAIT
D320	PUNCH, MARKING	FER A MARQUER A LA FRAPPE
D320	PUNCH, NAIL	CHASSE-CLOU
D180	PUNCH, OBLONG-HOLE	POINCON A TROU OBLONG
F180	PUNCH, PAPER	PERFORATEUR A PAPIER
D180	PUNCH, PIERCING	POINCON A PERFORATION
D180	PUNCH, RECTANGULAR DRIVE	POINCON A TROU RECTANGULAIRE
D180	PUNCH, ROUND-HOLE	POINCON A TROU ROND
D180	PUNCH, SCALLOPING	POINCON A FESTON
D180	PUNCH, SQUARE DRIVE	POINCON A TROU CARRE
D180	PUNCH, STRAP-END U	COUPE BOUT-DE-COURROIE EN U
D180	PUNCH, STRAP-END V	COUPE BOUT-DE-COURROIE EN V
B140	PUNK	AMADOU
I100	PUPPET, HAND	MARIONNETTE A GAINES
H060	PURIFICATOR	PURIFICATOIRE
C160	PURSE	BOURSE
C160	PURSE FRAME	ARMATURE DE BOURSE
C060	PUTTEE, MILITARY	BANDE MOLLETIERE MILITAIRE
I100	PUZZLE	CASSE-TETE
H060	PYX	CUSTODE
H060	PYXIS	PYXIDE
E500	QUADRANT	COMPAS QUART DE CERCLE
E180	QUADRANT, MILITARY GUNNER'S	NIVEAU DE POINTAGE D'ARTILLEUR MILITAIRE
B020	QUILT	COURTEPOINTE
I100	QUILT	COURTEPOINTE
G180	QUIRT	FOUET D'ECUYER
E180	QUIVER	CARQUOIS
F100	QUOIN	COIN DE SERRAGE
E180	QUOIN, MILITARY	COIN DE MIRE MILITAIRE
E180	QUOIN, MINIATURE MILITARY	COIN DE MIRE MILITAIRE MINIATURE
I020	QUOITS	PALET
D220	RABBLE	RABLE
E180	RACK, ARMS	RATELIER A ARMES
I080	RACK, BILLIARD CUE	SUPPORT DE QUEUES DE BILLARD
D220	RACK, BIT	RATELIER A MECHES
B060	RACK, BOOT	RATELIER A BOTTES
D100	RACK, COOLING	CLAYETTE A REFROIDIR
D320	RACK, DRAWKNIFE	RATELIER A PLANES

Class.
Code   **Object, suffix**   **Objet, suffixe**

Code	Object, suffix	Objet, suffixe
E340	RACK, DRYING	ETENDOIR A LINGE
F100	RACK, DRYING	SECHOIR
D320	RACK, GIMLET	RATELIER A VRILLES
B060	RACK, GUN	RATELIER D'ARMES
B060	RACK, HARNESS	RATELIER A HARNAIS
B060	RACK, HAT	PORTE-CHAPEAUX
B080	RACK, KEY	RATELIER A CLES
D100	RACK, KNIFE	RATELIER A COUTEAUX
H060	RACK, LAMPION	GRADIN A LAMPIONS
F180	RACK, LETTER	RATELIER A LETTRES
B060	RACK, MAGAZINE	PORTE-REVUES
D100	RACK, MEAT	PORTE-VIANDE
B060	RACK, MILITARY GUN	RATELIER D'ARMES MILITAIRE
E180	RACK, MILITARY SHOT	SUPPORT DE PROJECTILES MILITAIRE
D220	RACK, MOLD	RATELIER A MOULES
B080	RACK, NEWSPAPER	PORTE-JOURNAUX
F180	RACK, PEN	POSE-PLUMES
D100	RACK, PIE	GRILLE A TARTES
B080	RACK, PIPE	RATELIER A PIPES
B060	RACK, PLANT	ETAGERE A POTS DE FLEURS
G300	RACK, POLICE KEY	TABLEAU A CLES DE POLICE
D100	RACK, SCHNITZ	SECHE-FRUITS A CLAIRE-VOIE
D100	RACK, SPICE	SUPPORT A EPICES
D100	RACK, SPIT	PORTE-BROCHES A ROTIR
B080	RACK, SPOON	RATELIER A CUILLERES
F180	RACK, STAMP	PORTE-TIMBRES
D220 .	RACK, STOCK-METAL	RATELIER A METAL
B060	RACK, STORAGE	ETAGERE DE RANGEMENT
B140	RACK, STOVEPIPE	PORTE-OBJETS DE TUYAU DE POELE
E240	RACK, TEST TUBE	SUPPORT A EPROUVETTES
B080	RACK, TIE	SUPPORT A CRAVATES
D120	RACK, TOAST	PORTE-ROTIES
D220	RACK, TONGS	RATELIER A TENAILLES
J060	RACK, TOOL	RATELIER A OUTILS
C180	RACK, TOOTHBRUSH	PORTE-BROSSE A DENTS
B060	RACK, TOWEL	PORTE-SERVIETTES
D100	RACK, UTENSIL	PORTE-USTENSILES
D100	RACK, WINE	PORTE-BOUTEILLES A VIN
B060	RACK BAND, MILITARY GUN	ANSE DE RATELIER D'ARMES MILITAIRE
I080	RACKET, TENNIS	RAQUETTE DE TENNIS
B140	RADIATOR	RADIATEUR
F140	RADIO	RADIO
H080	RADIOGRAPH	RADIOGRAMME
G300	RAFT, LIFE	RADEAU DE SAUVETAGE
A040	RAIL, BAR	BARRE D'APPUI
C100	RAINCOAT	IMPERMEABLE
D020	RAKE	RATEAU
I100	RAKE	RATEAU
D220	RAKE, BLACKSMITH'S	RATEAU DE FORGERON
B140	RAKE, FIREPLACE	RACLETTE DE FOYER
D020	RAKE, GARDEN	RATEAU DE JARDINAGE
D020	RAKE, HAND HAY	RATEAU A FOIN A MAIN
E180	RAKE, HOT-SHOT	RATEAU A PROJECTILES CHAUFFES
E400	RAKE, NAIL	FOURCHE A CLOUS
B140	RAKE, STOVE	RACLETTE DE POELE
D100	RAMEKIN	RAMEQUIN
D220	RAMMER	FOULOIR
E180	RAMMER, MILITARY	REFOULOIR MILITAIRE
E180	RAMROD	BAGUETTE
E180	RAMROD, MILITARY	BAGUETTE MILITAIRE
E080	RAPIER	RAPIERE

Class. Code	Object, suffix	Objet, suffixe
E080	RAPIER, MILITARY	RAPIERE MILITAIRE
E080	RAPIER, MILITARY CANE	CANNE-EPEE MILITAIRE
D320	RASP	RAPE
D200	RASP	RAPE
D180	RASP	RAPE
D040	RASP, HOOF	RAPE A SABOT
D180	RASP, PEG	RAPE A CHEVILLE
G300	RATLINE	ENFLECHURE
I100	RATTLE	CRECELLE
H060	RATTLE	HOCHET
F120	RATTLE, GAS	CRECELLE A GAZ
B080	RATTRAP	RATIERE
C180	RAZOR	RASOIR
D220	REAMER	ALESOIR
D320	REAMER	ALESOIR
D220	REAMER, BOILER TUBE	ALESOIR POUR TUBES DE CHAUDIERE
D100	REAMER, JUICE	PRESSE A JUS
D320	REAMER, WHEELWRIGHT'S	ALESOIR DE CHARRON
D020	REAPER, MODEL	MOISSONNEUSE MODELE REDUIT
H080	RECEIPT	RECU
H080	RECEIPT, MILITARY	RECU MILITAIRE
B080	RECEIVER, CARD	PLATEAU A CARTES DE VISITE
C180	RECEIVER, HAIR	BOITE A CHEVEUX
F140	RECEIVER, TELEGRAPH	RECEPTEUR TELEGRAPHIQUE
H080	RECIPE	RECETTE
F120	RECORD, PHONOGRAPH	DISQUE DE PHONOGRAPHE
H080	RECORDS, MILITARY	ARCHIVES MILITAIRES
E300	RECTIFIER	RECTIFICATEUR
B140	REDUCER, STOVE LID	ANNEAU DE ROND DE POELE
D300	REED	PEIGNE
D300	REEL	DEVIDOIR
D160	REEL, CANDLE-DIPPING	SUPPORT DE PLONGE DES CHANDELLES
D200	REEL, CHALK	BOBINE A CORDE A LIGNER
D320	REEL, CHALK	DEVIDOIR DE CORDEAU CRAYEUX
D300	REEL, CLOCK	DEVIDOIR-COMPTEUR
E340	REEL, CLOTHESLINE	MOULINET DE CORDE A LINGE
D060	REEL, FISHING	MOULINET DE PECHE
D100	REFRIGERATOR	REFRIGERATEUR
E400	REGISTER, CASH	CAISSE ENREGISTREUSE
F100	REGLET	REGLETTE
E360	REGULATOR, GAS	REGULATEUR DE GAZ
E280	REGULATOR, VOLTAGE	GRADUATEUR DE TENSION
G180	REINS	GUIDE
E280	RELAY	RELAIS ELECTROMAGNETIQUE
H080	RELEASE, NEWS	COMMUNIQUE
H060	RELIC, RELIGIOUS	RELIQUE RELIGIEUSE
H060	RELIQUARY	RELIQUAIRE
H080	REPORT	RAPPORT
F100	RESHAPER, LINOTYPE MATRIX	MATRICE DE LINOTYPE
E280	RESISTOR	BATTERIE DE RESISTANCES
J060	RESPIRATOR	RESPIRATEUR
E380	RESPIRATOR	RESPIRATEUR
D120	REST, KNIFE	PORTE-COUTEAU
E180	REST, MUSKET	FOURQUINE
D100	REST, SPOON	SUPPORT A CUILLERE
E240	RETORT	CORNUE
E060	REVOLVER	REVOLVER
E060	REVOLVER, CENTER-FIRE	REVOLVER A PERCUSSION CENTRALE
E060	REVOLVER, MILITARY	REVOLVER MILITAIRE
E060	REVOLVER, MILITARY CENTER-FIRE	REVOLVER A PERCUSSION CENTRALE MILITAIRE
E060	REVOLVER, MILITARY PERCUSSION	REVOLVER A PERCUSSION MILITAIRE

Class. Code	Object, suffix	Objet, suffixe
E060	REVOLVER, PERCUSSION	*REVOLVER A PERCUSSION*
E060	REVOLVER, POLICE CENTER-FIRE	*REVOLVER A PERCUSSION CENTRALE DE POLICE*
E280	RHEOSTAT	*RHEOSTAT*
H080	RIBBON, COMMEMORATIVE	*RUBAN COMMEMORATIF*
H120	RIBBON, MEMBERSHIP	*RUBAN DE MEMBRE*
H120	RIBBON, MILITARY SERVICE	*RUBAN DE SERVICE MILITAIRE*
H120	RIBBON, POLICE SERVICE	*RUBAN DE SERVICE DE POLICE*
F180	RIBBON, TYPEWRITER	*RUBAN DE MACHINE A ECRIRE*
D100	RICER	*PRESSE-PUREE*
D020	RIDDLE, GRAIN	*SEPARATEUR A GRAIN*
D240	RIFFLES	*RIFLARD*
E060	RIFLE	*CARABINE*
E060	RIFLE, BREECHLOAD	*CARABINE A CHARGEMENT PAR LA CULASSE*
E060	RIFLE, CENTER-FIRE	*CARABINE A PERCUSSION CENTRALE*
E060	RIFLE, LONG	*CARABINE LONGUE*
E060	RIFLE, MILITARY BREECHLOAD	*CARABINE A CHARGEMENT PAR LA CULASSE MILITAIRE*
E060	RIFLE, MILITARY CENTER-FIRE	*CARABINE A PERCUSSION CENTRALE MILITAIRE*
E060	RIFLE, MILITARY FLINTLOCK	*CARABINE A SILEX MILITAIRE*
E060	RIFLE, MILITARY PERCUSSION	*CARABINE A PERCUSSION MILITAIRE*
E060	RIFLE, MILITARY RIM-FIRE	*CARABINE A PERCUSSION ANNULAIRE MILITAIRE*
E060	RIFLE, MINIATURE	*CARABINE MINIATURE*
E060	RIFLE, PERCUSSION	*CARABINE A PERCUSSION*
E060	RIFLE, POLICE CENTER-FIRE	*CARABINE A PERCUSSION CENTRALE DE POLICE*
E060	RIFLE, RIM-FIRE	*CARABINE A PERCUSSION ANNULAIRE*
E060	RIFLE BARREL	*CANON DE CARABINE*
E060	RIFLE BREECH MECHANISM	*BLOC DE CULASSE DE CARABINE*
C020	RING	*BAGUE*
B160	RING, CURTAIN	*ANNEAU DE RIDEAU*
D120	RING, DISH	*PORTE-PLAT CIRCULAIRE*
G180	RING, GIRTH	*ANNEAU DE SANGLE*
C160	RING, KEY	*PORTE-CLEFS*
G300	RING, LIFE	*BOUEE DE SAUVETAGE*
I100	RING, LIFE	*BOUEE DE SAUVETAGE*
C160	RING, MILITARY KEY	*PORTE-CLEFS MILITAIRE*
D120	RING, NAPKIN	*ANNEAU A SERVIETTE DE TABLE*
H120	RING, SIGNET	*CHEVALIERE*
D140	RING, SNUB	*ANNEAU D'ANCRAGE*
J060	RING, UTILITY	*ANNEAU TOUT USAGE*
D200	RIPPER, SLATER'S	*ARRACHE-ARDOISE*
D300	RIPPLE	*EGRENEUSE*
D320	RIPSAW	*SCIE A REFENDRE*
D220	RIVET	*RIVET*
J060	RIVET	*RIVET*
D100	ROASTER, APPLE	*GRILLE-POMMES*
D100	ROASTER, CHESTNUT	*GRILLE-MARRONS*
D100	ROASTER, COFFEE	*TORREFACTEUR A CAFE*
G180	ROBE, LAP	*COUVERTURE DE VOYAGE*
E180	ROD, CLEANING	*BAGUETTE DE FUSIL*
B160	ROD, CURTAIN	*TRINGLE A RIDEAU*
D060	ROD FERRULE, FISHING	*VIROLE DE CANNE A PECHE*
B160	ROD FINIAL, CURTAIN	*EMBOUT DE TRINGLE A RIDEAU*
D060	ROD, FISHING	*CANNE A PECHE*
A040	ROD, LIGHTNING	*PARATONNERRE*
E180	ROD, MILITARY CLEANING	*BAGUETTE DE FUSIL MILITAIRE*
E500	ROD, STADIA	*STADIA*
A040	ROD, STAIR	*TRINGLE D'ESCALIER*
D220	ROD, STIRRING	*RINGARD*
D060	ROD SWIVEL, FISHING	*EMERILLON DE CANNE A PECHE*
D180	ROLL, FILLET	*MOLETTE A FILET*
H080	ROLL, MILITARY MUSTER	*ROLE MILITAIRE*
D180	ROLL, PATTERN	*MOLETTE A MOTIF*

Class. Code	Object, suffix	Objet, suffixe
F080	ROLL-FILM	FILM EN ROULEAU
D260	ROLLER	ROULEAU
D020	ROLLER, GARDEN	ROULEAU DE JARDIN
D260	ROLLER, GRAINING	ROULEAU A DECOR
B160	ROLLER, SHADE	ENROULEUR DE STORE
C100	ROMPER	BARBOTEUSE
A020	ROOF	TOIT
G300	ROPE	CORDAGE
J060	ROPE	CORDE
I100	ROPE, JUMP	CORDE A SAUTER
G300	ROPE, SHIP'S BELL	CORDE DE CLOCHE DE NAVIRE
H080	ROSTER, MILITARY DUTY	TABLEAU DE SERVICE MILITAIRE
D100	ROTISSERIE	ROTISSOIRE
D160	ROULETTE	MOLETTE A MOTIF
D320	ROUTER	TOUPIE
C060	RUBBER	COUVRE-CHAUSSURE
J020	RUBBER FRAGMENT	FRAGMENT DE CAOUTCHOUC
G300	RUDDER	GOUVERNAIL
B020	RUFFLE, DUST	VOLANT DE LIT
B040	RUG	TAPIS
I100	RUG	TAPIS
B040	RUG, MILITARY MAGAZINE	TAPIS DE POUDRIERE MILITAIRE
B040	RUG, THROW	CARPETTE
D320	RULE, BENCH	REGLE D'ETABLI
F100	RULE, COMPOSING	LEVE-LIGNE
E560	RULE, FOLDING	REGLE PLIANTE
D140	RULE, LOG	REGLE DE CUBAGE
F040	RULE, PARALLEL	REGLES PARALLELES
F020	RULE, SLIDE	REGLE A CALCUL
F100	RULE, TYPESETTING	FILET POUR COMPOSITION
E560	RULER	REGLE
G120	RUNABOUT	BOGHEI
G120	RUNABOUT BRAKE	FREIN DE BOGHEI
G120	RUNABOUT CANOPY	TOIT DE BOGHEI
G120	RUNABOUT CONNECTING ROD	BARRE D'ACCOUPLEMENT DE BOGHEI
G120	RUNABOUT DASH BRACKET	CONSOLE DE GARDE-BOUE DE BOGHEI
G120	RUNABOUT SEAT	SIEGE DE BOGHEI
G120	RUNABOUT SHAFT	LIMON DE BOGHEI
G120	RUNABOUT TOE RAIL	REPOSE-PIEDS DE BOGHEI
B040	RUNNER	CHEMIN D'ESCALIER
B080	RUNNER, BENCH	CHEMIN DE BANC
B080	RUNNER, TABLE	CHEMIN DE TABLE
B100	RUSHLIGHT	CHANDELLE A MECHE DE JONC
E080	SABER	SABRE
E080	SABER, MILITARY	SABRE MILITAIRE
C060	SABOT	SABOT
E140	SABOT, CANNONBALL	SABOT DE BOULET DE CANON
C060	SABOT, FOUNDER'S	SABOT DE FONDEUR
C160	SABRETACHE	SABRETACHE
C160	SABRETACHE, MILITARY	SABRETACHE MILITAIRE
C160	SABRETACHE, POLICE	SABRETACHE DE POLICE
C140	SACHET	SACHET
C100	SACK	PEIGNOIR A COIFFER
H060	SACRARIUM	SACRARIUM
G180	SADDLE	SELLE
G180	SADDLE, HARNESS	SELLETTE
G180	SADDLE, MILITARY PACK	BAT MILITAIRE
G180	SADDLE, MILITARY RIDING	SELLE D'EQUITATION MILITAIRE
G180	SADDLE, PACK	BAT
G180	SADDLE, POLICE	SELLE DE POLICE
G180	SADDLEBAG	SACOCHE DE SELLE

Class. Code	Object, suffix	Objet, suffixe
H060	SADDLEBAG, CEREMONIAL	SACOCHE DE SELLE DE CEREMONIE
E340	SADIRON	FER A REPASSER AVEC POIGNEE AMOVIBLE
I100	SADIRON	FER A REPASSER AVEC POIGNEE AMOVIBLE
B060	SAFE	COFFRE-FORT
B080	SAFE, MATCH	PORTE-ALLUMETTES
C160	SAFE, MATCH	PORTE-ALLUMETTES
F080	SAFELIGHT	LAMPE INACTINIQUE
G300	SAIL	VOILE
I100	SAILBOAT	VOILIER
G280	SAILBOAT, INSTRUCTIONAL MODEL	VOILIER MODELE D'INSTRUCTION
G280	SAILBOAT, MODEL	VOILIER MODELE REDUIT
D100	SALAMANDER	COUVERCLE A BRAISER
E400	SALES-SAMPLE, BUCKLE	ECHANTILLON DE BOUCLES
E400	SALES-SAMPLE, BUTTON	ECHANTILLON DE BOUTONS
E400	SALES-SAMPLE, CARPET	ECHANTILLON DE TAPIS
E400	SALES-SAMPLE, CARTRIDGE	ECHANTILLON DE CARTOUCHES
E400	SALES-SAMPLE, CLOTH	ECHANTILLON D'ETOFFE
E400	SALES-SAMPLE, CROCHET HOOK	ECHANTILLON DE CROCHETS DE TRAVAIL AU CROCHET
E400	SALES-SAMPLE, FISHHOOK	ECHANTILLON D'HAMECONS
E400	SALES-SAMPLE, LACE	ECHANTILLON DE DENTELLE
E400	SALES-SAMPLE, LINOLEUM	ECHANTILLON DE LINOLEUM
E400	SALES-SAMPLE, PAINT	ECHANTILLON DE PEINTURE
E400	SALES-SAMPLE, PEN	ECHANTILLON DE PLUME
E400	SALES-SAMPLE, SEWING SUPPLIES	ECHANTILLON DE FOURNITURES DE COUTURE
E400	SALES-SAMPLE, WALLPAPER	ECHANTILLON DE PAPIER PEINT
D120	SALTCELLAR	SALIERE DE TABLE
D120	SALTSHAKER	SALIERE
D120	SALVER	PLATEAU D'ARGENT
H040	SAMPLER	BRODERIE
H040	SAMPLER, INSTRUCTIONAL MODEL	BRODERIE MODELE D'INSTRUCTION
C140	SASH	ECHARPE
H120	SASH	ECHARPE
C140	SASH, MILITARY	ECHARPE MILITAIRE
C160	SATCHEL	SACOCHE
D120	SAUCEBOAT	SAUCIERE
D100	SAUCEPAN	CASSEROLE
I100	SAUCEPAN	CASSEROLE
D100	SAUCEPAN LID	COUVERCLE DE CASSEROLE
D100	SAUCEPOT	POT A SAUCE
D120	SAUCER	SOUCOUPE
B080	SAUCER, FLOWERPOT	SOUCOUPE DE POT A FLEURS
E340	SAVER, SOAP	SAUPOUDROIR DE SAVON
D320	SAW	SCIE
I100	SAW	SCIE
D320	SAW, BAND	SCIE A RUBAN
D220	SAW, BAND	SCIE A RUBAN
D320	SAW, BENCH	SCIE D'ETABLI
D220	SAW, BLITZ	SCIE A DOSSERET
D320	SAW, BOW	SCIE A ARCHET
D320	SAW, COMPASS	SCIE PASSE-PARTOUT
D320	SAW, COPING	SCIE A CHANTOURNER
D320	SAW, CROSSCUT	SCIE DE TRAVERS
D320	SAW, DOVETAIL	SCIE A QUEUE D'ARONDE
D320	SAW, DOWEL	SCIE A DOSSERET
D320	SAW, FELLOE	SCIE A CADRE
D320	SAW, FLOORING	SCIE A PLANCHER
D320	SAW, FRAMED-PIT	SCIE DE LONG A CADRE
D240	SAW, ICE	SCIE A GLACE
D320	SAW, KEYHOLE	SCIE A GUICHET
D200	SAW, MASON'S	SCIE DE MACON
D100	SAW, MEAT	SCIE DE BOUCHER

Class. Code	Object, suffix	Objet, suffixe
D320	SAW, OPEN-PIT	SCIE DE LONG A LAME LIBRE
D020	SAW, PRUNING	SCIE D'ELAGAGE
E380	SAW, SURGICAL	SCIE CHIRURGICALE
D320	SAW, TENON	SCIE A TENON
D140	SAW, TWO-HANDED CROSSCUT	SCIE PASSE-PARTOUT A DEUX POIGNEES
D320	SAW BLADE, BENCH	LAME DE SCIE D'ETABLI
D320	SAW BLADE, CROSSCUT	LAME DE SCIE DE TRAVERS
D320	SAW HANDLE	MANCHE DE SCIE
D320	SAW HANDLE, CROSSCUT	MANCHE DE SCIE DE TRAVERS
D240	SAW HANDLE, ICE	POIGNEE DE SCIE A GLACE
D140	SAW HANDLE, TWO-HANDED CROSSCUT	MANCHE DE SCIE PASSE-PARTOUT A DEUX POIGNEES
D320	SAW-SET	TOURNE-A-GAUCHE POUR SCIE
D320	SAWHORSE	BANC DE SCIAGE
E180	SCABBARD, BAYONET	FOURREAU DE BAIONNETTE
E180	SCABBARD, DAGGER	FOURREAU DE DAGUE
E180	SCABBARD, MILITARY BACKSWORD	FOURREAU D'EPEE A UNE TRANCHE MILITAIRE
E180	SCABBARD, MILITARY BAYONET	FOURREAU DE BAIONNETTE MILITAIRE
E180	SCABBARD, MILITARY BROADSWORD	FOURREAU DE FORTE-EPEE MILITAIRE
E180	SCABBARD, MILITARY CANE RAPIER	FOURREAU DE CANNE-EPEE MILITAIRE
E180	SCABBARD, MILITARY CUTLASS	FOURREAU DE SABRE D'ABORDAGE MILITAIRE
E180	SCABBARD, MILITARY DIRK	FOURREAU DE POIGNARD MILITAIRE
E180	SCABBARD, MILITARY GLADIUS	FOURREAU DE GLAIVE MILITAIRE
E180	SCABBARD, MILITARY HANGER	FOURREAU DE SABRE COURT MILITAIRE
E180	SCABBARD, MILITARY HILTED KNIFE BAYONET	FOURREAU DE BAIONNETTE-COUTEAU A POIGNEE MILITAIRE
E180	SCABBARD, MILITARY HILTED SWORD BAYONET	FOURREAU DE BAIONNETTE-EPEE A POIGNEE MILITAIRE
E180	SCABBARD, MILITARY HILTED TRIANGULAR BAYONET	FOURREAU DE BAIONNETTE A POIGNEE/TRANCHE TRIANGULAIRE MILITAIRE
E180	SCABBARD, MILITARY PLUG KNIFE BAYONET	FOURREAU DE BAIONNETTE-COUTEAU A MANCHE MILITAIRE
E180	SCABBARD, MILITARY PLUG SWORD BAYONET	FOURREAU DE BAIONNETTE-EPEE A MANCHE MILITAIRE
H120	SCABBARD, MILITARY PRESENTATION SWORD	FOURREAU D'EPEE D'HONNEUR MILITAIRE
E180	SCABBARD, MILITARY RAPIER	FOURREAU DE RAPIERE MILITAIRE
E180	SCABBARD, MILITARY SABER	FOURREAU DE SABRE MILITAIRE
E180	SCABBARD, MILITARY SMALLSWORD	FOURREAU D'EPEE FINE MILITAIRE
E180	SCABBARD, MILITARY SOCKET CRUCIFORM BAYONET	FOURREAU DE BAIONNETTE A DOUILLE/TRANCHE CRUCIFORME MILITAIRE
E180	SCABBARD, MILITARY SOCKET KNIFE BAYONET	FOURREAU DE BAIONNETTE-COUTEAU A DOUILLE MILITAIRE
E180	SCABBARD, MILITARY SOCKET SPIKE BAYONET	FOURREAU DE BAIONNETTE-CRAMPON A DOUILLE MILITAIRE
E180	SCABBARD, MILITARY SOCKET SWORD BAYONET	FOURREAU DE BAIONNETTE-EPEE A DOUILLE MILITAIRE
E180	SCABBARD, MILITARY SOCKET TRIANGULAR BAYONET	FOURREAU DE BAIONNETTE A DOUILLE/TRANCHE TRIANGULAIRE MILITAIRE
E180	SCABBARD, MILITARY SWORD	FOURREAU D'EPEE MILITAIRE
E180	SCABBARD, MINIATURE SWORD	FOURREAU D'EPEE MINIATURE
E180	SCABBARD, POLICE SWORD	FOURREAU D'EPEE DE POLICE
E180	SCABBARD, SWORD	FOURREAU D'EPEE
F040	SCALE, ARCHITECT'S	ECHELLE D'ARCHITECTE
E560	SCALE, BALANCE	BALANCE
I100	SCALE, BALANCE	BALANCE
E560	SCALE, COMPUTING	REGLE A CALCULS
D100	SCALE, EGG	PESE-OEUFS
E560	SCALE, MILITARY COMPUTING	REGLE A CALCULS SMILITAIRE
E500	SCALE, NAVIGATIONAL	REGLE GRADUEE DE NAVIGATEUR
E560	SCALE, PLATFORM	BASCULE
E560	SCALE, SPRING	BALANCE A RESSORT
D100	SCALER, FISH	ECAILLEUR A POISSON
H120	SCALP	SCALP
E380	SCALPEL	SCALPEL
C080	SCARF	ECHARPE
B080	SCARF, BUREAU	JETE DE COMMODE
C140	SCARF, MILITARY NECK	FOULARD MILITAIRE
B080	SCARF, PIANO	JETE DE PIANO
D300	SCISSORS	CISEAUX
J060	SCISSORS	CISEAUX
C180	SCISSORS, BARBER'S	CISEAUX DE COIFFEUR
D300	SCISSORS, BUTTONHOLE	CISEAUX A BOUTONNIERES

Class. Code	Object, suffix	Objet, suffixe
D300	SCISSORS, EMBROIDERY	CISEAUX A BRODER
C180	SCISSORS, MANICURE	CISEAUX DE MANUCURE
E380	SCISSORS, SURGICAL	CISEAUX DE CHIRURGIE
B100	SCONCE	BOUGEOIR MURAL
B100	SCONCE, MIRRORED	BOUGEOIR MURAL A MIROIR
D100	SCOOP	PELLE A MAIN
I100	SCOOP	PELLE A MAIN
E560	SCOOP, BALANCE	NACELLE DE BALANCE
D120	SCOOP, CHEESE	PELLE A FROMAGE
D020	SCOOP, FEED	PELLE A FOURRAGE A MAIN
B140	SCOOP, FIREPLACE	PORTE-CHARBON DE FOYER
E340	SCOOP, ICE	PELLE A GLACE
D100	SCOOP, ICE-CREAM	CUILLERE A GLACE
D100	SCOOP, MELON	CUILLERE A MELON
D100	SCOOP, SALT	PELLE A SEL
D240	SCOOP, SAMPLING AMALGAMATING	PELLE D'ECHANTILLONNAGE-AMALGAMATION
E340	SCOOP, SNOW	POUSSE-NEIGE
E380	SCOOP, TREPANNING BONE	CURETTE POUR TREPANATION
H080	SCORECARD	TABLEAU D'AFFICHAGE DE POINTAGE
D320	SCORPER, CLOSED	PLANE RONDE
D320	SCORPER, OPEN	PLANE CINTREE
G280	SCOW	CHALAND
H080	SCRAPBOOK	ALBUM DE COUPURES
D220	SCRAPER	EBARDOIR
E260	SCRAPER	GRATTOIR
D180	SCRAPER	RACLOIR
D320	SCRAPER	RACLOIR
E340	SCRAPER, BOILER SCALE	RACLOIR DE CHAUDIERE A VAPEUR
B080	SCRAPER, BOOT	GRATTE-PIEDS
D100	SCRAPER, DOUGH	GRATTOIR A PATE
B140	SCRAPER, FIREPLACE	GRATTOIR DE FOYER
D100	SCRAPER, HOG	GRATTOIR DE PEAU DE PORC
E180	SCRAPER, MILITARY BARREL	CHAT MILITAIRE
E380	SCRAPER, PERIOSTEUM	GRATTOIR DE PERIOSTE
D320	SCRAPER, SHIPWRIGHT'S	RACLOIR DE CHARPENTIER NAVAL
E340	SCRAPER, SNOW	GRATTE A NEIGE
D140	SCRAPER, TREE	GRATTOIR D'ARBRE
D260	SCRAPER, WALL	GRATTE A MUR
B060	SCREEN	PARAVENT
B140	SCREEN, FIRE	PARE-ETINCELLES
B060	SCREEN, POLE	ECRAN DE CHEMINEE SUR PIED
D240	SCREEN, TROMMEL	TROMMEL CRIBLEUR
D320	SCREW	VIS
J060	SCREWDRIVER	TOURNEVIS
J060	SCREWDRIVER HANDLE	POIGNEE DE TOURNEVIS
D140	SCRIBE, TIMBER	TIRE-LIGNE DE BOIS
D320	SCRIBER	TIRE-LIGNE
H080	SCROLL	PARCHEMIN
E340	SCRUBBER	LAVETTE METALLIQUE
D200	SCUTCH	MARTEAU DE MACON
B140	SCUTTLE, COAL	SEAU A CHARBON
D020	SCYTHE	FAUX
D020	SCYTHE, CRADLE	JAVELEUR
D020	SCYTHE BLADE	LAME DE FAUX
D020	SCYTHE SNATH	MANCHE DE FAUX
G300	SEACOCK HANDLE	POIGNEE DE ROBINET
E400	SEAL, CARGO	PLOMB DE CARGAISON
H080	SEAL, DEED	SCEAU POUR LES ACTES NOTARIES
E400	SEALING WAX	CIRE A CACHETER
B100	SEARCHLIGHT	PROJECTEUR DE SIGNALISATION
B060	SEAT, LOVE	CAUSEUSE

Class. Code	Object, suffix	Objet, suffixe
D180	SEATIRON	LAME POUR PREMIERE SEMELLE
B060	SECRETARY	SECRETAIRE
B060	SECRETARY-BOOKCASE	SECRETAIRE-BIBLIOTHEQUE
G140	SEDAN	CHAISE A PORTEURS
D020	SEEDER, HAND CENTRIFUGAL	SEMOIR CENTRIFUGE A MAIN
D020	SEEDER, HAND SEEDBOX	SEMOIR A MAIN POUR PLATEAU DE SEMIS
D100	SEEDER, RAISIN	DENOYAUTEUR DE RAISINS
D020	SEEDER, SEEDBOX	SEMOIR POUR PLATEAU DE SEMIS
D240	SELENIUM	SELENIUM
F160	SEMAPHORE	SEMAPHORE
D240	SEPARATOR	TRIEUR
D100	SEPARATOR, CREAM	ECREMEUSE
D100	SEPARATOR, EGG	SEPARATEUR A OEUFS
D120	SERVER, CHEESE	RECIPIENT A FROMAGE
D120	SERVER, PIE	PELLE A TARTE
D120	SERVER, SALAD	ENSEMBLE DE FOURCHETTE ET DE CUILLERE A SALADE
D120	SERVICE, COFFEE	SERVICE A CAFE
D120	SERVICE, TEA	SERVICE A THE
I100	SERVICE, TEA	SERVICE A THE
H060	SET, ALTAR CARD	JEU DE CANONS D'AUTEL
B080	SET, ANTIMACASSAR	JEU DE TETIERES DE FAUTEUIL
D320	SET, AWL PAD	JEU D'ALENES INTERCHANGEABLES
I020	SET, BACKGAMMON	JEU DE TRICTRAC
C100	SET, BAPTISMAL	ENSEMBLE DE BAPTEME
D120	SET, BEVERAGE	SERVICE A BOIRE
I080	SET, BILLIARD	JEU DE BILLARD
I100	SET, BLOCK	JEU DE BLOCS
I020	SET, BOWLING	JEU DE QUILLES
C140	SET, BUCKLE	ENSEMBLE DE BOUCLES DE CEINTURE
B080	SET, BUREAU SCARF	ENSEMBLE DE JETES DE COMMODE
D220	SET, BUTTON DIE	ENSEMBLE DE MATRICES A BOUTONS
D100	SET, CANISTER	JEU DE BOITES DE RANGEMENT
D120	SET, CARVING	SERVICE A DECOUPER
I020	SET, CHECKER	JEU DE DAMES
I020	SET, CHESS	JEU D'ECHECS
I020	SET, CLOCK GOLF	JEU DE L'HORLOGE
C140	SET, CLOTHES BRUSH	TROUSSE DE BROSSES A VETEMENTS
C100	SET, COAT & BONNET	ENSEMBLE DE MANTEAU ET DE BEGUIN
C140	SET, COLLAR & CUFF	ENSEMBLE DE COL ET DE MANCHETTES
C140	SET, COLLAR & MUFF	ENSEMBLE DE COL ET DE MANCHON
C140	SET, COLLAR & SLEEVE	ENSEMBLE DE COL ET DE MANCHES
D120	SET, CONDIMENT	ENSEMBLE A CONDIMENTS
I020	SET, CRIBBAGE	JEU DE CRIBBAGE
I020	SET, CROKINOLE	JEU DE CROQUIGNOLES
I080	SET, CROQUET	JEU DE CROQUET
D120	SET, CRUET	ENSEMBLE DE BURETTES
H060	SET, CRUET	ENSEMBLE DE BURETTES
D120	SET, DAIRY	ENSEMBLE POUR LE LAIT ET LA CREME
D120	SET, DECANTER	ENSEMBLE DE CARAFES AVEC BOUCHON
F180	SET, DESK	NECESSAIRE DE BUREAU
D120	SET, DESSERT	SERVICE A DESSERT
I020	SET, DICE CUP	JEU DE DES A JOUER
D220	SET, DIE	ENSEMBLE DE MATRICES
F040	SET, DRAFTING INSTRUMENT	ENSEMBLE D'INSTRUMENTS DE DESSIN
C180	SET, DRESSER	ENSEMBLE D'ARTICLES DE COIFFURE
I020	SET, DUCK & EGGS	JEU DE CANARD ET DES OEUFS
E060	SET, DUELLING PISTOL	TROUSSE DE PISTOLETS DE DUEL
D120	SET, EGG	ENSEMBLE DE COQUETIERS
E380	SET, EMBALMING INSTRUMENT	TROUSSE D'INSTRUMENTS D'EMBAUMEMENT
D200	SET, FEATHER & PLUG	ENSEMBLE D'AIGUILLES ET DE COINS
I100	SET, FIGURE	GROUPE DE FIGURES

Class. Code	Object, suffix	Objet, suffixe
D120	SET, FLATWARE	*ENSEMBLE DE COUTELLERIE*
D120	SET, FORK & KNIFE	*ENSEMBLE DE FOURCHETTES ET DE COUTEAUX*
I020	SET, FORT	*JEU DE FORT*
H060	SET, FUNERAL DRAPERY	*ENSEMBLE DE DRAPERIES POUR FUNERAILLES*
I020	SET, GAME	*JEU*
D260	SET, GRAINING COMB	*ENSEMBLE DE PEIGNES A VEINER*
C180	SET, HAIRBRUSH	*JEU DE BROSSES A CHEVEUX*
E180	SET, LOADING TOOL	*ENSEMBLE D'OUTILS DE CHARGEMENT*
C180	SET, MANICURE	*TROUSSE DE MANUCURE*
I020	SET, MARBLE	*JEU DE BILLES*
E460	SET, MICROSCOPE	*ENSEMBLE DE MICROSCOPE*
C160	SET, MILITARY ACCOUTREMENT	*EQUIPEMENT MILITAIRE*
D220	SET, MILITARY BUTTON DIE	*ENSEMBLE DE MATRICES A BOUTONS MILITAIRES*
D220	SET, MILITARY DIE	*ENSEMBLE DE MATRICES MILITAIRE*
D120	SET, MILITARY FORK & KNIFE	*ENSEMBLE DE FOURCHETTES ET DE COUTEAUX MILITAIRE*
D100	SET, MILITARY MESS	*BATTERIE DE SEAUX DE CANTINE MILITAIRE*
D100	SET, MILITARY SKEWER	*ENSEMBLE DE BROCHETTES MILITAIRE*
D200	SET, MILL PICK	*ENSEMBLE D'HERMINETTES A MEULE*
I100	SET, NOAH'S ARK	*JEU D'ARCHE DE NOE*
I020	SET, OUIJA	*JEU DE OUIJA*
I020	SET, PACHISI	*JEU DE PACHISI*
I100	SET, PICTURE BLOCK	*JEU DE BLOCS A IMAGES*
F180	SET, POSTCARD	*JEU DE CARTES POSTALES*
C180	SET, RAZOR	*TROUSSE DE RASAGE*
D180	SET, SADDLER'S STITCHING AWL	*ENSEMBLE D'ALENES A COUDRE POUR SELLIER*
D120	SET, SALT & PEPPER	*ENSEMBLE DE SALIERE ET DE POIVRIERE*
E380	SET, SCALPEL	*JEU DE SCALPELS*
I020	SET, SCRABBLE	*JEU DE SCRABBLE*
C180	SET, SHAVING	*ENSEMBLE DE RASAGE*
I080	SET, SHUFFLEBOARD	*JEU DE GALET*
D100	SET, SKEWER	*ENSEMBLE DE BROCHETTES*
I020	SET, SOLITAIRE	*JEU DE SOLITAIRE*
I100	SET, STAMP	*JEU DE TIMBRES A IMPRIMER*
F180	SET, STAMP	*TROUSSE A TIMBRES A IMPRIMER*
F100	SET, STENCIL	*JEU DE POCHOIRS*
D180	SET, STUFFING ROD	*ENSEMBLE DE TIGES DE REMBOURRAGE*
D040	SET, SURGICAL INSTRUMENT	*TROUSSE CHIRURGICALE*
E380	SET, SURGICAL INSTRUMENT	*TROUSSE D'INSTRUMENTS DE CHIRURGIE*
E500	SET, SURVEYING INSTRUMENT	*TROUSSE D'ARPENTEUR*
C100	SET, SWEATER	*ENSEMBLE DE TRICOT*
I080	SET, TABLE TENNIS	*JEU DE TENNIS DE TABLE*
D120	SET, TABLEWARE	*SERVICE DE VAISSELLE*
D220	SET, TAP & DIE	*ENSEMBLE A FILETER*
I020	SET, TIDDLYWINK	*JEU DE LA PUCE*
C140	SET, TIE CLIP	*ENSEMBLE DE FIXE CRAVATE*
C180	SET, TOILET	*ENSEMBLE DE TOILETTE*
I100	SET, TOILET	*ENSEMBLE DE TOILETTE*
D100	SET, UTENSIL	*JEU D'USTENSILES*
I100	SET, WOODEN CONSTRUCTION	*JEU DE BLOCS DE CONSTRUCTION DE BOIS*
B060	SETTEE	*CANAPE*
D180	SETTER, GROMMET	*POINCON A OEILLET*
D220	SETTER, RIVET	*BOUTEROLLE*
D180	SETTER, RIVET	*FER A RIVET*
B060	SETTLE	*BANC A HAUT DOSSIER*
E500	SEXTANT	*SEXTANT*
E480	SHACKLE	*ENTRAVE*
G300	SHACKLE	*MANILLE*
E480	SHACKLE, MILITARY	*ENTRAVE MILITAIRE*
G300	SHACKLE, SWIVEL	*MANILLE D'EMERILLON*
B160	SHADE, SPRING-PULL	*STORE A RESSORT*
B140	SHAKER, GRATE	*BRASSEUR DE GRILLE DE POELE*

209

Class. Code	Object, suffix	Objet, suffixe
D120	SHAKER, PEPPER	POIVRIER
C180	SHAKER, POWDER	SAUPOUDROIR
D120	SHAKER, SUGAR	SUCRIER
C080	SHAKO, MILITARY	SHAKO MILITAIRE
C080	SHAKO CHIN STRAP, MILITARY	JUGULAIRE DE SHAKO MILITAIRE
B020	SHAM, PILLOW	COUVRE-OREILLER
I100	SHAM, PILLOW	COUVRE-OREILLER
C180	SHAPER, NAIL	GRATTE-ONGLES
F180	SHARPENER, PENCIL	TAILLE-CRAYONS
C180	SHARPENER, RAZOR BLADE	AFFILOIR DE LAMES DE RASOIR
D180	SHAVE, SKIRT	TRANCHET DE SELLIER
F120	SHAVER, EDISON DICTAPHONE	TOUR A CYLINDRE DE CIRE A DICTAPHONE
C100	SHAWL	CHALE
D300	SHEARS	GRANDS CISEAUX
D220	SHEARS, BENCH	CISAILLE D'ETABLI
D300	SHEARS, DRESSMAKER'S	GRANDS CISEAUX DE COUTURIERE
D040	SHEARS, FETLOCK	CISEAU A FANONS
D120	SHEARS, GRAPE	CISEAUX A RAISINS
D020	SHEARS, HEDGE	CISAILLE A HAIE
D020	SHEARS, PRUNING	CISAILLE A EMONDER
E380	SHEARS, RIB	COSTOTOME
D040	SHEARS, SHEEP	TONDEUSE A MOUTONS
E180	SHEATH	ETUI
E180	SHEATH, TOMAHAWK	ETUI A TOMAHAWK
G300	SHEAVE	REA
A020	SHED	GRANGE
B020	SHEET	DRAP
I100	SHEET	DRAP
D100	SHEET, COOKIE	PLAQUE A BISCUITS
B020	SHEET, MILITARY	DRAP MILITAIRE
B020	SHEET, MINIATURE	DRAP MINIATURE
E300	SHEET, STEAM BOILER	TOLE DE CHAUDIERE A VAPEUR
A040	SHELF	ETAGERE
E140	SHELL, ARTILLERY	BOMBE D'ARTILLERIE
E140	SHELL CASE, ARTILLERY	DOUILLE D'OBUS D'ARTILLERIE
E140	SHELL, SHOTGUN	CARTOUCHE DE FUSIL DE CHASSE
E140	SHELL, SHRAPNEL	OBUS
D020	SHELLER, CORN	EGRENEUSE DE MAIS
J020	SHERD	TESSON
J020	SHERD, HEAD	TESSON DE TETE
E180	SHIELD	BOUCLIER
E380	SHIELD, X-RAY	ECRAN A RAYONS
A040	SHINGLE	BARDEAU
C100	SHIRT	CHEMISE
I100	SHIRT	CHEMISE
C100	SHIRT, INSTRUCTIONAL MODEL	CHEMISE MODELE D'INSTRUCTION
C100	SHIRT, MILITARY	CHEMISE MILITAIRE
C100	SHIRT, POLICE	CHEMISE DE POLICE
C060	SHOE	SOULIER
I100	SHOE	SOULIER
C060	SHOE, CHILD'S	SOULIER D'ENFANT
C060	SHOE, MILITARY	SOULIER MILITAIRE
C060	SHOE HEEL	TALON DE SOULIER
C060	SHOE IRON	FER A SOULIER
C060	SHOE SOLE	SEMELLE DE SOULIER
C140	SHOEHORN	CHAUSSE-PIED
C060	SHOELACE	LACET DE SOULIER
C100	SHORTS	SHORT
E140	SHOT, BAR	BOULET RAME
E140	SHOT, CASE	BOITE A MITRAILLE
E140	SHOT, CHAIN	BOULET A CHAINE

Class. Code	Object, suffix	Objet, suffixe
E140	SHOT, LEAD	PLOMBS
E140	SHOT, MILITARY CASE	BOITE A MITRAILLE MILITAIRE
E140	SHOT, MILITARY CHAIN	BOULET A CHAINE MILITAIRE
E140	SHOT, MINIATURE CASE	BOITE A MITRAILLE MINIATURE
E060	SHOTGUN BREAKCATCH LEVER	LEVIER DE CULASSE DE FUSIL DE CHASSE
E060	SHOTGUN, CENTER-FIRE	FUSIL DE CHASSE A PERCUSSION CENTRALE
E060	SHOTGUN, DOUBLE-BARREL	FUSIL DE CHASSE A DEUX COUPS
E060	SHOTGUN, DOUBLE-BARREL CENTER-FIRE	FUSIL DE CHASSE A DEUX COUPS ET A PERCUSSION CENTRALE
E060	SHOTGUN, DOUBLE-BARREL PERCUSSION	FUSIL DE CHASSE A DEUX COUPS ET A PERCUSSION
E060	SHOTGUN, PERCUSSION	FUSIL DE CHASSE A PERCUSSION
J060	SHOVEL	PELLE
D220	SHOVEL, BLACKSMITH'S	PELLE DE FORGERON
J060	SHOVEL BLADE	LAME DE PELLE
E260	SHOVEL, ENTRENCHING	PELLE A TRANCHEE
B140	SHOVEL, FIREPLACE	PELLE DE FOYER
D020	SHOVEL, GRAIN	PELLE A GRAIN
J060	SHOVEL HANDLE	MANCHE DE PELLE
B140	SHOVEL, MINIATURE FIREPLACE	PELLE DE FOYER MINIATURE
E260	SHOVEL, POWER	PELLE MECANIQUE
D020	SHOVEL, SCOOP	PELLE CREUSE
B140	SHOVEL, STOVE	PELLE DE POELE
B120	SHOWER	DOUCHE
B120	SHOWER HEAD	POMME DE DOUCHE
D140	SHREDDER, BARK	BROYEUR D'ECORCE
H060	SHROUD	LINCEUIL
F080	SHUTTER, DARK-SLIDE	RIDEAU DE CHARGEUR
D300	SHUTTLE	NAVETTE
D300	SHUTTLE, NETTING	NAVETTE POUR FILETS
I080	SHUTTLECOCK	VOLANT
D020	SICKLE	FAUCILLE
B060	SIDEBOARD	BUFFET
B060	SIDEBOARD, MINIATURE	BUFFET MINIATURE
D100	SIEVE	CRIBLE
E180	SIEVE, MILITARY POWDER	TAMIS A POUDRE MILITAIRE
D100	SIFTER	TAMIS
E340	SIFTER, ASH	TAMIS A CENDRES
E180	SIGHT	MIRE
E180	SIGHT, MILITARY	MIRE MILITAIRE
E180	SIGHT, MILITARY ARTILLERY	MIRE D'ARTILLERIE MILITAIRE
E180	SIGHT, MILITARY TELESCOPE	MIRE TELESCOPIQUE MILITAIRE
H080	SIGN	ENSEIGNE
F160	SIGN, MILITARY TRAFFIC	PANNEAU DE SIGNALISATION MILITAIRE
H020	SIGN, PRICE	AFFICHE DE PRIX
H020	SIGN, TRADE	ENSEIGNE
F160	SIGN, TRAFFIC	PANNEAU DE SIGNALISATION
F160	SIGNAL, STORM	CONE DE TEMPETE
F180	SIGNET	SCEAU
J060	SINEW	BABICHE
B120	SINK	EVIER
D100	SINK, DRY	EVIER
D060	SINKER	PLOMB
I080	SKATE, ICE	PATIN A GLACE
I080	SKATE, ROLLER	PATIN A ROULETTES
I080	SKATE BLADE, ICE	LAME DE PATIN A GLACE
D100	SKEWER	BROCHETTE
D100	SKEWER, MILITARY	BROCHETTE MILITAIRE
G080	SKI	SKI
I080	SKI, SNOW	SKI
D220	SKID	PATIN
G300	SKID	SEMELLE DE HALAGE
G280	SKIFF	ESQUIF

Class. Code	Object, suffix	Objet, suffixe
D100	SKIMMER	ECUMOIRE
D220	SKIMMER	ECUMOIRE
D100	SKIMMER, CREAM	ECUMOIRE A CREME
C100	SKIRT	JUPE
H120	SKIRT	JUPE
I100	SKIRT	JUPE
C100	SKIRT, CHILD'S	JUPE D'ENFANT
D100	SLAB, CANDY MAKING	PLAQUE A CONFISERIE
I080	SLED	TRAINEAU
I080	SLED RUNNER	PATIN DE TRAINEAU
D220	SLEDGE	MASSE DE FORGERON
G140	SLEDGE	TRAINEAU
G120	SLEDGE	TRAINEAU A FARDEAUX
D220	SLEDGE, CROSS-PEEN	MASSE A DEVANT AVEC PANNE TRAVERSE
D220	SLEDGE, DOUBLE-FACE	MASSE A DEUX TETES
D200	SLEDGE, MASON'S BIT	MAILLET FENDEUR
D220	SLEDGE, MILITARY STRAIGHT-PEEN	MASSE A PANNE DROITE MILITAIRE
D220	SLEDGE HANDLE	MANCHE DE MASSE DE FORGERON
G140	SLEDGE RUNNER	PATIN DE TRAINEAU
C140	SLEEVE	MANCHE
G120	SLEIGH	TRAINEAU
I100	SLEIGH	TRAINEAU
G120	SLEIGH, MINIATURE	TRAINEAU MINIATURE
D120	SLICE, FISH	PELLE A POISSON
D100	SLICER, CHEESE	COUPE-FROMAGE
D100	SLICER, EGG	COUPE-OEUF
D100	SLICER, VEGETABLE	COUPE-LEGUMES
D320	SLICK	LISSOIR
D180	SLICKER	LISSOIR
D180	SLICKER, EDGE	LISSOIR DE BORD
G180	SLIDE, BREAST STRAP	BOUCLE COULISSANTE DE POITRAIL
E180	SLING	BRETELLE
E360	SLING	COURROIE
E180	SLING, MILITARY MUSKET	BRETELLE DE MOUSQUET MILITAIRE
E180	SLING, MILITARY RIFLE	BRETELLE DE FUSIL MILITAIRE
E180	SLING SWIVEL, MILITARY MUSKET	ANNEAU DE GRENADIERE MILITAIRE
E180	SLING THONG, MILITARY MUSKET	LANIERE DE BRETELLE DE MOUSQUET MILITAIRE
I100	SLINGSHOT	LANCE-PIERRE
C120	SLIP	CHEMISE
I100	SLIP	CHEMISE DE DESSOUS
C120	SLIP, CHILD'S	CHEMISE D'ENFANT
C120	SLIP YOKE	EMPIECEMENT DE CHEMISE
B080	SLIPCOVER	HOUSSE
C060	SLIPPER	PANTOUFLE
C060	SLIPPER, MILITARY MAGAZINE	PANTOUFLE DE POUDRIERE MILITAIRE
A080	SLUICE	VANNE
D240	SLUSHER	BENNE NIVELEUSE
E080	SMALLSWORD, MILITARY	EPEE FINE MILITAIRE
C100	SMOCK	SARRAU
D040	SMOKER, BEE	ENFUMOIR
G180	SNAP, HARNESS	MOUSQUETON DE HARNAIS
G180	SNAP, ROLLER	MOUSQUETON A ROULEAU
D120	SNIFTER	VERRE A DEGUSTATION
D220	SNIPS, SHEET METALWORKER'S	CISAILLE DE TOLIER
G140	SNOWSHOE	RAQUETTE
G140	SNOWSHOE FRAME	ARMATURE DE RAQUETTE
G140	SNOWSHOE LACING	COURROIE DE RAQUETTE
G140	SNOWSHOE, SALES MODEL	RAQUETTE MODELE DE VENTE
C160	SNUFFBOX	TABATIERE
E340	SOAP	SAVON
C060	SOCK	CHAUSSETTE

Class. Code	Object, suffix	Objet, suffixe
I100	SOCK	*CHAUSSETTE*
G180	SOCKET, WHIP	*PORTE-FOUET*
B060	SOFA	*SOFA*
D100	SPADE, BUTTER-WORKING	*PALETTE A MALAXER LE BEURRE*
D020	SPADE, DITCHING	*BECHE A FOSSE*
D020	SPADE, DRAIN-TILE	*BECHE DE PARIS*
D020	SPADE, GARDEN	*BECHE DE JARDINAGE*
D020	SPADE, PEAT	*PELLE A TOURBE*
C060	SPAT	*DEMI-GUETRE*
D100	SPATULA	*SPATULE*
D260	SPATULA	*SPATULE*
D100	SPATULA, MILITARY	*SPATULE MILITAIRE*
D200	SPATULA, PLASTERER'S	*SPATULE DE PLATRIER*
F120	SPEAKER	*HAUT-PARLEUR*
F120	SPEAKER, POLICE	*HAUT-PARLEUR DE POLICE*
E080	SPEAR	*FOENE*
E080	SPEAR, EEL	*FOENE A ANGUILLE*
E080	SPEAR, FISH	*FOENE A POISSON*
E080	SPEAR, MUSKRAT	*FOENE A RAT MUSQUE*
E380	SPECULUM	*SPECULUM*
E380	SPECULUM, AURAL	*SPECULUM POUR OREILLE*
H080	SPEECH .	*DISCOURS*
D100	SPIDER	*POELE A FRIRE A TROIS PIEDS*
J060	SPIGOT	*CHANTEPLEURE*
G240	SPIKE	*CRAMPON*
D320	SPIKE	*POINTE DE FER*
H120	SPIKE, POLICE HELMET	*POINTE DE CASQUE DE POLICE*
H120	SPIKE FERRULE, MILITARY HELMET	*RONDELLE DE POINTE DE CASQUE MILITAIRE*
D300	SPINDLE	*FUSEAU*
F180	SPINDLE	*PIQUE-NOTES*
B080	SPITTOON	*CRACHOIR*
E380	SPLINT	*ATTELLE*
D320	SPOKESHAVE	*RACLOIR DE RAIES*
D180	SPOKESHAVE	*VASTRINGUE*
E340	SPONGE	*EPONGE*
E180	SPONGE	*EPONGE*
E180	SPONGE, MILITARY	*EPONGE MILITAIRE*
E080	SPONTOON	*ESPONTON*
E080	SPONTOON, MILITARY	*ESPONTON MILITAIRE*
D300	SPOOL	*FUSETTE*
D300	SPOOLER	*BOBINEUSE*
D100	SPOON	*CUILLERE*
D120	SPOON	*CUILLERE*
I100	SPOON	*CUILLERE*
D240	SPOON	*CUILLERE DE SONDAGE*
D100	SPOON, BASTING	*CUILLERE A ARROSER*
D220	SPOON, BLACKSMITH'S	*CUILLERE DE FORGERON*
D100	SPOON, CADDY	*CUILLERE A BOITE A THE*
H060	SPOON, CEREMONIAL	*CUILLERE DE CEREMONIE*
D120	SPOON, COFFEE	*CUILLERE A CAFE*
H080	SPOON, COMMEMORATIVE	*CUILLERE COMMEMORATIVE*
D120	SPOON, DESSERT	*CUILLERE A DESSERT*
E380	SPOON, DOSE	*CUILLERE A MEDICAMENT*
C180	SPOON, EAR	*CURE-OREILLE*
D120	SPOON, GRAPEFRUIT	*CUILLERE A PAMPLEMOUSSE*
D120	SPOON, MARROW	*CUILLERE A MOELLE*
D100	SPOON, MEASURING	*CUILLERE A MESURER*
D120	SPOON, MILITARY	*CUILLERE MILITAIRE*
D100	SPOON, MILITARY	*CUILLERE MILITAIRE*
D120	SPOON, MINIATURE	*CUILLERE MINIATURE*
D120	SPOON, MUSTARD	*CUILLERE A MOUTARDE*

Class. Code	Object, suffix	Objet, suffixe
D120	SPOON, SALT	CUILLERE A SEL
D120	SPOON, SERVING	CUILLERE A SERVIR
D120	SPOON, SHERBET	CUILLERE A SORBET
D120	SPOON, SOUP	CUILLERE A SOUPE
D120	SPOON, SUGAR	CUILLERE A SUCRE
D120	SPOONER	PORTE-CUILLERES
I100	SPOONER	PORTE-CUILLERES
C160	SPORRAN, MILITARY	SPORRAN MILITAIRE
B100	SPOTLIGHT	PROJECTEUR
D140	SPOUT, SAP	CHALUMEAU A SEVE
D020	SPRAYER, HAND	VAPORISATEUR
E360	SPRING, SPIRAL	RESSORT SPIRALE
E340	SPRINKLER	ARROSOIR
D220	SPRINKLER, BLACKSMITH'S	ASPERSOIR DE FORGERON
D020	SPRINKLER, IRRIGATION	ARROSOIR DE PELOUSE
D220	SPRUE	BAGUETTE DE COULEE
D140	SPUD, BARKING	SARCLOIR A ECORCE
D020	SPUD, WEEDING	SARCLOIR A DESHERBER
G180	SPUR	EPERON
G180	SPUR, MILITARY	EPERON MILITAIRE
G180	SPUR, POLICE	EPERON DE POLICE
D320	SQUARE	EQUERRE
D320	SQUARE, BEVEL	FAUSSE EQUERRE
D320	SQUARE, CARPENTER'S	EQUERRE DE CHARPENTIER
D200	SQUARE, MASON'S	EQUERRE DE MACON
D200	SQUARE, MASON'S TRY	EQUERRE-NIVEAU DE MACON
D320	SQUARE, MITER	EQUERRE A ONGLET
D320	SQUARE, SET	EQUERRE A DESSIN
D320	SQUARE, TRY	EQUERRE A LAME D'ACIER
H020	SQUARE, TRY	EQUERRE A LAME D'ACIER
E340	SQUEEGEE	RACLETTE
D100	SQUEEZER, FRUIT	PRESSE-FRUITS
I100	STAGECOACH	DILIGENCE
G120	STAGECOACH	DILIGENCE
G120	STAGECOACH WHEEL	ROUE DE DILIGENCE
D220	STAKE, BEAK	TAS A BEC RECOURBE
D220	STAKE, BEAKHORN	BIGORNE
D220	STAKE, CANDLEMOLD	ENCLUME POUR MOULE A CHANDELLE
D220	STAKE, COOPER'S	ENCLUME DE TONNELIER
D220	STAKE, CREASING	ENCLUME CANNELEE A QUEUE
D220	STAKE, DOUBLE-HORN	ENCLUME A DEUX BECS CONIQUES ET A QUEUE
D220	STAKE, HATCHET	ENCLUME A QUEUE ET EN FORME DE HACHETTE
D220	STAKE, ROUND-HEAD	ENCLUME A TETE RONDE
D220	STAKE, SEAMING	ENCLUME POUR AGRAFAGE DES TOLES
D220	STAKE, SQUARE	ENCLUME A TETE CARREE
B060	STALL	STALLE
D220	STAMP	ETAMPE
H100	STAMP	TIMBRE
F180	STAMP	TIMBRE A ENCRER
F180	STAMP, CANCELLATION	TAMPON D'OBLITERATION
D180	STAMP, CLOSING	POINCON A REFOULER
F180	STAMP, DATE	TIMBRE DATEUR
F180	STAMP, MARKING	TAMPON A MARQUER
D180	STAMP, MILITARY BRANDING	FER A MARQUER MILITAIRE
F180	STAMP, NOTARY	SCEAU DE NOTAIRE
H100	STAMP, POSTAGE	TIMBRE-POSTE
H100	STAMP, TAX	TIMBRE-TAXE
H100	STAMP, TRADING	TIMBRE-PRIME
B140	STAND, BELLOWS	PORTE-SOUFFLET
D220	STAND, BLACKSMITH'S	SUPPORT DE PIECE FORGEE
B080	STAND, BOOK	SUPPORT A LIVRES

Class. Code	Object, suffix	Objet, suffixe
D120	STAND, CAKE	*ASSIETTE A GATEAUX SUR PIED*
D120	STAND, CARAFE	*DESSOUS DE CARAFE*
D100	STAND, CASK	*PORTE-BARIL*
H060	STAND, COFFIN	*SUPPORT DE CERCUEIL*
D220	STAND, CRUCIBLE	*SUPPORT A CREUSET*
D120	STAND, CRUET	*HUILIER*
E400	STAND, DISPLAY	*PRESENTOIR SUR PIED*
B140	STAND, FIRESET	*SUPPORT D'ENSEMBLE DE FOYER*
D180	STAND, LAST	*SUPPORT DE FORME A CHAUSSURE*
E120	STAND, MILITARY FALCONET	*FOURCHE DE FALCONET MILITAIRE*
H060	STAND, MISSAL	*LUTRIN*
F060	STAND, MUSIC	*PUPITRE A MUSIQUE*
D120	STAND, SERVING TRAY	*PORTE-PLATEAU DE SERVICE*
B060	STAND, SHAVING	*SUPPORT D'OBJETS DE RASAGE*
D040	STAND, SHOEING	*APPAREIL DE CONTENTION*
B080	STAND, SMOKER'S	*PRESENTOIR*
B060	STAND, TELEVISION	*TABLE DE TELEVISION*
D120	STAND, VEGETABLE DISH	*DESSOUS DE PLAT A LEGUMES*
B120	STAND, WATER HEATER	*SUPPORT DE CHAUFFE-EAU*
C020	STAND, WIG	*PORTE-PERRUQUE*
F180	STAPLE	*AGRAFE*
A040	STAPLE	*CRAMPON*
I080	STAPLE, LAWN TENNIS	*CRAMPON DE RUBAN MARQUEUR DE TENNIS*
F180	STAPLER	*AGRAFEUSE*
E180	STARTER, BULLET	*MAILLET A BALLES*
H080	STATEMENT, ACCOUNT	*ETAT DE COMPTE*
H080	STATEMENT, BANK	*ETAT DE COMPTE EN BANQUE*
F180	STATIONERY	*PAPETERIE*
H060	STATIONS OF THE CROSS	*CHEMIN DE LA CROIX*
H040	STATUE	*STATUE*
H060	STATUE, RELIGIOUS	*STATUE RELIGIEUSE*
H080	STATUTE	*STATUT*
C140	STAY, COLLAR	*SUPPORT DE COL DE CHEMISE*
D100	STEAMER	*MARMITE A VAPEUR*
E300	STEAMLINE	*TUYAU DE VAPEUR*
D220	STEEL	*AIGUISOIR*
B140	STEEL	*BRIQUET*
E560	STEELYARD	*CROCHET-BASCULE*
D120	STEIN	*POT A BIERE*
F100	STENCIL	*POCHOIR*
F180	STENCIL	*POCHOIR*
B080	STEPLADDER	*ESCABEAU*
B060	STEPS, BED	*ESCABEAU DE CHEVET*
G180	STEPS, CARRIAGE	*MARCHEPIED*
H080	STEREOGRAPH	*STEREOGRAPHE*
F160	STEREOSCOPE	*STEREOSCOPE*
D160	STICK, CANDLE DIPPING	*TIGE D'IMMERSION POUR BOUGIE*
F100	STICK, COMPOSING	*COMPOSTEUR*
I020	STICK, GAMBLING	*BATON DE JEU*
I080	STICK, LACROSSE	*BATON DE JEU DE CROSSE*
C140	STICK, MILITARY BUTTON	*PATIENCE MILITAIRE*
E180	STICK, MILITARY PORTFIRE	*PORTE-LANCE MILITAIRE*
C160	STICK, MILITARY SWAGGER	*BATON MILITAIRE*
F100	STICK, SIDE	*BLANC DE MARGE*
D680	STICK, SOAP	*PALETTE A SAVON*
F060	STICK, STAMPING	*BATON DE RYTHME*
D020	STICK, TOBACCO	*SECHOIR A TABAC*
H020	STICKER	*AUTOCOLLANT*
C140	STICKPIN	*EPINGLE DE CRAVATE*
D300	STILETTO	*POINCON*
E240	STILL	*DISTILLATEUR*

Class. Code	Object, suffix	Objet, suffixe
E240	STILL, SOLAR	DISTILLATEUR SOLAIRE
D100	STIRRER	MELANGEUR
G180	STIRRUP	ETRIER
D180	STIRRUP	TIRE-PIED
F100	STITCHER	PIQUEUSE AU FIL METALLIQUE
C140	STOCK	COL CRAVATE
D220	STOCK, DIE	PORTE-FILIERE
C140	STOCK, MILITARY	COL CRAVATE MILITAIRE
C060	STOCKING	BAS
H060	STOCKING, CHRISTMAS	BAS DE NOEL
C100	STOLE	ETOLE
H060	STONE, ALTAR	PIERRE D'AUTEL
I080	STONE, CURLING	PIERRE DE CURLING
D220	STONE, SCYTHE-SHARPENING	PIERRE A FAUX
J020	STONE, WORKED	PIERRE OUVREE
D020	STONEBOAT	TRAINEAU A FARDEAUX
B060	STOOL	TABOURET
B060	STOOL, MILITARY	TABOURET MILITAIRE
B060	STOOL, MILKING	BANC A TRAIRE
F060	STOOL, ORGAN	TABOURET D'HARMONIUM
F060	STOOL, PIANO	TABOURET DE PIANO
D320	STOP, BENCH	VALET D'ETABLI
E240	STOPPER	BOUCHON
B080	STOPPER, BOTTLE	BOUCHON DE BOUTEILLE
E180	STOPPER, MILITARY MUZZLE	OBTURATEUR DE MOUSQUET MILITAIRE
E340	STOPPER, SINK	BOUCHON D'EVIER
D100	STOVE	CUISINIERE
B140	STOVE	POELE
I100	STOVE	POELE
B140	STOVE, MILITARY	POELE MILITAIRE
B140	STOVE, MINIATURE	POELE MINIATURE
D100	STOVE, PORTABLE	CUISINIERE PORTATIVE
B140	STOVE, WOOD	POELE A BOIS
B140	STOVE DOOR	PORTE DE POELE
B140	STOVE DOOR, MILITARY	PORTE DE POELE MILITAIRE
B140	STOVE LEG	PIED DE POELE
B140	STOVE LID	ROND DE POELE
B140	STOVE URN	URNE DE POELE
B140	STOVEPIPE	TUYAU DE POELE
B140	STOVEPIPE COLLAR	COLLET DE TUYAU DE POELE
B140	STOVEPIPE DAMPER	REGISTRE DE TUYAU DE POELE
F040	STRAIGHTEDGE	REGLE DROITE
D100	STRAINER	EGOUTTOIR
D100	STRAINER, GRAVY	PASSOIRE A SAUCE
D060	STRAINER, ICE	ECUMOIRE A GLACONS
E340	STRAINER, LAUNDRY BLUEING	PASSOIRE A BLEU DE LESSIVE
D680	STRAINER, LYE	COULOIR A LESSIVE DE SOUDE
D100	STRAINER, MILITARY	EGOUTTOIR MILITAIRE
D100	STRAINER, MILK	PASSOIRE A LAIT
E340	STRAINER, SINK	FILTRE D'EVIER
D100	STRAINER, WHEY	PASSOIRE A PETIT LAIT
J060	STRAP	COURROIE
G180	STRAP, BREAST	COURROIE DE POITRAIL
G180	STRAP, CHOKE	LAISSE D'ETRANGLEMENT
G300	STRAP, DODGER	COURROIE DE PASSERELLE
G180	STRAP, HAME	COURROIE D'ATTELLE
G180	STRAP, SPUR	SANGLE D'EPERON
B100	STREETLAMP	REVERBERE
G140	STRETCHER	BRANCARD
D320	STRETCHER, CANOE CANVAS	TENDEUR POUR ARMATURE DE CANOT
E340	STRETCHER, CARPET	TENDEUR DE TAPIS

216

Class. Code	Object, suffix	Objet, suffixe
E340	STRETCHER, CURTAIN	TENDEUR DE RIDEAU
E260	STRETCHER, FENCE-WIRE	TENDEUR DE CLOTURES EN FIL DE FER
C140	STRETCHER, GLOVE	OUVRE-GANTS
E340	STRETCHER, GLOVE	TENDEUR DE GANTS
D300	STRETCHER, HAT	TENDEUR DE CHAPEAU
D180	STRETCHER, PELT	TENDEUR A PEAU
E340	STRETCHER, SOCK	TENDEUR DE BAS
E380	STRIPPER, RIB	RUGINE COSTALE
G140	STROLLER	POUSSETTE
B080	STRONGBOX	CASSETTE
B080	STRONGBOX, POLICE	CASSETTE DE POLICE
C180	STROP	CUIR A RASOIR
E180	STRUT, MILITARY TARGET	ETAI DE CIBLE MILITAIRE
C140	STUD	BOUTON DE COL
D100	STUFFER, SAUSAGE	ENTONNOIR A SAUCISSES
D120	SUGAR BOWL LID	COUVERCLE DE BOL A SUCRE
C100	SUIT	COSTUME
C100	SUIT, BATHING	MAILLOT DE BAIN
C100	SUIT, CHILD'S	COSTUME D'ENFANT
C100	SUIT, JUMP	COMBINAISON
I100	SUIT, JUMP	COMBINAISON
C100	SUIT, MILITARY MAGAZINE	COSTUME DE POUDRIERE MILITAIRE
C120	SUIT, UNION	HABIT DE DESSOUS
C160	SUITCASE	VALISE
B060	SUITE, BEDROOM	MOBILIER DE CHAMBRE A COUCHER
C080	SUNBONNET	CAPELINE
E540	SUNDIAL	CADRAN SOLAIRE
E500	SUNSTONE	AVENTURINE
D300	SUPPLIES, MILITARY SEWING	FOURNITURES DE COUTURE MILITAIRES
D300	SUPPLIES, SEWING	FOURNITURES DE COUTURE
E240	SUPPORT, RING	SUPPORT ANNULAIRE
C100	SURPLICE	SURPLIS
C140	SUSPENDERS	BRETELLE
C140	SUSPENDERS, MILITARY	BRETELLE MILITAIRE
C140	SUSPENDERS, POLICE	BRETELLE DE POLICE
D100	SWAB, BAKER'S OVEN	CHIFFON POUR FOUR DE BOULANGER
B160	SWAG	FESTON
D220	SWAGE	SUAGE
D220	SWAGE, BOTTOM	SUAGE INFERIEUR
D220	SWAGE, HALF-ROUND TOP	SUAGE DE FORGEAGE EN DEMI-ROND
D220	SWAGE, TOP	SUAGE SUPERIEUR
B080	SWATTER, FLY	TAPETTE A MOUCHES
C080	SWEATBAND	CUIRET
C100	SWEATER	CHANDAIL
E340	SWEEPER, CARPET	BALAI MECANIQUE
I100	SWEEPER, CARPET	BALAI MECANIQUE
D120	SWEEPER, CRUMB	RAMASSE-MIETTES
D300	SWIFT	GUINDRE
I060	SWING	BALANCOIRE
E300	SWITCH	COMMUTATEUR
F140	SWITCHBOARD, TELEPHONE	STANDARD
J060	SWIVEL, FLAG	EMERILLON DE DRAPEAU
I100	SWORD	EPEE
E080	SWORD	EPEE
E080	SWORD, HUNTING	EPEE DE CHASSE
E080	SWORD, MILITARY	EPEE MILITAIRE
H120	SWORD, MILITARY PRESENTATION	EPEE D'HONNEUR MILITAIRE
E080	SWORD, MINIATURE	EPEE MINIATURE
E080	SWORD, POLICE	EPEE DE POLICE
E080	SWORD BLADE, MILITARY	LAME D'EPEE MILITAIRE
E080	SWORD BOW	BRANCHE DE GARDE

Class. Code	Object, suffix	Objet, suffixe
E080	SWORD GUARD, MILITARY	GARDE D'EPEE MILITAIRE
E080	SWORD HILT	POIGNEE D'EPEE
E180	SWORD KNOT, MILITARY	DRAGONNE MILITAIRE
E180	SWORD KNOT, POLICE	DRAGONNE DE POLICE
E080	SWORD POMMEL	POMMEAU D'EPEE
D040	SYRINGE	SERINGUE
E380	SYRINGE	SERINGUE
D040	SYRINGE, DOSE	SERINGUE A DOSE
I080	SYSTEM, DIVER'S	EQUIPEMENT DE PLONGEE
D300	SYSTEM, PATTERN DRAFTING	SYSTEME DE DESSIN DES PATRONS
F040	T-SQUARE	EQUERRE EN T
H060	TABERNACLE	TABERNACLE
B060	TABLE	TABLE
I100	TABLE	TABLE
I020	TABLE, BAGATELLE	TABLE DE BILLIARD ANGLAIS
I100	TABLE, BILLIARD	TABLE DE BILLARD
I080	TABLE, BILLIARD	TABLE DE BILLARD
B060	TABLE, CARD	TABLE A JEU DE CARTES
B060	TABLE, CENTER	TABLE RONDE
B060	TABLE, CENTER PEDESTAL	GUERIDON
B060	TABLE, COFFEE	TABLE A CAFE
B060	TABLE, CONSOLE	TABLE-CONSOLE
B060	TABLE, CORNER	TABLE DE COIN
B060	TABLE, DINING	TABLE DE SALLE A MANGER
F040	TABLE, DRAFTING	TABLE A DESSIN
B060	TABLE, DRESSING	COIFFEUSE
B060	TABLE, FOLDING	TABLE PLIANTE
F100	TABLE, GALLEY	TABLE A GALEES
B060	TABLE, GAME	TABLE DE JEU
B060	TABLE, GARDEN	TABLE DE JARDIN
F100	TABLE, IMPOSING	MARBRE D'IMPOSITION
B060	TABLE, KITCHEN	TABLE DE CUISINE
B060	TABLE, LIBRARY	TABLE DE BIBLIOTHEQUE
B060	TABLE, MILITARY	TABLE MILITAIRE
B060	TABLE, MINIATURE	TABLE MINIATURE
B060	TABLE, MORTICIAN'S	TABLE D'EMBAUMEMENT
B060	TABLE, NIGHT	TABLE DE CHEVET
B060	TABLE, PIER	TABLE DE TRUMEAU
B060	TABLE, SERVING	DESSERTE
B060	TABLE, SEWING	TABLE A COUTURE
D100	TABLE, SPLITTING	TABLE A DEPECER
D100	TABLE, STEAM	TABLE CHAUDE A VAPEUR
B060	TABLE, TEA	TABLE A THE
B060	TABLE, TIER	TABLE A ETAGERE
B060	TABLE, TILT-TOP	TABLE A BASCULE
B060	TABLE, TRIPOD	TABLE A TROIS PIEDS
B060	TABLE, VESTING	TABLE POUR VETEMENTS SACERDOTAUX
B060	TABLE, WRITING	TABLE-BUREAU
B060	TABLE LEAF	PANNEAU DE TABLE
D120	TABLECLOTH	NAPPE
D120	TABLESPOON	CUILLERE DE TABLE
H080	TABLET	TABLETTE
E180	TACKLE, MILITARY CANNON	MOUFLE DE CANON MILITAIRE
H080	TAG, IDENTIFICATION	FICHE D'IDENTIFICATION
H080	TAG, MERCHANDISE	ETIQUETTE DE MARCHANDISE
F180	TAG, SHIPPING	ETIQUETTE D'EXPEDITION
H120	TALISMAN	TALISMAN
E260	TAMPER	DAME FRETTEE
D100	TAMPER	TAMPON
C160	TAMPER, PIPE	BOURRE-PIPE
E180	TAMPION, MILITARY	TAPE MILITAIRE

Class. Code	Object, suffix	Objet, suffixe
E180	TAMPION, MINIATURE MILITARY	TAPE MILITAIRE MINIATURE
F080	TANK, FILM-PROCESSING	BOITE NOIRE POUR DEVELOPPEMENT DE FILMS
G300	TANK, GASOLINE	RESERVOIR A ESSENCE
J060	TANK, H.P.G.	RESERVOIR DE CONTROLE A HAUTE PRESSION
J060	TANK, L.P.G.	RESERVOIR DE CONTROLE A BASSE PRESSION
E360	TANK, TEST	BAC D'ESSAIS
D100	TANK, WATER	RESERVOIR A EAU
D120	TANKARD	CHOPE
D120	TANTALUS	PORTE-LIQUEUR
D220	TAP	TARAUD
D320	TAP, SCREW	TARAUD
J060	TAPE, ADHESIVE	RUBAN ADHESIF
E380	TAPE, ADHESIVE	SPARADRAP
I080	TAPE, LAWN TENNIS	RUBAN MARQUEUR DE TENNIS
F120	TAPE, POLICE	BANDE MAGNETIQUE DE POLICE
H040	TAPESTRY	TAPISSERIE
J060	TARPAULIN	BACHE
D120	TAZZA	COUPE A FRUITS
D120	TEACUP	TASSE A THE
D100	TEAKETTLE	BOUILLOIRE
D100	TEAKETTLE LID	COUVERCLE DE BOUILLOIRE
D120	TEAPOT	THEIERE
D120	TEAPOT LID	COUVERCLE DE THEIERE
D120	TEASPOON	CUILLERE A THE
H080	TELEGRAM	TELEGRAMME
H080	TELEGRAM, POLICE	TELEGRAMME DE POLICE
F140	TELEPHONE	TELEPHONE
F140	TELEPHONE, MODEL	TELEPHONE MODELE REDUIT
E460	TELESCOPE	TELESCOPE
E200	TELESCOPE, ACHROMATIC	REFRACTEUR ACHROMATIQUE
E200	TELESCOPE, GALILEAN	LUNETTE DE GALILEE
E200	TELESCOPE, REFLECTING	TELESCOPE A REFLECTEUR
F140	TELEVISION	TELEVISEUR
D220	TEMPLATE	PATRON
D320	TEMPLATE, ANIMAL YOKE	PATRON A JOUG
D320	TEMPLATE, BOAT HULL	PATRON A CHARPENTE DE BATEAU
D320	TEMPLATE, COFFIN	PATRON A CERCUEIL
D300	TEMPLATE, MITTEN	PATRON A MOUFLE
D320	TEMPLATE, SNOWSHOE	PATRON A RAQUETTE
D300	TEMPLE	TEMPLET
A020	TEMPLE, MODEL	TEMPLE MODELE REDUIT
A020	TENT	TENTE
A020	TENT PEG	PIQUET DE TENTE
J020	TEXTILE FRAGMENT	FRAGMENT DE TISSU
E500	THEODOLITE	THEODOLITE
E520	THERMOGRAPH	THERMOGRAPHE
D100	THERMOMETER	THERMOMETRE
E380	THERMOMETER	THERMOMETRE
E420	THERMOMETER	THERMOMETRE
D100	THERMOMETER, MILK	THERMOMETRE A LAIT
D300	THIMBLE	DE
D180	THREAD, BOOTMAKER'S	LIGNEUL
E380	THREAD, SUTERING	FIL A SUTURE
G240	THROTTLE, STEAM LOCOMOTIVE	MANIPULATEUR DE LOCOMOTIVE A VAPEUR
B080	THROW	JETE
B080	THROW, TABLE	TAPIS DE TABLE
E180	THUMBSTALL, MILITARY GUNNER'S	CALE DE POUCE D'ARTILLEUR MILITAIRE
H100	TICKET	BILLET
C140	TIE, BOW	NOEUD PAPILLON
D040	TIE, CATTLE	COLLIER A BETAIL
C100	TIGHTS	COLLANT

Class. Code	Object, suffix	Objet, suffixe
A040	TILE	*TUILE*
D100	TILTER, TEAKETTLE	*VERSEUR DE THEIERE*
A020	TIMBER	*BOIS*
A020	TIMBER, INSTRUCTIONAL MODEL	*BOIS MODELE D'INSTRUCTION*
F080	TIMER, DARKROOM	*CHRONOMETRE DE CHAMBRE NOIRE*
D100	TIMER, KITCHEN	*MINUTERIE DE CUISINE*
H080	TIMETABLE	*HORAIRE*
G020	TIN	*BOITE EN FER-BLANC*
E400	TIN, ADHESIVE TAPE	*BOITE EN FER-BLANC POUR RUBAN ADHESIF*
E400	TIN, ALLSPICE	*BOITE EN FER-BLANC A POIVRE DE LA JAMAIQUE*
E400	TIN, ANALGESIC	*BOITE EN FER-BLANC POUR ANALGESIQUES*
E400	TIN, ANTACID	*BOITE EN FER-BLANC POUR ANTI-ACIDE*
E400	TIN, ANTISEPTIC	*BOITE EN FER-BLANC POUR ANTISEPTIQUE*
E400	TIN, APPLE & STRAWBERRY JAM	*BOITE EN FER-BLANC A CONFITURE DE POMMES ET DE FRAISES*
E400	TIN, ASBESTOS	*BOITE EN FER-BLANC A ASBESTE*
E400	TIN, BAKING POWDER	*BOITE EN FER-BLANC POUR LEVURE CHIMIQUE*
E400	TIN, BAKING SODA	*BOITE EN FER-BLANC A BICARBONATE DE SOUDE*
E400	TIN, BANDAGE	*BOITE EN FER-BLANC POUR BANDAGES*
E400	TIN, BEVERAGE MIX	*BOITE EN FER-BLANC A PREPARATION POUR BOISSON*
E400	TIN, BISCUIT	*BOITE EN FER-BLANC A BISCUITS*
E400	TIN, BOOT POLISH	*BOITE EN FER-BLANC DE CIRAGE A CHAUSSURES*
E400	TIN, BUTTER	*BOITE EN FER-BLANC A BEURRE*
E400	TIN, CAMPHOR	*BOITE EN FER-BLANC POUR CAMPHRE*
E400	TIN, CANDLE	*BOITE EN FER-BLANC POUR BOUGIES*
E400	TIN, CARBIDE	*BOITE EN FER-BLANC POUR CARBURE*
E400	TIN, CAULKING COMPOUND	*BOITE EN FER-BLANC POUR PRODUIT DE CALFEUTRAGE*
E400	TIN, CAYENNE	*BOITE EN FER-BLANC POUR CAYENNE*
E400	TIN, CELERY SALT	*BOITE EN FER-BLANC A SEL DE CELERI*
E400	TIN, CHALK	*BOITE EN FER-BLANC A CRAIES*
E400	TIN, CHEMICAL	*BOITE EN FER-BLANC POUR PRODUIT CHIMIQUE*
E400	TIN, CIGARETTE	*BOITE EN FER-BLANC POUR CIGARETTES*
E400	TIN, CIGARETTE PAPER	*BOITE EN FER-BLANC POUR PAPIER A CIGARETTES*
E400	TIN, CINNAMON	*BOITE EN FER-BLANC A CANNELLE*
E400	TIN, CLEANSER	*BOITE EN FER-BLANC POUR POUDRE A NETTOYER*
E400	TIN, CLOVE	*BOITE EN FER-BLANC A CLOUS DE GIROFLE*
E400	TIN, COCOA	*BOITE EN FER-BLANC A CACAO*
E400	TIN, COCONUT	*BOITE EN FER-BLANC A NOIX DE COCO*
E400	TIN, COFFEE	*BOITE EN FER-BLANC A CAFE*
E400	TIN, COLLAR STAY	*BOITE EN FER-BLANC A SUPPORTS DE COL*
E400	TIN, CONFECTION	*BOITE EN FER-BLANC A CONFISERIES*
E400	TIN, COSMETIC	*BOITE EN FER-BLANC POUR COSMETIQUES*
E400	TIN, COUGH DROP	*BOITE EN FER-BLANC POUR PASTILLES CONTRE LA TOUX*
E400	TIN, CREAM OF TARTAR	*BOITE EN FER-BLANC A CREME DE TARTRE*
E400	TIN, CURTAIN ROD	*BOITE EN FER-BLANC A TRINGLES A RIDEAU*
E400	TIN, DEODORANT	*BOITE EN FER-BLANC POUR DESODORISANT*
E400	TIN, FILM	*BOITE EN FER-BLANC POUR FILM*
E400	TIN, FILM PLATE	*BOITE EN FER-BLANC POUR PLAQUE PHOTOGRAPHIQUE*
E400	TIN, FOOD RATION	*BOITE EN FER-BLANC POUR VIVRES DE RESERVE*
E400	TIN, GASOLINE	*BOITE EN FER-BLANC A GAZOLINE*
E400	TIN, GINGER	*BOITE EN FER-BLANC A GINGEMBRE*
E400	TIN, GLUE	*BOITE EN FER-BLANC A COLLE*
E400	TIN, GRAVY MIX	*BOITE EN FER-BLANC A PREPARATION POUR SAUCE BRUNE*
E400	TIN, GUM ARABIC	*BOITE EN FER-BLANC A GOMME ARABIQUE*
E400	TIN, GUNPOWDER	*BOITE EN FER-BLANC A POUDRE A CANON*
E400	TIN, HACKSAW BLADE	*BOITE EN FER-BLANC A LAMES DE SCIE A METAUX*
E400	TIN, HAIR TONIC	*BOITE EN FER-BLANC POUR TONIQUE CAPILLAIRE*
E400	TIN, HONEY	*BOITE EN FER-BLANC A MIEL*
E400	TIN, INK	*BOITE EN FER-BLANC POUR ENCRE*
E400	TIN, INKPAD	*BOITE EN FER-BLANC POUR TAMPON ENCREUR*
E400	TIN, INSECTICIDE	*BOITE EN FER-BLANC POUR INSECTICIDE*
E400	TIN, JAM	*BOITE EN FER-BLANC A CONFITURE*

Class. Code	Object, suffix	Objet, suffixe
E400	TIN, KEROSENE	BOITE EN FER-BLANC A PETROLE
E400	TIN, LANTERN	BOITE EN FER-BLANC POUR LANTERNE
E400	TIN, LARD	BOITE EN FER-BLANC POUR LARD
E400	TIN, LAUNDRY SOAP	BOITE EN FER-BLANC A SAVON A LESSIVE
E400	TIN, LAXATIVE	BOITE EN FER-BLANC POUR LAXATIF
E400	TIN, LEATHER DRESSING	BOITE EN FER-BLANC POUR APPRET A CUIR
E400	TIN, LUBRICATING GREASE	BOITE EN FER-BLANC POUR GRAISSE LUBRIFIANTE
E400	TIN, LUBRICATING OIL	BOITE EN FER-BLANC POUR HUILE LUBRIFIANTE
E400	TIN, LYE	BOITE EN FER-BLANC A SOUDE DE LESSIVE
E400	TIN, MACE	BOITE EN FER-BLANC A MACIS
E400	TIN, MARJORAM	BOITE EN FER-BLANC A MARJOLAINE
E400	TIN, MATCH	BOITE EN FER-BLANC POUR ALLUMETTES
E400	TIN, MEAT EXTRACT	BOITE EN FER-BLANC POUR EXTRAIT DE VIANDE
E400	TIN, MEDICINAL	BOITE EN FER-BLANC POUR PRODUIT PHARMACEUTIQUE
E400	TIN, METAL POLISH	BOITE EN FER-BLANC POUR PRODUIT A POLIR LE METAL
E400	TIN, MILITARY DETONATING FUSE	BOITE EN FER-BLANC POUR DETONATEUR MILITAIRE
D120	TIN, MILITARY MESS	GAMELLE MILITAIRE
E400	TIN, MILITATY FRICTION TUBE	BOITE EN FER-BLANC A TUBE A FRICTION MILITAIRE
E400	TIN, MILK POWDER	BOITE EN FER-BLANC A LAIT EN POUDRE
E400	TIN, MOLASSES	BOITE EN FER-BLANC A MELASSE
E400	TIN, MUSTARD	BOITE EN FER-BLANC A MOUTARDE
E400	TIN, NON-ALCOHOLIC BEVERAGE	BOITE EN FER-BLANC A BOISSON NON-ALCOOLISEE
E400	TIN, NUTMEG	BOITE EN FER-BLANC A MUSCADE
E400	TIN, OINTMENT	BOITE EN FER-BLANC POUR ONGUENT
E400	TIN, PAINT	BOITE EN FER-BLANC A PEINTURE
E400	TIN, PAPER CLIP	BOITE EN FER-BLANC POUR ATTACHE-FEUILLES
E400	TIN, PEANUT	BOITE EN FER-BLANC A ARACHIDES
E400	TIN, PEANUT BUTTER	BOITE EN FER-BLANC A BEURRE D'ARACHIDES
E400	TIN, PEMMICAN	BOITE EN FER-BLANC A PEMMICAN
E400	TIN, PEPPER	BOITE EN FER-BLANC A POIVRE
E400	TIN, PERCUSSION CAP	BOITE EN FER-BLANC POUR AMORCES
E400	TIN, PETROLEUM JELLY	BOITE EN FER-BLANC A VASELINE
E400	TIN, PHONOGRAPH NEEDLE	BOITE EN FER-BLANC POUR AIGUILLES DE PHONOGRAPHE
E400	TIN, PIE FILLING	BOITE EN FER-BLANC A GARNITURE POUR TARTES
E400	TIN, PILL	BOITE EN FER-BLANC A PILULES
E400	TIN, PINE TAR	BOITE EN FER-BLANC A GOUDRON DE BOIS
E400	TIN, PIPE	BOITE EN FER-BLANC POUR PIPES
E400	TIN, PLUM JAM	BOITE EN FER-BLANC A CONFITURE DE PRUNES
E400	TIN, POULTRY GRIT	BOITE EN FER-BLANC A GRAVIER POUR VOLAILLE
E400	TIN, PUTTY	BOITE EN FER-BLANC A MASTIC
E400	TIN, RASPBERRY JAM	BOITE EN FER-BLANC A CONFITURE DE FRAMBOISES
E400	TIN, RIVET	BOITE EN FER-BLANC A RIVETS
E400	TIN, SAGE	BOITE EN FER-BLANC A SAUGE
E400	TIN, SALTPETER	BOITE EN FER-BLANC A SALPETRE
E400	TIN, SEWING NEEDLE	BOITE EN FER-BLANC POUR AIGUILLES A COUDRE
E400	TIN, SHAVING SOAP	BOITE EN FER-BLANC POUR SAVON A BARBE
E400	TIN, SHELLAC	BOITE EN FER-BLANC A SHELLAC
E400	TIN, SHORTENING	BOITE EN FER-BLANC A GRAISSE ALIMENTAIRE
E400	TIN, SKIN LOTION	BOITE EN FER-BLANC POUR LOTION POUR LA PEAU
E400	TIN, SNUFF	BOITE EN FER-BLANC A TABAC A PRISER
E400	TIN, SODA BISCUIT	BOITE EN FER-BLANC A CRAQUELINS
E400	TIN, SOLDER	BOITE EN FER-BLANC POUR SOUDURE
E400	TIN, SOLDER FLUX	BOITE EN FER-BLANC POUR FONDANT DE SOUDURE TENDRE
E400	TIN, SPICE	BOITE EN FER-BLANC A EPICES
E400	TIN, STARCH	BOITE EN FER-BLANC POUR EMPOIS
E400	TIN, STOVE POLISH	BOITE EN FER-BLANC POUR PATE A POLIR LE POELE
E400	TIN, STRAIGHT PIN	BOITE EN FER-BLANC POUR EPINGLES DROITES
E400	TIN, STRAWBERRY JAM	BOITE EN FER-BLANC A CONFITURE DE FRAISES
E400	TIN, SUGAR	BOITE EN FER-BLANC A SUCRE
E400	TIN, SUPPOSITORY	BOITE EN FER-BLANC A SUPPOSITOIRES
E400	TIN, SYRUP	BOITE EN FER-BLANC A SIROP

Class. Code	Object, suffix	Objet, suffixe
E400	TIN, TALCUM POWDER	BOITE EN FER-BLANC A POUDRE DE TALC
E400	TIN, TEA	BOITE EN FER-BLANC A THE
E400	TIN, TIRE PATCH	BOITE EN FER-BLANC POUR EMPLATRE DE REPARATION
E400	TIN, TOBACCO	BOITE EN FER-BLANC A TABAC
E400	TIN, TOILET SOAP	BOITE EN FER-BLANC POUR SAVON DE TOILETTE
E400	TIN, TOOTHPASTE	BOITE EN FER-BLANC POUR PATE DENTIFRICE
E400	TIN, TURPENTINE	BOITE EN FER-BLANC A TEREBENTHINE
E400	TIN, TYPEWRITER RIBBON	BOITE EN FER-BLANC A RUBANS DE MACHINE A ECRIRE
E400	TIN, VARNISH	BOITE EN FER-BLANC POUR VERNIS
E400	TIN, VEGETABLE OIL	BOITE EN FER-BLANC POUR HUILE VEGETALE
E400	TIN, VIOLIN FITTING	BOITE EN FER-BLANC A FOURNITURES DE VIOLON
E400	TIN, WATCH	BOITE EN FER-BLANC A MONTRE
E400	TIN, WOOD POLISH	BOITE EN FER-BLANC A LIQUIDE A POLIR LES BOIS
B140	TINDERBOX	BOITE A BRIQUET
B140	TINDERPISTOL	BRIQUET-PISTOLET
H080	TINTYPE	FERROTYPIE
H080	TINTYPE, MILITARY	FERROTYPIE MILITAIRE
D100	TOASTER	GRILLE-PAIN
C160	TOBACCO	TABAC
I080	TOBOGGAN	TOBOGGAN
B120	TOILET	TOILETTE
B120	TOILET FLUSH CHAIN	MANETTE DE CHASSE D'EAU
B120	TOILET SEAT	SIEGE DE TOILETTE
H100	TOKEN	JETON
H100	TOKEN, TRANSPORTATION	JETON DE TRANSPORT
E080	TOMAHAWK	TOMAHAWK
H060	TOMBSTONE	PIERRE TOMBALE
D220	TONGS	PINCE
D120	TONGS	PINCE
D140	TONGS	PINCES
E240	TONGS, BEAKER	PINCE A BECHER
D220	TONGS, BOLT	TENAILLES A BOULON
H060	TONGS, CENSOR CHARCOAL	PINCE A CHARBON DE BOIS POUR ENCENSOIR
D040	TONGS, CLINCHING	PINCE A RIVET DE MARECHAL-FERRANT
D220	TONGS, CLIP	PINCE DE FORGERON
D220	TONGS, CRUCIBLE	PINCE A CREUSET
B140	TONGS, FIREPLACE	PINCES DE FOYER
E240	TONGS, FLASK	PINCE A BALLON
D220	TONGS, FLAT	TENAILLES PLATES
D220	TONGS, HAMMER	TENAILLE A MARTELAGE
D220	TONGS, HOLLOW-BIT	PINCE-BUSE
D220	TONGS, HOOP	TENAILLES A BECS COURBES
E180	TONGS, HOT-SHOT	PINCES A PROJECTILE CHAUFFE
D100	TONGS, ICE	PINCE A GLACE
D100	TONGS, KITCHEN	PINCE DE CUISINE
E340	TONGS, LAUNDRY	PINCES A LESSIVE
B140	TONGS, MILITARY FIREPLACE	PINCES DE FOYER MILITAIRE
D220	TONGS, PICKUP	TENAILLES DE FORGERON
D220	TONGS, PINCER	TENAILLE-PINCE
E400	TONGS, SHELF	PERCHE A PINCE
D220	TONGS, SHOE	PINCE A FERRER
D220	TONGS, SIDE	PINCE A BECS DROIT ET COUDE
D120	TONGS, SUGAR	PINCE A SUCRE
D220	TONGS, TIRE	PINCE A BANDAGE DE ROUE
D220	TOOL, BOLT HEADING	BOULONNIERE
E180	TOOL, CARTRIDGE LOADING	SERTISSEUR
D320	TOOL, HOOP BENDING	OUTIL A CINTRER POUR CERCEAU
E180	TOOL, LOADING	OUTIL DE CHARGEMENT
D160	TOOL, LOOP	MIRETTE DOUBLE
E260	TOOL, MILITARY ENTRENCHING	PELLE-PIOCHE PLIANTE MILITAIRE
E180	TOOL, MILITARY HOT-SHOT	PORTE-BOULET CHAUFFE

Class. Code	Object, suffix	Objet, suffixe
D220	TOOL, NAIL HEADING	*CLOUTIERE*
D200	TOOL, PLASTERER'S MODELING	*OUTIL A MODELER DE PLATRIER*
C180	TOOTHBRUSH	*BROSSE A DENTS*
C180	TOOTHBRUSH, MILITARY	*BROSSE A DENTS MILITAIRE*
C180	TOOTHPICK	*CURE-DENT*
I100	TOP	*TOUPIE*
C080	TOQUE	*TOQUE*
D220	TORCH, GASOLINE	*CHALUMEAU A ESSENCE*
D220	TORCH, KEROSINE	*CHALUMEAU A PETROLE*
D220	TORCH, PROPANE	*CHALUMEAU A PROPANE*
E140	TORPEDO, DESIGN MODEL	*TORPILLE MODELE DE PROJET*
E140	TORPEDO, MODEL	*TORPILLE MODELE REDUIT*
H060	TOTEM	*TOTEM*
E380	TOURNIQUET	*TOURNIQUET*
E380	TOURNIQUET, MILITARY	*TOURNIQUET MILITAIRE*
E180	TOW, CLEANING	*ETOUPE*
C180	TOWEL	*SERVIETTE*
D040	TOWEL	*SERVIETTE*
C180	TOWEL, BATH	*SERVIETTE DE BAIN*
C180	TOWEL, BEACH	*SERVIETTE DE PLAGE*
H060	TOWEL, CEREMONIAL	*SERVIETTE DE CEREMONIE*
H080	TOWEL, COMMEMORATIVE	*SERVIETTE COMMEMORATIVE*
E340	TOWEL, DISH	*SERVIETTE A VAISELLE*
C180	TOWEL, FACE	*GANT DE TOILETTE*
C180	TOWEL, FINGERTIP	*SERVIETTE A MAIN*
C180	TOWEL, HAND	*ESSUIE-MAIN*
C180	TOWEL, POLICE	*SERVIETTE DE POLICE*
C180	TOWEL, ROLLER	*TOUAILLE*
A080	TOWER	*TOUR*
I100	TOY, DOLL	*JOUET DE POUPEE*
I100	TOY, MECHANICAL	*JOUET MECANIQUE*
I100	TOY, PULL	*JOUET A TIRER*
I100	TOY, TRUNDLE	*JOUET ROULANT*
G180	TRACE	*TRAIT*
A040	TRACK, DOOR	*COULISSE DE PORTE*
G240	TRACK SECTION	*SECTION DE RAIL DE CHEMIN DE FER*
D020	TRACTOR, FARM	*TRACTEUR AGRICOLE*
H100	TRADE ITEM, ARMBAND	*ARTICLE DE TRAITE BRASSARD*
H100	TRADE ITEM, AWL	*ARTICLE DE TRAITE ALENE*
H100	TRADE ITEM, AX	*ARTICLE DE TRAITE HACHE*
H100	TRADE ITEM, BASKET	*ARTICLE DE TRAITE PANIER*
H100	TRADE ITEM, BEAD	*ARTICLE DE TRAITE PERLE*
H100	TRADE ITEM, BELL	*ARTICLE DE TRAITE GRELOT*
H100	TRADE ITEM, BLANKET	*ARTICLE DE TRAITE COUVERTURE*
H100	TRADE ITEM, BROOCH	*ARTICLE DE TRAITE BROCHE*
H100	TRADE ITEM, BUTTON	*ARTICLE DE TRAITE BOUTON*
H100	TRADE ITEM, CASTOREUM	*ARTICLE DE TRAITE CASTOREUM*
H100	TRADE ITEM, COAT	*ARTICLE DE TRAITE MANTEAU*
H100	TRADE ITEM, CONE	*ARTICLE DE TRAITE CONE*
H100	TRADE ITEM, CURLER	*ARTICLE DE TRAITE PAPILLOTE*
H100	TRADE ITEM, EARRING	*ARTICLE DE TRAITE BOUCLE D'OREILLE*
H100	TRADE ITEM, FIGURINE	*ARTICLE DE TRAITE FIGURINE*
H100	TRADE ITEM, FISHHOOK	*ARTICLE DE TRAITE HAMECON*
H100	TRADE ITEM, HATCHET	*ARTICLE DE TRAITE HACHETTE*
H100	TRADE ITEM, HIDE	*ARTICLE DE TRAITE PEAU*
H100	TRADE ITEM, KETTLE	*ARTICLE DE TRAITE MARMITE*
H100	TRADE ITEM, KNIFE	*ARTICLE DE TRAITE COUTEAU*
H100	TRADE ITEM, KNIFE SHEATH	*ARTICLE DE TRAITE GAINE DE COUTEAU*
H100	TRADE ITEM, MIRROR	*ARTICLE DE TRAITE MIROIR*
H100	TRADE ITEM, MUSKET	*ARTICLE DE TRAITE FUSIL*
H100	TRADE ITEM, PELT	*ARTICLE DE TRAITE FOURRURE*

Class. Code	Object, suffix	Objet, suffixe
H100	TRADE ITEM, PENDANT	ARTICLE DE TRAITE PENDENTIF
H100	TRADE ITEM, PIGMENT	ARTICLE DE TRAITE PIGMENT
H100	TRADE ITEM, PISTOL	ARTICLE DE TRAITE PISTOLET
H100	TRADE ITEM, RING	ARTICLE DE TRAITE BAGUE
H100	TRADE ITEM, SHELL	ARTICLE DE TRAITE COQUILLAGE
H100	TRADE ITEM, TOBACCO	ARTICLE DE TRAITE TABAC
H100	TRADE ITEM, TOKEN	ARTICLE DE TRAITE JETON
H100	TRADE ITEM, WIRE	ARTICLE DE TRAITE LACET
D100	TRAMMEL	CREMAILLERE
D100	TRAMMEL, MINIATURE	CREMAILLERE MINIATURE
F140	TRANSCEIVER	EMETTEUR-RECEPTEUR
H080	TRANSCRIPT	TRANSCRIPTION
E300	TRANSFORMER	TRANSFORMATEUR
E280	TRANSISTOR	TRANSISTOR
F140	TRANSMITTER	TRANSMETTEUR
F140	TRANSMITTER, RADIO	RADIOEMETTEUR
F140	TRANSMITTER, TELEGRAPH	EMETTEUR TELEGRAPHIQUE
H080	TRANSPARENCY	TRANSPARENT
H080	TRANSPARENCY, LANTERN-SLIDE	DIAPOSITIVE DE LANTERNE A PROJECTION
D060	TRAP	PIEGE
D060	TRAP, FISH	FILET DE MADRAGUE
D060	TRAP CHAIN	CHAINE DE PIEGE
D220	TRAVELER	ROUE A MESURER
D120	TRAY, BED	TABLE DE MALADE
D120	TRAY, BREAD	PLATEAU A PAIN
B100	TRAY, CANDLESNUFFER	PLATEAU A MOUCHETTES
H060	TRAY, CEREMONIAL	PLATEAU DE CEREMONIE
H080	TRAY, COMMEMORATIVE	PLATEAU COMMEMORATIF
F180	TRAY, DESK	BOITE A COURRIER
C180	TRAY, DRESSER	PLATEAU DE COMMODE
D120	TRAY, FLATWARE	PLATEAU A COUTELLERIE
E380	TRAY, KIDNEY	CUVETTE RENIFORME A PANSEMENTS
F100	TRAY, MATRIX	PORTE-MATRICES
E400	TRAY, MONEY	PLATEAU A MONNAIE
F080	TRAY, PRINT-PROCESSING	PLATEAU DE DEVELOPPEMENT D'EPREUVES
F100	TRAY, REGLET	PORTE-REGLETTES
D120	TRAY, SERVING	PLATEAU DE SERVICE
E400	TRAY, STORAGE	BAC DE RANGEMENT
E300	TREADLE	PEDALE
D180	TREE, BOOT	TIRE-BOTTE
C140	TREE, SHOE	EMBAUCHOIR
E380	TREPHINE	TREPHINE
F040	TRIANGLE	EQUERRE A DESSINER
E240	TRIANGLE	TRIANGLE
I100	TRICYCLE	TRICYCLE
D180	TRIMMER, EDGE	ROGNOIR
D040	TRIMMER, HOOF	BOUTOIR
F100	TRIMMER, SAW	ROGNOIR
B100	TRIMMER, WICK	COUPE-MECHE
D220	TRIP-HAMMER	MARTEAU A BASCULE
F080	TRIPOD	TREPIED
E240	TRIPOD	TREPIED
E500	TRIPOD, SURVEYOR'S	TREPIED D'ARPENTEUR
D120	TRIVET	TREPIED
E340	TRIVET	TREPIED
I100	TRIVET	TREPIED
H120	TROPHY	TROPHEE
D100	TROUGH, DOUGH	PETRIN
D100	TROUGH, MINIATURE DOUGH	PETRIN MINIATURE
D200	TROUGH, MIXING	AUGE A MORTIER
D140	TROUGH, SAP	AUGE A SEVE

Class. Code	Object, suffix	Objet, suffixe
D200	TROWEL	*TRUELLE*
D020	TROWEL, GARDEN	*DEPLANTOIR DE JARDINAGE*
D200	TROWEL, POINTING	*TRUELLE A JOINTS*
D200	TROWEL, SMOOTHING	*TRUELLE A LISSER*
I100	TRUCK	*CAMION*
G220	TRUCK, TRAIN	*BOGIE DE TRAIN*
I100	TRUMPET	*TROMPETTE*
C160	TRUMPET, EAR	*CORNET ACOUSTIQUE*
F060	TRUMPET, NATURAL	*TROMPETTE SANS PISTONS*
I100	TRUNK	*COFFRE*
C160	TRUNK	*MALLE*
C160	TRUNK, MILITARY	*MALLE MILITAIRE*
G020	TUB	*BAC*
E400	TUB, CONFECTION	*BAQUET A CONFISERIES*
E400	TUB, LARD	*BAQUET A LARD*
G020	TUB, MILITARY	*BAC MILITAIRE*
B140	TUB, MILITARY COAL	*BAC A CHARBON MILITAIRE*
D100	TUB, MILITARY SALTING	*SALOIR MILITAIRE*
E400	TUB, PICKLE	*BAQUET A CORNICHONS*
E400	TUB, RASPBERRY JAM	*BAQUET A CONFITURE DE FRAMBOISES*
D100	TUB, SALTING	*SALOIR*
D220	TUB, SLACK	*BAC A TREMPER*
F060	TUBA	*TUBA*
G020	TUBE	*TUBE*
E400	TUBE, COSMETIC	*TUBE A COSMETIQUES*
E400	TUBE, DENTURE ADHESIVE	*TUBE A CIMENT POUR PROTHESE DENTAIRE*
E400	TUBE, DEODORANT	*TUBE A DESODORISANT*
E400	TUBE, FLAVORING	*TUBE A ESSENCE*
E400	TUBE, GLUE	*TUBE A COLLE*
D200	TUBE, GROUTING	*COFFRAGE*
E400	TUBE, GUN GREASE	*TUBE A GRAISSE DE FUSIL*
E400	TUBE, MEDICINAL	*TUBE A PRODUIT PHARMACEUTIQUE*
E140	TUBE, MILITARY FRICTION	*TUBE A FRICTION MILITAIRE*
E400	TUBE, PAINT	*TUBE A PEINTURE*
E400	TUBE, SHAVING SOAP	*TUBE A SAVON A BARBE*
F120	TUBE, SPEAKING	*PORTE-VOIX*
H060	TUBE, SUCKING	*TUYAU ASPIRANT*
E240	TUBE, TEST	*EPROUVETTE*
D100	TUBE, THIEF	*TUBE D'ECHANTILLON DE DOSAGE*
E400	TUBE, TOOTHPASTE	*TUBE DE PATE DENTIFRICE*
E280	TUBE, X-RAY	*TUBE A RAYONS X*
E300	TUBE-EXPANDER	*CHAMBRE A EXPANSION*
E240	TUBING	*TUBES*
G180	TUG, HARNESS	*PORTE-BRANCARD*
G180	TUG, SHAFT	*BRACELET DE BRANCARD*
D120	TUMBLER	*VERRE SANS PIED*
H080	TUMBLER, COMMEMORATIVE	*VERRE SANS PIED COMMEMORATIF*
G180	TUMPLINE	*COURROIE DE PORTAGE*
C100	TUNIC	*TUNIQUE*
C100	TUNIC, MILITARY	*TUNIQUE MILITAIRE*
C100	TUNIC, POLICE	*TUNIQUE DE POLICE*
C080	TUQUE	*TUQUE*
C080	TURBAN	*TURBAN*
D120	TUREEN	*SOUPIERE*
D120	TUREEN LID	*COUVERCLE DE SOUPIERE*
E360	TURNBUCKLE	*TENDEUR*
D180	TURNER, SEAM	*LISSOIR DE COUTURE*
G300	TURNTABLE	*RIDOIR*
D220	TUYERE	*TUYERE*
C180	TWEEZERS	*BRUCELLES*
E240	TWEEZERS	*BRUCELLES*

Class. Code	Object, suffix	Objet, suffixe
D320	TWIBIL	HACHE A DOUBLE TRANCHANT
D300	TWISTER	TORDEUSE
D040	TWISTER, NOSE	SERRE-NEZ
F100	TYPE	CARACTERE
F180	TYPEWRITER, MANUAL	MACHINE A ECRIRE MANUELLE
C160	UMBRELLA	PARAPLUIE
I100	UMBRELLA	PARAPLUIE
B040	UNDERLAY	SOUS-COUCHE
C120	UNDERSHIRT	TRICOT DE CORPS
C100	UNIFORM	UNIFORME
C100	UNIFORM, MILITARY	UNIFORME MILITAIRE
D220	UPSETTER, TIRE/AXLE	MACHINE A REFOULER LES ESSIEUX ET LES BANDAGES
C180	URINAL	URINAL
C180	URINAL, MILITARY	URINAL MILITAIRE
B080	URN	URNE
D120	URN, COFFEE	FONTAINE A CAFE
D120	URN, TEA	FONTAINE A THE
B160	VALANCE	CANTONNIERE
J060	VALVE	SOUPAPE
E300	VALVE, STEAM	SOUPAPE DE VAPEUR
E300	VALVE, STEAM BOILER	VALVE DE CHAUDIERE A VAPEUR
E160	VAMBRACE	CANON D'AVANT-BRAS
E380	VAPORIZER	VAPORISATEUR
B080	VASE	VASE
H060	VASE	VASE
D120	VASE, CELERY	VASE A CELERI
H080	VASE, COMMEMORATIVE	VASE COMMEMORATIF
D100	VAT, BUTTER	CUVE A BEURRE
D100	VAT, FISH	CUVE A POISSON
D120	VEGETABLE DISH LID	COUVERCLE DE PLAT A LEGUMES
C080	VEIL	VOILE
H060	VEIL	VOILE
H060	VEIL, CHALICE	VOILE DE CALICE
H060	VEIL, CIBORIUM	PAVILLON DE CIBOIRE
C100	VEIL, HUMERAL	VOILE HUMERAL
H060	VEIL, TABERNACLE	PAVILLON DE TABERNACLE
G140	VELOCIPEDE	VELOCIPEDE
A040	VENTILATOR	VENTILATEUR
G280	VESSEL, MINIATURE CARGO	NAVIRE MINIATURE
G280	VESSEL, MODEL 3-MAST GENERAL CARGO	NAVIRE A CARGAISONS DIVERSES A 3 MATS MODELE REDUI
G280	VESSEL, MODEL BARK CARGO	NAVIRE A CARGAISONS BASQUE MODELE REDUIT
G280	VESSEL, MODEL CARGO	NAVIRE A CARGAISONS MODELE REDUIT
G280	VESSEL, MODEL SCHOONER CARGO	NAVIRE A CARGAISONS GOELETTE MODELE REDUIT
G280	VESSEL, MODEL SQUARE-RIGGED CARGO	NAVIRE A CARGAISONS A PHARE CARRE MODELE REDUIT
I100	VICTORIA	VICTORIA
I100	VILLAGE	VILLAGE
F060	VIOLIN	VIOLON
F060	VIOLIN STRING	CORDE DE VIOLON
F060	VIOLONCELLO	VIOLONCELLE
D220	VISE	ETAU
D320	VISE	PRESSE
D220	VISE, BENCH	ETAU D'ETABLI
D180	VISE, COLLAR	ETAU A COLLIER
D220	VISE, HAND	ETAU A MAIN
D220	VISE, LEG	PIED D'ETAU
E180	VISE, MILITARY SHELL	ETAU A OBUS MILITAIRE
D220	VISE, PIPE	ETAU A TUYAUX
D320	VISE, SAW SHARPENING	ETAU POUR AIGUISER LES SCIES
Z999	VOID-REGISTRATION NUMBER REPLACED BY ANOTHER	NUL - NO. D'ENREGISTREMENT REMPLACE PAR UN AUTRE
Z999	VOID-UNUSED REGISTRATION NUMBER	NUL - NO. D'ENREGISTREMENT NON UTILISE
H080	VOUCHER, AUDITOR'S	PIECE JUSTIFICATIVE

Class. Code	Object, suffix	Objet, suffixe
H080	VOUCHER, BANK	*BON DE COMPTE EN BANQUE*
E140	WAD, GUN	*BOURRE DE FUSIL*
E180	WAD-HOOK, MILITARY	*CROCHET A BOURRE MILITAIRE*
I100	WAGON	*CHARIOT*
G120	WAGON	*CHARIOT*
G120	WAGON AXLE	*ESSIEU DE CHARIOT*
G120	WAGON AXLE-BED	*SUPPORT D'ESSIEU DE CHARIOT*
G120	WAGON BODY-HANGER	*SUSPENSION DE CAISSE DE CHARIOT*
G120	WAGON BOLSTER PLATE	*COUSSINET D'ESSIEU AVANT DE CHARIOT*
G120	WAGON BRAKESHOE	*SABOT DE FREIN DE CHARIOT*
G120	WAGON CAP	*CAPUCHON DE TIMON DE CHARIOT*
G120	WAGON, DELIVERY	*VOITURE DE LIVRAISON*
G120	WAGON HITCH	*ATTACHE DE WAGON*
G120	WAGON HOUND	*BRAS DE JONCTION DE LIMONIERE DE CHARIOT*
G120	WAGON KING BOLT	*PIVOT D'ESSIEU AVANT DE CHARIOT*
G120	WAGON SEAT SPRING	*RESSORT DE SIEGE DE CHARIOT*
G120	WAGON SHAFT	*LIMON DE CHARIOT*
G120	WAGON SHAFT BRACE	*LIEN CINTRE POUR LIMONIERE DE CHARIOT*
G120	WAGON SHAFT COUPLING	*TRAVERSE DE LIMONIERE DE CHARIOT*
G120	WAGON SPRING	*RESSORT DE CHARIOT*
G120	WAGON TONGUE	*TIMON DE CHARIOT*
G120	WAGON TURNTABLE	*PLATE-FORME PIVOTANTE DE CHARIOT*
G120	WAGON WHEEL	*ROUE DE CHARIOT*
G120	WAGON WHEEL HUB	*MOYEU DE ROUE DE CHARIOT*
C100	WAISTCOAT	*GILET*
H120	WAISTCOAT	*GILET*
C100	WAISTCOAT, MILITARY	*VESTE MILITAIRE*
C100	WAISTCOAT, POLICE	*VESTE DE POLICE*
C160	WALKER	*TROTTE-BEBE*
A020	WALL	*MUR*
C160	WALLET	*PORTEFEUILLE*
A040	WALLPAPER	*PAPIER PEINT*
A040	WALLPAPER FRAGMENT	*FRAGMENT DE PAPIER PEINT*
I020	WALTES	*JEU DE WALTES*
H060	WAND, DANCE	*BAGUETTE DE DANSE*
B060	WARDROBE	*GARDE-ROBE*
B080	WARMER, BED	*BASSINOIRE*
D100	WARMER, BRANDY	*CHAUFFE-COGNAC*
B080	WARMER, FOOT	*CHAUFFE-PIEDS*
C160	WARMER, HAND	*CHAUFFE-MAINS*
D100	WARMER, PLATE	*CHAUFFE-ASSIETTES*
E340	WASHBOARD	*PLANCHE A LAVER*
I100	WASHBOARD	*PLANCHE A LAVER*
E340	WASHBOILER	*CHAUDRON A LESSIVE*
C180	WASHCLOTH	*DEBARBOUILLETTE*
D320	WASHER	*RONDELLE*
E360	WASHER, TURNBUCKLE	*RONDELLE POUR TENDEUR*
B060	WASHSTAND	*TABLE DE TOILETTE*
I100	WASHSTAND	*TABLE DE TOILETTE*
B060	WASHSTAND, MILITARY	*TABLE DE TOILETTE MILITAIRE*
E340	WASHTUB	*BAQUET A LESSIVE*
B080	WASTEBASKET	*CORBEILLE A PAPIER*
I100	WATCH, PENDANT	*MONTRE PENDENTIF*
E540	WATCH, POCKET	*MONTRE DE POCHE*
D040	WATERER, LIVESTOCK	*ABREUVOIR A BETAIL*
E300	WATERWHEEL AXLE	*ESSIEU DE ROUE A AUBES*
F180	WAX, SEALING	*CIRE A CACHETER*
E420	WEATHERVANE	*GIROUETTE*
D200	WEDGE	*COIN A REFENDRE*
D320	WEDGE, CLEAVING	*COIN DE REFENTE*
D320	WEDGE, HANDLE	*COIN DE POIGNEE*

Class. Code	Object, suffix	Objet, suffixe
D020	WEEDER, ROD	EXTIRPATEUR A TRINGLES
E560	WEIGHT, BALANCE	CONTREPOIDS
B160	WEIGHT, CURTAIN	POIDS DE RIDEAU
A040	WEIGHT, DOOR	CONTREPOIDS DE PORTE
G180	WEIGHT, HITCHING	POIDS D'ATTACHE
D300	WEIGHT, LOOM	POIDS A METIER
C140	WEIGHT, MILITARY PANTS	POIDS DE PANTALON MILITAIRE
D060	WEIGHT, MINIATURE NET	LEST MINIATURE
D060	WEIGHT, NET	LEST
G280	WHALEBOAT	BALEINIER
J020	WHALEBONE FRAGMENT	FRAGMENT D'OS DE BALEINE
D320	WHEEL, CAULKING	ROULETTE A CALFATAGE
D180	WHEEL, CROW	ROULETTE DENTELEE
D300	WHEEL, FLAX SPINNING	ROUET A CHANVRE
D100	WHEEL, JAGGING	VIDELLE
D300	WHEEL, SPINNING	ROUET
G300	WHEEL, STEERING	ROUE DE GOUVERNAIL
G080	WHEEL, STEERING	VOLANT D'ORIENTATION DU TRAIN AVANT
D300	WHEEL, TRACING	ROULETTE A POINTILLER
D300	WHEEL, WOOL SPINNING	ROUET A LAINE
G140	WHEELBARROW	BROUETTE
I100	WHEELBARROW	BROUETTE
G140	WHEELBARROW WHEEL	ROUE DE BROUETTE
D220	WHETSTONE	PIERRE A AIGUISER
G180	WHIFFLETREE	PALONNIER
H040	WHIMSEY	BABIOLE
G180	WHIP	FOUET
E480	WHIP	FOUET
E480	WHIP, MILITARY	FOUET MILITAIRE
I100	WHIRLIGIG	TOURNIQUET
D100	WHISK	FOUET
F120	WHISTLE	SIFFLET
I100	WHISTLE	SIFFLET
H060	WHISTLE, CEREMONIAL	SIFFLET DE CEREMONIE
H120	WHISTLE, MILITARY	SIFFLET MILITAIRE
G300	WHISTLE, STEAM	SIFFLET A VAPEUR
D300	WHORL, SPINDLE	VOLANT DE FUSEAU
B100	WICK	MECHE
B140	WICK	MECHE
D320	WICKER	BANDES POUR VANNERIE
C020	WIG	PERRUQUE
A020	WIGWAM	WIGWAM
A020	WIGWAM, MODEL	WIGWAM MODELE REDUIT
H080	WILL	TESTAMENT
D300	WINDER, BOBBIN	MACHINE A BOBINER
D060	WINDER, FISHING	CARET DE PECHE
G080	WINDER, KITE LINE	DEVIDOIR DE FICELLE DE CERF-VOLANT
D300	WINDER, LACE	BOBINEUSE A DENTELLE
E360	WINDER, MOTOR	DEVIDOIR
D300	WINDER, THREAD	DEVIDOIR DE FIL
G300	WINDLASS	GUINDEAU
E360	WINDLASS	TREUIL
D320	WINDLASS, HOOPING	BRIDE DE SERRAGE
I100	WINDMILL	EOLIENNE
A040	WINDOW	FENETRE
A040	WINDOW, SALES MODEL	FENETRE MODELE DE VENTE
A040	WINDOWPANE	CARREAU
A040	WINDOWPANE, LEADED	VITRAIL
F180	WIPER, PEN	ESSUIE-PLUME
J060	WIRE	FIL METALLIQUE
J020	WOOD FRAGMENT	FRAGMENT DE BOIS

Class.
Code | **Object, suffix** | **Objet, suffixe**

Code	Object, suffix	Objet, suffixe
J020	WOOD, WORKED	*BOIS OUVRE*
B140	WOODBIN	*BOITE A BOIS*
B140	WOODBIN, MILITARY	*BOITE A BOIS MILITAIRE*
J060	WORKBENCH	*ETABLI*
D100	WORKER, BUTTER	*MALAXEUR A BEURRE*
E180	WORM	*TIRE-BOURRE*
E180	WORM, MINIATURE	*TIRE-BOURRE MINIATURE*
H060	WREATH	*COURONNE MORTUAIRE*
H040	WREATH, FLORAL	*COURONNE DE FLEURS*
D220	WRENCH, ALLEN	*CLE ALLEN*
D220	WRENCH, BOX	*CLE POLYGONALE*
D220	WRENCH, CARRIAGE NUT	*CLE CARREE*
D220	WRENCH, CRESCENT	*CLE A MOLETTE*
E480	WRENCH, FIRE HOSE	*ENROULEUR DE MANCHE A INCENDIE*
B100	WRENCH, LAMP	*CLE DE LAMPE*
E180	WRENCH, MILITARY NIPPLE	*CLE DE CHEMINEE MILITAIRE*
D220	WRENCH, MONKEY	*CLE ANGLAISE*
D220	WRENCH, OPEN-END	*CLE OUVERTE*
D220	WRENCH, PIPE	*SERRE-TUBE*
D220	WRENCH, SLIP	*CLE A MACHOIRES MOBILES*
D220	WRENCH, SOCKET	*CLE A DOUILLE*
D220	WRENCH, TAP	*TOURNE-A-GAUCHE*
D220	WRENCH, TORQUE	*CLE DYNAMOMETRIQUE*
E340	WRINGER, CLOTHES	*ESSOREUSE A VETEMENTS*
E340	WRINGER, MOP	*ESSOREUSE A VADROUILLE*
C140	WRISTLET	*BRACELET DE POIGNET*
E540	WRISTWATCH	*MONTRE-BRACELET*
E560	YARDSTICK	*VERGE*
I100	YO-YO	*YO-YO*
G140	YOKE	*PALANCHE*
G180	YOKE, ANIMAL	*JOUG*
D200	ZAX	*COUTEAU D'ARDOISIER*

BIBLIOGRAPHY

1: Iconographic reference

2: Scientific definition and terminology

3: Documentary work on uses and evolution of objects

*: Reference material

GENERAL WORKS

3 Abrahamson, Una, **God Bless our Home, Domestic Life in Nineteenth Century Canada,** Burns & MacEachern Limited, Toronto, 1966.

1 , 2 **The American Heritage Dictionary of the English Language,** William Morris, ed., Houghton Mifflin Company, Boston, 1981.

1 **The Antique Dealers Pocketbook,** Charles Scribner's Sons, New York, 1972.

1 , 2 **Antiques in the Home,** A Golden Hands Book, Gabrielle Weaver, ed., Marshall Cavendish Publications, London, 1974.

2 **Atlas linguistique de l'Est du Québec,** Québec, 1980.

* **Le Bélisle: Dictionnaire de la langue française au Canada,** Louis-Alexandre Bélisle, ed., Leland, Montréal, 1957.

* Bergeron, Yves, **L'ethnologie au Québec,** Ministère des Affaires culturelles, Québec, 1987.

1 , 2 , 3 Blanchard, l'abbé Étienne, **2000 mots par l'image. Les mots illustrés,** Le Devoir, Montréal, 1917.

2 , 3 Blanchard, l'abbé Étienne, **En garde! Termes anglais et anglicismes,** Beauchemin, Montréal, 1913.

1 Blanchard, l'abbé Étienne, **Vocabulaire bilingue par l'image,** Les frères des écoles chrétiennes, Montréal, 1948.

1 , 2 Bragonier Jr., Reginald, and David Fisher, **What's What, A Visual Glossary of the Physical World,** Hammond, Maplewood, N.J., 1981.

1 , 2 , 3 Byrn, Edward W., **The Progress of Invention in the Nineteenth Century,** Scientific American Office, Munn & Co., New York, 1900.

1 Caverhill, Learmont & Co., **Wholesale Hardware, General Supplies, Tools & Equipment for Railroads-Shipyards-Steamships-Auto Transports-Public Utilities-Contractors-Industrial plants,** Montréal, n.d.

1 , 2 Clabburn, Pamela, **The Needleworker's Dictionary,** William Morrow & Company, New York, 1976.

* Cowie, Donald, and Keith Henshaw, **Antique Collector's Dictionary,** Arc Books, New York, 1971.

1 Cumberland General Store, **Wish and Want Book,** No 376, Crossville, Tenn., 1976.

1 Cumberland General Store, **Wish and Want Book,** No 481, Crossville, Tenn., 1981.

2 **Dictionnaire étymologique,** Larousse, Paris, 1971.

2 **Dictionnaire du français plus,** CEC, Montréal, 1987.

2 **Dictionnaire Militaire, Anglais-Français, Français-Anglais,** J.C. Murchie, director, Edmond Clouthier, Printer to the King's Most Excellent Majesty, Ottawa, 1945.

2 , 3 **Dictionnaire technique général Anglais-Français,** J.-Gérard Belle-Isle, ed., Beauchemin, Montréal, 1977.

1 , 2 **Dictionnaire Thématique Visuel,** Jean-Claude Corbeil, director, Québec/Amérique, Can., 1986.

* Du Berger, Jean, in association with Simonne Dubois-Ouellet, **Pratiques culturelles traditionnelles,** CÉLAT, Québec, 1989.

1 , 2   **Duden français, Dictionnaire en images,** Bibliographisches Institut Manheim/Wein/Zurich.

*   Dunn, Oscar, **Glossaire franco-canadien,** Presses de l'université Laval, Québec, 1976.

1 , 3   Dupont, Jean-Claude, **Contribution à l'ethnographie des côtes de Terre-Neuve,** Centre d'études nordiques, Presses de l'université Laval, Québec, 1968.

1 , 3   Dupont, Jean-Claude, **Histoire populaire de l'Acadie,** Lémeac, Québec, 1978.

1 , 2   **Encyclopedia of Antiques,** Octopus Books, London, 1976.

*   **Encyclopédie ou Dictionnaire raisonné des sciences, des arts et des métiers,** Samuel Faulche & Compagnie, Neufchastel, 1765.

1   **L'Encyclopédie Diderot et D'Alembert. Recueil de planches, sur les sciences, les arts libéraux, et les arts mécaniques avec leur explication: Ébeniste en meubles et voitures,** Inter-Livres, Paris, 1989.

*   **Encyclopédie Universalis,** France, 1974.

1 , 3   Genest, Bernard, René Bouchard, Lise Cyr, and Yvan Chouinard, **Les artisans traditionnels de l'est du Québec,** Ministère des Affaires culturelles, Québec, 1979.

1 , 2   Genêt, Nicole, Luce Vermette, and Louise Décarie-Audet, **Les objets familiers de nos ancêtres,** Éditions de l'Homme, Montréal, 1974.

2 , 3   Gérin, Léon, **Vocabulaire pratique de l'anglais au français,** Albert Lévesque, Montréal, 1937.

1 , 2 , 3   Giedion, Siegfried, **La mécanisation au pouvoir. Contribution à l'histoire anonyme,** CCI/Centre Georges Pompidou, Paris, 1980.

*   Gould, Mary Earle, **Early American Wooden Ware & Other Kitchen Utensils,** Charles E. Tuttle Co., Rutland, Vt., 1971.

2   **Le Grand Robert de la langue française,** Paul Robert, Dictionnaires Le Robert, Paris, 1986.

3   Hardy, Jean-Pierre de David-Thierry Ruddel, **Les apprentis à Québec 1660-1815,** Presses universi-taires du Québec, Montréal, 1977.

2   **Harrap's New Standard French and English Dictionary,** Jean Edmond Mansion, ed., 4 vols., George G. Harrap & Co., London, 1981.

1   Harrod's Stores, **Victorian Shopping: Harrod's Catalogue, 1895,** facs. of 1895 ed., David & Charles, Newton Abbot, Eng., 1972.

1   Hudson's Bay Company, **The Autumn and Winter Catalogue 1910-1911 of the Hudson's Bay Company,** reprint of 1910 ed., Watson & Dwyer Publishing, Winnipeg, 1977.

*   Jenkins, Dorothy H., **A Fortune in the Junk Pile, a Guide to Valuable Antiques,** Crown Publishers, New York, 1964.

1   The J.H. Ashdown Hardware Company Limited, **Wholesale Hardware,** E.W. Rugg Co., (printer), Winnipeg, 1904.

2   **Larousse 3 volumes en couleurs, Dictionnaire encyclopédique,** Larousse, Paris, 1970.

1 , 2 , 3   Lecoq, Raymond, **Les objets de la vie domestique,** Berger-Levrault, Paris, 1979.

1 , 2   Leloir, Maurice, **Dictionnaire du Costume et de ses accessoires, des armes et des étoffes, des orig-ines à nos jours,** Grund, Paris, 1951.

3   Leroi-Gourhan, André, **Évolution et techniques** (vol. 1, **L'Homme et la matière,** vol. 2, **Milieu et techniques**), Albin Michel, Paris, 1943 and 1973.

3   Leroi-Gourhan, André, **Le geste et la parole** (vol. 1, **Techniques et langage,** vol. 2, **La mémoire et les rythmes**), Albin Michel, Paris, 1964-1965.

*   Lessard, Michel, and Huguette Marquis, **Encyclopédie des antiquités du Québec, Trois siècles de production artisanale,** Éditions de l'Homme, Montréal, 1971.

2 , 3   Lorrain, Léon, **Les étrangers dans la cité,** Presses du Mercure, Montréal, 1936.

2   M.A.D.L.C., **Dictionnaire militaire ou recueil alphabétique de tous les termes propres à la guerre,** Tome 1, 1st ed., revised, corrected and expanded by M.E., George Conrad Walther, Librairie du Roi, Dresde, 1751.

1   Marshall Field & Co., **Illustrated Catalogue, Holiday Goods, Druggists' Sundries, Stationery, Small Wares, Etc.,** Adams, Quiney, Franklin, Chicago, 1892.

2   **Military Dictionary, English-French, French-English,** J.C. Murchie, director, Edmond Cloutier, Printer to the King's Most Excellent Majesty, Ottawa, 1945.

*   Miller, Robert W., **Pictorial Guide to Early American Tools and Implements,** Wallace-Homestead Book Company, Des Moines, 1980.

1 , 2 , 3   Minhinnick, Jeanne, **At Home in Upper Canada,** Clarke, Irwin & Co., Toronto, 1970.

1 , 2   Ministère de la culture, **Objets civils domestiques, Principes d'analyse scientifique, Vocabulaire,** Imprimerie Nationale, Paris, 1984.

1   Montgomery Ward & Co., **Catalogue and Buyers' Guide, No 57, Spring and Summer 1895,** reprint of 1895 ed., Dover Publications, New York, 1969.

1   Norvell-Shapleigh Hardware Co., **Mail Order Catalogue,** St-Louis, C.1900.

1 , 2   **The Oxford-Duden Pictorial French-English Dictionary,** Clarendon Press, Oxford, 1984.

1 , 3   Patterson, Pat, and Frances Patterson, **Harvests Past, Domestic and Agricultural Hand Tools, and Rural Life in the Ottawa Valley 1860-1875,** The Boston Mills Press, Erin, Ont., 1989.

1 , 2   Pegler, Martin M., **The Dictionary of Interior Designs,** Fairchild Publications, New York, 1983.

2   **Le Petit Robert 1, Dictionnaire alphabétique et analogique de la langue française,** Paul Robert, Dictionnaires Le Robert, Paris, 1987.

*   Pinto, Edward H., **Treen or Small Woodware Through the Ages,** B.T. Batsford, London, 1949.

*   Poiré, Paul, **Nouveau dictionnaire des sciences et de leurs applications,** 2 Tomes, Supplément, Delagrave, Paris, 1924.

1   Russell and Erwin Manufacturing Compagny, **Illustrated Catalogue of American Hardware of the Russel and Erwin Manufacturing Company,** reprint 1865 ed., Association for Preservation Technology, U.S.A., 1980.

*   Savage, George, **Dictionary of 19th Century Antiques and Later Objects D'Art,** Nelson Foster & Scott, Don Mills, Ont., 1978.

1   Sears, Roebuck and Company, **1897 Sears Roebuck Catalogue,** Chelsea House Publishers, New York, 1976.

1 , 2   Seymour, John, **Arts et traditions de la maison,** France Loisirs, Paris, 1988.

1 , 2   Seymour, John, **Métiers oubliés,** Sté Nlle des Éditions du Chêne, Paris, 1985.

*   Stevens, Gerald, **In A Canadian Attic,** The Ryerson Press, Toronto, 1966.

1 , 2   **The Stoddart Visual Dictionary,** Jean-Claude Corbeil, ed.-in-chief, Stoddart Publishing, Toronto, 1986.

1   T. Eaton Co., **The 1901 Editions of the T. Eaton Co. Limited Catalogues for Spring and Summer, Fall and Winter,** cat. 46 and 47, facs. of 1901 ed., The Musson Book Co., Toronto, 1970.

1 , 2   Vermette, Luce, **La vie domestique aux Forges du Saint-Maurice,** History and Archeology No 58, Canadian Parks Service, Environment Canada, Ottawa, 1982.

1 , 2   **Webster's Third New International Dictionary of the English Language Unabridged,** G. & C. Merriam Company, Springfield, Mass., 1981.

1 , 2   Wheeler, Robert C., **A Toast to the Fur Trade, A Picture Essay on Its Material Culture,** Wheeler Productions, St.Paul, 1985.

*   Wilson, William Philip, **The Canadian Guidebook: Antique Collecting in Ontario,** Greey de Pencier Publications, Toronto, 1974.

1 , 2 , 3   Wintersgill, Donald, **The Book of English Antiques 1700-1830,** William Collins Sons & Co., London, 1975.

*   Wood, Violet, **Victoriana, A Collector's Guide,** G. Bell and Sons, London, 1960.

1   Woodward Stores, **The Shopping Guide of the West: Woodward's catalogue 1898-1953,** J.J. Douglas, Vancouver, 1977.

See also:

- The **Manuscript Reports and Research Bulletins** series published by the Canadian Parks Service.

- The **Studies in Archaeology, Architecture and History** series published by the Canadian Parks Service.

- The **Canadian Historic Sites: Occasional Papers in Archaeology and History** series published by the Canadian Parks Service.

- The **Cahiers du patrimoine** published by the Ministère des Affaires culturelles du Québec.

- The catalogues of large department stores such as Eaton's, Sears Roebuck and Hudson's Bay Company.

- Specialized catalogues and technical encyclopedias for early tools and 19th century North American specialized working machines.

01
STRUCTURES

1 , 2   Blumenson, John J. G., **Identifying American Architecture, A Pictorial Guide to Styles and Terms,** 1600-1945, AASLH, Nashville, 1979.

Dubé, Philippe, **Deux cents ans de villégiature dans Charlevoix,** Presses de l'université Laval, Québec, 1986.

1 , 2   Fleming, John, Hugh Honour, and Nikolaus Pevsner, **The Penguin Dictionary of Architecture,** 3rd ed., Penguin Books, 1980.

Habitation rurale au Québec, Jean-Claude Dupont, director, Hurtubise, HMH, Montréal, 1978.

1 , 2   Haggar, Reginald G., **A Dictionary of Art Terms,** Hawthorn Books, New York, 1962.

1 , 2   Humphreys, Barbara A., and Meredith Sykes, **The Buildings of Canada, a Guide to Pre-20th-Century Styles in Houses, Churches and Other Structures,** Parks Canada, Environment Canada, Ottawa, 1980.

1 , 2   Laframboise, Yves, **L'architecture traditionnelle au Québec. La maison aux XVIIe et XVIIIe siècles,** Éditions de l'Homme, Montréal, 1975.

2   Martin, Judy, **Longman Dictionary of Art, A Handbook of Terms, Techniques, Materials, Equipment and Processes,** Longman Group, Harlow, Essex, Eng., 1986.

*   Zevi, Bruno, **The Modern Language of Architecture,** Douglas S. McIntire, Vancouver, 1978.

A020: BUILDING

2   Adam-Villeneuve, Francine, and Cyrille Felteau, **Les moulins à l'eau de la Vallée du Saint-Laurent,** Éditions de l'Homme, Montréal, 1978.

1 , 2 , 3   Bergeron, Michel, and Paul-Aimé Lacroix, **Les dépendances agricoles à l'Île d'Orléans,** Coll. Dossiers, No 40, Ministère des Affaires culturelles, Direction du patrimoine, Québec, 1979.

1 , 2   **Book Making in Diderot's Encyclopédie: a facsimile reproduction of articles and plates,** facs. of 1751 ed., intro. by G.G. Barber, Gregg International Publishers, Westmead, Eng., 1973.

1 , 2 , 3   Carpentier, Paul, **La maison-bloc à Saint-Esprit, Habitation rurale à Québec,** Cahiers du Québec/Hurtubise, HMH, Montréal, 1978.

1 , 2 , 3   Dorion, Jacques, **Les écoles de rang au Québec,** Éditions de l'Homme, Montréal, 1979.

1 , 2 , 3   Gauthier, Raymonde, **Les manoirs du Québec,** Fides, Québec, 1976.

         Gauthier-Larouche, Georges, **Évolution de la maison traditionnelle dans la région de Québec,** PUL, Québec, 1974.

1 , 2 , 3   Hatton, E. M., **The Tent Book,** Houghton Mifflin Company, Boston, 1979.

*   King, Thomas B., **Glass in Canada,** The Boston Mills Press, Erin, Ont., 1987.

1 , 2 , 3   Léonidoff, Georges-Pierre, **Architecture traditionnelle de camps forestiers, Habitation rurale au Québec,** Cahiers Québec/Hurtubise, HMH, Montréal, 1978.

1 , 2 , 3   Lessard, Michel, and Huguette Marquis, **Encyclopédie de la maison québécoise,** Éditions de l'Homme, Montréal, 1972.

1 , 2 , 3   Noppen, Luc, **Les églises du Québec (1600-1850),** Fides, Québec, 1977.

1 , 2 , 3 , *   Noppen, Luc, Claude Paulette, and Michel Tremblay, **Québec: trois siècles d'architecture,** Libre Expression, Québec, 1979.

2 , 3 , *   Séguin, Robert-Lionel, **Les Granges du Québec,** Quinze, Montréal, 1976.

A040: BUILDING COMPONENT

1   Arthur, Eric, and Thomas Ritchie, **Iron, Cast and Wrought Iron in Canada from the Seventeenth Century to the Present,** University of Toronto Press, Toronto, 1982.

*	Barrows, Claire M., **Living Walls: how to appreciate and install wallpaper and wall coverings,** The Wallcoverings Council, New York, 1968.
3	Hartley, Dorothy, **Food in England,** Macdonald General Books, London, 1979.
1	Robert Marples & Son Tool Manufacturers, **Price List,** 4th ed., Hermitage Works, Sheffield, C.1904.

B040: FLOOR COVERING

1 , 2	Mathieu, Jocelyne, **Faire ces tapis à la mode de l'Île d'Orléans,** Basile, Montréal, 1980.
2	Robinson, George, **Carpets, Pitman's Common Commodities and Industries,** Sir Isaac Pitman & Sons, London, 1966.

B060: FURNITURE

*	**Ameublement terminologie,** Cahier No 113 du Centre technique du bois, 10 av. Saint-Mandré, Paris.
1 , 2	Barber, Edwin Atlee, Luke Vincent Lockwood and Hollis French, **The Ceramic, Furniture and Silver Collectors' Glossary,** Da Capo, New York, 1976.
1	Brunhammer, Yvonne, and Monique Fayet, **Meubles et ensembles, époque Louis XIII et Louis XIV,** Charles Massin, Paris, 1966.
*	Burgess, Fred. W., **Antique Furniture,** George Routledge & Sons, London, 1915.
	Davis, Kenneth and Thom Henvey, **Restoring Furniture,** Orbis Publishing, London, 1978.
*	Dobson, Henry, and Barbara Dobson, **The Early Furniture of Ontario & the Atlantic Provinces,** M. F. Feheley Publishers Co., Toronto, 1974.
1 , 2	**Encyclopedia of Antiques,** Octopus Books, London, 1976.
*	**L'Encyclopédie des styles d'hier et d'aujourd'hui,** Denoël, Paris, 1969.
*	Filbee, Marjorie, **Dictionary of Country Furniture,** Hearst Books, New York, 1977.
1 , 2 , 3	Gloag, John, **A Short Dictionary of Furniture: Containing 1764 Terms Used in Britain and America,** Studio Publications in association with T. Y. Cromwell, New York, 1955.
1	Janneau, Guillaume, **Meubles et sièges,** Les arts décoratifs, Flammarion, Paris, France, 1965.
1 , 3	Joy, Edward T., **The Country Life Book of English Furniture,** Country Life, London, 1966.
1	Lea, Zilla Rider, **The Ornamented Chair, Its Development in America (1700-1890),** Charles E. Tuttle Co., Rutland, Vt., 1962.
*	Legouix, Michèle, **Guide pratique des styles en ameublement,** Solar, Paris, 1980.
*	Lucie-Smith, Edward, **Furniture: A Concise History,** Oxford University Press, New York, 1979.
	Martin, Paul-Louis, **La berçante québécoise,** Boréal Express, Montréal, 1973.
1	Naeve, Milo M., **Identifying American Furniture, A Pictorial Guide to Styles and Terms Colonial To Contemporary,** 2nd ed., revised and expanded, AASLH, Nashville, 1989.
1 , 2	Palardy, Jean, **Les meubles anciens du Canada français,** Le Cercle du Livre de France, Montréal, 1963.

1 , 2   Shackleton, Philip, **The Furniture of Old Ontario,** Macmillan of Canada, Toronto, 1973.

Smith, Jean, and Elizabeth Smith, **Le grand livre des antiquités,** Éditions de l'Homme, Montréal, 1976.

1 , 2   Sparkes, Ivan G., **English Windsor Chairs,** Shire Album 70, Shire Publications, Aylesbury, Eng., 1980.

*   Stevens, Gerald, **The Canadian Collector, Glass-Pottery-Furniture-Firearms of the Nineteenth Century,** The Ryerson Press, Toronto, 1957.

1 , 2   Tardieu, Suzanne, **Le mobilier rural traditionnel français,** Aubier-Flammarion, Paris, 1976.

B080: HOUSEHOLD ACCESSORY

1 , 2   Newman, Harold, **An Illustrated Dictionary of Glass,** Thames & Hudson, London, 1977.

B100: LIGHTING DEVICE

1 , 2 , 3   Adams, W.H. Davenport, **Lighthouses and Lightships: A Descriptive and Historical Account of Their Mode of Construction and Organization,** T. Nelson and Sons, London 1871.

1 , 2   Darbee, Herbert C., **A Glossary of old lamps and lighting devices,** Technical Leaflet 30, AASLH, Nashville, 1965.

1 , 2   Hague, Douglas B., and Rosemary Christie, **Lighthouses: their architecture, history and archaeology,** Gomer Press, Llandysul, 1975.

1 , 2 , 3   Hayward, Arthur H., **Colonial Lighting,** 3rd enl. ed., Dover Publications, New York, 1962.

*   Hebard, Helen Brigham, **Early Lighting in New England, 1620-1861,** Charles E. Tuttle Co., Rutland, Vt., 1964.

*   McKearin, George S., and Helen McKearin, **American Glass,** Crown Publishers, New York, 1968.

*   O'Dea, W. T., **A Short History of Lighting,** Science Museum, London, 1958.

*   Russell, Loris S., **A Heritage of light: lamps and lighting in the Canadian home,** University of Toronto Press, Toronto, 1968.

1 , 2   Russell, Loris S., **Lighting the Pioneer Ontario Home,** R.O.M. Series #12, Toronto, 1966.

*   Spence, Hilda, and Kevin Spence, **A Guide to Early Canadian Glass,** Longmans Canada, Don Mills, Ont., 1966.

1 , 2 , 3   Stevens, Gerald, **Early Canadian Glass,** The Ryerson Press, Toronto, 1960.

1 , 2   Thwing, Leroy, **Flickering Flames, A History of Domestic Lighting through the Ages,** Charles E. Tuttle Co., Rutland, Vt., 1963.

1 , 2   Trudel, Jean, **Silver in New France,** National Gallery of Canada, Ottawa, 1974.

1 , 2   Witney, Dudley, **The Lighthouse,** McClelland and Stewart, Toronto, 1975.

1 , 2 , 3   Woodhead, E. I., C. Sullivan, and G. Gusset, **Lighting Devices in the National Reference Collection, Parks Canada,** National Historic Parks and Sites, Parks Canada, Environment Canada, Ottawa, 1984.

B140: TEMPERATURE CONTROL DEVICE

1   Arthur, Eric and Thomas Ritchie, **Iron, Cast and Wrought Iron in Canada from the Seventeenth Century to the Present,** University of Toronto Press, Toronto, 1982.

3   Hartley, Dorothy, **Food in England,** Macdonald General Books, London, 1979.

*   King, Thomas B., **Glass in Canada,** The Boston Mills Press, Erin, Ont., 1987.

1 , 2 , 3 Moussette, Marcel, **Le chauffage domestique au Canada des origines à l'industrialisation,** Presses de l'université Laval, Québec, 1983.

B160: WINDOW OR DOOR COVERING

1 , 2 , 3 Mathieu, Jocelyne, "**Les textiles dans l'intérieur domestique. Étude comparative Perche-Québec, XVIIe - XVIIIe siècles**", *Canadian Folklore,* Vol. 1-2, Folklore Studies Association of Canada, 1983, Québec.

03
PERSONAL ARTIFACTS

2 , 3   Audet, Bernard, **Le costume paysan dans la région de Québec au XVIIe siècle,** Leméac, Montréal, 1980.

1 , 3   Barbeau, Marius, **Assomption Sash,** Bulletin No 93, Anthropological Series No 24, facs. of 1937 ed., National Museums of Canada, Ottawa, 1954.

*   Barthorp, Michael, **The British Army on Campaign 1816-1853,** Men-At-Arms Series No 193, Osprey Publishing, London, 1987.

1 , 3   Boucher, François, **20,000 Years of Fashion, The History of Costume and Personal Adornment,** Harry N. Abrams, New York, 1967.

1 , 2 , 3 Boulton, James J., **Uniforms of the Canadian Mounted Police,** Turner-Warwick Publications, North Battleford, Sask., 1990.

1 , 2 , 3 Brasser, Ted J., **Bo'jou Neejee!: Profiles of Canadian Indian Art,** National Museum of Man, Ottawa, 1976.

*   Brinckerhoff, Sidney B., **Boots and Shoes of the Frontier Soldier 1865-1893,** Museum Monograph No 7, Arizona Historical Society, Tucson, 1976.

1   Charlebois, Mariette, **Dentelles liturgiques du Québec, 1865-1965,** musée Beaulne, Coaticook, Québec, 1985.

*   Collard, Eileen, **Early Clothing in Southern Ontario,** The Mississauga Press, Burlington, Ont., 1969.

2   **Courtaulds Vocabulary of Textile Terms,** 2nd ed., Stephen Austin and Sons, Hertford, Eng., 1972.

1 , 2 , 3 Cunnington, C. Willett, and Phillis Cunnington, **The History of Underclothes,** Faber and Faber, London, 1981.

1 , 2 , 3 Cunnington, C. Willett, Phillis Cunnington, and Charles Beard, **A Dictionary of English Costume, 900-1900,** Adam & Charles Black, London, 1960.

1 , 2   Dammann, Gordon, **A Pictorial Encyclopedia of Civil War Medical Instruments and Equipment,** Pictorial Histories Publishing Company, Missoula, Ont., 1983.

1 , 2 Dupré, Céline, **Vocabulaire de la chaussure: français-anglais,** Cahiers de l'Office de la langue française, Gouvernement du Québec, Québec, 1982.

1 , 2 Dupré, Céline, **Vocabulaire de l'habillement: français-anglais,** Cahiers de l'Office de la langue française, Gouvernement du Québec, Québec, 1984.

1 , 3 Fosten, Bryan, **Wellington's Infantry (1)** and (2), Men-At-Arms Series No 114-119, Osprey Publishing, London, 1981 and 1982.

3 Fosten D.S.V. and R.J. Marion, **The British Army 1914-18,** Men-At-Arms Series No 81, Osprey Publishing, London, 1978.

1 , 2 , 3 Hartman, Sheryl, **Indian Clothing of the Great Lakes: 1740-1840,** Eagle View Publishing Company, Odgen, Vt., 1991.

3 , * Hook, Jason, **The American Plains Indians,** Osprey Publishing, London, 1985.

***** Hook, Jason, **The Apaches,** Osprey Publishing, London, 1987.

1 , 2 Lee, Rev. Frederick George, **A Glossary of Liturgical and Ecclesiastical Terms,** Bernard Quaritch, London, 1877.

1 , 2 **Liturgische Geräte, Kreuse Und Reliquiare Der Christliche Kirchen, Objets lithurgiques, croix et reliquaires des églises chrétiennes,** Rieth, Rudulf und Renate, editors, Wissenschaftlich Kommission Documentationsstelle Tübingen, Strasbourg, 1972.

2 Mayer-Thurman, Crista C., **Raiment For The Lord's Service, A Thousand Years of Western Vestments,** The Art Institute of Chicago, Chicago, 1975.

2 Mayo, Janet, **A History of Ecclesiastical Dress,** B. T. Batsford, London, 1984.

1 , 2 , 3 **Les métiers du cuir,** Jean-Claude Dupont, and Jacques Mathieu, directors, Ethnologie de l'Amérique Française, Presses de l'université Laval, Québec, 1981.

1 Palmer, Thomas France, **Dictionary of Technical Textile Terms (Tri-Lingual), Vol. I, English-French-Spanish,** Hirschfeld Brothers, London, 1920.

***** Pocknee, Cyril E., **Liturgical Vesture, Its Origins and Development,** A. R. Mowbray & Co., London, 1960.

1 , 3 Prat, Jean H., **Fourrure et peltiers à travers les âges,** Tigre, Paris, 1952.

1 , 2 , 3 Ribeiro, Aileen, **Dress in Eighteenth-Century Europe 1715-1789,** Holmes & Meier Publishers, New York, 1985.

1 , 2 , 3 Ross, David, and René Chartrand, **Cataloguing Military Uniforms,** The New Brunswick Museum, Saint John, 1977.

1 , 2 , 3 Ross, David, and Robin May, **The Royal Canadian Mounted Police 1873-1987,** Men-At-Arms Series No 197, Osprey Publishing, London, 1988.

1 , 2 Roulin, Dom E., **Linges, insignes et vêtements liturgiques,** P. Lethielleux, Paris, 1930.

2 , 3 Séguin, Robert-Lionel, **Le costume civil en nouvelle-France,** National Museums of Canada, Ottawa, 1968.

***** Severin, Elizabeth, **The Interpreter's Companion or A Handbook of Clothing for Army Women,** Parks Canada, Ottawa, 1987.

1 , 2 , 3 **The Spirit Sings: A Catalogue of the Exhibition,** Glenbow Museum, McClelland and Stewart, Toronto, 1987.

1	**The Spirit Sings: Artistic Traditions of Canada's First Peoples,** Glenbow Museum, McClelland and Stewart, Toronto, 1987.
1 , 2	The Textile Institute, **Textile Terms and Definitions,** 7th ed., edited by C.A. Farnfield and C.J. Alvey, Manchester, Eng., 1975.
1 , 2	The Textile Institute, **Textile Terms and Definitions,** 8th ed., edited by S.R. Beech, C.A. Farnfield, P.A. Wharton and J.A. Wilkins, Manchester, Eng., 1986.
1 , 2	**Vocabulary of Basic Terms for Cataloguing Costume,** ICOM International Committee for the Museums and Collections of Costume, pp. 119-151, 1982.
1 , 2 , 3	Wilcox, R. Turner, **The Dictionary of Costume,** Charles Scribner's Sons, New York, 1969.
1 , 2 , 3	Wilcox, R. Turner, **The Mode in Footwear,** Charles Scribner's Sons, New York, 1948.
1 , 3	Wright, Merideth, **Put On Thy Beautiful Garments, Rural New England Clothing 1783-1800,** The Clothes Press, East Montpelier, Vt., 1990.

C080: CLOTHING, HEADWEAR

1 , 3	Dreher, Denise, **From the Neck Up, An Illustrated Guide to Hatmaking,** Madhatter Press, Minneapolis, 1981.

C120: CLOTHING, UNDERWEAR

1 , 2 , 3	Cunnington, C. Willett, and Phillis Cunnington, **The History of Underclothes,** Faber and Faber, London, 1981.
3	Ribeiro, Aileen, **Dress in Eighteenth-Century Europe 1715-1789,** Holmes & Meier Publishers, New York, 1985.

C160: PERSONAL GEAR

2	Corti, Egon Ceasar, **A History of Smoking,** Harrap, London, 1931.
1 , 2 , 3	Bennion, Elizabeth, **Antique Medical Instruments,** Sotheby Parke Bernet, London, 1979.
2,*	**Encyclopédie du tabac et des fumeurs,** Éditions Temps, Paris, 1975.
1	Kephart, Horace, **Camping & Woodcraft, A Handbook for Vacation Campers and for Travelers in the Wilderness,** 2 Vols., The Macmillan Company, New York, 1970.
1 , 2	Richie, C. France, **Cataloguing Procedures for Smoking Pipe Artifacts,** 1st ed., Artifact Cataloguing Guide, National Historic Parks and Sites, Parks Canada, Ottawa, 1979.

C180: TOILET ARTICLE

1 , 3	Bennion, Elizabeth, **Antique Medical Instruments,** Sotheby Parke Bernet, London, 1979.
1 , 2	Cox, James Stevens, **An Illustrated Dictionary of Hairdressing & Wigmaking,** Batsford Academic and Educational, London, 1984.
1 , 3	Doyle, Robert A., **Straight Razor Collecting, An Illustrated History and Price Guide,** Collector Books, Paducah, Ky., 1980.

1 , 2 , 3   Durbin, Gail, **Wig, Hairdressing and Shaving Bygones,** Shire Album 117, Shire Publications, Aylesbury, Eng., 1984.

04/05/06
TOOLS AND EQUIPMENT

1   Caverhill, Learmont & Co., **Wholesale Hardware, General Supplies, Tools & Equipment for Railroads-Shipyards-Steamships-Auto Transports-Public Utilities-Contractors-Industrial Plants,** Montréal, n.d.

1 , 2   The Diagram Group, **Handtools of Arts and Crafts, The Encyclopedia of the Fine, Decorative and Applied Arts,** Harrap, London, 1981.

1 , 2   Hodges, Henry, **Artifacts, An Introduction to Early Materials and Technology,** John Baker Publishers, London, 1964.

1 , 3   Hummel, Charles France, **With Hammer in Hand, The Dominy Craftsmen of East Hampton, New York,** The University Press of Virginia, Charlottesville, 1982.

1   Lee Valley Tools, **Garden Tools,** Canada, Summer 1990.

3   Lemieux, Germain, **La vie paysanne 1860-1900,** Prise de Parole/ FM, Sudbury, 1982.

3   Pomerleau, Jeanne, **Métiers ambulants d'autrefois,** Guérin, Montréal, 1990.

1 , 2   Rempel, John I., **Tools of the Woodworker: Hard planes,** Technical Leaflet 24, History News, Vol. 19, No. 12, AASLH, Nashville, October 1964.

1   Robert Marples & Son Tool Manufacturers, **Price List,** 4th ed., Hermitage Works, Sheffield, Eng., C.1904.

1   R. Timmins & Sons, **Tools For the trades and crafts, an eighteenth century pattern book,** K. Roberts Publishing, Fitzwilliam, N.H., 1976.

1 , 2 , 3   Salaman, R.A., **Dictionary of Tools Used in the Woodworking and Allied Trades, C.1700-1970,** Charles Scribner's Sons, New York, 1977.

1 , 2   Seymour, John, **The Forgotten Crafts,** Alfred A. Knopf, New York, 1986.

1 , 2   Seymour, John, **The Forgotten Household Crafts,** Alfred A. Knopf, New York, 1987.

1   Sloan, Eric, **A Museum of Early American Tools,** Ballantine Books, New York, 1964.

1 , 3   Velter, André and Marie-José Lamothe, **Le livre de l'outil,** Messidor, Paris, 1986.

D020: AGRICULTURAL T&E

3   Audet, Bernard, **"Avoir feu et lieu dans l'Île d'Orléans au XVIIe siècle",** Doctoral thesis, Université Laval, Québec, 1990.

1 , 2   Bridgen, Roy, **Agricultural Hand Tools,** Shire Album 100, Shire Publications, Aylesbury, Eng., 1983.

3   Government of Ontario, **The British Farmer's and Farm Labourer's Guide to Ontario, The Premier Province of the Dominion of Canada, 1880,** Crimming Atlas Reprints, Port Elgin, Ont., 1974.

1 , 2   Kline, John B., **A Tool Collectors' Guide, Tobacco Farming And Cigar Making Tools,** John B. Kline, n.p., 1975.

2 , 3   Létourneau, Firmin, **Histoire de l'agriculture (Canada français),** Imprimerie populaire, Montréal, 1953.

1 , 2   Partridge, Michael, **Farm Tools Through the Ages,** New York Graphic Society, Boston, 1973.

        Provencher, Jean, **Le patrimoine agricole et horticole au Québec,** Commission des biens culturels, Québec, 1984.

1 , 2 , 3   Séguin, Robert-Lionel, **L'Équipement aratoire et horticole du Québec ancien (XVIIe, XVIIIe et XIXe siècle),** Tomes I and II, Guérin, Montréal, 1989.

        Séguin, Robert-Lionel, **L'équipement de la ferme canadienne,** Ducharme, Montréal, 1959.

1 , 2   Tait, Lyal, **Tobacco In Canada,** T. H. Best Printing, n.p., 1968.

D040: ANIMAL HUSBANDRY T&E

1 , 2 , 3   Bérubé, André, François Duranleau, Thiery Rudell, and Serge St.Pierre, **Le forgeron de campagne: un inventaire d'outils,** History Division Paper No 12, Mercury Series, National Museum of Man, National Museums of Canada, Ottawa, 1975.

1 , 2   C.M. Moseman and Brother, **Mosemans' Illustrated Catalog of Horse Furnishing Goods,** reprint of 1893 ed., Dover Publications, New York, 1987.

1 , 2 , 3   Cyr, Lise, and Yvan Chouinard, **Le forgeron Émile Asselin,** Coll. Dossiers No 14, Ministère des Affaires culturelles, Direction générale du patrimoine, Québec, 1976.

1 , 2 , 3   Dupont, Jean-Claude, **L'artisan forgeron,** Collection Formart, Série Histoire des métiers d'art, La documentation québécoise, Ministère des Communications, Presses de l'université Laval, Québec, 1979.

        Frère Isidore, **L'élevage du cheval,** La Trappe, Oka, 1940.

1 , 2   Genest, Bernard, in collaboration with Françoise Dubé, **Arthur Tremblay, forgeron du village,** Série Arts et Métiers, Ministère des Affaires culturelles, Québec, 1978.

1 , 2 , 3   Hardy, Jean-Pierre, **Le forgeron et le ferblantier,** Collection Histoire Populaire du Québec, Boréal Express, Montréal, 1978.

1 , 2 , 3   Lemieux, Germain, **La vie paysanne 1860-1900,** Prise de Paroles/FM, Sudbury, 1982.

1 , 2   Munsey, Cecil, **The Illustrated Guide to Collecting Bottles,** Hawthorn Books, New York, 1970.

1 , 2 , 3   Séguin, Robert-Lionel, **L'équipement de la ferme canadienne,** Ducharme, Montréal, 1959.

1 , 2 , 3   Séguin, Robert-Lionel, **L'équipement aratoire et horticole du Québec ancien (XVIIe, XVIIIe and XIXe siècle),** Tomes I and II, Guérin, Montréal, 1989.

2 , 3   Séguin, Robert-Lionel, **La civilisation traditionnelle de l'«habitant» aux XVIIe et XVIIIe siècles,** Fides, Montréal, 1967.

1 , 2 , 3   Smith, K.R. Bradley, **Blacksmiths' and Farriers' Tools at Shelburne Museum, - A History of their Development from Forge to Factory,** Museum Pamphlet Series, No 7, The Shelburne Museum, Shelburne, Vt., 1991.

1 , 2   Watson, Aldren A., **The Village Blacksmith,** T. Y. Crowell Co., New York, 1968.

1 , 2   Wylie, William N. T., **The Blacksmith In Upper Canada, 1784-1850: A Study of Technology, Culture and Power,** Langdale Press, Gananoque, Ont., 1990.

D060: FISHING & TRAPPING T&E

3 ~~Bergeron, Yves et Pierre Lessard, **Gaspé: A Sea Ledger,** musée de Gaspé, Gaspé, 1987.~~

1 , 2 Blair, Carvel Hall and Willite Dyer Ansel, **A Guide to Fishing Boats and Their Gear,** Cornell Maritime Press, Cambridge, 1968.

3 Brown, Mike, **The Great Lobster Chase: The Real Story of Maine Lobsters and the Men Who Catch Them,** International Marine Publishing Company, Camden, Maine, 1985.

Chiasson, Père Anselme, **Les Îles-de-la-Madeleine, vie matérielle et sociale,** Leméac, Montréal, 1981.

1 , 2 Duhamel Du Monceau, Henri Louis, **Traité général des pesches, et histoire des poissons qu'elles fournissent, tant pour la subsistance des hommes, que pour plusieurs autres usages qui ont rapport aux arts et au commerce,** Sayant & Lyon, Dessaint, Paris, 1769-1782.

2,* Dupont, Jean-Claude, **Contribution à l'ethnographie des côtes de Terre-Neuve,** Centre d'études nordiques, Presses de l'université Laval, Québec, 1968.

1 , 2 , 3 Dupont, Jean-Claude, **Histoire populaire d'Acadie,** Leméac, Montréal, 1979.

Hubert, Paul, **Les Îles-de-la-Madeleine,** Imprimerie générale, Rimouski, 1926.

1 , 2 , 3 Jenson, L. B., **Fishermen of Nova Scotia,** Petheric Press, Halifax, 1980.

2 , 3 Lafleur, Normand, **La vie traditionnelle du coureur de bois aux XIXe et XXe siècles,** Leméac, Montréal, 1973.

2 , 3 Larocque, Paul, **Pêche et coopération au Québec,** Éditions du Jour, Montréal, 1978.

2 , 3 Martin, Paul-Louis, **Histoire de la chasse au Québec,** Boréal Express, Montréal, 1980.

1 , 2 , 3 McCullough, A.B., **The Commercial Fishery of the Canadian Great Lakes,** Studies in Archaeology, Architecture, and History, National Historic Parks and Sites, Canadian Parks Service, Environment Canada, Ottawa, 1985.

1 , 2 , 3 Moussette, Marcel, **La Pêche sur le Saint-Laurent, Répertoire des méthodes et des engins de capture,** Boréal Express, Montréal, 1979.

1 , 2 Nova Scotia Department of Fisheries, **Sea, Salt & Sweat, A Story of Nova Scotia and the Vast Atlantic Fisheries,** Nova Scotia Communications and Information Centre, Halifax, 1977.

1 , 2 , 3 Provencher, Paul, **Guide du trappeur,** Éditions de l'Homme, Montréal, 1973.

2 , 3 Saint-Pierre, Serge, **Les méthodes de chasse en Nouvelle-France aux XVIIe et XVIIIe siècles, dans Armes, chasse et trappage,** J.-C. Dupont, and J. Mathieu, directors, CÉLAT, Québec, 1987.

D100: FOOD PROCESSING T&E

1 , 2 Barber, Edwin Atlee, Luke Vincent Lockwood, and Hollis French, **The Ceramic, Furniture and Silver Collectors' Glossary,** Da Capo, New York, 1976.

3 Blanchette, Jean-François, **L'importance des artefacts dans l'étude des modes d'alimentation en Nouvelle-France entre 1720-1760,** History and Archeology No 52, Parks Canada, Ottawa, 1981.

Boucher, Francis and Yves Lacasse, **La fabrication traditionnelle du beurre,** musée Laurier, Arthabaska, Québec, 1981.

*   Brown, John Hull, **Early American Beverages,** Charles E. Tuttle Co., Rutland, Vt., 1966.

1   Burke, James H., **The Warner collector's guide to American sterling silver and silver-plate Hollowware,** Warner Books, New York, 1982.

1 , 2   Duhamel Du Monceau, Henri Louis, **Traité général des pesches, et histoire des poissons qu'elles fournissent, tant pour la subsistance des hommes, que pour plusieurs autres usages qui ont rapport aux arts et au commerce,** Sayant & Lyon, Dessaint, Paris, 1769-1782.

2 , 3   Dupont, Jean-Claude, **Le fromage de l'Île d'Orléans,** Collection Traditions du geste et de la parole, III, Leméac, Montréal, 1977.

2 , 3   Dupont, Jean-Claude, **Le pain d'habitant,** Collection Traditions du geste et de la parole, I, Leméac, Montréal, 1974.

2 , 3   Dupont, Jean-Claude, **Le sucre du pays,** Collection Traditions du geste et de la parole, II, Leméac, Montréal, 1975.

1 , 2   Fearn, Jacqueline, **Domestic Bygones,** Shire Album 20, Shire Publications, Aylesbury, Eng., 1977.

1 , 2 , 3   Franklin, Linda Campbell, **From hearth to cookstove, America in the kitchen: an American domestic history of gadgets and utensils made or used in America from 1700 to 1930: a guide for collectors,** 2nd ed., House of Collectibles, Orlando, Fla., 1978.

3   Godden, Geoffrey A., **An Illustrated Encyclopeadia of British Pottery and Porcelain,** Herbert Jenkins, London, 1968.

1 , 3   Gould, Mary Earle, **Early American Wooden Ware & Other Kitchen Utensils,** Charles E. Tuttle Co., Rutland, Vt., 1971.

3   Hartley, Dorothy, **Food in England,** Macdonald General Books, London, 1979.

1 , 2   Ingram, Arthur, **Dairying Bygones,** Shire Album 29, Shire Publications, Aylesbury, Eng., 1987.

*   Lafrance, Marc, and Yvon Desloges, **Goûter à l'histoire. Les origines de la gastronomie québécoise,** Éditions de la Chenelière, Montréal, 1989.

1 , 2   Mondock, Judi, and Lorin Buckner, **The Canning Corner, An encyclopedia of canning utensils including photographs, prices and patents...,** Privately published by Judi Mondock, Philadelphia, and Lorin Buckner, Grand Haven, Mich., 1974.

1 , 2   Munsey, Cecil, **The Illustrated Guide to Collecting Bottles,** Hawthorn Books, New York, 1970.

1 , 2   Newman, Harold, **An Illustrated Dictionary of Silverware,** Thames and Hudson, London, 1987.

*   Pinto, Edward H., **Treen or Small Woodware Through the Ages,** B. T. Batsford, London, 1949.

3   Prévost, Robert, Suzanna Gagné, and Michel Phaneuf, **L'histoire de l'alcool au Québec,** Stanké/Société des alcools du Québec, Montréal, 1986.

3   Rousseau, François, **L'Oeuvre de chère en Nouvelle-France,** Presses de l'université Laval, Québec, 1983.

*   Séguin, Robert-Lionel, **Le menu quotidien en Nouvelle-France,** Liberté, 10, 7, January and February 1969.

1 , 3   Séguin, Robert-Lionel, **Les moules du Québec,** Bulletin No 188, History Bulletin Series No 1, National Museums of Canada, Ottawa, 1963.

*   Stevens, G. France, **Canadian Glass C.1825-1925,** Ryerson Press, Toronto, 1967.

*   Unitt, Doris, and Peter Unitt, **Treasury of Canadian Glass,** 2nd ed., Clock House, Peterborough, Ont., 1969.

D120: FOOD SERVICE T&E

1 , 2   Barber, Edwin Atlee, Luke Vincent Lockwood, and Hollis French, **The Ceramic, Furniture and Silver Collectors' Glossary,** Da Capo, New York, 1976.

1 , 2 , 3   Bennion, Elizabeth, **Antique Medical Instruments,** Sotheby Parke Bernet, London, 1979.

*   Bly, John, **Discovering Hall Marks on English Silver,** Shire Album 38, Shire Publications, Aylesbury, Eng., 1979.

*   Brown, John Hull, **Early American Beverages,** Charles E. Tuttle Co., Rutland, Vt., 1966.

1   Burke, James H., **The Warner collector's guide to American sterling silver and silver-plate Hollowware,** Warner Books, New York, 1982.

2 , 3   Collard, Elizabeth, **Nineteenth-Century Pottery and Porcelain in Canada,** 2nd ed., McGill-Queen's University Press, Kingston, 1984.

1 , 2   **A Gather of Glass, Glass Through the Ages in the Royal Ontario Museum,** C. Peter Kaellgren, ed., R.O.M., Toronto, 1977.

3   Godden, Geoffrey A., **An Illustrated Encyclopeadia of British Pottery and Porcelain,** Herbert Jenkins, London, 1968.

1 , 2   Jones, Olive, and Catherine Sullivan, **The Parks Canada Glass Glossary for the Description of Containers, Tableware, Flat Glass and Closures,** Parks Canada, Environment Canada, Ottawa, 1985.

1 , 2   King, Thomas B., **Glass in Canada,** The Boston Mills Press, Erin, Ont., 1987.

1 , 2 , 3   McKearin, George S., and Helen McKearin, **American Glass,** Crown Publishers, New York, 1968.

1 , 2   Newman, Harold, **An Illustrated Dictionary of Glass,** Thames and Hudson, London, 1977.

1 , 2   Newman, Harold, **An Illustrated Dictionary of Silverware,** Thames and Hudson, London, 1987.

1 , 2   Revi, Albert Christian, **American Pressed Glass and Figure Bottles,** Thomas Nelson & Sons, Nashville, 1964.

1   Rottenburg, Barbara Lang, and Judith Tomlin, **Glass Manufacturing in Canada: A Survey of Pressed Glass Patterns,** History Division No 33, Mercury Series, National Museum of Man, National Museums of Canada, Ottawa, 1982.

2 , 3   Séguin, Robert-Lionel, **Les ustensiles en Nouvelle-France,** Leméac, Montréal, 1971.

1   Spence, Hilda and Kevin Spence, **A Guide to Early Canadian Glass,** Longmans Canada, Don Mills, Ont., 1966.

*   Stevens, Gerald, **The Canadian Collector, Glass-Pottery-Furniture-Firearms of the Nineteenth Century,** The Ryerson Press, Toronto, 1957.

*   Stenvens, Gerald, **Early Canadian Glass,** The Ryerson Press, Toronto, 1960.

*   Stevens, Gerald, **Early Ontario Glass,** R.O.M./University of Toronto, 1965.

1   Trudel, Jean, **Silver in New France,** National Gallery of Canada, Otttawa, 1974.

*   Unitt, Doris, and Peter Unitt, **Treasury of Canadian Glass,** 2nd ed., Clock House, Peterborough, Ont., 1969.

*   Zerwick, Chloe, **A Short History of Glass,** The Corning Museum of Glass, Corning, New York, 1980.

D140: FORESTRY T&E

1 , 2 , 3   Bérubé, André, François Duranleau, Thiery Ruddell, et Serge St-Pierre, **Le forgeron de campagne: un inventaire d'outils,** History Division Paper No 12, Mercury Series, National Museum of Man, National Museums of Canada, Ottawa, 1975.

2   Des Chênes, Jude, **Vocabulaire de l'acériculture, Terminologie technique et industrielle, Vocabulaire français-anglais,** Cahiers de l'Office de la langue française, Publications du Québec, Québec, 1988.

1 , 2 , 3   **Exercices des métiers du bois,** Jean-Claude Dupont, and Jacques Mathieu, directors, Cahiers du CÉLAT, No 4, Québec, February 1986.

1 , 2 , 3   Fortier, Luc, and Maurice Vallée *et al.,* **Métiers du bois et outils anciens au centre du Québec (1815-1925),** Les Cahiers de la Société historique de Drummondville, La Société historique du centre du Québec, Drummondville, Qué., 1980.

1 , 2   Jones, Olive R., **Cylindrical English and Beer Bottles 1735-1850,** Studies in Archaeology, Architecture and History, Canadian Parks Service, Environment Canada, Ottawa, 1986.

2 , 3   Lafleur, Normand, **La drave en Mauricie,** Bien Public, Trois-Rivières, 1973.

2 , 3   Lafleur, Normand, **La vie traditionnelle du coureur de bois aux XIXe et XXe siècles,** Leméac, Montréal, 1973.

D160: GLASS, PLASTICS, CLAYWORKING T&E

1 , 2 , 3   **Exercices des métiers de la pierre et de l'argile,** Jean-Claude Dupont, director, in collaboration with Christine Godin, Cahiers du CÉLAT, No 9, Québec, March 1988.

1 , 2   Jones, Olive, and Catherine Sullivan, **The Parks Canada Glass Glossary for the Description of Containers, Tableware, Flat Glass and Closures,** Parks Canada, Environment Canada, Ottawa, 1985.

*   Kendrick, Grace, **The Antique Bottle Collector, Including Latest Price Guide,** Pyramid, New York, 1976.

1   Ketchum, William C., Jr., **A Treasury of American Bottles,** Rutledge Books, A & W Visual Library, New York, 1975.

*   King, Thomas B., **Glass in Canada,** The Boston Mills Press, Erin, Ont., 1987.

1 , 2 , 3   Kulasiewicz, Frank, **Glassblowing,** Watson-Guptill Publications, New York, 1974.

1 , 3   Littleton, Harvey K., **Glassblowing, A Search for Form,** Van Nostrand Reinhold Company, New York, 1971.

1 , 2 , 3   McKearin, George S., and Helen McKearin, **American Glass,** Crown Publishers, New York, 1968.

1, 2   Munsey, Cecil, **The Illustrated Guide to Collecting Bottles,** Hawthorn Books, New York, 1970.

1, 3   Séguin, Robert-Lionel, **Les moules du Québec,** Bulletin No 188, History Bulletin Series No 1, National Museums of Canada, Ottawa, 1963.

*   Stevens, Gerald, **Early Canadian Glass,** The Ryerson Press, Toronto, 1960.

*   Stevens, Gerald, **Early Ontario Glass,** R.O.M. Series No 2, R.O.M./University of Toronto, Toronto, 1965.

1, 2, 3   Wilkinson, R., **The Hallmarks of Antique Glass,** Richard Madley, London, 1968.

*   Zerwick, Chloe, **A Short History of Glass,** The Corning Museum of Glass, Corning, New York, 1980.

D180: LEATHER, HORN, SHELLWORKING T&E

1, 2, 3   Chouinard, Yvan, **Disciple de Saint-Crépin, René Simard, artisan-cordonnier,** Ministère des Affaires culturelles, Québec, 1977.

1, 2, 3   Labelle, Ronald, **Tanneurs et tanneries du Bas-Saint-Laurent,** National Museums of Canada, Ottawa, 1979.

1, 2, 3   **Les métiers du cuir,** Jean-Claude Dupont, and Jacques Mathieu, directors, Ethnologie de l'Amérique Française, Presses de l'université Laval, Québec, 1981.

1, 2, 3   Prat, Jean H., **Fourrure et pelletiers à travers les âges,** Tigre, Paris, 1952.

1, 2   **Saddlery and Harness-Making with Numerous Engravings and Diagrams,** J.A. Allen and Company, London, 1962.

1, 2, 3   Salaman, R.A., **Dictionary of leather-working tools, C.1700-1950 and the tools of allied trades,** MacMillan Publishing Company, New York, 1986.

1, 2, 3   Simard, Hélène, **Trois générations de cordonniers à Saint-Jean-Port-Joli,** National Museums of Canada, Ottawa, 1976.

D200: MASONRY & STONEWORKING T&E

2, 3   Desruisseaux, Jacques, **L'industrie de la pierre à Saint-Marc-des-Carrières,** *mémoire de licence* presented to the Department of Geography, Université Laval, 1968.

1, 2   **Exercises des métiers de la pierre et de l'argile,** Jean-Claude Dupont, director, in collaboration with Christine Godin, Cahiers du CÉLAT, No 9, Québec, March 1988.

1, 2   Hammond, Martin, **Bricks and Brickmaking,** Shire Album 75, Shire Publications, Aylesbury, Eng., 1981.

1, 2, 3   Gaumond, Michel, and Paul-Martin, **Les maîtres potiers du bourg Saint-Denis,** Ministère des Affaires culturelles, Québec, 1978.

2, 3   Godin, Christine, **"L'exercice du métier de potier par les Dion de l'Ancienne-Lorette: de l'artisanat à la manufacture 1850-1915",** MA thesis, Université Laval, Québec, 1981.

2, 3   Labelle, Ronald, **"L'ethnohistoire du métier de tailleur de pierre à Saint-Marc-des-Carrières, comté de Portneuf",** MA thesis, Université Laval, Québec, 1980.

2, 3   Laframboise, Yves, **"Technologie traditionnelle de la taille de la pierre à Québec aux XVIIIe et XIXe siècles",** MA thesis, Université Laval, Québec, 1979.

*   Langlois, Jacques, **Répertoire des artisans potiers québécois, 1655-1916,** Coll. Dossiers No 37, Ministère des Affaires culturelles, Québec, 1978.

1 , 2   McKee, Harley J., **Introduction to Early American Masonry Stone, Brick, Mortar and Plaster,** National Trust for Historic Preservation, Washington, 1973.

D220: METALWORKING T&E

1   Arthur, Eric, and Thomas Ritchie, **Iron, Cast and Wrought Iron in Canada from the Seventeenth Century to the Present,** University of Toronto Press, Toronto, 1982.

1 , 2   Bailey, Jocelyn, **The Village Blacksmith,** Shire Album 24, Shire Publications, Aylesbury, Eng., 1987.

1 , 2 , 3   Bérubé, André, François Duranleau, Thiery Ruddell, and Serge St-Pierre, **Le forgeron de campagne: un inventaire d'outils,** History Division Paper No 12, Mercury Series, National Museum of Man, National Museums of Canada, Ottawa, 1975.

*   Clarke, Mary Stetson, **Pioneer Iron Works,** Chilton Book Company, Philadelphia, 1968.

1   Couture, Georges, Léon Lesage, and Hector Poiré, **Initiation à la fonderie,** Ministère du Bien-Être Social et de la Jeunesse, Office des cours par correspondance, Montréal, n.d.

1 , 2 , 3   Cyr, Lise, and Yvan Chouinard, **Le forgeron Émile Asselin,** Coll. Dossiers No 14, Ministère des Affaires culturelles, Québec, 1976.

1 , 2 , 3   Dupont, Jean-Claude, **L'artisan forgeron,** Collection Formart, Série Histoire des métiers d'art, La documentation québécoise, Ministère des Communications, Presses de l'université Laval, Québec, 1979.

1 , 2 , 3   Fortier, Luc, and Maurice Vallée *et al.,* **Métiers du bois et outils anciens au centre du Québec (1815-1925),** Les Cahiers de la Société historique de Drummondville, La Société historique du centre du Québec, Drummondville, Qué., 1980.

1 , 2 , 3   Genest, Bernard, in collaboration with Françoise Dubé, **Arthur Tremblay, forgeron de village,** Série Arts et Métiers, Ministère des Affaires culturelles, Québec, 1978.

1 , 3   Hardy, Jean-Pierre, **Le forgeron et le ferblantier,** Collection Histoire Populaire du Québec, Boréal Express, Montréal, 1978.

1 , 2 , 3   Hardy, Jean-Pierre, **Un ferblantier de campagne (1875-1950),** National Museums of Canada, Ottawa, 1975.

1 , 3   Hasluck, Paul N., **The Pattern Maker's Handybook, A practical manual on patterns for founders embracing information on the tools, materials and appliances employed in their construction,** The Musson Book Co., Toronto, 1887.

*   Miller, Robert W., **Pictorial Guide to Early American Tools and Implements,** Wallace-Homestead Book Company, Des Moines, 1980.

*   Overman, Fred., **The Moulder's And Founder's Pocket Guide: A Treatise on...,** A. Hart, Late Carey & Hart, Philadelphia, 1853.

1 , 3   **Practical Blacksmithing, A Collection of Articles...,** reprint of 1889,1890 and 1891 eds., M.T. Richardson, ed., Weathervane Books, New York, 1978.

1 , 2 , 3   Smith, K.R. Bradley, **Blacksmiths' and Farriers' Tools at Shelburne Museum, - A History of their Development from Forge to Factory,** Museum Pamphlet Series, No 7, The Shelburne Museum, Shelburne, Vt., 1991.

1   Trudel, Jean, **Silver in New France,** National Gallery of Canada, Ottawa, 1974.

3   Unglik, Henry, **Cast Irons from Les Forges du Saint-Maurice, Québec: A Metallurgical Study,** Studies in Archaeology, Architecture and History, National Historic Parks and Sites, Parks Canada, Environment Canada, Ottawa, 1990.

1 , 2   Watson, Aldren A., **The Village Blacksmith,** T. Y. Crowell Co., New York, 1968.

1 , 2 , 3   Wylie, William N. T., **The Blacksmith in Upper Canada, 1784-1850: A Study of Technology, Culture and Power,** Langdale Press, Gananoque, Ont., 1990.

D240: MINING & MINERAL HARVESTING T&E

1 , 2 , 3   **Exercices des métiers de la pierre et de l'argile,** Jean-Claude Dupont, director, in collaboration with Christine Godin, Cahiers du CÉLAT, No 9, Québec, March 1988.

D260: PAINTING T&E

2   **Dictionary of Terms used in the Paper, Printing and Graphics Arts Industries,** Howard Smith Division, Domtar Pulp & Paper, n.p., n.d.

1 , 2   **A Graphic Arts Production Handbook,** Pocket Pal, 12th ed., International Paper Co., New York, 1979.

1 , 2   Mayer, Ralph, **A Dictionary of Art Terms and Techniques,** T. Y. Crowell Co., New York, 1969.

1 , 2 , 3   Porter, John R., **L'Art de la dorure Au Québec du XVIIe siècle à nos jours,** Galarneau, Québec, 1975.

D280: PAPERMAKING T&E

1 , 2   **Book Making in Diderot's Encyclopédie: a facsimile reproduction of articles and plates,** facs. of 1751 ed., intro. by G.G. Barber, Gregg International Publishers, Westmead, Eng., 1973.

1 , 2 , 3   Charland, Jean-Pierre, "**Les pâtes et papiers au Québec, 1880-1980: Technologies, travail et travailleurs,**" Documents de recherche No 23, Institut québécois de recherche sur la culture, 1990.

2   **Dictionary of Terms Used in the Paper, Printing, and Graphic Arts Industries,** Howard Smith Division, Domtar Pulp & Paper, n.p. n.d.

1 , 2   Glaister, Geoffrey Ashal, **Glossary of the book: terms used in paper-making, printing, bookbinding and publishing with notes on illuminated manuscripts, bibliophiles, private presses and printing societies,** George Allen and Unwin, London, 1960.

2 , 3   **A Graphic Arts Production Handbook,** Pocket Pal, 12th ed., International Paper Co., New York, 1979.

3   Simard, Cyril, **Les papiers Saint-Gilles, Héritage de Félix-Antoine Savard,** Presses de l'université Laval, Québec, 1988.

D300: TEXTILEWORKING T&E

*   Atwater, Mary Meigs, **The Shuttle-Craft Book of American Hand-Weaving,** The MacMillan Company, New York, 1928.

1 , 2   Audet, Bernard, **Le costume paysan dans la région de Québec au XVIIe siècle,** Leméac, Montréal, 1980.

1 , 2   Bays, Carter, **"Collecting Early Hand-Operated Sewing Machines",** *The Antique Trader Weekly,* 20 Jan. 1982, Dubuque, Iowa.

    Bériau, O.-A., **La teinturerie domestique,** Leméac, Montréal, 1980.

1 , 2   Brent, Martha Eckmann, **"A Stitch In Time: Sewing Machine Industry of Ontario, 1860-1897",** *Material History Bulletin* No 10, Spring 1980, Ottawa.

1 , 2   Burnham, Dorothy K., **Warp and Weft, A Textile Terminology,** R.O.M., Toronto, Ont., 1980.

1 , 3   Burnham, Dorothy K., **L'art des étoffes. Le filage et le tissage traditionnels au Canada,** National Museums of Canada, Ottawa, 1981.

3   Burnham, Harold, and Dorothy K., **Keep me Warm one Night. Early Handweaving in Eastern Canada,** University of Toronto Press, Toronto, 1972.

3   Buxton-Keenlyside, Judith, **Selected Canadian Spinning Wheels In Perspective: An Analytical Approach,** History Division Paper No 30, Mercury Series, National Museum of Man, National Museums of Canada, Ottawa, 1981.

1 , 2 , 3   Carufel, Hélène de, **Le Lin,** Leméac, Montréal, 1980.

1 , 2 , 3   Chiasson, Père Anselme, **L'histoire des tapis "hookés" de Chéticamp et de leurs artisans,** Éditions de Lescarbot, Yarmouth, N.S., 1985.

*   Corbman, Dr. Bernard P., **Textiles: Fiber to Fabric,** 5th ed., McGraw-Hill Ryerson, Toronto, 1979.

    Courtaulds Vocabulary of Textile Terms, 2nd ed., Stephen Austin and Sons, Hertford, Eng., 1964.

*   Dan River, **A Dictionary of Textile Terms,** 10th ed., Dan River Mills Incorporated, Danville, Va., 1967.

1 , 2 , 3   Dreher, Denise, **From The Neck Up, An Illustrated Guide to Hatmaking,** Madhatter Press, Minneapolis, 1981.

1 , 2 , 3   Fortier, Luc, and Maurice Vallée *et al.,* **Métiers du bois et outils anciens au centre du Québec (1815-1925),** Les Cahiers de la Société historique de Drummondville, La Société historique du centre du Québec, Drummondville, Qué., 1980.

1 , 3   Frost, S. Annie, **The Ladies' Guide to Needle Work, Embroidery Etc., Being A Complete Guide To All Kinds Of Ladies' Fancy Work,** Adams & Bishop, New York, 1877.

1 , 3   Groves, Sylvia, **The History of Needlework Tools And Accessories,** Country Life Books, David and Charles, Newton, Abbot, Eng., 1973.

1 , 2   Houart, Victor, **Sewing Accessories: An Illustrated History,** Souvenir Press, London, 1984.

1 , 2   Johnson, Eleanor, **Needlework Tools, A guide to collecting,** Shire Album 38, Shire Publications, Aylesbury, Eng., 1986.

1 , 2 , 3   Mathieu, Jocelyne, **"Les textiles dans l'intérieur domestique. Étude comparative Perche-Québec, XVIIe-XVIIIe siècles",** *Canadian Folklore,* Vol. 1-2, Folklore Studies Association of Canada, 1983, Québec.

1 , 2   McClelland, Mary Elizabeth, **Felt, Silk & Straw Handmade Hats, Tools And Processes,** Tools of the Nation Maker, Vol. III, The Bucks County Historical Society, Doylestown, Pa., 1977.

2 , 3   Musée du Québec, **La fabrication artisanale des tissus, appareils et techniques,** Ministère des Affaires culturelles, Québec, 1974.

* Palmer, Thomas France, **Dictionary of Technical Textile Terms (Tri-Lingual), Vol. I., English-French-Spanish,** Hirschfeld Brothers, London, 1920.

1 , 2 , 3 Prat, Jean H., **Fourrure et Pelletiers à travers les âges,** Tigre, Paris, 1952.

1 , 2 Russell, Loris S., "**Early Canadian Sewing Machines**", *Canadian Collector,* Canadian Antiques and Fine Arts Society, September/October 1976, Toronto.

1 , 2 Salaman, R.A., **Dictionary of leather-working tools, C.1700-1950 and the tools of allied trades,** Macmillan Publishing Company, New York, 1986.

1 , 2 Sanctuary, Anthony, **Rope, Twine And Net Making,** Shire Album 51, Shire Publications, Aylesbury, Eng., 1980.

2 Simard, Cyril, **Artisanat québécois, Tome 1: les bois et les textiles,** Éditions de l'Homme, Montréal, 1975.

The Textile Institute, **Textile Terms and Definitions,** 7th ed., Edited by C.A. Farnfield, and P.J. Alvey, Manchester, Eng., 1975.

* The Textile Institute, **Textile Terms and Definitions,** 8th ed., Edited by S.R. Beech, C.A. Farnfield, P. A. Wharton, and J.A. Wilkins, Manchester, Eng., 1986.

D320: WOODWORKING T&E

1 Alex. Mathieson & Sons Saracen Tools Works, **Illustrated price list of wood working tools manufactured by Alex. Mathieson & Sons, Ltd., of Glasgow, (Scotland),** reprint of 1899 ed., K. Roberts Publishing Co., Hartford, Conn. 1979.

1 , 2 , 3 Baines, Anthony, **Woodwind Instruments and their history,** Faber and Faber, London, 1967.

* Bernier, Jacques, **Les intérieurs domestiques des menuisiers et charpentiers de la région de Québec, 1810-1819,** History Division Paper No 23, Mercury Series, National Museum of Man, National Museums of Canada, Ottawa, 1977.

* Bernier, Jacques, **Quelques boutiques de menuisiers et charpentiers au tournant du XIXe siècle,** History Division Paper No 17, Mercury Series, National Museum of Man, National Museums of Canada, Ottawa, 1976.

* Brisson, Réal, **La charpenterie navale à Québec sous le régime français,** Institut québécois de recherche sur la culture, Québec, 1983.

1 , 2 **Catalogue of Coopers' Tools Including Turpentine Tools Manufactured by The L. & I. J. White Co. Edge Tools And Machine Knives,** L.J. White Co., Buffalo, 1912.

1 , 2 , 3 **Exercises des métiers du bois,** Jean-Claude Dupont, and Jacques Mathieu, directors, Cahiers du CÉLAT, No 4, Québec, February 1986.

1 , 2 , 3 Fortier, Luc, and Maurice Vallée, *et al.,* **Métiers du bois et outils anciens au centre du Québec (1815-1925),** Les Cahiers de la Société historique de Drummondville, La Société historique du centre du Québec, Drummondville, Qué., 1980.

1 , 2 , 3 Genest, Bernard, in collaboration with Françoise Dubé, **Arthur Tremblay, forgeron de village,** Série Arts et Métiers, Ministère des Affaires culturelles, Québec, 1978

1 , 3 Hasluck, Paul N., **The Pattern Maker's Handybook, A practical manual on patterns for founders embracing information on the tools, materials and appliances employed in their construction,** The Musson Book Co., Toronto, 1887.

1 , 2 , 3   Hubbard, Frank, **Three Centuries of Harpsichord Making,** Harvard University Press, Cambridge, 1967.

1 , 2   Kilby, Kenneth, **The Cooper and His Trade,** Linden Publishing Co., Fresno, Calif., 1989.

Lemieux, Germain, **La vie paysanne 1860-1900,** Prise de Parole/FM, Sudbury, 1982.

1 , 2   Marcil, Eileen, **Les Tonneliers du Québec,** History Division Paper No 34, Mercury Series, National Museum of Man, National Museums of Canada, Ottawa, 1983.

1 , 3   Smith, Roger K., **Patented Transitional & Metallic Planes In America 1827-1927,** The North Village Publishing Co., Lancaster, Mass., 1981.

E020: ACOUSTICAL T&E

1 , 2   Diagram Group, **Musical Instruments of the World,** Facts On File Publications, New York, 1976.

E060-E180: ARMAMENT T&E

1 , 2   Blackmore, Howard L., **British Military Firearms,** Arco Publishing Co., New York, 1961.

1   Boulton, James J., **Uniforms of the Canadian Mounted Police,** Turner-Warwick Publications, North Battleford, Sask., 1990.

1 , 2   Bryce, Douglas, **L'armement du Machault, une frégate française du XVIIIe siècle,** Parks Canada, Ottawa, 1984.

1 , 2   Credland, Arthur G., **Whales and Whaling, The Arctic Fishery,** Shire Album 80, Shire Publications, Aylesbury, Eng., 1982.

1 , 2 , 3   **Encyclopaedia of Firearms,** Harold Leslie Peterson, ed., Connoisseur, London, 1964.

*   **Exercices et évolutions d'infanterie tels que révisés par ordre de sa Majesté 1861,** Translated from the English, printed by G. Desbarats and M. Cameron, Québec, 1863.

1 , 2 , 3   Eyell, Edward C., **Handguns of the World, Military Revolvers and Self-Loaders from 1870 to 1945,** Stackpole Books, Harrisburgh, Pa., 1981.

1 , 2   Foulkes, Charles, Captain, and C. Hopkinson, **Sword, Lance & Bayonet, A record of the Arms of the British Army & Navy,** 2nd ed., Arms and Armour Press, London, 1968.

1 , 2   Gooding, S. James, **An Introduction to British Artillery in North America,** Museum Restoration Service, Ottawa, 1972.

1 , 2 , 3   Hogg, Ian V., **Artillery In Color, 1920-1963,** Arco Publishing Co., New York, 1980.

1 , 2 , 3   Hogg, Ian V., **The Complete Illustrated Encyclopedia of the World's Firearms,** A&W Publishers, New York, 1978.

1 , 2 , 3   Leloir, Maurice, **Dictionnaire du costume et de ses accessoires, des armes et des étoffes des origines à nos jours,** Grund, Paris, 1970.

*   Lenk, Torsten, **The Flintlock: its origin and development,** Translated by G.A. Urquart, The Holland Press, London, 1965.

1 , 2   Peterson, Harold Leslie, **Arms and Armor in Colonial America, 1426-1783,** The Stackpole Company, Harrisburg, Pa., 1956.

2   Rattenbury, Richard, **Management of Firearms Collections: Identification and Classification,** Technical Leaflet 136, AASLH, Nashville, 1981.

1 , 2   Robson, Brian, **Swords of the British Army, The Regulation Patterns, 1788-1914,** Arms and Amour Press, London, 1975.

2 , 3   Saint-Pierre, Serge, **Les méthodes de chasse en Nouvelle-France aux XVIIᵉ-XVIIIᵉ siècles, dans Armes, chasse et trappage,** J.C. Dupont, and J. Mathieu, directors, Cahiers du CÉLAT, Québec, 1987.

*   Stevens, Gerald, **The Canadian Collector, Glass-Pottery-Furniture-Firearms of the Nineteenth Century,** The Ryerson Press, Toronto, 1957.

E200: ASTRONOMICAL T&E

1 , 2   **An Inventory of the Navigation and Astronomy Collections In the National Maritime Museum, Greenwich, With a List of Instruments Used at the Royal Observatory 1676-1950 and of Other Special Collections,** Department of Navigation, Department of Astronomy, National Maritime Museum, Greenwich, 1973.

1 , 2   Mills, John FitzMaurice, **Encyclopedia of Antique Scientific Instruments,** Facts On File Publications, New York, 1983.

E240: CHEMICAL T&E

1 , 2   Richardson, Lillian C., and Charles G. Richardson, **The Pill Rollers, A Book on Apothecary Antiques and Drug Store Collectibles,** 1st ed., Old Fort Press, Fort Washington, Md., 1979.

E280: ELECTRICAL & MAGNETIC T&E

2   Dubuisson, Bernard, **Encyclopédie, pratique de la construction et du bâtiment,** Vol. 2, Quillet, Paris, 1968.

1 , 2   Gordon, Bob, **Early Electrical Appliances,** Shire Album 124, Shire Publications Ltd., Aylesbury, Eng., 1984.

1 , 3   IEEE Canadian Region, **Electricity-The Magic Medium,** The Institute of Electrical and Electronics Engineers, Thornhill, Ont., 1985.

2 , 3   Kirk, R. E., and D. F. Othner, **Encyclopedia of Chemical Technology,** Wiley Interscience, John Wiley & Sons, New York, 1967.

2 , 3   Knapp, France, **Chemical Technology, Chemistry, Applied to the Arts and to Manufacture,** Lee and Blanchard, Philadelphia, 1848.

1 , 3   Meadowcroft, Wm. H., **The ABC of Electricity,** Exelcior Publishing House, New York, 1888.

1 , 2   Munsey, Cecil, **The Illustrated Guide to Collecting Bottles,** Hawthorn Books, New York, 1970.

E340: MAINTENANCE T&E

1 , 2   Arthur, Eric, and Thomas Ritchie, **Iron, Cast and Wrought Iron in Canada from the Seventeenth Century to the Present,** University of Toronto Press, Toronto, 1982.

1 , 2   Fearn, Jacqueline, **Domestic Bygones,** Shire Album 20, Shire Publications, Aylesbury, Eng., 1977.

1 , 2 , 3   Glissman, A.H., **The Evolution of the Sad-Iron,** A. H. Glissman, Carlsbad, Calif., 1970.

1 , 2 , 3   Hardy, Jean-Pierre, **Le forgeron et le ferblantier,** Collection Histoire Populaire du Québec, Boréal Express, Montréal, 1978.

1 , 2   Sambrook, Pamela, **Laundry Bygones,** Shire Album 107, Shire Publications, Aylesbury, Eng., 1983.

E380: MEDICAL & PSYCHOLOGICAL T&E

1 , 2 , 3   Bennion, Elizabeth, **Antique Medical Instruments,** Sotheby Parke Bernet, London, 1979.

1 , 2   Dammann, Gordon, **A Pictorial Encyclopedia of Civil War Medical Instruments and Equipment,** Pictorial Histories Publishing Company, Missoula, Mont., 1983.

1 , 2 , 3   Fréal, Jacques, **Les pots d'apothicaire en France du XVIe au XIXe siècle,** Garnier, France, 1982.

1   Hartz, **Aesculap, General Surgical Catalogue 1974,** The J. F. Hartz Co., Scarborough, Ont., Printed by the Ets. W. Todt Kg, D-773 Villingen, Germany, n.d.

1 , 2   Jackson, W.A., **The Victorian Chemist and Druggist,** Shire Album 80, Shire Publications, Aylesbury, Eng., 1981.

1   Lawton, **Surgical Instrument Catalog,** The Lawton Co., Moonachie, N.J., 1970.

1 , 2 , 3   Lessard, Renald, **Se soigner au Canada aux XVIIe et XVIIIe siècles,** History Division Paper No 43, Mercury Series, Canadian Museum of Civilization, National Museums of Canada, Hull, Qué., 1989.

1 , 2 , 3   Lyons, Albert, and R. Joseph Petrucelli II, **Medicine, An Illustrated History,** Harry N. Abrams, New York, 1978.

1 , 2   Munsey, Cecil, **The Illustrated Guide to Collecting Bottles,** Hawthorn Books, New York, 1970.

1 , 2   Richardson, Lillian C., and Charles G. Ricardson, **The Pill Rollers, A Book on Apothecary Antiques and Drug Store Collectibles,** 1st ed., Old Fort Press, Fort Washington, Md., 1979.

*   Stevens, Gerald, **Early Canadian Glass,** The Ryerson Press, Toronto, 1960.

1 , 3   **Technology and American Medical Practice, 1880-1930: An Anthology of Sources,** J. D. Howell, ed., Garland Publishing, New York, 1988.

E400: MERCHANDISING T&E

1 , 3   Bennion, Elizabeth, **Antique Medical Instruments,** Sotheby, Parke Bernet, London, 1979.

1   C.M. Moseman and Brother, **Mosemans' Illustrated Catalog of Horse Furnishing Goods,** reprint of 1893 ed., Dover Publications, New York, 1987.

1 , 3   Fréal, Jacques, **Les pots d'apothicaire en France du XVIe au XIXe siècle,** Garnier, France, 1982.

*   Godden, Goeffrey A., **An Illustrated Ecyclopaedia of British Pottery and Porcelain,** Herbert Jenkins, London, 1968.

1 , 2   Hedges, A.A.C., **Bottles and Bottle Collecting,** Shire Album 6, Shire Publications, Aylesbury, Eng., 1975.

1 , 2   Jones, Olive, and Catherine Sullivan, **The Parks Canada Glass Glossary for the Description of Containers, Tableware, Flat Glass and Closures,** Parks Canada, Environment Canada, Ottawa, 1985.

*   Kendrick, Grace, **The Antique Bottle Collector, Including Latest Price Guide,** Pyramid, New York, 1976.

1 , 2   Ketchum, William C., Jr., **A Treasury of American Bottles,** Rutledge Books, A&W Visual Library, New York, 1975.

1   McKearin, George S., and Helen McKearin, **American Glass,** Crown Publishers, New York, 1968.

1   Mondock, Judi, and Lorin Buckner, **The Canning Corner, An encyclopedia of canning utensils including photographs, prices and patents...,** Privately published by Judi Mondock, Philadelphia, and Lorin Buckner, Grand Haven, Mich., 1974.

1 , 2   Munsey, Cecil, **The Illustrated Guide to Collecting Bottles,** Hawthorn Books, New York, 1970.

1 , 2   Newman, Harold, **An Illustrated Dictionary of Glass,** Thames and Hudson, London, 1977.

1   Putnam, Hazel E., **Bottle Identification,** Old Time Bottle Publishing, Salem, Or., 1965.

1 , 2   Revi, Albert Christian, **American Pressed Glass and Figure Bottles,** Thomas Nelson & Sons, Nashville, 1964.

*   Spence, Hilda, and Kevin Spence, **A Guide to Early Canadian Glass,** Longmans Canada, Don Mills, Ont., 1966.

1   Zumwalt, Betty, **Ketchup, Pickels, Sauces, 19th Century Food In Glass,** MakWest Publishers, Fulton, Calif., 1980.

E420: METEOROLOGICAL T&E

1 , 2   Mills, John FitzMaurice, **Encyclopedia of Antique Scientific Instruments,** Facts On File Publications, New York, 1983.

E460: OPTICAL T&E

1 , 2   **An Inventory of the Navigation and Astronomy Collections In the National Maritime Museum, Greenwich, With a List of Instruments Used at the Royal Observatory 1676-1950 and of other Special Collections,** Department of Navigation, Department of Astronomy, National Maritime Museum, Greenwich, 1973.

1 , 2   Mills, John FitzMaurice, **Encyclopedia of Antique Scientific Instruments,** Facts On File Publications, New York, 1983.

E500: SURVEYING & NAVIGATIONAL T&E

1 , 2   **The American Neptune, Instruments of Navigation**, Pictorial Supplement XVII, The Peabody Museum, Salem, Mass., 1975.

1 , 2   **An Inventory of the Navigation and Astronomy Collections In the National Maritime Museum, Greenwich, With a List of Instruments used at the Royal Observatory 1676-1950 and of other Special Collections**, Department of Navigation, Department of Astronomy, National Maritime Museum, Greenwich, 1973.

1 , 2   Mills, John FitzMaurice, **Encyclopedia of Antique Scientific Instruments**, Facts On File Publications, New York, 1983.

1 , 2   Pearsall, Ronald, **Collecting And Restoring Scientific Instruments**, Arco Publishing Co., New York, 1974.

1 , 2 , 3   Randier, Jean, **Marine Navigation Instruments,** Translated from the French by John E. Powell, Murray, London, 1980.

1 , 2   Wynter, Harriet, and Anthony Turner, **Scientific Instruments**, Studio Vista, London, 1975.

E540: TIMEKEEPING T&E

3   **Canadian Clocks and Clockmakers**, G. Edmond Burrows, Oshawa, 1973.

1 , 2   Mills, John FitzMaurice, **Encyclopedia of Antique Scientific Instruments**, Facts On File Publication, New York, 1983.

*   Pomerleau, Jeanne, **Métiers ambulants d'autrefois**, Guérin, Montréal, 1990.

E560: WEIGHTS & MEASURES T&E

1 , 2 , 3   Fortier, Luc, and Maurice Vallée *et al.*, **Métiers du bois et outils anciens au centre du Québec (1815-1925)**, Les Cahiers de la Société historique de Drummondville, La Société historique du centre du Québec, Drummondville, Qué., 1980.

1 , 2   Graham, J. T., **Scales And Balances, a guide to collecting,** Shire Album 55, Shire Publications, Aylesbury, Eng., 1981.

1 , 2   Graham, J. T., and Maurice Stevenson, **Weights and measures and their marks, a guide to collecting**, 2nd ed., Shire Album 44, Shire Publications, Aylesbury, Eng., 1987.

1 , 2   Ingram, Arthur, **Dairying Bygones**, Shire Album 29, Shire Publications, Aylesbury, Eng., 1987.

1 , 2 , 3   Kisch, Bruno, **Scales And Weights, A Historical Outline**, Yale University Press, New Haven, 1965.

1 , 2   Lyons, Albert, and R. Joseph Petrucelli II, **Medicine, An Illustrated History**, Harry N. Abrams, New York, 1978.

1 , 2   Mills, John FitzMaurice, **Encyclopedia of Antique Scientific Instruments**, Facts On File Publications, New York, 1983.

1 , 2   Richardson, Lillian. C., and Charles G. Richardson, **The Pill Rollers, A Book on Apothecary Antiques and Drug Store Collectibles**, 1st ed., Old Fort Press, Fort Washington, Md., 1979.

F040: DRAFTING T&E

1 , 2 Mills, John FitzMaurice, **Encyclopedia of Antique Scientific Instruments**, Facts On File Publications, New York, 1983.

F060: MUSICAL T&E

1 , 2 , 3 Baines, Anthony, **Brass instruments, their history and development**, Faber and Faber, London, 1978.

1 , 2 , 3 Baines, Anthony, **Woodwind instruments and their history**, Faber and Faber, London, 1967.

1 , 2 , 3 Bielefeldt, Catherine C., **The Wonders of the Piano, The Anatomy of the Instrument**, Belwin-Mills Publishing Corp., Melville, N.Y., 1984.

1 , 2 , 3 Carse, Adam, **Musical Wind Instruments**, Da Capo, New York, 1965.

1 , 2 , 3 Diagram Group, **Musical Instruments of the World**, Facts On File Publications, New York, 1976.

1 , 2 , 3 Hubbard, Frank, **Three Centuries of Harpsichord Making**, Harvard University Press, Cambridge, 1967.

1 , 2 , 3 Paganelli, Sergio, **Musical Instruments from the Renaissance to the 19th century**, Cassell Publishers, London, 1988.

F080: PHOTOGRAPHIC T&E

1 , 2 , 3 Jenkins, Reese V., **Images and Enterprise, Technology and the American Photographic Industry 1839 to 1925,** The John Hopkins University Press, Baltimore, 1975.

* Lessard, Michel, **Les livernois photographes**, Musée du Québec, Québec, 1987.

3 Pomerleau, Jeanne, **Métiers ambulants d'autrefois**, Guérin, Montréal, 1990.

1 , 2 , 3 Stroebel, Leslie, and Hollis N. Todd, **Dictionary of Contemporary Photography**, Morgan & Morgan, New York, 1974.

F100: PRINTING T&E

1 , 2 **Book Making in Diderot's Encyclopédie: a facsimile reproduction of articles and plates,** facs. of 1751 ed., intro. by G.G. Barber, Gregg International Publishers, Westmead, Eng., 1973.

2 **Dictionary of Terms Used in the Paper, Printing, and Graphic Arts Industries**, Howard Smith Division, Domtar Pulp & Paper, n.p., n.d.

1 , 2 Glaister, Geoffrey Ashal, **Glossary of the book: terms used in paper-making, printing, bookbinding and publishing with notes on illuminated manuscripts, bibliophiles, private presses and printing societies**, George Allen and Unwin, London, 1960.

2 **A Graphic Arts Production Handbook**, Pocket Pal, 12th ed., International Paper Co., New York, 1979.

1, 2   Mayer, Ralph, **A Dictionary of Arts Terms and Techniques**, T.Y. Crowell Co., New York, 1969.

1   Wroth, Lawrence C., **The Colonial Printer**, Dominion Books, The University Press of Virginia, Charlottesville, 1964.

F120: SOUND COMMUNICATION T&E

1, 2   Diagram Group, **Musical Instruments of the World**, Facts On File Publications, New York, 1976.

F140: TELECOMMUNICATION T&E

*   Mellor, Alec, **La fabuleuse aventure du téléphone**, Montparnasse, Paris, 1975.

1   Robert Marples & Son Tool Manufacturers, **Price List**, 4th ed., Hermitage Works, Sheffield, Eng., C.1904.

F160: VISUAL COMMUNICATION T&E

1, 3   By Authority of the Department of Marine and Fisheries, **Rules And Regulations For The Guidance of Lightkeepers And Of Engineers In Charge Of Fog Alarms In The Dominion Of Canada...**, 3rd ed., Government Printing Bureau, Ottawa, 1 Jan. 1904.

1   **Royal Canadian Sea Cadet Manuel,** reprint of 1954 ed., Royal Canadian Sea Cadets, Ottawa, 1971.

07
DISTRIBUTION & TRANSPORTATION

1   Arthur, Eric, and Thomas Ritchie, **Iron, Cast and Wrought Iron in Canada from the Seventeenth Century to the Present,** University of Toronto Press, Toronto, 1982.

2, 3   Blouin, Charles, **Les ponts de glace de l'Île d'Orléans**, Vol. 3, Culture et Tradition, Québec, 1978.

2, 3   Brunhes-Delamarre, Mariel, and Roger Henniger, **Transports ruraux, guide ethnologique 3**, musée national des arts et traditions populaires, Paris, 1972.

1, 2, 3   **The Rand McNally Encyclopedia of Transportation**, Rand McNally, Chicago, 1976.

*   Sanfaçon, Roland, **Le premier chemin royal de Québec à Montréal sur la rive nord du fleuve Saint-Laurent**, Presses de l'université Laval, Québec, 1956.

G120: LAND TRANSPORTATION, ANIMAL POWERED

1, 2, 3   Berkebile, Don H., **Carriage Terminology: An Historical Dictionary**, Smithsonian Institution Press, Washington, 1978.

1   C.M. Moseman and Brother, **Mosemans' Illustrated Catalog of Horse Furnishing Goods**, reprint of 1893 ed., Dover Publications, New York, 1987.

          Corriveau, Claude, **Les voitures à chevaux au Québec**, Septentrion, Sillery, Qué., 1991.

1, 2   **Exercices des métiers du bois**, Jean-Claude Dupont, and Jacques Mathieu, directors, Cahiers du CÉLAT, No 4, Québec, February 1986.

1 , 2 , 3   Hardy, Jean-Pierre, **Le forgeron et le ferblantier**, Collection Histoire Populaire du Québec, Boréal Express, Montréal, 1978.

1 , 2   Hart, Edward, **The Harness Horse**, Shire Album 53, Shire Publications, Aylesbury, Eng., 1981.

1 , 2   Leclerc, Paul-André, **Les voitures à chevaux à la campagne**, musée François-Pilote, La Pocatière, Qué., 1978.

1 , 2 , 3   Lemay, Pierre, **Le traîneau à chiens d'hier à aujourd'hui**, L'Aurore, Montréal, 1977.

1 , 2 , 3   **Les métiers du cuir**, Jean-Claude dupont, and Jacques Mathieu, directors, Ethnologie de l'Amérique Française, Presses de l'université Laval, Québec, 1981.

1 , 3   Milnes, Herbert, **Settlers Traditions**, Boston Mills Press, Cheltenham, Ont., 1980.

3   Pomerleau, Jeanne, **Métiers ambulants d'autrefois**, Guérin, Montréal, 1990.

1 , 3   **Saddlery and Harness-Making with Numerous Engravings and Diagrams**, Paul N. Hasluck, ed., J.A. Allen and Company, London, 1962.

1 , 2   Salaman, R.A., **Dictionary of leather-working tools, C.1700-1950 and the tools of allied trades**, Macmillan Publishing Company, New York, 1986.

G140: LAND TRANSPORTATION, HUMAN POWERED

1 , 2 , 3   Carpentier, Paul, **La raquette à neige**, Boréal Express, Sillery, Qué., 1976.

1 , 2 , 3   Hardy, Jean-Pierre, **Le forgeron et le ferblantier**, Collection Histoire Populaire du Québec, Boréal Express, Montréal, 1978.

1 , 2   Ingram, Arthur, **Dairying Bygones**, Shire Album 29, Shire Publications, Aylesbury, Eng., 1987.

G280: WATER TRANSPORTATION EQUIPMENT

1 , 2   Blair, Carvel Hall, and Willits Dyer Ansel, **A Guide to Fishing Boats and Their Gear**, Cornell Maritime   Press, Cambridge, 1968.

*   Davis, Charles G., **The Ship Model Builder's Assistant**, Marine Research Society, Salem, Mass., 1926.

1 , 3   Gillmer, Thomas C., **Working Watercraft, a Survey of the Surviving Local Boats of America and Europe**, International Marine Publishing Company, Camden, Maine, 1972.

1 , 2   Grant, Ruth Fulton, **The Canadian Atlantic Fishery**, The Ryerson Press, Toronto, 1934.

1   Jenson, L. B., **Fishermen of Nova Scotia**, Petheric Press, Halifax, 1980.

1   MacKean, Ray, and Robert Percival, **The Little Boats, Inshore Fishing Craft of Atlantic Canada**, Brunswick Press, Fredericton, C.1979.

1 , 2 , 3   McCullough, A.B., **The Commercial Fishery of the Canadian Great Lakes,** Studies in Archaeology, Architecture, and History, National Historic Parks and Sites, Canadian Parks Service, Environment Canada, Ottawa, 1985.

1 , 2   zu Mondfeld, Wolfram, **Encyclopédie Navale des Modèles Réduits, Guide du collectionneur et du modéliste**, Gérard Watelet, Pygmalion, France, 1979.

*   Nova Scotia Department of Fisheries, **Sea, Salt & Sweat, A Story of Nova Scotia and the Vast Atlantic Fisheries**, Nova Scotia Communications and Information Centre, Halifax, 1977.

1 , 2 , 3   **The Oxford Companion to Ships and the Sea**, Peter Kemp, ed., Oxford University Press, Oxford, 1988.

1 , 2   Paasch, Capt H., **Illustrated Marine Encyclopedia**, Ratinckx Frères, Antwerp, 1890.

1   **Royal Canadian Sea Cadet Manual,** reprint of 1954 ed., Royal Canadian Sea Cadets, Ottawa, 1971.

1 , 2   Zimmerly, David W., **An Illustrated Glossary of Kayak Terminology**, National Museum of Man, The Canadian Museums Association, Ottawa, n.d.

G300: WATER TRANSPORTATION ACCESSORY

*   Brewington, M.V., **Shipcarvers of North America**, Dover Publications, New York, 1972.

H020: ADVERTISING MEDIUM

1   Dumas Antoine, **À l'enseigne d'antan. Aperçu des enseignes en usage aux XVIIIe et XIXe siècles à Québec et à Montréal**, Pelican, Québec, 1970.

1 , 2   Hornung, Clarence P., **Handbook Of Early Advertising Art, Mainly From American Sources**, 3rd ed., Pictorial Volume, Dover Publications, New York, 1956.

1 , 2   Munsey, Cecil, **The Illustrated Guide to Collecting Bottles**, Hawthorn Books, New York, 1970.

1 , 2   Richardson, Lillian C., and Charles G. Richardson, **The Pill Rollers, A Book on Apothecary Antiques and Drug Store Collectibles**, 1st ed., Old Fort Press, Fort Washington, Md., 1979.

*   Stevens, Gerald, **Early Canadian Glass**, The Ryerson Press, Toronto, 1960.

H040: ART

*   **Artisans et paysans de France, recueil d'études d'art populaire**, F.X. le Roux, Paris, 1946.

*   Barbeau, Marius, **Maîtres artisans de chez-nous**, Éditions du Zodiaque, Montréal, 1942.

*   Barbeau, Marius, **Trésors des Anciens Jésuites**, Bulletin No 153, Anthropological Series No 43, National   Museum of Canada, Ottawa, 1957.

1 , 2 , 3   Blanchette, Jean-François, **From the heart: folk art in Canada**, Canadian Centre for Folk Culture Studies of the National Museum of Man, McClelland and Stewart, Ottawa, 1983.

1 , 2 , 3   Carpentier, Paul, **Les croix de chemin: au-delà du signe**, National Museums of Canada, Ottawa, 1981.

1 , 2 , 3   Carpentier, Paul, **La légende dans l'art québécois**, musée du Québec, Québec, 1979.

1 , 2   De Grobois, Louise, Raymonde Lamothe, and Lise Nantel, **Les Patenteux du Québec**, Éditions du Partis-Pris, Montréal, 1974.

1 , 2   **Dictionary of Terms used in the Paper, Printing and Graphic Arts Industries**, Howard Smith Division, Domtar Pulp & Paper, n.p., n.d.

1 , 2 , 3   Doyon-Ferland, Madeleine, **Les arts populaires. Esquisses du Canada français**, Montréal, 1967.

1 , 2   Dupont, Jean-Claude, **L'art populaire au Canada français, Ethnologie québécoise**, Cahiers du Québec/Hurtubise, HMH, Montréal, 1972.

Gauvreau, Jean-Marie, **Artisans du Québec**, Bien Public, Trois-Rivières, 1940.

1 , 2 , 3   Genest, Bernard, in collaboration with René Bouchard, **Un monde peuplé d'animaux, Wilfrid Richard et les siens, sculpteurs**, musée de la civilisation/Agenda Québec Agenda, Québec, 1986.

*   Godden, Geoffrey A., **An Illustrated Encyclopaedia of British Pottery and Porcelain**, Herbert Jenkins, London, 1968.

1 , 2   **A Graphic Arts Production Handbook**, Pocket Pal, 12th ed., International Paper Co., New York, 1979.

1   Haggar, Reginald G., **A Dictionary of Art Terms**, Hawthorn Books, New York, 1962.

1 , 2   Harper, J. Russel, **L'art populaire: l'art naïf au Canada**, National Gallery of Canada, Ottawa, 1973.

1 , 2 , 3   Latour, Thérèse, **Les arts populaires du Québec**, Ministère des Affaires culturelles, Québec, 1975.

2 , 3   Latour, Thérèse, **Trésors d'art populaire québécois**, Ministère des Affaires culturelles, Québec, 1980.

1 , 2 , 3   Lessard, Michel, and Huguette Marquis, **L'art traditionnel au Québec, Trois siècles d'ornements populaires**, Éditions de l'Homme, Montréal, 1975.

1 , 2   Martin, Judy, **Longman Dictionary of Art: A Handbook of Terms, Techniques, Materials, Equipment and Processes**, Longman Group, Harlow, Essex, Eng., 1986.

1 , 2   Mayer, Ralph, **A Dictionary of Art Terms and Techniques**, T.Y. Crowell Co., New York, 1969.

2 , 3   **Questions d'art populaire**, John R. Porter, director, Cahiers du CÉLAT, CÉLAT, Québec, 1984.

1 , 2 , 3   Rivière, Georges-Henri, and Denise Gluck, **Arts populaires des pays de France**, D. Cuénot, Paris, 1975.

1 , 3   Schiffer, Margaret, **Chrismas Ornaments, A Festive Study**, Schiffer Publishing, Exton, Pa., 1984.

*   Simard, Cyril, **Artisanat québécois**, Éditions de l'Homme, Montréal, 1975.

1 , 2 , 3 , *   Simard, Jean, **Les arts sacrés au Québec**, De Mortagne, Boucherville, Qué., 1989.

1 , 2 , 3   Simard, Jean, Bernard Genest, Francine Labonté, and René Bouchard, **Pour passer le temps. Artistes populaires du Québec**, Coll. Les Cahiers du patrimoine, No 17, Ministère des Affaires culturelles, Québec, 1985.

H060: CEREMONIAL ARTIFACT

*   **American Church Silver of the Seventeenth and Eighteenth Centuries With a Few Pieces of Domestic Plate Exhibited At the Museum of Fine Arts, July to December, 1911**, Museum of Fine Arts, Boston, 1911.

*   **Church Silver of Colonial Virginia, An Exhibition Organized By The Virginia Museum of Fine Arts**, George A. Cruger, ed., Richmond, 1970.

1   Fox, Ross Allen C., **Quebec and Related Silver at The Detroit Institute of Arts**, Published for the Founders Society, Detroit Institute of Arts, by Wayne State University Press, Detroit, 1978.

1 , 2   Lee, Rev. Frederick George, **A Glossary of Liturgical and Ecclesiastical Terms**, Bernard Quaritch, London, 1877.

1 , 2 , 3   Lessard, Pierre, **Les images dévotes. Leur utilisation traditionnelle au Québec**, Presses de l'université Laval, Québec, 1981.

1 , 2   **Liturgische Geräte, Kreuse Und Reliquiare Der Christlische Kirchen, Objets lithurgiques, croix et reliquaires des églises chrétiennes**, Rieth, Rudulf und Renate, eds., Wissenschaftlich Kommission Documentationsstelle Tübingen, Strasbourg, 1972.

2   Mayer-Thurman, Crista C., **Raiment for the Lord's Service, A Thousand Years of Western Vestments**, The Art Institute of Chicago, Chicago, 1975.

1 , 2   Roulin, Dom E., **Linges, Insignes et Vêtements Liturgiques**, Lethielleux, Paris, 1930.

1 , 3   Séguin, Robert-Lionel, **Les moules du Québec**, Bulletin No 188, History Bulletin Series No 1, National Museums of Canada, Ottawa, 1963.

1 , 2 , 3   Simard, Jean, **Les arts sacrés au Québec**, De Mortagne, Boucherville, Qué., 1989.

2 , 3   Simard, Jean, in association with Jocelyne Milot, and René Bouchard, **Un patrimoine méprisé. La religion populaire des Québécois**, Cahiers du Québec/Hurtubise, HMH, Montréal, 1979.

1 , 2   Trudel, Jean, **Silver in New France,** National Gallery of Canada, Ottawa, 1974.

H080: DOCUMENTARY ARTIFACT

1 , 2   Munsey, Cecil, **The Illustrated Guide to Collecting Bottles**, Hawthorn Books, New York, 1970.

H100: EXCHANGE MEDIUM

1 , 2 , 3   **Canada, Stamps and Stories, The Canadian Heritage Through the Fascinating World of Stamps, With a Catalogue of the Postage Stamps of Canada,** R. Harvey Warm, ed.-in-chief, Canada Post Office, Ottawa, 1975.

1 , 2 , 3   McCullough, A.B., **Money and Exchange in Canada to 1900,** Dunburn Press Limited in cooperation with Parks Canada and the Canadian Government Publishing Centre, Toronto, 1984.

1 , 2   **The Story of Canada's Currency**, 3rd ed., printed for the Bank of Canada, 1981.

H120: PERSONAL SYMBOL

*   Barthorp, Michael, **The British Army on Campaign 1816-1853**, Men-At-Arms Series No 193, Osprey Publishing, London, 1987.

1   Boulton, James J., **Uniforms of the Canadian Mounted Police**, Turner-Warwick Publications, North Battleford, Sask., 1990.

1 , 2 , 3   Brasser, Ted J., **Bo'jou Neejee!: Profiles of Canadian Indian Art**, National Museum of Man, Ottawa, 1976.

3   Chappell, Mike, **British Battle Insignia: 1914-1918**, Men-At-Arms Series No 182, Osprey Publishing, London, 1986.

*   Chappell, Mike, **The Canadian Army at War**, Men-At-Arms Series No 164, Osprey Publishing, London, 1985.

1 , 3   Fosten, Bryan, **Wellington's Infantry (1) and (2)**, Men-At-Arms Series No 114-119, Osprey Publishing, London, 1981 and 1982.

3   Fosten D.S.V., and R.J. Marion, **The British Army 1914-18**, Men-At-Arms Series No 81, Osprey Publishing, London, 1978.

1 , 2 , 3   Hartman, Sheryl, **Indian Clothing of the Great Lakes: 1740-1840**, Eagle View Publishing Company, Odgen, Vt., 1991.

3 , *   Hook, Jason, **The American Plains Indians**, Osprey Publishing, London, 1985.

*   Hook, Jason, **The Apaches**, Osprey Publishing, London, 1987.

2 , 3   Lessard, Pierre, **Les images dévotes. Leur utilisation traditionnelle au Québec**, Presses de l'université Laval, Québec, 1981.

1 , 2 , 3   Ross, David, and René Chartrand, **Cataloguing Military Uniforms**, The New Brunswick Museum, Saint- John, 1977.

1 , 3   Ross, David, and Robin May, **The Royal Canadian Mounted Police 1873-1987**, Men-At-Arms Series No 197, Osprey Publishing, London, 1988.

1   **Royal Canadian Sea Cadet Manual,** reprint of 1954 ed., Royal Canadian Sea Cadets, Ottawa, 1971.

2 , 3   Simard, Jean, in association with Jocelyne Milot, and René Bouchard, **Un patrimoine méprisé. La religion populaire des Québécois**, Cahiers du Québec/Hurtubise, HMH, Montréal, 1979.

1 , 2 , 3   **The Spirit Sings: A Catalogue of the Exhibition**, Glenbow Museum, McClelland and Stewart, Toronto, 1987.

1   **The Spirit Sings: Artistic Traditions of Canada's First Peoples**, Glenbow Museum, McClelland and Stewart, Toronto, 1987.

I020: GAME

1 , 2   Bell, R. C., **Board and Table Game Antiques**, Shire Album 60, Shire Publications, Aylesbury, Eng., 1981.

2   Doyon-Ferland, Madeleine, **Jeux, rythmes et divertissements traditionnels**, text collated and edited by Andrée Paradis, Leméac, Montréal, 1980.

1 , 2 , 3   Italiano, Carlo, **Les traîneaux de mon enfance**, Les Livres Toundra, Ottawa, 1974.

1 , 2 , 3   King, Constance Eileen, **The Encyclopedia of Toys**, Crown Publishers, New York, 1978.

1 , 2 , 3   Tremblay, Katherine, and Louise Renaud, **Les jeux et jouets de Place-Royale**, Groupe Harcart, Publications du Québec, Gouvernement du Québec, Québec, 1990.

1 , 3   Whitehouse, J.R.B., **Table Games of Georgian and Victorian Days**, revised 2nd ed., Priory Press, Royston (Herts.), 1971.

I100: TOY

1 , 2 , 3   King, Constance Eileen, **The Encyclopedia of Toys**, Crown Publishers, New York, 1978.

2 , 3   Séguin, Robert-Lionel, **Les jouets anciens du Québec**, Leméac, Montréal, 1976.

1 , 2 , 3   Tremblay, Katherine, and Louise Renaud, **Les jeux et jouets de Place-Royale**, Groupe Harcart, Publications du Québec, Gouvernement du Québec, Québec, 1990.

OTHER NOMENCLATURES

Baudrillard, Jean, **Le système des objets**, Denoël Gonthier, Paris, 1968.

Blackaby, James R., Patricia Greeno, and The Nomenclature Committee, **The Revised Nomenclature for Museum Cataloguing, A Revised and Expanded Version of Robert G. Chenhall's System for Classifying Man-Made Objects**, AASLH Press, Nashville, 1978.

Chenhall, Robert G., **Nomenclature for Museum Cataloguing, A System for Classifying Man-Made Objects**, AASLH, Nashville, 1978.

De Verville, M., director, **Système descriptif des objets domestiques français**, Musée nationaux, Paris, 1977.

Hertforshire Simple Name List, Museum Documentation Association, Hertforshire Curators' Group, Standing Committee for Museums in Hertforshire, 1984.

Murdock, George P. et al., **Outline of Cultural Materials**, Human Relations Area Files, New Haven, 1961.

Royal Commission on the Historical Monuments of England, **Thesaurus of Archaeological Terms**, 1986.

Social History and Industry Classification (SHIC), **A Subject Classification for Museum Collections**, SHIC Working Party, The Centre for Cultural Tradition and Language, University of Sheffield, 1983.

Système descriptif des objets domestiques français, Musée national des arts et traditions populaires, Centre d'ethnologie française, Musées nationaux, 1977.